WEST VIRGINIA'S WAR

THE CIVIL WAR IN THE GREAT INTERIOR

Series Editors
Martin J. Hershock and Christine Dee

The Civil War in the Great Interior is a series of short documentary histories on the Civil War in the midwestern states. Each volume presents fresh primary sources that will aid professors and students, as well as the informed general reader, in exploring the social, political, and military impact of the Civil War.

Ohio's War: The Civil War in Documents, edited by Christine Dee

Missouri's War: The Civil War in Documents, edited by Silvana R. Siddali

Indiana's War: The Civil War in Documents, edited by Richard F. Nation and Stephen E. Towne

Kansas's War: The Civil War in Documents, edited by Pearl T. Ponce

Illinois's War: The Civil War in Documents, edited by Mark Hubbard

Michigan's War: The Civil War in Documents, edited by John W. Quist

West Virginia's War: The Civil War in Documents, edited by William Kerrigan

WEST VIRGINIA'S WAR

The Civil War in Documents

~

EDITED BY WILLIAM KERRIGAN

Ohio University Press

Athens

Ohio University Press, Athens, Ohio 45701
ohioswallow.com
© 2025 by Ohio University Press
All rights reserved

To obtain permission to quote, reprint, or otherwise reproduce or distribute material from Ohio University Press publications, please contact our rights and permissions department at (740) 593-1154 or (740) 593-4536 (fax).

The Ohio University Press European Union safety representative may be contacted about General Product Safety Regulation (GPSR) concerns at Mare Nostrum Group B.V., Mauritskade 21D, 1091 GC Amsterdam, The Netherlands, or by email at gpsr@mare-nostrum.co.uk.

Printed in the United States of America
Ohio University Press books are printed on acid-free paper ∞ ™

Library of Congress Cataloging-in-Publication Data

Names: Kerrigan, William editor
Title: West Virginia's war : the Civil War in documents / edited by William Kerrigan.
Description: Athens : Ohio University Press, [2025] | Series: Civil War in the great interior | Includes bibliographical references and index.
Identifiers: LCCN 2024062351 | ISBN 9780821426401 paperback | ISBN 9780821426418 pdf
Subjects: LCSH: West Virginia—History—Civil War, 1861–1865 | West Virginia—History—Civil War, 1861–1865—Sources
Classification: LCC E536 .W47 2025 | DDC 973.7/454—dc23/eng/20250410
LC record available at https://lccn.loc.gov/2024062351

Contents

List of Illustrations — xi
Series Editors' Preface — xiii
Preface — xv
Acknowledgments — xix
Introduction — 1

One

Virginia's West   8

The Two Virginias — 14
Freedwoman Jennie Small Recalls Life in Slavery — 16
The Constitutional Convention of 1829–30 — 17
"The peasantry of the west" — 19
"A constitution, which perpetuates that inequality of power" — 20
"If West Virginia shall call for a law to remove slavery from her side of the Blue Ridge" — 21
The Reform Constitution of 1851 — 24
The New Constitution — 25
The Harpers Ferry Insurrection — 26
"Poor doomed Harpers Ferry" — 29
John Brown Writes Mary Ann Brown of His Impending Execution — 31
Thomas Jackson Observes Brown's Execution — 32
Correspondence between Margaretta Mason and Lydia Marie Child on Brown's Raid — 34
"That this slavery agitation shall cease" — 37
The Response from the Far West — 39

Two

The Revolution of 1860   42

"There are special reasons why citizens of Virginia should be Republicans" — 46
"This time next year she will have to do her own work" — 47
The Last Returned Fugitive Slave: Newspaper Accounts — 48
To the Cleveland Union-Savers — 51

The Union Men of Harrison County	52
Woods Speaks at the Secession Convention	53
"Every Union man is denounced as an abolitionist!"	54
Virginia Convention Votes	56
The Position of Western Virginia	57
A Betrothed Couple Take Different Sides	59
A Union "More Odious Than Any Tyranny"	64
The Free-Soilers of Ceredo Stand Their Ground	66

Three

Opening Gambits 68

Confederate Recruitment Begins	73
The Armory at Harpers Ferry	74
Switching Allegiances	76
A Minister Fears Slave Insurrection	76
Reuben Put on Trial for Planning Slave Insurrection	78
"The people of Greenbrier are amongst the most loyal of the State"	81
"The freedom purchased by your father's blood"	83
"I have ordered troops to cross the Ohio river"	84
"Repress all attempts at negro insurrection"	85
Battle of Philippi	86
"You were there on a regular *drunk*"	88
"The Union men are greatly in ascendancy here"	89
"We are enemies to none but armed rebels"	90
"We do not doubt that you will in due time sweep the rebels from western Virginia"	91
"All the sons of bitches in the Confederate Army"	92
The Kanawha Valley	93

Four

The Rules of War 96

"Our houses have been forcibly entered and robbed"	99
A Virginia "Sassesh"	101
Battelle Calls for West Virginia Leadership	102
"A glorious tramp"	103
In Pursuit of Confederate Bushwhackers	105
Greybacks and Bushwhackers	109
Virginia Ranger Act	111

Contents   vii

The Squirrel Hunters	112
"Poor heart-broken looking creatures"	114
Rutherford B. Hayes Encounters "Contrabands"	114
A Loyal Black Farmer Makes a Postwar Claim	117
General Jackson Gives God the Glory	119
Harpers Ferry Contraband Camp Stereograph	120
"With the influx of rebel troops came the human hyenas in search of living prey"	121
The Fate of Harpers Ferry's Contraband Community	124
Confederates Occupy Charleston in 1862	125
Confederate Major General's Public Order	127

Five

The Movement for Statehood   128

"The peculiar situation of Northwestern Virginia"	131
The Wheeling Conventions	133
"You have been convened in extraordinary session"	135
The Statehood Referendum	136
"They are afflicted with madness"	137
Senator Willey's Concerns	139
Gradual Emancipation and Statehood	140
"You have deserted our just and holy cause"	141
"A strange ceremony"	142
"I believe the admission of West Virginia into the Union is expedient"	142
A Soldier Votes for West Virginia	144
"Admitted into the Union on an equal footing"	145
"The Bogus Government"	146
Biographies of Some of the First West Virginia Legislators	147
"One 'who treads alone'"	151

Six

Women and the War   153

The Ladies of Wheeling Contribute to the Cause	156
Ladies at Morgantown	156
Disreputable Women	157
Lady Visitors from Parkersburg	158
Disloyal Women Locked Up	158
A Profane Confederate Woman	159

Union Soldiers Search a Pro-Confederate Home	160
"Rebel beaux could not shine with the Union girl"	162
"I drew out my pistol and shot him"	163
The Bustle	165
"Abe's sagacious Grimalkins"	166
A Confederate Woman in Barbour County	169
Quartering Troops	173
A Union woman Travels Through West Virginia	174
"A spy sent from Princeton"	175
"An ideal specimen of the 'female Southern Confederacy'"	175
"Bogus Soldiers"	176
"In the shape of a female"	177
"Wants Hoops"	179

Seven

Enduring a Long War   181

Enduring War in the 7th (West) Virginia	184
The 7th (West) Virginia Responds to War Critics	185
The Daily Lives of Soldiers	188
Excerpts from *The Knapsack,* 1863	190
"A burning river, carrying destruction to our merciless enemy"	192
Troop Transfer across West Virginia	194
Local Newspapers on the Troop Transfer	200
Election of 1864	200
"The very existence of the State of West Virginia"	202
A Refugee Crisis in the Lower Shenandoah Valley	204

Eight

Revolution and Counterrevolution   206

Loyal West Virginians Prepare for the Return of Defeated Confederates	209
West Virginians Respond to the Assassination of Lincoln	210
"A great many reb Soldiers in the place"	211
"They had better not return amongst us"	212
West Virginia's First Governor Confronts Postwar Challenges	213
Emerging Resistance to Radical Republican Rule	217
Jefferson County Voters Turned Away from the Polls in 1869	219
Accusations of Voter Suppression in Jefferson County	221
"West Virginia Redeemed!"	221

"A party . . . dangerous to our existence as a State"	224
The Flick Amendment	225
Low Turnout for the Flick Amendment Vote	226
Building a New West Virginia	227
"Shall we not show ourselves worthy of our own emancipation?"	229
John Henry	230
Booker T. Washington: *Up from Slavery*	232

Nine

Memory · 235

Stonewall Jackson Statue Unveiled on the State Capitol Grounds	238
The Mountaineer Statue	243
Union Soldier Monument Installation	247
Charleston Installation of Sad Lincoln	251
Stonewall Jackson Statue Restored and Relocated	254
Timeline	257
Discussion Questions	261
Notes	265
Selected Bibliography	273
Index	279

Illustrations

Abraham Lincoln Walks at Midnight	1
Map of Virginia: Showing the Distribution of Its Slave Population from the Census of 1860	8
Life in eastern and western Virginia	15
Votes by county representatives on Virginia secession	56–57
Anna Kennedy Davis and John James Davis, 1862	63
Major turnpikes and railroads in West Virginia, 1860	72
A Virginia "Sassesh"	101
The Squirrel Hunters	113
Contraband camp, Harpers Ferry, VA	120
The *Spirit of Jefferson* celebrates the end of Republican rule in the state	222
J. H. Diss Debar, *The West Virginia Hand Book and Immigrant's Guide*	228
Stonewall Jackson statue on statehouse grounds	239
The Mountaineer Monument on West Virginia State Capitol grounds	243
The Union soldier monument	248

Series Editors' Preface

The Civil War in the Great Interior series focuses on the Middle West, as the complex region has come to be known, during the most critical era of American history. In his annual message to Congress in December 1862, Abraham Lincoln identified "the great interior region" as the area between the Alleghenies and the Rocky Mountains, south of Canada and north of the "culture of cotton." Lincoln included in this region the states of Ohio, Indiana, Michigan, Wisconsin, Illinois, Missouri, Kansas, Iowa, Minnesota, and Kentucky; the area that would become West Virginia; and parts of Tennessee and the Dakota, Nebraska, and Colorado Territories. This area, Lincoln maintained, was critical to the "great body of the republic" not only because it bound together the North, South, and West but also because its people would not assent to the division of the Union.

This series examines what was, to Lincoln and other Americans in the mid-nineteenth century, the most powerful, influential, and critical area of the country. It considers how the people of the Middle West experienced the Civil War and the role they played in preserving and redefining the nation. These collections of historical sources—many of which have never been published—explore significant issues raised by the sectional conflict, the Civil War, and Reconstruction. The series underscores what was unique to particular states and their residents while recognizing the values and experiences that individuals in the Middle West shared with other Northerners and, in some cases, with Southerners.

Within these volumes are the voices of a diverse cross section of nineteenth-century Americans, including African Americans, European immigrants, Native Americans, and women. Editors have gathered evidence from farms and factories, rural and urban areas, and communities throughout each state to examine the relationships of individuals, their communities, the political culture, and the events on the battlefields. The volumes present readers with layers of evidence that can be combined in a multitude of patterns to yield new conclusions and raise questions about prevailing interpretations of the past.

The editor of each volume provides a narrative framework through brief chapter introductions and background information for each document, as well as a timeline. As these volumes cannot address all aspects of the Civil War experience for each state, they include selected bibliographies to guide readers in further research. Documents were chosen for what they reveal about the past, but each also speaks to the subjective nature of history and the decisions that historians face when weighing the merits and limits of each piece of evidence they uncover. The diverse documents included in these volumes also expose readers to the craft of history and to the variety of source materials historians utilize as they explore the past.

Much of the material in these works will raise questions, spark debates, and generate discussion. Whether read with an eye toward the history of the Union war effort, a particular state or region, or the Civil War's implications for race, class, and gender in America, the volumes in the Civil War in the Great Interior help us consider—and reconsider—the evidence from the past.

Martin J. Hershock

Christine Dee

Preface

West Virginia is the only state created in the midst of the Civil War. When Abraham Lincoln signed off on the bill establishing the state, he justified it as an expedient measure during a national crisis. The roots of division within Virginia stretched back to its first constitution, which jealously protected the powers of elites in the state's east. The west differed from the east in geography and in the ways the people earned their daily bread. But separation was not foreordained. Even as a variety of social, economic, and political factors pulled eastern and western Virginians apart, other factors kept the state bound together. Without the Civil War, West Virginia might still be just "western Virginia." The issues that splintered the nation in 1861—slavery, resentment of the slave power, and disagreement on the value of the Union—formed the allegiances of western Virginians just as they did for Americans in other regions. But West Virginia's experience of the war and its aftermath was unique. Sometimes described as the "fifth border state," West Virginia was no state at all until 1863. That fundamental fact meant that the people of western Virginia faced a set of distinctive circumstances as they navigated through the conflict and sought to restore peace in its aftermath.

The documents in this book were selected in an effort to represent the experiences of a diverse range of western Virginians across a diverse landscape. The social, cultural, and economic realities differed in West Virginia's Northern and Eastern Panhandles and also in its northern and southern counties. What Wheeling residents thought about and experienced in the war was distinct from what those in Harpers Ferry, in the Kanawha Valley, and in southern counties like Greenbrier experienced. Black and White, male and female, slaveholding and nonslaveholding western Virginians all understood the conflict differently as well. I have attempted to capture a broad range of perspectives on (West) Virginia from the antebellum era all the way to the present, when West Virginians are still struggling with how to remember and honor this tumultuous period. The Civil War, after all, is a central part of West Virginia's origin story.

I have endeavored to keep the documents as close to their original form as possible. Ellipses are used to indicate places where I have removed some words for the sake of brevity. The spellings in the original are retained except in cases where that spelling might make it difficult for the reader to discern meaning. For some sources, missing commas or other punctuation have been added and words have been capitalized or uncapitalized when the condition in the original was distracting enough to interfere with the reader's ability to comprehend the meaning of the author. Brackets are occasionally employed to fill in missing or partial words.

The introduction provides an overview of the history of western Virginia and its relationship to the rest of the state. Chapter 1 examines the sources of some of the tension between the eastern and western counties of Virginia up to 1859 and John Brown's raid on Harpers Ferry. Documents in chapter 2 examine the growing political crisis in the aftermath of the raid and through the secession winter of 1860–61. Documents in chapter 3 explore the moves western Virginians—Black and White, those loyal to the Union and those to Virginia—made during the early months of the war, as well as the efforts of Union and Confederate military officials to control the region. Chapter 4's documents examine the experiences of western Virginians during military occupation, as well as the perspective of soldiers from the occupying armies, while chapter 5 is devoted to the long process of separation from Virginia and the movement to statehood. Chapter 6 focuses on the varied ways western Virginia's women experienced the war. Women's perspectives on the war are infused through the chapters, but collecting a variety of documents regarding women in one chapter allows for a deeper look at the distinctive experiences of women in wartime (West) Virginia. Documents in chapter 7 explore how soldiers and civilians endured war as the conflict continued into its final years. Chapter 8 examines the distinctive postwar experiences of West Virginia in the eras that historians often refer to as Reconstruction and the Gilded Age and shows that those period titles do not fit the West Virginia experience very well. Chapter 9 examines Civil War memory by focusing on the four Civil War statues that currently occupy space on the statehouse grounds. In addition to images of each statue, and transcriptions of any text on the monuments, I have provided newspaper accounts of the events surrounding their dedication.

A word on the geographic names I deploy throughout the book. As the state of West Virginia is a midwar creation, deciding what terms to use in referring to the place has been challenging. I deploy "western Virginia" to refer to the counties of the Shenandoah Valley and the Trans-Allegheny region. All these counties shared common frustrations with eastern Virginia's political dominance before the war, but many cast their lot with the east once the war began. I occasionally use "(West) Virginia" to refer to institutions committed to the Union that identified as part of "West Virginia" after statehood was secured. For example, the 7th Virginia Infantry Regiment was renamed the 7th West Virginia midway through the war. I use the term "West Virginia" to refer to those counties that became part of the new state in 1863. At times I also use other geographic descriptors, including "southwestern Virginia," "northwestern Virginia," "the Northern Panhandle," and "the Eastern Panhandle." In many cases there is no perfect term to describe the time and place I am referring to, but it is my hope that my choices do not distract or confuse the reader.

Acknowledgments

I would like to thank Marty Hershock, series editor, for inviting me to take on this project at the peak of the pandemic after L. Diane Barnes, who had initially planned to write this volume, moved on from her position as a professor of history at Youngstown State University to bigger things. Diane generously shared the files she had compiled for this project with me, including scans of some archival documents that I used in this volume. For that I am very grateful, as I began this project at a time when every relevant archive was closed to the public. Dedicated staff at several archives agreed to send me scans of documents while their physical archives were still shuttered. I want to thank the staff of the West Virginia and Regional History Center in Morgantown, West Virginia; the archivists at the Ohio History Connection in Columbus, Ohio; and the Gilder Lehrman Institute in New York for providing me with digital access during those trying times.

The William L. Clements Library at the University of Michigan awarded me a Melhorn Fellowship to do archival work with one of my gifted undergraduate students, Casey Wood. Casey is one of those increasingly rare people under thirty who writes in cursive script—in fact, Casey produces elegant cursive. That talent was invaluable as we worked our way through manuscripts written in primitive nineteenth-century cursive and documents that were often heavily stained or weathered. Casey proved a master detective in deciphering smudged and scribbled diary and journal entries, and without his assistance several compelling documents in this collection would not have appeared in this volume.

I am grateful to the leadership of Muskingum University for continuing its commitment to supporting faculty research and writing with regular sabbatical leaves. While most of the research for and writing of this volume occurred in the summer, part of my fall 2022 sabbatical was devoted to revising this work.

An early version of this manuscript was field-tested by students enrolled in my Civil War History course, and their feedback has proven immensely valuable in making this a more undergraduate-friendly volume. The regular Civil War study tours I offer to my undergraduates with my colleague Tom McGrath have provided me with repeated opportunities to visit and study many of the places featured in this volume, including Wheeling, Harpers Ferry and the Eastern Panhandle, Greenbrier County and Lewisburg, and Charleston. Other locations I was able to visit on solo trips. An excellent dissertation written by

Adam Zucconi of Richard Bland College helped me rethink the politics of West Virginia statehood, and Dr. Zucconi generously shared with me one of the documents that made it into this volume. I did not have the opportunity to meet Wheeling historian Jon-Erik Gilot until the volume was nearly finished, but he provided some useful responses to last-minute questions.

I am also deeply indebted to the anonymous readers who provided very useful feedback on early drafts of this manuscript, and to Ricky Huard and Beth Pratt at Ohio University Press for their patient and steady stewardship of this manuscript through the stages of peer review and publication. Also, Tyler Balli's careful and judicious copyediting and suggestions have made this a much better volume.

Many colleagues and friends also assisted me during this process. Stephen Van Horn, professor of geology at Muskingum, constructed the maps that show how county representatives voted in the Virginia Secession Convention in April 1861. Erin Stevic assisted me with some last-minute technical issues on maps. Many friends and colleagues have provided support and encouragement to me during the long process from first draft to publication. I appreciate the incredible support of my colleagues in the History Department—Laura Hilton, Alistair Hattingh, Karen Dunak, and Tom McGrath—but also colleagues beyond my department and institution, including David Turrill, Arjun Sondhi, Tom German, and Greg Wilson.

Finally, I am extremely grateful for the support of my wife, Katie, and my son, Liam, during the research and writing process.

Introduction

THE CENTENNIAL of West Virginia in 1963 passed without a monument celebrating the event on the state capitol's grounds. Eleven years later, however, on June 20, 1974, a bronze statue of Abraham Lincoln, the president who gave birth to the state, was dedicated on the lawn between the capitol and the Kanawha River. Designed by sculptor Fred Torrey, the bronze statue was inspired by Vachel Lindsay's somber poem about the president, "Abraham Lincoln Walks at Midnight." Lindsay's poem depicts "a mourning figure" walking alone at night.

> His head is bowed. He thinks on men and kings.
> Yea, when the sick world cries, how can he sleep?
> Too many peasants fight, they know not why,
> Too many homesteads in black terror weep.
>
> The sins of all the war-lords burn his heart.
> He sees the dreadnaughts scouring every main.
> He carries on his shawl-wrapped shoulders now
> The bitterness, the folly and the pain.[1]

Abraham Lincoln Walks at Midnight, by Fred Torrey. Photo by William Kerrigan.

The mood of Torrey's Lincoln monument departed significantly from the other three Civil War monuments already present on the capitol grounds. The first one honored one of West Virginia's most notable opponents of statehood: Thomas "Stonewall" Jackson. This statue to the state's most famous Confederate had been dedicated sixty-four years earlier in 1910. Perhaps the Lincoln statue reflected the post-heroic mood of the whole country in 1974, as the nation extracted itself from a long and bloody conflict in Vietnam. But the Lincoln statue also reveals something about West Virginia's fraught and unresolved understanding of its own origin story.

The state of West Virginia was born in conflict. Forced to choose between their identities as Americans or as Virginians, the region's White residents did not all agree on which allegiance to prioritize. With the war's end, many western Virginians who had taken up arms for the Confederacy returned to their prewar communities, where their civil status was uncertain. Some victims of violence on both sides nursed grievances, making the challenge of reintegrating former Confederates more vexing. In the postwar era, West Virginia's experience of Reconstruction differed from that of Virginia and other defeated Confederate states. The issue of White Confederate disenfranchisement took center stage in the new state, and challenges to the rights of freedmen and freedwomen were overshadowed by this first concern. It is worth asking whether the term "Reconstruction" makes sense for explaining the postwar transformation of West Virginia, a state that did not exist before the war began.[2] By 1872, former Confederates in the state had reclaimed their political rights and helped shape the young state's first constitutional revision. By that point West Virginia was moving into a new era of industrial development that accelerated political realignments even while the memories of the conflict were still fresh.

The earliest histories of the state portrayed western Virginians as hostile to the institution of slavery and overwhelmingly loyal to the Union. This idea of Union-loving West Virginia was embedded in Theodore F. Lang's *Loyal West Virginia*, first published in 1895, which lifted up the state's Unionist heroes and downplayed the presence of slavery in the region. Early estimates of the number of western Virginians who enlisted either in the Union or Confederate army reinforced the loyalty theme. At their highest thirty-two thousand western Virginians were counted as enlisting on the Union side, and only about seven thousand on the Confederate side. But those numbers have been adjusted as historians have adopted more sophisticated counting methods. The presence of many Ohio and Pennsylvania men in many of the (West) Virginia units has adjusted the Union-side numbers to as low as twenty thousand, and more thorough attempts to count western Virginians in Confederate units has raised that number to rough equality with the Union enlistments.[3]

Yet even the debate over the numbers of western Virginians enlisting in regular Confederate and Union units misrepresents the nature of the Civil War, especially in places like western Virginia. The fate of the region was not simply determined by soldiers in regular units; many western Virginians joined home guards—that is, informal partisan ranger units—or operated as "bushwhackers," which operated beyond the control of the governments to which they claimed allegiance. Recent scholarship on irregular warfare has drawn attention to the important role these actors played in determining the war's outcome, and while irregular warfare occurred throughout the nation during the Civil War, in certain areas, including Missouri, Arkansas, and in many parts of Appalachia, unregulated violence was widespread. This certainly characterized the war experience of western Virginians. "It is impossible to understand the Civil War without appreciating the scope and impact of the guerilla conflict," historian Daniel E. Sutherland writes. "Guerillas helped check invading armies at every turn."[4] Traditional "drums and trumpets" histories of the Civil War focused almost entirely on formal battlefields, depicting the war as a great chess match between opposing generals. In such histories, places like western Virginia were largely invisible, as the region's battles were generally small affairs, with the lone exception of the mass surrender of Union forces at Harpers Ferry in the fall of 1862.

These traditional histories largely ignore not just irregular fighters but civilians, including women and enslaved and free African Americans, and do not assess these people's impact on the war's outcome. But western Virginia's story invites us to question these old narratives. The Civil War's outcome was to a large extent determined by the actions of noncombatants. Women encouraged or discouraged the participation of sons and husbands. They supported armies in a variety of ways, from knitting clothes for soldiers and quietly resisting occupiers to serving as spies and even in some cases taking up arms.[5] Enslaved African Americans, "through small, isolated actions, . . . engaged in a continuing struggle to assert their humanity in daily dramas: in understated forms of challenges, such as malingering or stealing, and property crime; or in overstated forms, such as violent and open resistance to slaveholder authority," notes historian William A. Link. Pursuing their own interests, enslaved people shaped the behaviors and political decisions of their enslavers before and during the Civil War. Free Black farmers and laborers, who had navigated a precarious status before the war, also faced new risks and challenges in the war years.[6]

West Virginia's marginalization in traditional Civil War histories was not just the result of their emphasis on the conflict's mega-battles. As West Virginia is the only fully Appalachian state, its residents faced the burden of two powerful, simplistic stereotypes—one positive, one negative. Historians Kenneth

Noe and Shannon Wilson identify the first of these as "the myth of Unionist Appalachia." The idea of West Virginians' dependable and consistent loyalty to the liberty-loving Union has been reified in the state's motto, adopted in 1872, *Montani semper liberi* (Mountaineers Are Always Free). The West Virginia coat of arms, displayed on the cover of this volume, also centers free White laborers in the West Virginia story. The freedom-loving mountaineer was celebrated in early histories and memorialized in the Mountaineer Monument on capitol grounds and on the campus of West Virginia University, which elevated the Mountaineer to mascot status in the late 1920s.

Noe and Wilson identify "the myth of savage Appalachia" as the second stereotype the state has been burdened with. According to this myth, the Civil War spawned senseless, persistent, and bloody feuds between uncivilized mountain families, portrayed most famously by the Hatfield-McCoy feud along the West Virginia–Kentucky border. Lang's *Loyal West Virginia* identified three classes of persons in the state. The first two classes, enterprising residents of cities and towns and farmers, had many noble qualities, according to Lang, but he had nothing positive to say about the third: "the Improvident Mountaineer," who occupied the hills and hollows. Negative depictions of western Virginia's mountain people may have been magnified and spread by occupying armies during the war, as soldiers from out of state attributed guerrilla violence to this class of West Virginians. The imposition of both positive and negative caricatures of groups of people deemed different and exotic is not uncommon and finds a parallel in the stereotypes of American Indians as "noble savages."[7]

A flurry of recent scholarship on border states in the Civil War has invited some scholars to also consider western Virginia as a "border state," even though it did not exist as a political unit at the outset of the war. A border state is defined generally as a state where slavery existed in 1861 but did not formally join the Confederacy. Missouri, Kentucky, Maryland, and Delaware all fit this description, and recent border state scholarship has considered West Virginia as "the fifth border state" when it formally joined the Union in 1863.[8] Western Virginians, like other border state residents, were more likely to experience a tension between the two driving issues of the war: the future of slavery and the value of the Union.

A spate of recent scholarship on border states has illuminated that many residents of this region mapped out a political viewpoint that was both proslavery and pro-Union. For many western Virginians at the outset of the war, there was no contradiction in these positions. For example, Waitman T. Willey, one of the most vocal defenders of the Union during the Virginia Secession Convention, argued that leaving the Union presented a greater threat to the institution of slavery than remaining in it: "Let us look at this matter. You dissolve the

Union. What then? The common national obligation is destroyed. Will not the negro find it out? The motives to flee across the line would be increased, because the negro would know that whenever he crosses that line, he will be free. There will be no fugitive slave law for his recovery, and he will know it."[9] The recent border state scholarship also highlights how border state Unionists reacted to the shifting war aims of the North, as emancipation became a second objective, and how they experienced and remembered the war and Reconstruction.[10]

In 1860 western Virginia was a region, not a state. Virginia, with over sixty-three thousand square miles of land, was larger than any other state east of the Mississippi. It ranked fifth among all states in total population and seventh in free population. Over half a million enslaved persons lived in Virginia in 1860, and each counted for representation purposes as three-fifths a person, meaning that Virginia's fifteen electoral votes in 1860 made it the fourth-most powerful state in the 1860 presidential election. Since the time of the American Revolution, Virginia had played an outsized role in shaping the young nation, both politically and culturally. Seven of the first fifteen American presidents were born in the state. Within the slaveholding states, Virginia remained the largest in both total population and in the number of enslaved people who toiled within its borders. Three in ten Virginians were by law the property of White enslavers. Slavery was central to Virginia's economy. Free White Virginians in all regions of the state, whether they were enslavers or not, were generally proud of Virginia's influence in the nation and favored the institution of slavery. Abolitionism had no toehold in Virginia.

A state as expansive as Virginia in 1860 was not without its cultural and economic diversity. As early as 1816, when the Virginia legislature established the Fund for Internal Improvements, it divided the state into four divisions: the Tidewater, the Piedmont, the Valley, and the Trans-Allegheny region. These divisions reflected distinctive regions within the state, and over time each vied to extend or preserve its political power within the state.[11] The longest-settled of these—the Tidewater—encompassed the counties along the Atlantic coast and inland tributaries to the fall line, where the first rapids obstructed river navigation. Many of the oldest Virginia families resided in this region. They had extensive landholdings and commanded large numbers of enslaved laborers, initially required to cultivate the labor-intensive tobacco crops, the foundation of much of the region's wealth. By the early nineteenth century, declining soil fertility was undermining the profitability of the crop, but those first families maintained much of their wealth and political power.

To the west of the Tidewater, the Piedmont region starts where the land begins to rise. A fertile region of plains and gently rising hills, by the nineteenth century the Piedmont had begun to eclipse the Tidewater in agricultural productivity, with tobacco and wheat the most important crops. Some of the United States' most important early leaders, notably Thomas Jefferson and James Madison, made the Piedmont their home. Both the Tidewater and Piedmont regions depended heavily on enslaved labor on the eve of the Civil War.

Between the Blue Ridge Mountains and the Alleghenies, a broad valley extended toward the southwest. Called the Shenandoah Valley for the river that flows northeasterly through its northern region, it is also known as the Great Valley. Many of the Great Valley's migrants did not arrive from eastern Virginia but instead filtered down through the region from Pennsylvania. Roughly one in five persons living in the Shenandoah Valley was unfree in 1860, a decline from earlier decades when enslaved people constituted more than a quarter of the region's population. The region's economy was rapidly diversifying both in agriculture and industry, but products produced by enslaved workers remained central to the Valley's economy. At its northern end, where the Shenandoah River flowed into the Potomac, the towns of Martinsburg and Harpers Ferry were emerging as significant centers of trade and industry, a development accelerated by the arrival of the Chesapeake and Ohio Canal and the Baltimore and Ohio Railroad, which provided those communities easy access to eastern markets.[12]

West of the Valley, Virginia's Trans-Allegheny region stretched northwest to the Ohio River and southwest to the Cumberland Gap, a notch in the long ridge of the Cumberland Mountains that became an important gateway for White settlement in Kentucky and Tennessee. Many residents of the Trans-Allegheny part of the region had multigenerational ties to the eastern regions of Virginia. Others were more recent arrivals from Northern states. It was mostly a land of ridges and hollows and was generally, but not entirely, ill-suited for large-scale plantation agriculture. Instead, Trans-Allegheny Virginia was characterized by small farms and limited animal grazing, but it also contained significant pockets of industry near Wheeling, at Harpers Ferry, along the Kanawha River near Charleston, and along the Monongahela River.

While the percentage of enslaved people in the Trans-Allegheny region was generally lower than in the Valley and the east, slavery was still present nearly everywhere in the region. Its importance to local western economies varied greatly. In the Northern Panhandle, more than 5 percent of the population was enslaved in 1820, and people were still occasionally bought and sold on the streets of Wheeling in the years just before the Civil War. The institution was nevertheless rapidly disappearing in this narrow strip of land wedged between the free states of Pennsylvania and Ohio. By 1860 enslaved persons amounted to only a fraction of 1 percent of the region's population. In the Monongahela Valley, small numbers of enslaved people toiled on farms and in factories or as domestic servants in the homes of middle-class Whites. Many White families who owned no enslaved people nevertheless depended upon the institution, leasing house servants annually from local enslavers. About 13 percent of the population of Kanawha County was unfree. Many of these enslaved laborers were owned by eastern Virginia planters, leased annually to the owners of the salt factories along the Kanawha River to do the hard and dangerous work of converting briny water to salt.[13] Further south, in Greenbrier and Monroe Counties, more than 10 percent of the population was unfree. While these counties were characterized by mountainous terrain, in the pockets of flatter lands White residents attempted to replicate the plantation slavery of the east, and many plantations with ten or more enslaved laborers were present. South of Monroe County, where the Valley splintered into a series of ridges and narrow bottomlands, counties along the line of the recently completed Virginia and Tennessee Railroad were rapidly transferring to a slave-based commercial economy. Nearly three in ten persons residing in Pulaski County in 1860 were unfree. In an acknowledgment that this new rail line was accelerating southwestern Virginia's distinctions from northwestern Virginia, in 1860 the Board of Public Works divided the Trans-Allegheny region into northwest and southwest divisions.[14]

Geography, economy, cultural ties, political allegiances, and views about slavery and the slaveholding elite would all influence the allegiances of western Virginians during the war, as would the presence or absence of one military force or another. With the war's end, autonomous West Virginia would have to grapple with the challenges of resolving the political and civil rights of the newly freed men and women and of those who had supported the failed Confederacy. They would also have to craft the origin story of a state born in conflict.

ONE

Virginia's West

*B*EFORE THERE was West Virginia, there was Virginia's west. In 1860, Virginia stretched from the Chesapeake's eastern shore to the Ohio River in the northwest, and the Cumberland Gap in the southwest. The geographic diversity of the state allowed for numerous ways of getting a living, and its challenging geography made travel between its eastern and western regions quite difficult. Like many of Britain's North American colonies, Virginia's original charter was somewhat vague on its western boundaries. As a result, colonial eastern Virginians held expansive notions of what lands in the interior rightly belonged to them. Many members of Virginia's Tidewater elite made use of their extensive political influence to secure claims to large tracts of land in the west well before the

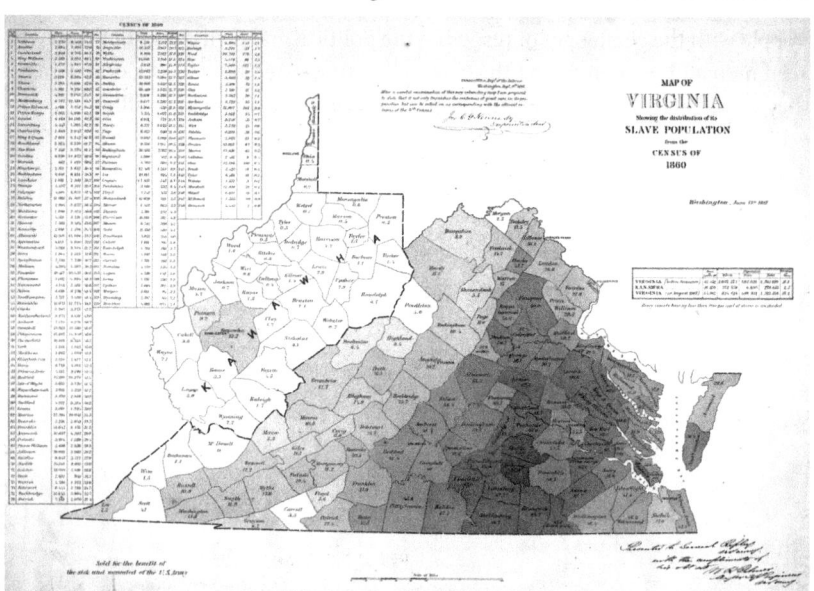

Map of Virginia: Showing the Distribution of Its Slave Population from the Census of 1860 (Washington: Henry S. Graham, 1861), Library of Congress.

American Revolution. Young George Washington, not born into an elite family, was able to amass paper claims to large swaths of western land through military service, survey work, and his rising social capital. In July of 1773 he advertised ten thousand acres of land south of the Ohio between the Kanawha and Little Kanawha Rivers for leases to settlers "upon moderate terms." Potential tenants would have to clear, fence, and plant at least three acres of unbroken land for each fifty leased, plant and enclose five acres of meadow, and plant "at least fifty good fruit trees," all within two years. In exchange for this hard work, which was necessary for Washington to complete his legal claim to the land, Washington would not charge these tenants any rent for those first two years, an offer he believed would be attractive to many young families of modest means. He was incorrect. The ambitious poor had easier options for securing land for themselves and did not take up his offer. Desperate to improve the land to secure his title, Washington was forced to hire an overseer and to purchase several indentured servants to make these improvements. But many of these servants ran away rather than complete this backbreaking work.[1] Washington and the elite easterners who made use of their financial, social, and political capital to secure vast claims in western Virginia struggled to convert their paper claims to profits. Migrants of lesser means who moved into western Virginia often occupied land on the principle of squatter's rights, resulting in a jumble of conflicting land claims that made it difficult for anyone to secure titles. This reality created opportunities for lawyers, who moved into incipient communities and offered their services to sort these conflicting claims out. The eastern-dominated government retained the power to establish county courts and appoint local officials until 1851, so it behooved these lawyers to find eastern patrons to affirm their local authority. The eastern elite jealously protected their political power for decades after the Revolution, even as the population stagnated in the east and accelerated west of the Blue Ridge. The unequal relationship between east and west, and efforts by westerners to correct this, shaped the state's politics before the Civil War.[2]

The eastern elite expected to rule. Virginia's revolutionary founders drafted a state constitution which ensured that large slaveholders would maintain political power well into the future. In apportioning representation, they counted enslaved people to keep the balance of power in the east. In addition, property qualifications kept many poorer White Virginians from voting entirely. The late 1820s saw the rise of Andrew Jackson to the presidency and elevated the principle of universal White male suffrage across the nation, but Virginia's planter elite resisted this wave for a long time. In two state constitutional conventions, the first in 1829–30 and the second in 1850–51, western Virginians pressed for the end of property qualifications for voting and fairer political representation for the west in state government. In the first of these conventions, western representatives achieved no meaningful reform. While the 1830 constitution passed, it was roundly rejected by westerners.

In 1848 Virginians elected John B. Floyd to the governorship. A native of Virginia's southwest, Floyd pushed for another constitutional convention to address the grievances of most of his fellow western Virginians. The 1850–51 convention yielded several significant victories for westerners that would have a profound effect on Virginia politics. First, the eastern elite agreed to end property qualifications for voting, making Virginia the second to last state to embrace universal White male suffrage. This significantly increased the voting population, energized partisan politics, and resulted in higher levels of voter engagement across the state. Second, the introduction of popular elections for the governor's office ensured that western Virginians would now have a stronger voice in Virginia politics. Floyd's successor in the governor's office was Joseph Johnson, a native of Harrison County in the northwest. The last two governors of the undivided state also represented western interests. Henry A. Wise (1856–60) was an easterner but a vocal advocate of western issues, and John Letcher (1860–64) hailed from the Shenandoah Valley. Westerners welcomed additional reforms, including the popular election of county court officials—replacing the appointment system that tended to enforce official local loyalty to eastern elite—and the end of "plural voting," which allowed some of the state's largest landholders to vote in more than one county.[3]

Despite these gains, many westerners remained unconvinced that the eastern elite would embrace true equality between east and west. The convention protected the taxation system, which capped the assessment of slave property at $300—at a time when some enslaved people were sold for $1,500—while other taxable forms of property were assessed at market value. Furthermore, the convention promised to reexamine legislative reapportionment at a later date, allowing the east to maintain its majority control of the state assembly until 1865. The eastern elite continued to protect its interests against a west it viewed as a threat. Harrison County resident John S. Carlile, who opposed Virginia's secession in 1861 and emerged as one of the earliest advocates of West Virginia statehood, later stated that the limited victories of the 1850–51 convention "clearly disclosed" to his mind "the utter incompatibility" of northwest Virginians' interests and of "remaining in connection with the eastern portion of the state."[4] Some of Carlile's own wealth was in slave property, but he had come to conclude that the large planters of the east would never extend true equality to Trans-Allegheny Virginians.

Westerners did not seek fairer political representation simply as an end in itself. There were critical issues the Trans-Allegheny west faced that the eastern-dominated state government did not prioritize. Emerging industries in the west—including ironworks in the Monongahela Valley and salt manufacturing along the Kanawha River—required improved roads, canals, and railroads to thrive. Agriculturalists interested in shifting away from subsistence to commercial farming also needed efficient ways to get their goods to distant markets. Eastern politicians, who already benefited from improved transportation systems in their own areas, were slow to agree to taxes to support those needs in the west. Support for improved turnpike connections between the regions was halting. Funding for George Washington's planned James River and Kanawha Canal came so slowly that it was just half-finished in 1850. Stingy when it came to financing transportation investments that would strengthen the connections between western Virginia resources and eastern Virginia markets, state legislators also blocked proposals by the Baltimore and Ohio Railroad to extend its lines into western Virginia, because they feared Richmond would lose trade to rival city Baltimore. Only in the southwestern reaches of the Trans-Allegheny region did Richmond respond effectively to calls from the west for transportation improvements, completing the Virginia and Tennessee Railroad from Lynchburg to Bristol, Tennessee, in 1856. In fact, by that investment, the eastern elite may have purchased the loyalty of Virginia's southwest. While much of the Trans-Allegheny northwest remained opposed to secession even after Fort Sumter, the Trans-Allegheny southwest leaders aligned with the eastern elite and supported secession. As historian Kenneth Noe has explained, "Linked to Richmond's markets, Southwest Virginians also were linked in 1861 to Richmond's cause."[5] The general failure of eastern politicians to understand the mutual benefits of internal improvements to both east and west was one reason westerners sought more balanced political representation in state government.[6]

As significant as the divides were between eastern and western Virginians, other forces united the citizens of the sections. They shared a common pride in the history of their state and its founding heroes—Washington, Jefferson, and Madison. That the state had birthed seven presidents before the Civil War spoke to its prestige and power. A substantial number of Trans-Allegheny Virginians hailed from families that had roots in the state going back generations. Partisan politics, too, cut across the sectional grain in Virginia, and by expanding voter participation across the state, the 1851 constitution strengthened partisan identities in the state. At base, adherents of the Jacksonian Democratic Party and the rival Whigs represented two different responses to the societal changes wrought by the market and transportation revolutions. Those who welcomed these changes tended to find a home in the Whig Party. Those with a greater ambivalence about these changes often aligned with the Jacksonian Democrats. These alignments were imperfect, however, and as historian Daniel W. Crofts notes, "antebellum southerners voted more as members of a community than as individuals." Ties of kinship and patronage shaped political allegiances at the local level, sometimes in ways that defied the conflicting ideologies of the parties.[7]

The political revolution ushered in by Andrew Jackson also served to unite Virginians of east and west in specific ways. First, the Jacksonian idea that race, not class, should bestow the full rights of citizenship—white supremacy—was shared by nearly all White Virginians, whether they held enslaved peoples or not. In addition, Jackson's victory, created new political identities that spanned the regions of the state. With each party taking sides on issues of the day and dispensing patronage to loyal members, many Virginians would come to see party distinction as more significant than geographic divide. Eastern and western Democrats united to thwart the plans of eastern and western Whigs, who did the same. These party identities became so strong that even after the political parties shifted again, the labels "Whig" and "Jackson man" continued to have resonance for many years.[8]

One issue that almost never divided White Virginians—easterners from westerners, or Whigs from Democrats—was the morality of slavery. Abolitionism— the belief that slavery was morally wrong and ought to be abolished everywhere— emerged as a small but vocal movement in many Northern states around 1830. But even in states where slavery did not exist, abolitionist ideas sparked violent responses from many Northern Whites. While violence against abolitionists became less common in the North after 1850, at no time before the Civil War were abolitionist ideas held by a majority of White people in the Northern states. In Virginia, abolitionism was not significantly active anywhere before the Civil War. Any public assertion that slavery as an institution was less than a positive good for both master and slave was likely to have severe consequences for the utterer. Speech that questioned the morality of slavery in a state where 30 percent of the population was enslaved was widely understood as having the potential to incite "servile insurrection" against free White people.

An alternative antislavery viewpoint—free-soil ideology—had gained traction among many White Northerners by the 1840s and was a core component of the Republican Party's ideology when it emerged in the North in the middle of the 1850s. Free-soil ideology generally avoided making moral statements about the justness of slavery and did not universally reject white supremacy. Instead, it focused on restricting the growth of slavery to the states where it already existed and argued that the institution was inefficient and less productive than free-labor systems. Free-soilism implied that slavery might simply die out eventually because of its inefficiency, and therefore avoided discussion of whether it should be dismantled where it already existed. Free-soilism did inspire anger in many of its followers, not by stoking moral outrage at the plight of the enslaved but by encouraging resentment of the "slave power" or "slaveocracy," which had controlled the national government for too long, all to protect the institution that made slaveholders wealthy. The passage of the Fugitive Slave Act of 1850, which gave slave hunters extraordinary powers to disrupt life in Northern communities as they sought to capture runaways, and the passage of the Kansas-Nebraska Act, which appeared to open the entire West for exploitation by the slaveocracy, fueled resentment against slaveholding elites across the North in the 1850s.

Most White Virginians, however, failed to distinguish abolitionism from free-soil ideas and treated each with the same contempt and fear. Nevertheless, two aspects of free-soil thinking had some purchase in western Virginia before the Civil War. The first was the notion that slavery was an inefficient and unproductive labor system, inferior to free-labor systems. The second was the idea that a small but powerful slaveholding elite held the reins of power and used that power to elevate their own interests. While western Virginians may have been loath to associate themselves publicly with a Northern antislavery movement, elements of the free-soil critique certainly resonated—and were infrequently uttered—in the west in the two decades before the Civil War. Henry Ruffner's 1847 call for ending slavery in western Virginia is one example and is included in this chapter's primary sources.[9]

The rise of the free-soil Republican Party in the North in the middle of the 1850s unsettled most White Virginians. (Two exceptions to this are discussed in chapter 2—residents in Virginia's Northern Panhandle and in the tiny free-soil community of Ceredo in Virginia's far west.) Most Virginians were insulted by what they perceived as the anti-Southernism of Republican rhetoric and viewed the party's rise as a dark and ominous development. Partisan rivalries in the state fueled this reaction, as Virginia politicians of both parties postured to be the fiercest protector of the state against "Black Republicanism."

Exaggerated reactions to the rise of the Republican Party set the context for understanding Virginia's response to events in Harpers Ferry on the night of October 16, 1859. That evening, abolitionist John Brown, accompanied by eighteen armed men, both Black and White, entered Harpers Ferry under cover of darkness. They seized the two bridges into town and the US armory and arsenal, and emancipated the enslaved people of two local enslavers. Brown hoped to spark a wider insurrection that would emancipate all the enslaved people of Virginia. By the time Brown was captured on the morning of October 18, sixteen people had been killed, including ten of Brown's men.

The subsequent trial and execution of Brown polarized the nation but mostly united White Virginians. Southern slaveholders laid the blame on Northern politicians who promoted antislavery ideas. In Harpers Ferry, fears of a wider conspiracy meant that any residents with Northern roots found themselves under suspicion. Shortly after the raid, Harpers Ferry resident Mary Mauzy and two other local women paid a visit to a local teacher who was "a Yankee by birth, but has been for several years in the South" in order to assess where her loyalties lay.

Mauzy noted that the teacher "pretends to have no sympathy with Old Brown and his party" and that she expressed the view that if other Northerners visited the South and saw slavery as it really existed, they might change their negative views of the South and its institution. Mauzy appeared to accept the teacher's expression of solidarity with her Southern neighbors and concluded that she liked the teacher "as well as I expected. She has been attending our Church and we felt it our duty to give her some attention."[10] Perhaps Mary was convinced, but her visit testified to the anxiety and suspicion Brown's raid engendered in the community. Many Northerners condemned Brown's raid, and the Republican Party distanced itself from his actions. But expressions of Northern sympathy with the martyred Brown confirmed many White Virginians' worst fears—that Northern radicals were intent on promoting servile insurrections across the South.

THE TWO VIRGINIAS

> Connecticut-born Henry Howe found success as an author producing thick gazetteers filled with historical facts and observations about various states, including New York, Ohio, and Virginia. The first printing of his Virginia volume was released in 1845 and contained this sketch alongside his observations about life in the western part of the state.

LIFE IN WESTERN VIRGINIA.

Much of Western Virginia is yet a new country, and thinly settled; and in some of the more remote and inaccessible counties, the manner of living and the habits of the people are quite primitive. Many of these mountain counties are so far from markets, that it is a common saying among the inhabitants that they can only sell those things which will "*walk away*"—meaning cattle, horses, swine, &c. Of the latter, immense droves are sent to the east annually from this country, and Tennessee, Kentucky, and Ohio. The feeding of the swine, as they pass through the country in the autumn each year, supplies a market for much of the corn which is produced. Aside from this, there is but little inducement for each one to raise more grain than his own family will consume; and consequently, there is but little room for enterprise on the part of the agriculturalist. His products, when they sell at all, bring but a trivial sum. For instance, corn, the chief product, brings but from 17 to 25 cents per bushel; oats, 12 ½ cts. do.; pork, beef, and venison, $2 to $2 50 neat per 100 lbs.; and other things in proportion. This pay, too, is frequently in store-goods, on which the merchant, owing to his small amount of custom, charges heavy profits. For foreign luxuries, the

Life in eastern and western Virginia. From Henry Howe, *Historical Collections of Virginia* [. . .] (Charleston, SC: W. R. Babcock, 1849).

agriculturalist pays the highest prices,—the expense of transportation from the north—where they are usually purchased by the merchant—to the wild parts of Western Virginia, being three or four cents per pound: so for bulky articles, as sugar, coffee, &c., the consumer is obliged to pay several cents a pound more than an inhabitant of the older portions of the state. He, however, graduates his wants to his means; and although he may not have the fine house, equipage, dress, &c., of the wealthy planter, yet he leads a manly life, and breathes the pure air of the hills with the contented spirit of a freeman. Living

> "Far from the maddening crowd's ignoble strife,
> *His* sober wishes never *learn* to stray;
> Along the cool, sequestered vale of life,
> *He keeps* the noiseless tenor of his way."

The inhabitants of the mountain counties are almost perfectly independent. Many a young man with but a few worldly goods, marries, and, with an axe on one shoulder and a rifle on the other, goes into the recesses of the mountains, where land can be had for almost nothing. In a few days he has a log-house and a small clearing. Visit him some fine day thirty years afterwards, and you will find he has eight or ten children—the usual number here—a hardy, healthy set; forty or fifty acres cleared, mostly cultivated in corn; a rude square log bin, built in cob-house fashion, and filled with corn in *the cob,* stands beside his cabin; near it is a similar structure, in which is a horse; and scattered about are half a dozen hay-ricks; an immense drove of hogs, and some cattle, are roaming at large in the adjoining forest. And if it is what is called *"mast year"*—that is, if the forests abound in nuts, acorns, &c.—these animals will be found to be very fat, and display evidence of good living.

Enter the dwelling. The lady of the house, and all her children, are attired in homespun. Her dress is large, of convenient form, and entirely free from the fashionable lacing universal elsewhere. It is confined together with buttons, instead of hooks and eyes. She looks strong and healthy—so do her daughters—and as rosy and blooming as "flowers by the way-side." Her sons, too, are a sturdy-looking set, who soon (if not now) will be enabled to fell a tree or shoot a deer with facility. The house and furniture are exceedingly plain and simple, and, with the exception of what belongs to the cupboard, principally manufactured in the neighborhood. The husband is absent, hunting. At certain seasons of the year, what time he can spare on his little farm he passes in the excitement of the chase, and sells the skins of his game.

Henry Howe, *Historical Collections of Virginia* [. . .] (Charleston, SC: W. R. Babcock, 1849), 152–53

FREEDWOMAN JENNIE SMALL RECALLS LIFE IN SLAVERY

Howe's depiction of western Virginia includes no depiction of slavery in the region. But in fact enslaved people were present in almost every western Virginia county. The voices of enslaved western Virginians are mostly absent from the archives, but in the 1930s the Works Progress Administration collected interviews with people born in slavery. The brief interviews, most often conducted by White interviewers, are an important, if flawed, record of slavery through the eyes of the enslaved. Jennie Small recounted her early life in slavery in Pocahontas County, western Virginia, before the war.

INTERVIEW OF EX-SLAVE FROM VIRGINIA

Jennie Small,
Ex-slave, over 80 years of age.
(Reported by Rev. Edward Knox)

    I was born in Pocahontas County, Virginia in the drab and awful surroundings of slavery.

    The whipping post and cruelty in general made an indelible impression in my mind. I can see my older brothers in their tow-shirts that fell knee-length, which was sometimes their only garment, toiling laboriously under a cruel lash as the burning sun beamed down upon their backs. Pappy McNeal (we called the master Pappy) was cruel and mean. Nothing was too hard, too sharp, or too heavy to throw at an unfortunate slave. I was very much afraid of him; I think as much for my brothers' sakes as for my own. Sometimes in his fits of anger, I was afraid he might kill someone.

However, one happy spot in my heart was for his son-in-law who told us: "Do not call Mr. McNeal the master, no one is your master but God, call Mr. McNeal, mister." I have always had a tender spot in my heart for him.

There are all types of farm work to do and also some repair work about the barns and carriages. It was one of these carriages my brother was repairing when the Yankees came, but I am getting ahead of my story.

I was a favorite of my master. I had a much better sleeping quarters than my brothers. Their cots were made of straw or corn husks. Money was very rare, but we were all well-fed and kept. We wore tow-shirts which were knee-length, and no shoes. Of course, some of the master's favorites had some kind of footwear.

There were many slaves on our plantation. I never saw any of them auctioned off or put in chains. Our master's way of punishment was the use of the whipping post. When we received cuts from the whip he put soft soap and salt into our wounds to prevent scars. He did not teach us any reading or writing; we had no special way of learning; we picked up what little we knew.

When we were ill on our plantation, Dr. Wallace, a relative of Master McNeal, took care of us. We were always taught to fear the Yankees. One day I was playing in the yard of our master, with the master's little boy. Some Yankee Soldiers came up and we hid, of course, because we had been taught to fear the soldiers. One Yankee soldier discovered me, however, and took me on his knee and told me that they were our friends and not our enemies; they were here to help us. After that I loved them instead of fearing them. When we received our freedom, our master was very sorry, because we had always done all their work, and hard labor.

<small>Federal Writers' Project, "Slave Narratives: A Folk History of Slavery in the United States from Interviews with Former Slaves," vol. 12, Ohio Narratives, 1941, manuscript / mixed material, https://www.loc.gov/item/mesn120/</small>

THE CONSTITUTIONAL CONVENTION OF 1829–30

Frustrated by the disproportionate political power of the eastern counties, western Virginians pressed for political reform in 1829. During a constitutional convention over the winter of 1829–30, westerners pressed for the end of property qualifications for voting for White males and an end to the practice of apportioning representation by counting both the free and enslaved population of each district. Although enslaved people could not vote, their numbers secured majority power for the slaveholding elite of the east even as the population of the west exploded. Western representatives also sought to end policies that taxed slave "property" at less than its market value while not providing similar relief to other forms of property. The westerners came away from the convention with no meaningful gains and a growing anger at the arrogance of eastern politicians.

THE CONVENTION.

The Whig states that the committee on the Legislative department is equally divided on the subject of exclusive white representation. The Convention itself is considered to be about equally divided on this question—the most difficult one which is likely to be made. The eastern Virginians have over three hundred thousand slaves—the country west of the Blue Ridge has not more than one tenth part of that number. The claim to include the slaves in the number of persons to be represented will be tenaciously maintained. On the other hand it will be opposed by those who regard these 300 000 slaves as having no more part in the government than so many cattle.

Wheeling Compiler, October 21, 1829

* * *

23 OCTOBER 1829

W. Campbell of Brooke, submitted resolutions, which are read as follows:

1. Resolved, that all persons now by law possessed of the right of suffrage, have sufficient evidence of permanent common interests with, and attachment to, the community, and have the right of suffrage.

2. Resolved, that all free white males of twenty-three years of age, born within this Commonwealth, and resident therein, have sufficient evidence of permanent common interest with, and attachment to, the community, and have the right of suffrage.

3. Resolved, that every free white male of 21 years of age, not included in the two preceding resolutions, who is now a resident, or who may hereafter become, a resident within this Commonwealth, who is desirous of having the right of suffrage in this Commonwealth, shall, in open court, as may be prescribed

by law, make a declaration of his intention to become a permanent resident in this State, and if such person shall, six months after making such declaration, solemnly promise to submit to, and support the government of this Commonwealth, and if he shall not have been convicted of any high crime or misdemeanors against the laws of this Commonwealth, such person shall be considered as having permanent common interests with, and attachment to, the community, and shall have the right of suffrage.

<small>Journal, Virginia Constitutional Convention of 1829–30, acc. no. 35181, p. 91, Library of Virginia, Richmond</small>

"THE PEASANTRY OF THE WEST"

Richmond delegate Benjamin Watkins Leigh defended the conservative position during the 1829–30 convention that voting should be restricted to men of property and that the political power of the eastern elite should be preserved. His address to the convention provoked deep resentment for its comparison of western farmers to "peasants." It was an insult that was not soon forgotten in the region.

The resolution of the Legislative Committee, proposes to give the west power of taxation over the east, though it be apparent, that, in some respects, concerning as well the objects of taxes as the subjects of appropriation, the west has not only no common interest with the east, but a contrary or different interest. The interest of the west is contrary to ours, in regard *to slaves* considered as a subject of taxation, certainly and obviously. The unavoidable inequality of taxation upon all subjects, and the unavoidable equality of benefit from the revenue, give the west an interest to augment, and the east an interest to reduce, the amount of taxes. And as those internal improvements, those roads and canals, which seem in the opinions of many, to be the only objects of Government, let any man survey the face of the country, and deny, if he can, that different, more extensive, and more expensive, works of the kind, are wanted, and even projected, in the west and the north, than are wanted or have ever entered into the imagination of the east and the south. They would expend thousands where we would expend hundreds; that is, of our money; for if the expenditure was to be of their own, I cannot doubt they would grudge it as much as we do, or more.... We are asked ... in a tone as if they thought the request the most reasonable in the world, to give them power to tax us three times as much as themselves, when their great object can only be, to apply the revenue (after providing for, perhaps stinting, the civil list) to those internal improvements they have so much at heart.... I should be sorry to say any thing offensive to gentlemen from any quarter—but I must follow the lights of my own mind, and declare it as my opinion, that the cunning of man, or of the devil, cannot devise a more vexatious and grinding tyranny for any people, than to subject them to taxation by those, who have not the same interest with them, much more who have interests contrary to or different from theirs.

The resolution of the Legislative Committee, proposes to give full representation to the labour of the west, with an exemption from taxation, while the labour of the east will be subjected to taxation deprived of representation.

The complaint seems to shock gentlemen—I shall repeat my words. (He repeated them)—in every civilized country under the sun, some there must be who labour for their daily bread, either by contract with, or subjection to others, or for themselves. Slaves, in the eastern part of this State, fill the places of the peasantry of Europe... in the present state of the population beyond the Alleghany, there must be some peasantry, and as the country fills up, they will scarcely have more—that is, men who tend the herds and dig the soil, who have neither real nor personal capital of their own, and who earn their daily bread by the sweat of their brow. These, by this scheme, are all to be represented—but none of our slaves. And yet, *in political economy,* the latter fill exactly the same place. Slaves, indeed, are not and never will be comparable with the hardy peasantry of the mountains, in intellectual power, in moral worth, in all that determines man's degree in the moral scale, and raises him above the brute.... But I ask gentlemen to say, whether they believe, that those who are obliged to depend on their daily labour for daily subsistence, can, or do ever enter into political affairs? They never do—never will—never can.... Now, what real share, so far as mind is concerned, does any man suppose the peasantry of the west—that peasantry, which it must have when the country is as completely filled up with day-labourers as ours is of slaves—can or will take in affairs of the State?

Proceedings and Debates of the Virginia State Convention of 1829–30 (Richmond: Samuel Shepherd, 1830), 158–59

"A CONSTITUTION, WHICH PERPETUATES THAT INEQUALITY OF POWER"

The Wheeling Compiler *summarized the frustration of many westerners on the failure of the constitutional convention to make any progress on issues that mattered to the west.*

This constitution is GIVEN to the West, much in the same manner as the constitution of France was given by Louis XVIII. The King, though a minority of the nation, held the sovereign power; and he gave the nation such a constitution as suited his own views. The Eastern division of Virginia held an unequal share of power. The Convention question was carried chiefly by the vote of the West; but the apportionment of members was made by the East, and made to secure a majority of Eastern members. It has passed a modification of the constitution, which has been carried by the vote of the East against the West. No Western man voted for it, except Cook, of the Valley. With this exception, all the Delegates from the West, with three from the Loudoun, and two from the Bedford district, were against the adoption of the new constitution. The final vote was, yeas 55, nays 41—including Mr. Doddridge, who was sick and absent when the question was taken, and also including Mr. Stanard, of Richmond, who was the only anti-convention man who voted with the nays. A considerable majority of the Convention voted for the constitution; but that majority represented only a MINORITY of the white population of the state. The 55 members who passed the constitution, according to the tables heretofore published, represented 334,925 whites. The 41 members in the negative, represented 348,336 whites. Thus the MINORITY has GIVEN to the MAJORITY a constitution, which perpetuates that inequality of power which was sought to be obviated by a revision of the old constitution.

<small>Wheeling Compiler, January 27, 1830</small>

"IF WEST VIRGINIA SHALL CALL FOR A LAW TO REMOVE SLAVERY FROM HER SIDE OF THE BLUE RIDGE"

Henry Ruffner, president of the Shenandoah Valley's Washington College, was born into a slave-owning family. The family relied upon enslaved laborers at its salt manufactory in Malden on the Kanawha River. Despite this family legacy, Ruffner eventually concluded that slavery was bad for western Virginia, and in an address to the Franklin Society of Lexington, Virginia, he argued that ending slavery in western Virginia would bring greater prosperity to the region. While Ruffner avoided the moral arguments against slavery deployed by Northern abolitionists, the speech, which was published in pamphlet form shortly after it was delivered, was extremely controversial and was probably responsible for his resignation as president of Washington College the following year.

ADDRESS TO THE PEOPLE OF WEST VIRGINIA

Fellow-Citizens,

Now is the time, when we of West Virginia should review our public affairs, and consider what measures are necessary and expedient to promote the welfare of ourselves and our prosperity. Three years hence another census of the United

States will have been completed. Then it will appear how large a majority we are of the citizens of this Commonwealth, and how unjust it is that our fellow-citizens of East Virginia, being a minority of the people, should be able, by means of their majority in the Legislature, to govern both East and West for their own advantage. You have striven in vain to get this inequality of representation rectified. The same legislative majority has used the power of which we complain, to make all our complaints fruitless, and to retain the ascendancy now when they represent a minority of the people, which they secured to themselves eighteen years ago, while they yet represented the majority. . . .

You claim the white basis of representation, on the republican principle that *the majority shall rule.* You deny that slaves, who constitute no part of the political body, shall add political weight to their masters, either as individual voters or as a mass of citizens. But the slaveholding interest, which is supreme in the East, is also powerful in some parts of the West. Let this be considered as a *perpetual* and *growing* interest in our part of the State, and it may throw so much weight on the side of the Eastern principle of representation, when the hour of decision comes, as to produce a compromise, and to secure to the East a part in at least what she claims on the ground of her vast slave property. But let all the West, on due consideration, conclude that slavery is a pernicious institution, and must be gradually removed; then, united in our views on all the great interests of our West Virginia, we shall meet the approaching crisis with inflexible resolution; and West Virginia can and must succeed in her approaching struggle for her rights and her prosperity. . . .

We disclaim all intention to interfere with slavery in East Virginia. We leave it to our brethren there, to choose for themselves, whether they will let the institution remain as it is, or whether they will modify it or abolish it, in one way or another. . . . All that we ask of our Eastern brethren, in regard to this matter, is, that if West Virginia shall call for a law to remove slavery from her side of the Blue Ridge, East Virginia shall not refuse her consent, because the measure may not be palatable to herself. . . . By allowing West Virginia her just share of representation, and, if she call for it, a law for the removal of slavery, East Virginia will do more to harmonize the feelings of the State, then she ever has done, or can do by a continued refusal. West Virginia being then secured in her essential rights and interests, will not desire a separation, nor be disposed to disturb the harmony of the Commonwealth. . . .

There are certain drugs, of which large doses are poisonous, but small ones are innocent or even salutary. Slavery is not of this kind. Large doses of it kill, it is true; but smaller doses, mix them as you will, are sure to sicken and debilitate the body politic. . . . Our own West Virginia furnishes conclusive evidence, that slavery, in all quantities and degrees, has a pernicious influence on the public welfare.... We have now seen how slavery, when in full operation, first checks, and then stops, the growth of population; and finally turns it into a decline. We have seen also that slavery, when in partial operation, or mixed with a larger proportion of free labor, hangs like a dead weight upon a country, and makes it drag heavily onwards in the march of population....

[I]n agriculture, slave labor is proved to be far less productive than free labor,—*slavery is demonstrated to be not only unprofitable, but deeply injurious to the public prosperity.*... Agriculture in the slave States may be characterized in general by two epithets—*extensive—exhaustive*—which in all agricultural countries forebode two things—*impoverishment—depopulation.* The general system of slaveholding farmers and planters, in all times and places, has been, and now is, and ever will be, to cultivate much land, badly, for present gain—in short, to kill the goose that lays the golden egg. They cannot do otherwise with laborers who work by compulsion, for the benefit only of their masters, and whose sole interest in the matter is, to do as little and to consume as much as possible....

Of all the States in the Union, not one has on the whole such various and abundant resources for manufacturing, as our own Virginia, both East and West.... What must you think has caused Virginians in general to neglect their superlative advantages for manufacturing industry?...

We glory in Wheeling, because she only, in Virginia, deserves to be called a manufacturing town. For this her citizens deserve to be crowned—not with laurel—but with the solid gold of prosperity. But how came it, that Wheeling, and next to her, Wellsburg—of all the towns in Virginia—should become manufacturing towns? Answer: They breathe the atmosphere of free States, almost touching them on both sides.—But again; seeing that Wheeling, as a seat for manufactures, is equal to Pittsburgh, ... why is Wheeling so far behind Pittsburgh, and comparatively so slow in her growth?—Answer: She is in a country in which slavery is established by law.

Thus it appears, fellow-citizens, by infallible proofs, that West Virginia, in all her parts and in all her interests, has suffered immensely from the institution of slavery....

Now fellow-citizens, it is for you to determine whether the slavery question shall be considered, discussed and decided, at this critical, this turning point of your country's history: or whether it shall lie dormant until the doom of West Virginia is sealed. May heaven direct your minds to the course dictated by patriotism, by humanity and by your own true interest.

A Slaveholder of West Virginia.

Henry Ruffner, *Address to the People of West Virginia: Shewing That Slavery Is Injurious to the Public Welfare, and That It May Be Gradually Abolished without Detriment to the Rights and Interests of Slaveholders* (Lexington, VA: R. C. Noel, 1847)

THE REFORM CONSTITUTION OF 1851

Western Virginians forced another constitutional convention in 1850. There they pressed state leaders to count only free White persons when apportioning representation, to drop property qualifications for voting, and to end the unfair state property taxation laws, which capped the taxable value of slave property at $300, well below market value, but did not do the same for other forms of property, including land. Monongalia County residents pushed Waitman T. Willey, their representative to the nine-month-long convention, to fight for these issues. The slaveholding elite of the east continued to smell an abolitionist plot in the efforts of westerners to balance political power in the state, so western advocates of equal representation were often on the defensive and felt compelled to deny they had any sympathy with abolitionism. At the same time, the eastern elite's unwillingness to share control increased the resonance among western Virginians of free-soil complaints about the slave power.

Phila. Dec 2 1850

My Dear Sir

Your favor is received, for wh[ich] please accept my thanks. I had incidentally heard of your becoming a public man thro' Mr. Joseph Price, and was about writing you at Richmond, when, from the papers I learned of the convention's adjournment. I trust you will be true to the interests of W. Va. in the adjustment of the sectional question wh[ich] will probably agitate your conv[ention]. I am far from being an abolitionist. I believe the negroes of Richmond or Charleston are better off than the negroes of Phila[delphia] but my soul abhors Southern nullification.

Very truly yrs

W. W. Arnett

W. W. Arnett to Waitman T. Willey, p. 122, Charles H. Ambler Papers, West Virginia and Regional History Center, West Virginia University, Morgantown

* * *

Washington City Jan[uar]y 22 1851

Dear Sir:

I fear you will not succeed in getting the White basis. I have heard that the *valley* will play false in the hour of need, and I shall not be surprised if such turns out to be the fact. Can not something be done to awaken the Eastern members to a perception of the *Free Soil* tendencies of the West, more particularly, the North West? One thing is certain as fate, that should the representation be fixed, in the new Constitution, upon the mixed basis, our people will be dissatisfied with it. They will naturally begin to enquire into the subject, and as they come to be more fully acquainted with it, and begin to *feel* and know that it is the *slave power* that is ruling over them and destroying that equality which ought to exist between the different sections of the same State, the feeling in favor of slavery which [is] with us, is but a mere *prejudice,* will quickly die away, and in its stead will rise hostility to the *peculiar institution,* which will in the end make Virginia a free state, and give a blow to slavery in the Union from which it will never recover.

Respectfully yours
George S. Ray

George S. Ray to Waitman T. Willey, p. 122, Charles H. Ambler Papers, West Virginia and Regional History Center, West Virginia University, Morgantown

THE NEW CONSTITUTION

In the long constitutional convention of 1850–51, westerners secured a partial victory with the end of property qualifications for White male voting. The new constitution called for a reapportionment in 1865 and every ten years after but left it to future politicians to determine whether apportionment would be made on "the white basis" or "the mixed basis." The unfair cap on taxation of slave property also remained in place.

ARTICLE III.

Qualification of Voters.

1. Every white male citizen of the commonwealth, of the age of twenty-one years, who has been a resident of the state for two years, and of the county, city or town where he offers to vote, for twelve months next preceding an election, and no other person, shall be qualified to vote for members of the General Assembly and all officers elected by the people. . . .

2. The General Assembly . . . shall cause every city or town, the white population of which exceeds five thousand, to be laid off into convenient wards, and a separate place of voting to be established in each, and thereafter no inhabitant of such city or town shall be allowed to vote except in the ward in which he resides.

3. No voter, during the time for holding any election at which he is entitled to vote, shall be compelled to perform military service, except in time of war or public danger; to work upon the public roads, or to attend any court as suitor, juror or witness; and no voter shall be subject to arrest under any civil process during his attendance at elections, or in going to and returning from them.

4. In all elections votes shall be given openly, or *viva voce,* and not by ballot; but dumb persons entitled to suffrage may vote by ballot. . . .

Apportionment of Representation.

5. It shall be the duty of the General Assembly, in the year one thousand eight hundred and sixty-five, and in every tenth year thereafter, in case it can agree upon a principle of representation, to re-apportion representation in the Senate and House of Delegates in accordance therewith; and in the event the General Assembly, at the first or any subsequent period of re-apportionment, shall fail to agree upon a principle of representation, and to re-apportion representation in accordance therewith, each House shall separately propose a scheme of representation, containing a principle or rule for the House of Delegates, in connection with a principle or rule for the Senate. . . .

New Constitution of the Commonwealth of Virginia (Richmond: William Culley, 1851)

THE HARPERS FERRY INSURRECTION

John Brown's raid on the federal arsenal at Harpers Ferry sent shockwaves throughout the nation. The Senate appointed a select committee to conduct interviews, gather information, and issue an authoritative report on the events. Virginia senator James M. Mason, a slaveholder whose home in the Shenandoah Valley town of Winchester, not far from Harpers Ferry, was tasked with chairing the committee.

As to the attack itself at Harper's Ferry, the committee find that Brown first appeared in that neighborhood early in July, 1859. He came there under the assumed name of Isaac Smith, attended by two of his sons and a son-in-law. He gave out in the neighborhood that he was a farmer from New York, who desired to rent or purchase land in that vicinity, with a view to agricultural pursuits, and soon afterwards rented a small farm on the Maryland side of the river, and some four or five miles from Harper's Ferry, having on it convenient houses, and began farming operations in a very small way. . . . He lived in an obscure manner, and attracted but little attention, and certainly no suspicion whatever as to his ulterior objects. Whilst there, he kept some two or three of his party, under assumed names, at Chambersburg, Pennsylvania, who there received, and from time to time forwarded to him, the arms of different kinds of which he was subsequently found in possession. Cook, one of his men spoken of above, it appears, had resided at Harper's Ferry and its neighborhood for some twelve months before Brown appeared, pursuing various occupations. He left the Ferry a few days before the attack was made, and joined Brown at his country place. The whole number assembled with Brown at the time of the invasion were twenty-one men, making with himself in all twenty-two.

On Sunday night, the 16th of October, 1859, between 11 and 12 o'clock at night, Brown, attended by probably eighteen of his company, crossed the bridge connecting the village of Harper's Ferry with the Maryland shore, and, on reaching the Virginia side, proceeded immediately to take possession of the buildings of the armory and arsenal of the United States. These men were armed, each, with a Sharp's rifled carbine, and with revolving pistols. The inhabitants of the village asleep, the presence of this party was not known until they appeared and demanded admittance at the gate leading to the public works, which was locked. The watchman in charge states that on his refusal to admit them, the gate was opened by violence and the party entered, made him prisoner, and established themselves immediately in a strong brick building used as an engine-house, with a room for the watchmen adjoining it. . . . Their next movement was to take possession, by detached parties of three or four, of the arsenal of the United States, where the public arms were chiefly deposited, a building not far from the engine-house; and by another party, of the workshops and other buildings of the armory, about half a mile off, on the Shenandoah river, called "Hall's rifle works." They thus seized Colonel Lewis W. Washington, with several of his slaves, (negro men,) at his residence, some five or six miles distant; and in like manner a gentleman named Allstadt, who lived near the road leading from Colonel Washington's to the Ferry, two or three miles distant from the latter, with some five or six of his slaves, (also negro men.) . . . During Monday, a large portion of the arms, consisting of carbines, pistols, in boxes, and pikes, were brought off in the wagon and deposited in a school-house about a mile from the village of Harper's Ferry, on the Maryland side.

The first alarm that was given, indicating the presence of the hostile party, appears to have been on the arrival there of the mail train of cars on the Baltimore and Ohio railroad, on its way from Wheeling to Baltimore, and which arrived at Harper's Ferry at its usual hour, about half past one o'clock in the morning. On the arrival of Brown's party, he had stationed two men, well armed, on the bridge, with directions to permit none to pass. This bridge is a viaduct for the railroad to cross the river, having connected with it a bridge for ordinary travel. When the train arrived, it was arrested by this guard, and very soon afterwards a negro named Hayward, a free man who lived at Harper's Ferry and was in the service of the railroad company as a porter, was shot by this guard and died in a few hours. His statement was, as shown in the testimony of John D. Starry, one of the witnesses, "that he had been out on the railroad bridge, looking after a watchman who was missing, and he had been ordered to halt by some men who were there; and instead of doing that, he turned to go back to the office, and as he turned they shot him in the back." The alarm, however, did not extend to the inhabitants of the town, the scene of operations, so far, being near the river, at points occupied by the railroad structures and the public works; the principal part of the town being somewhat remote from that quarter. The train of cars, after being detained some hours, was permitted to proceed on its way to Baltimore.

When daylight came, as the inhabitants left their houses, consisting chiefly of workmen and others employed in the public works, on their way to their usual occupations, and unconscious of what had occurred during the night, they were seized in the streets by Brown's men and carried as prisoners to the engine-house, until, with those previously there, they amounted to some thirty or forty in number. Pikes were put in the hands of such of the slaves as they had taken, and they were kept under the eyes of their captors, as sentinels, near the buildings they occupied. But their movements being conducted at night, it was not until the morning was well advanced that the presence and character of the party was generally known in the village. The nearest towns to Harper's Ferry were Charlestown, distant some ten miles, and Martinsburg, about 20. As soon as information could reach those points, the citizens assembled, hurriedly enrolled themselves into military bands, and with such arms as they could find, proceeded to the Ferry. Before their arrival, however, it would seem that some four or five of the marauders, who were stationed at "Hall's rifle works," were driven out by the citizens of the village, and either killed or captured. In the course of the day, an attack was made on the engine and watch-house by those of the armed citizens of the adjoining country who had thus hurriedly arrived, and the prisoners in the watch-house, adjoining the engine-house, were liberated. The attacking parties were fired on by the marauders in the engine-house, and some were severely wounded.... The engine-house is a strong building, and was occupied by Brown, with seven or eight of his men.

During the day it appears that all of Brown's party, who were not with him in the engine-house, were either killed or captured, except those who were on the Maryland side engaged in removing the arms, as above stated. Before, however, they were thus captured or destroyed, they shot and killed two persons, citizens of Virginia, in the streets.... The party immediately under Brown remained barricaded in the engine-house during the whole of that day, (Monday.) They had confined with them ten most respectable and valuable citizens, kept, as stated by Brown, in the nature of "hostages," for the security of his own party, he assuming that a regard for the safety of the "hostages" would deter their friends and neighbors from attempting their rescue by force.

During the day an irregular fire was kept up against the engine-house by the people who assembled, and which was returned by the party within through loop-holes made in the wall, or through the doorway, partially opened.

In this manner two of Brown's party were killed at the doorway; and in the afternoon a gentleman of the village, Mr. Beckham, was killed by a shot from the engine-house....

[A]s soon as intelligence could be conveyed to Washington of the state of things at Harper's Ferry, the marines on duty at the navy-yard were ordered to the scene of action, under the command of Colonel Robert E. Lee, of the army... [who] found it necessary to carry the house by storm, the party within refusing to surrender except on terms properly held inadmissible. In this affair one marine was killed, and another slightly wounded.... The armory and other public works of the United States were in the possession and under the control of this hostile party more than thirty hours; that besides the resistance offered by them to the military force of Virginia, they resisted by force the lawful authority of the United States sent there to dispossess them, killing one, and wounding another of the troops of the United States, and as shown that, before they were thus overpowered, they killed in the streets three of the citizens of Virginia who were alone and not even in military array, beside the negro who was killed by them on their first arrival.

Report [of] the Select Committee of the Senate Appointed to Inquire into the Late Invasion and Seizure of the Public Property at Harper's Ferry (Washington, D.C.: GPO, 1860), 3–7

"POOR DOOMED HARPERS FERRY"

Mary and George Mauzy were residents of Harpers Ferry at the time of the raid. George was an agent for a riverboat company, and while the family did not own property in slaves, they were among the many middle-class nonslaveholding western Virginians who leased domestic servants from slaveowners. Mary describes the atmosphere in the town in the wake of the failed insurrection, and George adds his own thoughts in this letter to their daughter in England. One of their children mentioned in the letter, George Jr., was about four years old at the time of the raid.

Harpers Ferry, November 8, 1859

My dear Genie,

My conscience chides for not writing to you sooner but if you knew how much my mind is constantly excited you would not I am sure blame me. I seem as if I cannot collect my ideas sufficiently to write a letter. Ere this you have received our letters of the 18th Oct with the papers giving full statement of the recent insurrection. I can imagine your feelings at receiving such news from your home—poor doomed Harpers Ferry. We little dreamed that our quiet peaceful streets should ever be the scene of Battle, and now I can hardly realize it. The streets are filled with Soldiers, and on Sunday when Mr. White preached there were a great many in Church. You can imagine how strange it looked, and oh such a sermon as dear Mr. White preached and such prayers, it seems as if he had received inspiration. Everyone said he was not himself, his congregation was carried away. My dear Genie how I wish for you at such times, you always enjoyed those beautiful sermons so much. He spoke of the dangers through which we had passed, of our preservation, of the loss of those we were wont to meet in our midst . . . in such a beautiful and touching manner. . . .

George talks as much as ever about you. He is the most affectionate little fellow a dozen times during the day he will say Ma let me kiss you. He has improved very much since you saw him. He grows very straight. I made him a blue jacket with gilt buttons, on Saturday evening he wore it and the boys called him Captain of the Marines. He says tell sister I've a pistol and I am going to shoot Niggers with it. His papa gave him a double barrel Pistol and some times he will hold it and let him shoot it off. Every one children and all seems to have a warlike feeling. . . .

It will be an awful time when old Osswattomie is executed, every one dreads the time to come. I always shuddered at the thought of seeing any one hung, but I believe I could stand and witness their execution without feeling any horror. To think how they came as a Thief in the night and dragged persons from their Beds & made them prisoners. . . .

My dear Genie I must close as your Pa wishes to write some . . .

Affectionately your Ma

* * *

Dear children:

Your kind letter of the 21st ult. was recd on the 7th Inst. for which we are very thankful. I am rather at a loss to know what to write about—as Mary has occupied so much ground. . . .

We have good reason to be very thankfull to an all wise & overuling Providence for bringing us out of this contemplated insurrection & servile war....

I tell you some of these fellows are as hard to kill as any grisley bear, even old Brown, he is cut & hacked all to pieces within yet he is as fierce as a lion. They are a hard set of customers, they are all perfect Infidels having no faith in the Bible, and are all imbued with freeloveism, Socialism, Spiritualism & every other ism that was ever thought of by man or Devil, & hence this recklessness of Character....

Yours as ever

Geo Mauzy

Mary E. Mauzy and George Mauzy to Mrs. Eugenie Burton, November 8, 1859, typescript, Boyd B. Stutler Collection, West Virginia State Archives, Charleston

JOHN BROWN WRITES MARY ANN BROWN OF HIS IMPENDING EXECUTION

During his confinement in a Charles Town, Virginia, jail, Brown wrote dozens of letters to family and acquaintances in which he remained steadfast in defense of his actions.

JOHN BROWN TO MARY ANN BROWN

Jefferson Co.
Charlestown, Va, 31st Oct. 1859.

My Dear Wife, & Children every one

I suppose you have learned before this by the newspapers that Two weeks ago today we were fighting for our lives at Harpers ferry: that during the fight Watson was mortally wounded; Oliver killed, Wm Thompson Killed, & Dauphin slightly wounded. That on the following day I was taken prisoner immediately after which I received several Sabre cuts in my head; & Bayonet stabs in my body. As nearly as I can learn Watson died of his wound on Wednesday the 2d or on Thursday the 3d day after I was taken. Dauphin was killed when I was taken; & Anderson I suppose also. I have since been tried, & found guilty of Treason, &c; and of murder in the first degree. I have not yet received my sentence. No others of the company with whom you were acquainted were so far as <u>I can learn</u> either killed or taken. Under all these terible calamities; I feel quite cheerful in the assurance that God reigns; & will overrule all for his glory; & the best possible good. I feel <u>no</u> consciousness of guilt in the matter: nor even mortifycation on account of my imprisonment; & irons; & I feel perfectly assured that very soon no member of my family will feel any possible disposition to "blush on my account." Already dear friends at a distance with kindest sympathy are cheering me with the assurance that posterity at least: will do me justice. I shall commend you all together with my beloved; but bereaved daughters in law to their sympathies which I have no doubt will soon reach you. I also commend you all to him "whose mercy endureth for forever": to the God of my fathers "whose I am; & whom I serve." "He will never leave you nor forsake you" unless you forsake him. Finally my dearly beloved be of good comfort. Be sure to remember & to follow my advice & my example too: . . . it has been consistent with the holy religion of Jesus Christ in which I remain a most firm, & humble believer. Never forget the poor nor think any thing you bestow on them to be lost, to you even though they may be as black as Ebedmelch the Ethiopian eunuch who cared for Jeremiah in the pit of dungeon; or as black as the one to whom Phillip preached Christ. Be sure to entertain strangers for thereby some have. "Remember them that are in bonds as bound with them." I am in the charge of a jailor like the one who took charge of "Paul & Silas"; & you may rest assured that both kind hearts & kind faces are more or less about me: whilst thousands are thirsting for my blood. "These light afflictions which are but for a moment shall work out for us a far more exceeding & eternal weight of Glory." I hope to be able to write you again. My wounds are doing well. Copy this, & send it to your sorrow stricken brothers Ruth; to comfort them. Write me a few words in regard to the welfare of all. God Allmighty bless you all: & make you "joyful in the midst of all your tribulations." Write to John Brown, Charlestown, Jefferson Co, Va, care of Capt John Avis Your Affectionate Husband & Father.

John Brown

PS Yesterday Nov 2d I was sentenced to be hanged on 2 Decem next. Do not grieve on my account. I am still quite cheerful.

God bless you all Your Ever

J Brown

John Brown to Mary Ann Brown, October 31, 1859, typescript, John Brown / Boyd S. Stutler Collection, Ms 78-1, West Virginia Archives and History, https://archive.wvculture.org/hiStory/jbexhibit/bbsms02-0044.html

THOMAS JACKSON OBSERVES BROWN'S EXECUTION

Thomas Jackson was born in Clarksburg, Virginia (now West Virginia), on January 21, 1824. He was a class of 1846 West Point graduate and first

experienced combat in the Mexican-American War. In 1859 he was a professor of natural philosophy and an artillery instructor at the Virginia Military Institute in Lexington. After Brown's raid, Jackson accompanied a group of VMI cadets to Charles Town and was present and on duty to witness Brown's hanging. Like Brown, Jackson was a man of deep religious faith, but when the Civil War broke out, he cast his lot with slavery and the Confederacy. At the first battle of Manassas, he earned the nickname "Stonewall" Jackson for his heroics, and he would become the most revered Confederate military leader born in western Virginia. He is commemorated by statues in Clarksburg and on the grounds of the West Virginia State Capitol grounds in Charleston. He described the execution of Brown in a letter to his wife Mary Anna Jackson.

THOMAS JACKSON TO MARY ANNA JACKSON

December 2 [1859] John Brown was hung to-day at about half-past eleven A.M. He behaved with unflinching firmness. The arrangements were well made under the direction of Colonel Smith. The gibbet was erected in a large field, south-east of the town. Brown rode on the head of his coffin from his prison to the place of execution. The coffin was of black walnut, enclosed in a box of poplar of the same shape as the coffin. He was dressed in a black frock coat, black pantaloons, black vest, black slouch hat, white socks, and slippers of predominating red. There was nothing around his neck but his shirt collar. The open wagon in which he rode was strongly guarded on all sides. Captain Williams (formerly assistant professor at the Institute) marched immediately in front of the wagon. The jailer, high sheriff, and several others rode in the same wagon with the prisoner. Brown had his arms tied behind him, and ascended the scaffold with apparent cheerfulness. After reaching the top of the platform, he shook hands with several who were standing around him. The sheriff placed the rope around his neck, then threw a white cap over his head, and asked him if he wished a signal when all should be ready. He replied that it made no difference, provided he was not kept waiting too long. In this condition he stood for about ten minutes on the trap-door, which was supported on one side by hinges and on the other (the south side) by a rope. Colonel Smith then announced to the Sheriff "all ready," which apparently was not comprehended by him, and the colonel had to repeat the order, when the rope was cut by a single blow, and Brown fell through about five inches, so as to bring his knees on a level with the position occupied by his feet before the rope was cut. With the fall his arms, below the elbows, flew up horizontally, his hands clenched;

and his arms gradually fell, but by spasmodic motions. There was very little motion of his person for several moments, and soon the wind blew his lifeless body to and fro. His face, upon the scaffold, was turned a little east of south, and in front of him were the cadets, commanded by Major Gilman. My command was still in front of the cadets, all facing south. One howitzer I assigned to Mr. Truheart on the left of the cadets, and with the other I remained on the right. Other troops occupied different positions around the scaffold, and altogether it was an imposing but very solemn scene. I was much impressed with the thought that before me stood a man, in the full vigor of health, who must in a few moments enter eternity. I sent up a petition that he might be saved. Awful was the thought that he might in a few minutes receive the sentence "Depart, ye wicked, into everlasting fire!" I hope that he was prepared to die, but I am doubtful. He refused to have a minister with him. His wife visited him last evening. His body was taken back to the jail, and at six o'clock P.M. was sent to his wife at Harper's Ferry. When it reached Harper's Ferry, the coffin was opened, and his wife saw the remains, after which it was again opened at the depot before leaving for Baltimore, lest there should be an imposition.

Life and Letters of General Thomas J. Jackson (Stonewall Jackson) by His Wife Mary Anna Jackson (New York: Harper & Brothers, 1892), 130–32.

CORRESPONDENCE BETWEEN MARGARETTA MASON AND LYDIA MARIE CHILD ON BROWN'S RAID

Margaretta Mason was the wife of James M. Mason, the Virginia senator who wrote the Fugitive Slave Act of 1850 and chaired the Senate select committee in charge of the investigation of the John Brown insurrection. The Masons owned property and enslaved people in Frederick County, Virginia, not far south from Harpers Ferry, and on several plantations in other parts of the state. Lydia Maria Child was an abolitionist and a bestselling author. Her request to Virginia's governor that she be able to visit Brown while he was imprisoned enraged Margaretta Mason, who wrote to Child. Excerpts from Mason's and Child's letters follow.

Letter of Mrs. Mason.
Alto, King George's Co., Va., Nov. 11th, 1859.

Do you read your Bible, Mrs. Child? If you do, read there, "Wo unto you, hypocrites," and take to yourself with two-fold damnation that terrible sentence; for, rest assured, in the day of judgment it shall be more tolerable for those thus scathed by the awful denunciation of the Son of God, than for you.

You would sooth with sisterly and motherly care the hoary-headed murderer of Harper's Ferry! A man whose aim and intention was to incite the horrors of a servile war—to condemn women of your own race, ere death closed their eyes on their sufferings from violence and outrage, to see their husbands and fathers murdered, their children butchered, the ground strewed with the brains of their babes. The antecedents of Brown's band prove them to have been the offspring of the earth; and what would have been our fate had they found as many sympathizers in Virginia as they seem to have in Massachusetts?

Now, compare yourself with those your "sympathy" would devote to such ruthless ruin, and say, on that "word of honor, which never has been broken," would *you* stand by the bedside of an old negro, dying of a hopeless disease, to alleviate his sufferings as far as human aid could? Have *you* ever watched the last, lingering illness of a consumptive, to soothe, as far as in you lay, the inevitable fate? Do *you* soften the pangs of maternity in those around you by all the care and comfort you can give? Do *you* grieve with those *near* you, even though their sorrows resulted from their own misconduct? Did *you* ever sit up until the "wee hours" to complete a dress for a motherless child, that she might appear on Christmas day in a new one, along with her more fortunate companions? *We* do these and more for our servants, and why? Because we endeavor *to do our duty in that state of life it has pleased God to place us.* In his revealed word we read our duties to them—theirs to us are there also— "Not only to the good and gentle, but to the forward."— (Peter 2:18.) Go thou and do likewise, and keep away from Charlestown. If the stories read in the public prints be true, of the sufferings of the poor of the North, you need not go far for objects of charity. "Thou hypocrite! take first the beam out of thine own eye, then shalt thou see clearly to pull the mote out of thy neighbor's." But if, indeed, you do lack objects of sympathy near you, go to Jefferson county, to the family of George Turner, a noble, true-hearted man, whose devotion to his friend (Col. Washington) causing him to risk his life, was shot down like a dog. Or to that of old Beckham, whose grief at the murder of his negro subordinate made him needlessly expose himself to the aim of the assassin Brown. And when you can equal in deeds of love and charity to those *around* you, what is shown by nine-tenths of the Virginia plantations, then by your "sympathy" whet the knives for our throats, and kindle the torch that fires our homes. *You* reverence Brown for his clemency to his prisoners! Prisoners! and how taken? Unsuspecting workmen, going to their daily duties; unarmed gentlemen, taken from their beds at the dead hour of the night, by six men doubly and trebly armed. Suppose he had hurt a hair on their heads, do you suppose one of the band of desperadoes would have left the engine-house alive? And did he not know that his treatment of them was his only hope of life then, or of clemency afterward?

Of course he did. The United States troops could not have prevented him from being torn limb from limb.

I will add, in conclusion, no Southerner ought, after your letter to Governor Wise and to Brown, to read a line of your composition, or to touch a magazine which bears your name in its lists of contributors; and in this we hope for the "sympathy," at least of those at the North who deserve the name of woman.

M. J. C. Mason

Reply of Mrs. Child.
Wayland, Mass., Dec. 17th, 1859.

Prolonged absence from home has prevented my answering your letter so soon as I intended. I have no disposition to retort upon you the "twofold damnation" to which you consign me. On the contrary, I sincerely wish you well, both in this world and the next. If the anathema proved a safety valve to your own boiling spirit, it did some good to you, while it fell harmless upon me. Fortunately for all of us, the Heavenly Father rules His universe by laws, which the passions or the prejudices of mortals have no power to change.

As for John Brown, his reputation may be safely trusted to the impartial pen of History; and his motives will be righteously judged by Him who knoweth the secrets of all hearts. Men, however great they may be, are of small consequence in comparison with principles; and the principle for which John Brown died is the question at issue between us.

You refer me to the Bible, from which you quote the favorite text of slaveholders: "Servants, be subject to your masters with all fear; not only to the good and gentle, but also to the froward."—1 Peter 2:18.

Abolitionists also have favorite texts, to some of which I would call your attention. "Remember those that are in bonds, as bound with them."—Hebrews 13:3.

"Hide the outcasts. Bewray not him that wandereth. Let mine outcasts dwell with thee. Be thou a covert to them from the face of the spoiler."—Isa. 16:3, 4.

"Thou shalt not deliver unto his master the servant which is escaped from his master unto thee. He shall dwell with thee where it liketh him best. Thou shall not oppress him."—Deut. 23:15, 16. . . .

If the appropriateness of these texts is not apparent, I will try to make it so, by evidence drawn entirely from *Southern* sources. The Abolitionists are not such an ignorant set of fanatics as you suppose. They *know* whereof they affirm. They are familiar with the laws of the Slave States, which are alone sufficient to inspire abhorrence in any humane heart or reflecting mind not perverted by the prejudices of education and custom. I might fill many letters with significant extracts from your statute-books; but I have space only to glance at a few, which indicate the *leading* features of this system you cherish so tenaciously.

The universal rule of the slave State is that "the child follows the condition of its *mother*." This is an index to many things. Marriages between white and colored people are forbidden by law; yet a very large number of the slaves are brown or yellow....

Your laws uniformly declare that "a slave shall be deemed a chattel personal in the hands of his owner, to all intents, constructions, and purposes whatsoever." This, of course, involves the right to sell his children, as if they were pigs; also, to take his wife from him, "for any intent or purpose whatsoever." Your laws also make it death for him to resist a white man, however brutally he may be treated, or however much his family may be outraged before his eyes. If he attempts to run away, your laws allow any man to shoot him....

<small>*Correspondence between Lydia Maria Child and Gov. Wise and Mrs. Mason, of Virginia* (New York: American Anti-Slavery Society, 1860), 16, 18–20</small>

"THAT THIS SLAVERY AGITATION SHALL CEASE"

Alexander Boteler was a resident of Harpers Ferry and represented that district in Congress. When the Thirty-Sixth Congress convened just three days after John Brown was hanged, proslavery politicians were determined to block the election of John Sherman (a Republican from Ohio) to the speakership, as they blamed the party for inciting the Harpers Ferry insurrection. Sherman had additionally antagonized slavery's defenders in Congress by allowing his name to be attached to a reprint of Hinton Rowan Helper's antislavery screed, The Impending Crisis, *in 1859. Republicans held a plurality of seats in the Thirty-Sixth Congress, but not enough to secure an easy victory for Sherman, their preferred speaker. After forty-four ballots, and two months of deliberation, William Pennington, a Whig-turned-Republican and a newly elected representative from New Jersey, was finally elected to the speakership. On January 25, Boteler pleaded with his fellow congressmen to unite against the election of a Republican speaker for the sake of the nation.*

Mr. BOTELER. Mr. Clerk, I have no set speech to make . . . but I do protest against the continuance of this most unnecessary discussion. For myself, the House will do me the justice to say that I have possessed my seat in silence upon this floor during the seven weary weeks we have been in session, whilst this exciting discussion has been going on, and whilst the infamous Abolition outrage upon the district I have the honor to represent has been the fruitful inspiration of almost every gentleman who has risen to address the House. Mr. Clerk, I was present at that horrible Harper's Ferry raid; I was a witness to that abominable outrage; I saw the blood of my friends shed in the streets of Harper's Ferry; and if there is a man here who has a right to discuss that subject, it is myself; and yet I have forborne. I have remained silent for various reasons . . . [but] when I have heard gentlemen on the other side of the floor stand up and derisively refer to that infamous outrage, I have been hardly able to retain my seat and refrain from the expression of my indignation in terms which would not have sounded parliamentary. My mind, sir, has again and again, during this discussion, gone back to that gloomy October evening, when I stood by the side of a friend, and laid my hand upon his brow where the death-damp was gathering, while the blood was gushing from his noble heart, and I have been often disposed to say, in apology for my forbearance:

> "Oh! pardon me, thou bleeding piece of earth,
> That I am meek and gentle with these butchers!"

For I tell you, sir, that in my opinion, the leaders of the Abolition party, who are seeking to control the organization of this House, and to obtain possession of the Government, are as much the murderers of my friends at Harper's Ferry as were old John Brown and his deluded followers; and I think that the committee engaged in the investigation in my State, and the investigation on the part of the Senate, will prove that the agitation of the slavery question by the great leaders of the Republican party has been the direct cause of the Harper's Ferry invasion.

I tell you further, sir, the Commonwealth of Virginia has come to the determination that this shall be the end of it; that this slavery agitation shall cease, so far as she is concerned; that her territory shall be protected from a repetition of that bloody raid. She has taken some indemnity for the past and means to have security for the future. And, sir, to make her determination good, she has buckled on her armor, and her borders are now bristling with bayonets, for she feels compelled to take the guardianship of her rights and her honor into her own hands. Heretofore she has trusted to the tie of consanguinity; heretofore she has relied upon the linked shields of all the States for her protection; but, sir, at the moment when she dreamed not of it, she has been smitten upon the cheek. Our honored old mother has been struck a blow which roused her children from their false security and rallied them to her rescue. We now discover that we must depend upon our own right arm to protect our State from further outrage, so long as there remains a "Republican" organization in Congress and the country. And, men of the North, why will you persist in maintaining that organization? What good do you expect to effect by it? You formed it, so you have said, for the sole purpose of making Kansas a free State. You have Kansas, and when she comes into this Union, she will come in "free." If there be any other purpose that you expect to accomplish by it, it must be to transfer your "irrepressible conflict" from the Territories to the States. . . .

The election which returned these gentlemen here took place a month before the John Brown raid. The people of the North know, they must know now, they cannot fail now to see, what is the inevitable tendency of this slavery agitation. They have been told by you, the politicians, you the leaders—and we have allowed ourselves to be deluded by the syren song sung in our ears—that you do not intend to interfere with slavery within the States. Personally, I believe you do not. Personally, there is not a leader among you all—not even Fred Douglass—who can be found with courage enough to come into the southern States and interfere with slavery there. But, from year to year, you have beaten the drum of abolitionism in all the highways and byways of the North. From your pulpit and press and forum, in season and out of season, you have preached to the rising generation that slavery is a curse; and that anti-slavery sentiment has stimulated others, less careful of their personal safety, to come amongst us with a hostile intent, to steal our slaves and incite them to insurrection. . . .

I trust, Mr. Clerk, that this discussion will now cease. I trust that all will make an effort, by balloting, and by a succession of ballotings, to organize the House. I trust that we will go on in our efforts, day after day, until we do effect an organization, and proceed to perform the duties which we were sent here to discharge; that the great heart of our country will cease to pulsate with the anxiety which now causes it to throb; and that we will each, in our own appropriate sphere, do what we can to make ourselves more worthy of the inestimable blessings which a good God has given us, and which can only be enjoyed by a *free,* a *virtuous,* and *united* people. (Applause.)

Speech of Hon. Alexander R. Boteler, of Virginia, on the Organization of the House, Delivered in the House of Representatives, January 25, 1860 (Washington, D.C.: William H. Moore, 1860)

THE RESPONSE FROM THE FAR WEST

In the wake of John Brown's raid, Virginia residents along the state's Ohio River border expressed unity with eastern Virginians. On December 12, 1859, the citizens of Guyandotte assailed "the recent audacious and unprovoked aggression of John Brown and his associates upon the laws and dignity of our State" and declared, that all Virginians, "whether living upon the banks of the Ohio, or the shores of the Chesapeake," were united against the invasion of Northern abolitionists.[11] Yet they drew different conclusions from easterners about how to best strengthen the state against future external attacks. Cabell County residents believed the best way to do so was by unifying the state through infrastructure. In January 1860 they appealed to the state legislature to quickly complete the Covington and Ohio Railroad and to simultaneously begin construction of the road on its eastern and western ends. Their plea was largely ignored. The legislature continued to only modestly fund this critical railway and allocated no resources to begin construction on its western end.

LAST APPEAL OF THE PEOPLE OF CABELL COUNTY AND VICINITY, TO THE RICHMOND LEGISLATURE, JANUARY, 1860.

To the General Assembly of Virginia:

Whereas the undersigned, being legal voters, residing along the western, and in the present alarming crisis—the frontier border of the State, and separated at present . . . about six days journey from our Capitol—the only proper place to look for succor in time of need; and whereas the recent audacious assault upon Harper's Ferry appeals to our people to fortify and strengthen by all means in their power—we would respectfully, but earnestly urge upon your Honorable body, the imperative necessity of completing at once the Covington and Ohio Railroad to the Kentucky line—for the following reasons:

FIRST: It will bring that portion of the cis-Alleghany branch of the family, now so alien by position, but not as yet in affection, in close and easy communication with the Maternal head—to promptly give and receive succor, and exchange daily congratulations and favors—which tend so much to make a Great People in heart and purpose, ONE.

SECOND: While we regard all the great interests of the State, and every section thereof, entitled to equal protection and favor from the Legislature; and reflect that our broad, and as yet—for want of adequate outlets—very imperfectly developed section of the country—has for many years been subjected to heavy, and in some instances, unequal and unjust taxation—to help build up Railroads and Canals in other parts of the State—we feel it to be our just right, arising from adequate consideration already rendered, to have the Covington and Ohio Railroad promptly completed.

THIRD: But rising above sectional and personal considerations, we say the sound policy of the State, and whole South, repeat the demand. The State, because it will unite more closely to the Maternal head, by bonds of interest and affection, a large and growing section, now the most exposed, and yet beyond the reach of giving, or receiving seasonable aid—and thereby increase her Military strength. It will place her Commercial and Manufacturing cities in direct, expeditious and cheap communication with the great West—the produce and trade of which have mainly built up, and now sustain in all their pride and greatness, the cities of the North. . . .

FOURTH: The completion of this road will give to itself and the entire system of Improvements . . . a vital and highly remunerative existence—that soon shall extinguish Public Debt. To delay, therefore, seems to us in this point of view merely, as unwise and suicidal. . . .

FIFTH: It is equally as necessary, in our mind, that the appropriation should be expended simultaneously, and in equal proportions at least, at the East and West ends. For an additional million expended during the next two years in tunnelling the Alleghanies, will scarcely be perceptible to anybody, while that sum expended on the Western end, will save the half million now going fast to decay, open a cheap outlet to the Ohio to a large portion of our people, for their Mineral and Agricultural products, and from the easy grade of this section, will overcome to some extent the obstacles that now separate us.

Reprinted in Granville Parker, *The Formation of the State of West Virginia* (Wellsburg, WV, 1875), 3–5

TWO

The Revolution of 1860

"*P*OOR DELUDED old Brown was hung yesterday," the *Wheeling Daily Intelligencer* noted on December 3, 1859. "He died, as it was expected he would die, firm, fearless, and resigned, without a favor to ask or a word to retract. While we condemn, we cannot help pitying such a man. A man of so much frankness, such high personal courage, so much magnanimity as he evinced, was intended for a more honorable end than the gallows. Poor old fellow, the path's of his life were dark and tangled, he lost his way, and he died like Abner, 'as the fool dieth.'"[1]

Such a sympathetic take on John Brown was quite unusual for a Virginia newspaper. But the *Wheeling Daily Intelligencer* was something of an outlier. Founded as a Whig newspaper in 1852, it was acquired in 1856 by Archibald W. Campbell and John F. McDermot and began describing itself as a "liberal and independent journal" willing to present diverse viewpoints on issues of the day. The *Intelligencer* benefitted from its owners' investment in new printing technology but also its location on the National Road and its access to improved telegraph communication. The paper's ability to report on big news events sometimes just twenty-four hours after they occurred, its large, seven-column, four-page format—which provided plentiful room for both news and financially sustaining advertisement—allowed it to thrive. By the 1860s, it was the sole daily paper in western Virginia, and its circulation of more than three thousand dwarfed any other paper in the region. With Wheeling's location on the Ohio River, just across from the free state of Ohio and just fifteen miles to the west of Pennsylvania, it is no surprise that the *Intelligencer* became an important platform for introducing free-soil ideas to Virginia's west, though the paper's viewpoints were not likely shared by the majority of its northwest Virginia neighbors. By 1858, Republican Party leaders were providing financial support for the paper, and its editorial position became increasingly Republican. The *Intelligencer* and the *Wellsburg Herald,* which published farther up the state's Northern Panhandle and had a much smaller circulation, may have been the only two Virginia newspapers to endorse Abraham Lincoln for president in 1860.[2]

The *Intelligencer* was not the only expression of free-soil ideology in the state of Virginia before 1860. In 1857, about two hundred miles to the south and west of Wheeling, a Massachusetts activist named Eli Thayer established the small free-soil community of Ceredo on the Virginia side of the Ohio River, near present-day Huntington, West Virginia. Thayer had previously started the Massachusetts Emigrant Aid Society in 1854 to encourage antislavery families to move to Kansas to secure that territory as a free state. Ceredo was his second and bolder experiment, as it attempted to establish free-soil ideas in the nation's most powerful slave state. The Ceredo colony might be viewed as a conservative effort at reform by example. If a community without slavery could prove prosperous in Virginia, it might persuade other Virginians to abandon the institution of slavery. The name of the town was a reference to Ceres, the goddess of grain, and meant to evoke a bountiful community of free laborers. Nevertheless, the community's neighbors in both Kentucky and Virginia eyed it suspiciously as a den of abolitionists, and a document near the end of this chapter examines the Ceredo colonists' experiences when the secession crisis emerged.[3]

Beyond the Northern Panhandle and the tiny settlement at Ceredo, criticisms of slavery were generally not tolerated across the state of Virginia, and Brown's attempt to launch a "servile war" at Harpers Ferry affirmed the idea that antislavery opinions were dangerous and should not be tolerated. Western Virginia politicians had long been put on the defensive whenever they questioned the power or policies favored by the eastern planter class. The accusation of holding abolitionist viewpoints took on a new severity after Brown's raid, and during the secession crisis western representatives were frequently accused of being abolitionists or "Black Republicans," even when they couched their dissenting opinions in proslavery language.

While Americans began 1860 talking about Brown's raid and subsequent hanging, attention soon turned toward the upcoming presidential election in the fall. Both the Republican and Democratic Parties began the year with some internal dissension. For the Republicans, Brown's employment of violence in the antislavery cause resulted in some members of the party backing away from abolitionist-leaning language and probably allowed Lincoln, something of a dark horse candidate, to eventually defeat more well-known rivals like William H. Seward and Salmon P. Chase, whose reputations as radicals on slavery now cost them support. Dissension in the Democratic Party ran deeper, and attempts to hold together its Northern and Southern wings ultimately failed, with the party splintering into two factions over the issue of slavery in the territories.

The Northern wing nominated Illinois senator Stephen Douglas, who continued to try to find a viable middle ground on the issue, while Southern Democrats nominated John C. Breckinridge on a platform aggressively defending the rights of enslavers to extend that institution into the West. A hastily formed coalition calling itself the Constitutional Union Party nominated Tennessean John Bell. Composed mostly of Southerners who had been part of the now-defunct Whig Party, the Constitutional Union Party's platform was distilled into a single phrase: "The Constitution of the Country, the Union of the States, and the enforcement of the laws."[4]

In Virginia, Lincoln took just over 1 percent of the state's vote, most of this coming from the northern and western counties. Douglas drew some adherents in a handful of western counties adjacent to free states. But across the state the race came down to a contest between Breckinridge and Bell, with the Constitutional Unionist candidate winning a plurality of the popular vote, thus securing all Virginia's Electoral College votes in a winner-take-all system. Bell's victory obscured how closely divided Virginia voters were between the Southern-rights and compromise candidate. Virginians from the Tidewater to the Trans-Allegheny region were not of one mind, and neither Virginia's subsequent secession nor the western Virginia movement to secede from the seceders was foreordained.

Following the Republican victory, talk of secession occupied public gatherings across the state, including the western counties. As the secession winter of 1860–61 turned into springtime conflict, western voices opposed to the war and in favor of remaining with the Union gained strength. Despite the popularity of the Southern-rights Democrat Breckinridge in many western counties in 1860, when Richmond called for a statewide convention to discuss secession in the spring of 1861, western Virginians largely opposed leaving the Union. An April 4 vote at the Secession Convention revealed substantial opposition to secession in both the Shenandoah Valley and the Trans-Allegheny regions of the state. Following South Carolina's assault on federal forces at Fort Sumter on April 12 and Lincoln's call to raise a force of seventy-five thousand men from state militias to respond to the aggression, support for secession increased across all regions of Virginia. On April 17, much to the dismay of many representatives from the northwestern counties, the Secession Convention endorsed secession with a vote of 88 to 55, with many representatives of the Shenandoah Valley and southwestern Virginia counties flipping from opposition to support; secession was to be effective as soon as voters across the state had an opportunity to vote on the issue.[5] Virginia governor Henry Wise did not wait for the formality of a public referendum before making Virginia secession a reality, ordering forces to seize the strategic town of Harpers Ferry. Unionists in the west began exploring alternative plans for a loyal Virginia government, with some even calling for a separate state.[6]

A state referendum to endorse or reject the convention's call for Virginia secession was scheduled for May 23. Mindful that a majority of representatives from northwestern Virginia had voted against the pro-secession majority on April 17, the convention looked for an olive branch in the hopes of securing yes votes in the west. It endorsed an amendment to the Virginia constitution which declared that "taxation shall be equal and uniform throughout the Commonwealth, and all property shall be taxed in proportion to its value," and added it to the language of the secession referendum.[7] For many westerners, this very late change of heart regarding this decades-old inequity must have seemed too little, too late.

For White western Virginians, the decision to support or reject Virginia's secession was personal and sometimes placed them at odds with their family members. Thomas Jackson, the Clarksburg-born professor at the Virginia Military Institute, cast his lot with the Confederacy, a decision his sister Laura Jackson Arnold, still living in Harrison County, publicly condemned. She never saw her brother again.[8] Clarksburg native John James Davis opposed secession, while his Maryland-born fiancée, Anna Kennedy, supported it, but their relationship survived nonetheless. Their correspondence on the issue is included in this chapter. In other cases, the decisions that individual western Virginians made alienated them from their own communities and resulted in a forced separation from their families. Judge Samuel Woods of Barbour County attended the Secession Convention and endorsed Virginia's separation, a choice that forced him into exile from his family for part of the war, as Barbour County remained under the control of Union officials.

In the midst of the secession crisis, enslaved Virginians continued to make choices to determine their own fate. In early December an enslaved woman named Lucy Bagby, living in Wheeling, slipped away in the hopes of securing freedom in Ohio. Eventually captured and brought before a judge in Cleveland, Bagby was to be the last person returned to slavery under the Fugitive Slave Act. The emerging secession crisis hung over the deliberations about Bagby's fate, and the White officials who cooperated in Bagby's reenslavement congratulated themselves on what they viewed as a noble effort to sacrifice this young woman for the sake of the nation. Black abolitionist Frances Ellen Watkins Harper savaged these men in her poem "To the Cleveland Union-Savers," a document included in this chapter. Bagby's case reminded both White and Black western Virginians that the institution of slavery was still protected by federal power, even as some White politicians were telling their constituents that the recent election result was slavery's death knell.

"THERE ARE SPECIAL REASONS WHY CITIZENS OF VIRGINIA SHOULD BE REPUBLICANS"

Lincoln received very few votes across Virginia, and in Wayne County, along the Kentucky border, a handful of voters who had the audacity to cast a ballot for the Republican faced threats of violence from their neighbors. For the most part, support for Lincoln was limited to small groups of voters in the Northern Panhandle counties. At least one element of the Republican Party's rhetoric, however, resonated with a western Virginian who had long resented the arrogance and power of slaveholding eastern elites.

The Wellsburg *Herald* of yesterday, has a long article giving reasons why, first, citizens of Virginia should not vote for either of the Democratic tickets, and second, why they should not vote for Bell and Everett. The article closes as follows:

But why should citizens of Virginia vote for Lincoln? In the first place, as citizens of Virginia they should vote for him like any other citizen of the United States, because his principles are broad and national, and are such as if carried out would best develope the national prosperity.

But there are special reasons why citizens of Virginia should be Republicans.— They should vote for Lincoln and Hamlin, if for no other reason, because they have been told in some quarters that they would not be allowed to vote that ticket. Whenever the question is brought up in this shape and a portion of the people are told that they shall vote as it pleases them, then that one principle of our government that is thus brought in question becomes of more importance to the citizen than all the other questions involved in the canvass. *The right to vote as a man pleases is the very corner stone of free institutions, and the man who will not assert it, and, if need be, defend it at the price of his blood, does not deserve the name of a free man.* When he relinquishes that right under threats or menaces, he becomes a very slave and deserves to be treated as a slave. Yet, in certain portions of our State, not very remote, this right is denied and it has been publicly proclaimed that *no man shall vote for Lincoln.* To this proclamation only one answer can be given, and that must be given at the polls, at any cost, and the threat treated with the contempt it deserves. Virginians should not only vote for Lincoln and Hamlin to demonstrate their independence when it is called in question, but they should vote for them to demonstrate their abhorrence of the treasonable sentiments of the secession Democracy. Republicanism in the South is the antipodes of Breckinridge Democracy, and the larger the vote for Lincoln and Hamlin the sharper the rebuke to the disunionists.—A large Lincoln vote, would of all things demonstrate the lack of sympathy between Virginia and the cotton States and dampen the ardor of these latter States in favor of disunion. . . .

Besides these reasons of a more general nature, the domestic policy of Virginia has been shaped for many years back to foster the slave interest at the expense of all others, and it has become necessary for the development of Western Virginia that a different system should prevail. To institute such a policy, vote for Lincoln and Hamlin and help organize a political party in Western Virginia that will counteract the slaveholding oligarchy. It can be done—all that is necessary is to organize the elements on a national foundation and give them backbone enough to hold them upright; and if the people say so, it will be done and our iniquitous laws be modified peaceably, quietly and without disturbance.

Wheeling Daily Intelligencer, November 3, 1860

"THIS TIME NEXT YEAR SHE WILL HAVE TO DO HER OWN WORK"

In the wake of Lincoln's election, a number of Southern states began to organize for secession. South Carolina left the Union in December 1860, and six other states followed before the end of February. Lewis County native William C. Tavenner was in New Orleans in December, but eager to know what people back home might do, he wrote to his family in western Virginia. Tavenner later served in the 17th Virginia Cavalry.

New Orleans, Dec. 24th 1860

Dear Ma

I have not yet heard from any of you. I think this is the third letter that I have commenced with these words but they are true.

I have no news to tell you, and only write to let you know how we all are. [I]t is not my regular day for writing but I do not expect I will be able to write on Wednesday as it is always a busy day with us and tomorrow being Christmas (a holiday) will make it more so.

I wish you would send me the Weston Herald some times so that I may form some idea of what you Lewis County people intend doing—whether you will secede with the Southern States or with the Northern States. I expect that you had better all go up to Kanawha to live, as it is far out of the world that any army would never think of going up there, and that, by doing so you will be safe from the abolitionists that may come into your country.

There is a young gentleman here (one of my most intimate friends) that got a letter from his mother some days ago. She was staying with Aunt Mary—she said she and Aunt M were sitting in a room. Aunt Mary asleep

and she reading when one of the negroes that were in the room thinking that Mrs. Wedderbon wasn't listening, said of Aunt M— "Poor old lady she has an easy time <u>now</u>, but this time next year she will have to do her own work." I suppose there must be a great deal of excitement now in Va and in all the border states. There is a great excitement here but it is not from <u>fear</u>. . . .
Write to me often and let me know all the news. Give my love to all.

Your aff[ectionate] Son

William C. Tavenner

William C. Tavenner to his mother, December 24, 1860, William C. Tavenner Collection, West Virginia and Regional History Center, West Virginia University, Morgantown

THE LAST RETURNED FUGITIVE SLAVE: NEWSPAPER ACCOUNTS

Lucy Bagby was about eighteen when she escaped from Wheeling resident William Goshorn in 1860. Goshorn was determined to learn of her whereabouts and get her back, and suspicion soon fell upon Phillip Herbert, a free Black Wheeling resident who left for Pittsburgh shortly after Bagby's disappearance. Herbert was arrested and questioned about her disappearance, which mobilized Wheeling's free Black population to come to his defense. Goshorn ultimately learned that Bagby was in Cleveland, and he used the force of the Fugitive Slave Act to secure her return. Bagby's escape and forcible return occurred after the election of Lincoln but before his inauguration. She was the last person returned to slavery under the Fugitive Slave Act of 1850. The Wheeling Daily Intelligencer *regularly reported on the story as it unfolded.*

EXCITEMENT AMONG THE COLORED FOLKS.

On Saturday afternoon one Phil Herbert, a negro who has been confined in jail for several weeks charged with assisting in the escape of Lucy, a slave girl belonging to Mr. Wm. Goshorn, had a hearing in the Sheriff's office before Col. Knox. Thirty-one negroes, of all hues of the rainbow and sundry other hues, ages, sexes, and conditions, were examined, and we do not suppose that ever in this knowing world did an equal number of colored folks know less upon any one stated subject. They knew the slave girl Lucy, (or the "young lady," as they called her,) some slightly, some intimately and some otherwise. They knew Phil only slightly. One or two even knew that Phil went to Pittsburgh about the same time that the girl disappeared, but they didn't know what he went for, or if they did they wouldn't tell. Col. Knox discharged Phil and admonished him to be careful in the future, and he said he would. All afternoon the negroes were marching in and out of the Sheriff's office, single file, and the colored population were never before in such a flurry. No set of witnesses ever told off their stories so glibly, and we never before saw so much ivory.

Wheeling Daily Intelligencer, December 10, 1860

* * *

THE FUGITIVE SLAVE LUCY.

They had some very interesting proceedings in the U. S. Court room at Cleveland, on Thursday morning, just before the surrendering of Mr. Goshorn's slave girl, Lucy. There was a large number of people present. Judge Spaulding, counsel for the girl, in withdrawing the defense, said among other things:

"Nothing now remains that may impede the performance of your painful duty, sir, unless I be permitted to trespass and say to this assemblage 'we are this day offering to the majesty of Constitutional law an homage that takes with it a virtual surrender of the finest feelings of our nature—the vanquishing of many of our strictest resolutions—the mortification of a freeman's pride, and, I almost said, the contravention of a Christian's duty to his God.[']"

Mr. Barlow, counsel for Mr. Goshorn, said, as reported in the *Herald,* "that the course of his friend Judge Spalding was patriotic. The right of slavery, or the Constitutionality of the fugitive slaw law, is not involved here. The latter question has been decided. The duty of the Court is to give effect to the law. In justice to the claimants, I must say they are actuated by no mercenary motives. Neither do they come to wake the prejudices of the North. Virginia now stands in a commanding position, and wishes to show the Southern people that the Northern people will execute the laws, and be faithful to the Union. The citizens of Cleveland have come up to their duty manfully; no man has laid a straw in the way of the enforcement of the law, and for my friend I thank them."

Marshal Johnson read sundry provisions of the United States laws, and said he had no alternative—he must obey them. The girl could be purchased in Wheeling, and he would give $100 for that purpose. Mr. Barlow asked permission for the older Mr. Goshorn to speak, when that gentleman arose and said:

"Language would not express his gratitude to the citizens for his treatment. His mission was an unpleasant one, but it may be oil poured upon the waters of our nation's troubles. I would the task of representing Virginia had fallen to better hands. The South had been looking for such a case as this. I have no office to gain, I want to save the Union. We must do it if our servants will not. We have charged the North with persuading away our servants—I hope God will forgive them. How pleasant it would be if I could come among you with this same girl as my servant, and enjoy your hospitality as I have now. He continued at some length."

Before leaving Cleveland the Messrs. Goshorn sent the following card to the Cleveland *Herald:*

"Before leaving Cleveland for home, we feel it a duty to the citizens of Cleveland, as well as to ourselves, to express our unfeigned gratitude for the uniform kindness with which we have been treated. Nothing but courtesy has been shown us by all of your citizens, who have even shielded us from the insults of your colored population—as an instance of which we will refer to an incident which occurred this morning at the breakfast table of the Weddell House. A negro waiter refused to serve us, and upon the fact being known to Col. Ross, the proprietor of the House, the waiter was promptly discharged, and ordered to leave the house."

"We again thank you all.
JNO. GOSHORN.
WM. S. GOSHORN."

Wheeling Daily Intelligencer, January 26, 1861

* * *

RETURN OF THE FUGITIVE SLAVE, LUCY.

Last evening the U. S. Marshall from the Northern District of Ohio, Mr. Johnson, arrived in this city, having in charge the fugitive slave, Lucy, owned by Mr. W. S. Goshorn. The Marshall was accompanied by Chas. B. Flood, Editor of the Cleveland *National Democrat,* and Mr. Grey, also connected with one of the Cleveland papers, and a half a dozen other gentlemen, all of whom put up at the McLure House. Mr. Goshorn speaks in high terms of praise of the efficiency of the Marshall, and is also under obligations to other officers and citizens for their activity in seeing the law enforced. There was no attempt made, even by the negroes, to rescue the girl upon her leaving Cleveland. At the town of Lima, however, on the line of the road, a large crowd of negroes, some of whom, it was said, were armed for a rescue, but although the Conductor whistled down brakes he considered it unadvisable to stop. After leaving Lima a negro and a white man, both of whom were armed, were arrested and disarmed by the Marshall, upon the suspicion that they meditated a rescue. The Cleveland gentlemen were entertained last evening at the house of Mr. Goshorn.

—*Wheeling Daily Intelligencer,* January 25, 1861

TO THE CLEVELAND UNION-SAVERS

Francis Ellen Watkins Harper was an African American poet, author, and lecturer who was active in the abolitionist and women's rights movement. The poem below was her response to the Cleveland court decision to return Lucy Bagby to slavery in Wheeling.

To the Cleveland Union-Savers

An Appeal From One of the Fugitive's Own Race

Men of Cleveland, had a vulture
Clutched a timid dove for prey;
Would ye not with human pity,
Drive the gory bird away?

Had you seen a feeble lambkin,
Shrinking from a wolf so bold,
Would ye not to shield the trembler,
In your arms, have made its fold?

But when she, a hunted sister,
Stretched her hands that ye might save,
Colder far than Zembla's regions,
Was the answer that ye gave.

On your Union's bloody altar,
Was your helpless victim laid;
Mercy, truth, and justice shuttered,
But your hands would give no aid.

And ye sent her back to torture,
Stripped of freedom, robbed of right,
Thrust the wretched, captive stranger,
Back to Slavery's gloomy night.

Sent her back where men may trample
On her honors and her fame,
And upon her lips so dusky,
Press the cup of woe and shame.

There is blood upon your city,
Dark and dismal is the stain;
And your hands would fail to cleanse it,
Though you should Lake Erie drain.

There's a curse upon your Union,
Fearful sounds are in the air;
As if thunderbolts were forging,
Answers to the bondsman's prayer.

Ye may bind your trembling victims,
Like the heathen priests of old;
And may barter manly honor
For the Union and for gold.

But ye cannot stay the whirlwind,
When the storm begins to break;
And our God doth rise in judgment,
For the poor and needy's sake.

And your guilty, sin-cursed Union,
Shall be shaken to its base,
Till ye learn that simple Justice
Is the right of every race.

—Frances Ellen Watkins Harper

Anti-Slavery Bugle (Salem, OH), February 23, 1861

THE UNION MEN OF HARRISON COUNTY

In January of 1861, Union men in Harrison County gathered to express their views on the impending secession crisis. Some citizens of the western counties were concerned they would be bullied to acquiesce to the demands of powerful eastern slaveholding interests.

Meeting at the Court House on Saturday, [January] 19th [1861].
On Saturday, a portion of the people of Harrison county assembled at the Court House, for the purpose of recommending two suitable persons to be voted for by the friends of the Union for members of the Convention, which is to assemble on the 13th of February, 1861.

Upon motion, Maj. Charles Lewis was called to the Chair; and upon motion of Wm. A. Harrison, Esq., Dr. David Davisson was appointed Secretary.

The Chairman in a few appropriate remarks explained the object of the meeting.

Wm. A. Harrison, Esq., then addressed the meeting, taking a bold and decided stand in favor of the Union as formed by the revolutionary fathers, and against secession.

Mr. Harrison then read the proceedings of an enthusiastic Union meeting held on Friday evening at Shinnston, in which members of all political parties participated, declaring their devotion to the Union and their opposition to secession.

Jno. J. Davis., Esq., then offered the following resolutions as a basis for the action of the meeting.

Resolved, That we will support no man as a delegate to the convention to be held in Richmond, on the 13th day of February next, who is not unequivocally opposed to secession, and will not so pledge himself.

Resolved, That we will support no man who will not pledge himself to oppose and vote against the appointment of persons to represent this State in any convention, having for its object the establishment of a provisional or other government, or of persons to any body convened for the purpose of forming a Southern Confederacy or government.

Resolved, That we will support no man who will not pledge himself to vote against any ordinance, resolution, or motion, that has for its object the withdrawal of the State from the Federal Union.

Resolved, That we will support no man who will not pledge himself to vote against any resolution to be laid down as an *ultimatum,* and the refusal of which, by the other States, to be considered just cause for seceding from the Union.

Resolved, That we will not support any man who believes that the Convention to assemble at Richmond, on the 13th of February, 1861, or any other State authority, can absolve the citizens of this State from their allegiance to the General Government; and that we will support no man who does not believe that the Federal Government has the right of self-preservation.

Resolved, That we will support no man who will not oppose all deliberation and discussion by the members of said Convention in secret secession.

The above resolutions were adopted unanimously.

Wheeling Daily Intelligencer, January 24, 1861

WOODS SPEAKS AT THE SECESSION CONVENTION

Judge Samuel Woods of Barbour County was one of the western men who spoke in favor of secession at the Virginia Convention. Woods would serve the Confederacy during the war, leaving behind a wife and children in a western Virginia community occupied by Union forces.

Mr. WOODS—

I offer the following resolutions, and move their reference to the Committee on Federal Relations. . . .

1. Resolved, That the allegiance which the citizens of Virginia owe to the Federal Government of the United States of America is subordinate to that due, to Virginia, and may, therefore, be lawfully withdrawn by her whenever she may deem it her duty to do so. 2. That in case the State of Virginia should exercise this authority, her citizens would be in duty bound to render allegiance and obedience to her alone. 3. That Virginia recognizes no authority in any government, State or Federal, to coerce her or any of her citizens, to render allegiance to the government of the United States, after she may, in the exercise of her sovereign power, have withdrawn from it; and that she will regard any attempt at coercion as equivalent to a declaration of war against her, to be resisted at "every hazard and to the last extremity." 4. That the States of South Carolina, Georgia, Florida, Alabama, Mississippi, Louisiana and Texas, having severally and formally withdrawn the allegiance of their respective people from the United States of America, a faithful, earnest desire to avert civil war, and the sound conservative sentiment of the country, alike indicate to the Government of the United States the *necessity* and *policy* of acknowledging their independence.

Mr. WOODS

Representing, as I do, sir, the conservative sentiment of the county of Barbour, to the suffrages of whose voters I am indebted for the honor of a seat upon this floor, I have sought this opportunity of presenting to this Convention the views embodied in these resolutions, which have been fully canvassed, carefully considered, and which I believe to express the sentiments of my people. . . .

<small>George H. Reese, ed., *Proceedings of the Virginia State Convention of 1861, February 13–May 1* (Richmond: Virginia State Library, 1965) 1:129–31</small>

"EVERY UNION MAN IS DENOUNCED AS AN ABOLITIONIST!"

As pro-secession views gained an upper hand in Richmond, a delegate to the Virginia Secession Convention from Morgantown described the growing intolerance of dissenting ideas.

The editor of the Morgantown *Star,* who is a delegate to the Virginia Convention, writes home to his paper in the following strain. We are glad to perceive that there is some indication of manhood in the 10th Congressional District, and hope it may grow and spread over North-western Virginia: Richmond, March 9, 1861.

Dear "Star:"—I have been waiting and waiting for something tangible to be done by this Convention, in order that I might communicate it to your readers, but in vain. When I first came here, I supposed that something would be done soon to relieve the anxiety and suspense of the people of Virginia, as there was such a large majority of Union men in the Convention, but I have been doomed to disappointment. Your readers cannot imagine the state of things here from the reports of the proceedings of the Convention in the newspapers. . . . Every means is used to intimidate the members of this Convention. Meetings are held nightly. Bands are hired who parade the streets followed by a motley crew of free negroes, boys and mad caps who go around to the different Hotels, calling upon the well-known secessionists for speeches—cheering South Carolina, &c, &c. Every allusion to the Union is hissed, and every Union man is denounced as an abolitionist! The members from the North West are compelled to daily hear citizens of Richmond, who are allowed privileged seats, point them out with the remark that "there is where the abolitionists sit," "these are the abolitionists," &c.—Even Alfred M. Barbour, who represents a county containing 5,000 slaves, is compelled frequently to hear himself pointed out by some vagabond on the street as an abolitionist, and simply because he is a Union man. How long, oh, how long will free people of the West submit to this thing?

When Mr. Willey made his speech the other day, he was hissed by a person in the galleries. Mr. W. retorted in a masterly manner. The President ordered the galleries cleared, but Mr. W. begged him not to do so, as he thought he had squared the account with the goose who hissed. Mr. Willey sustained his well earned reputation in his speech. His arguments against secession were unanswerable. The best compliment I can pay him is to say that he received the most universal attention, from both the Convention and the galleries, of any gentleman who has yet spoken.

Mr. Carlile, on Thursday, made a speech of two hours length, which struck the secessionists like a thunderbolt.

It was decidedly the boldest speech of the session. . . .

As Mr. Carlile was leaving the Convention, accompanied by two very respectable ladies from his boarding house, he was hissed by the crowd.—And this is your great city of Richmond where free speech is guaranteed to every man by the bill of rights and the laws of his country.

I learn that Mr. O. Jennings Wise told a member of the Convention a few days ago that if this Convention did not pass an ordinance of secession, it ought to be driven from its hall at the point of the bayonet. . . .

The Union men have no paper here to represent or defend them. *The Enquirer, Examiner* and *Dispatch* are violent disunion papers, and the *Whig,* quasi

Union. So the people of the Northwest will see, as anticipated by me. That the representatives from that section have not a very pleasant berth. The Convention ought to adjourn to some other place; but too many of the members are timid. They fear the denunciations of the papers here and the name of abolitionist. When will men become bold, free and independent again?

The members of the Convention from your Congressional district are as firm as the eternal hills, with the exception of Hall, of Wetzel, who is an out and out secessionist. Mr. Hall was elected by a plurality of seven votes, and four Union candidates in the field. He evidently represents but a meager minority of his people, and cannot be called a representative man. If he misrepresents the feelings of his people they ought to speak out. He was presented this evening with a splendid gold-headed cane, by the young men of Richmond, for his defence of the honor of Virginia, by advocating secession and denouncing the North-Western members as untrue to the institutions of the State. . . .

Hastily yours, M. M. D.

Reprinted in *Wellsburg Herald,* March 22, 1861

VIRGINIA CONVENTION VOTES

County representatives to the Virginia Secession Convention took two votes on Virginia secession. In the first vote on April 4, secession was defeated. On April 12 South Carolina forces fired on Fort Sumter, and on April 15 Lincoln called for state militias to suppress the rebellion. Two days later, the Virginia Convention took a second vote on secession, which passed.

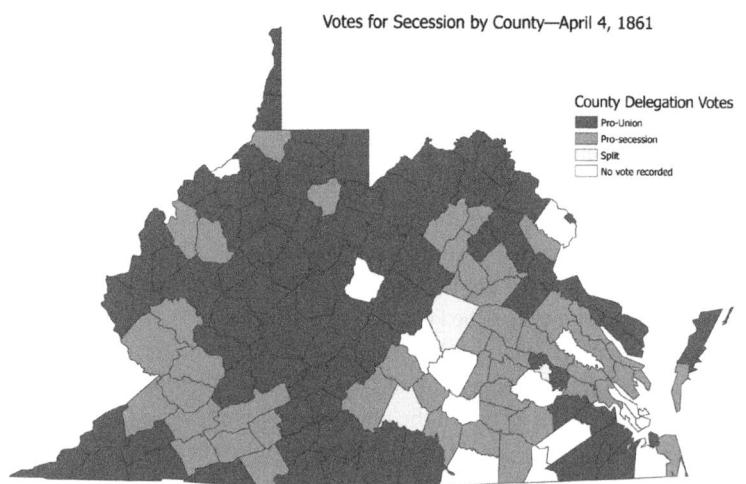

Votes for Secession by County—April 4, 1861

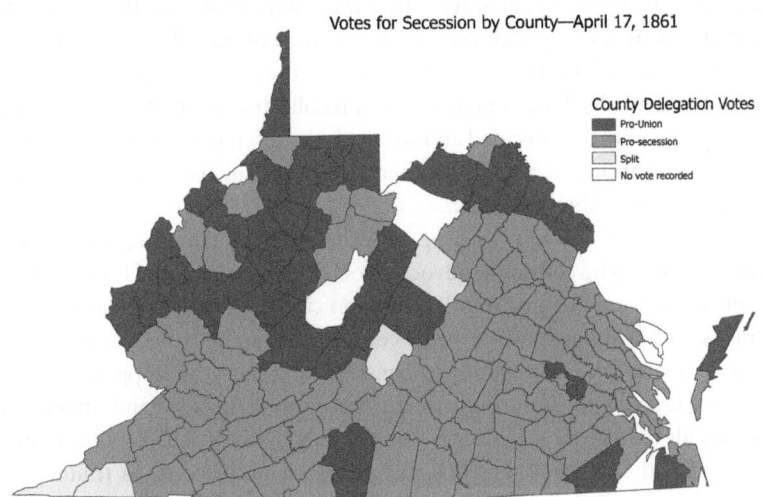

Votes by county representatives on Virginia secession on April 4, 1861, and April 17, 1861. Maps created by Stephen Van Horn from data gathered from the digital collection "Secession Convention Proceedings," University of Richmond, https://secession.richmond.edu/.

THE POSITION OF WESTERN VIRGINIA

Lincoln's response to South Carolina's attack on a federal fort was to call up the militia of the loyal states. For Virginians who sought to carve a path of neutrality between the seceded states and the federal government, Lincoln's call made neutrality no longer viable. A Charleston newspaper expressed its concern over Lincoln's proclamation calling forth the state militia.

In utter disregard and contempt of every overture and prayer of Virginia, for peace, and without any authority of Congress, Mr. Lincoln and his advisers have declared war against the South. He has issued his proclamation for seventy-five thousand militiamen, and has had the audacity to call upon the border Slave States for a portion of them, designating three regiments as Virginia's quota. The various governors of the slave States have each responded promptly to the call, that they would furnish no men or money for any purpose so wicked in its ends and so unconstitutional in its means as the proposed subjugation of the South. The free States have all offered their sinews of war and powers of destruction with eagerness and alacrity. The Virginia Convention has passed the ordinance of secession. Four hundred federal troops, stationed at Harper's Ferry, Va., after destroying ten thousand rifles and firing the public buildings, fled before the Virginians made their appearance. No doubt some of the gallant four hundred were familiar with John Brown's by-paths across the neighboring hills, and others of them may also have retained a vivid recollection of the latter end of the martyr. At any rate they decided and so acted that discretion was the better part of valor. The Virginians soon thereafter arrived, extinguished the flames and secured about four thousand rifles.

The Northern cities, in keeping with their usual fanaticism, are perfectly furious; any one who refuses to advocate coercion is in danger of losing his life. Federal soldiers are flocking into Washington city by thousands; negroes are in the ranks with white men. Civil war is commenced, and it behooves every man who loves his species now calmly to consider how can it be stopped. We have heretofore urged with all our little might, that prompt, decided and unanimous action by all the border slave States was the only possible means of preventing bloodshed and civil strife. For that, many men denounced us as traitors. We hope we may be pardoned for presenting once more with renewed energy and infinitely increased weight the same argument as applicable to our present disturbed condition. The immediate and unanimous voice of all the slave States in defense of themselves and the South, may yet cause the North to reflect before they rush headlong into this internecine strife. We are fain to believe that those in authority at Washington have made the issue simply to satisfy their party whether or not the Union is permanently divided. The Black Republican horde cried that the rebels must be demolished. In order to preserve his party organization at the North, Mr. Lincoln was forced to terminate the dreadful and doubtful inaction of his administration. The suspense caused by the delay and deliberation policy paralyzed every energy of the country as effectually as actual war would have done: it afforded no satisfactory response to those who persisted in reiterating the question "have we a government?" Mr. Lincoln drafted just about the same number of men from each of the slave States as he had votes last fall, respectively in them. If those States had sustained him, then his plan would have been to have subjugated the seven seceded states.

If the border States are not lost to every sentiment of honor and all knowledge of interest, if their people are not divided among themselves, Mr. Lincoln and his party will soon be convinced of the advantages of peace, and will speedily acknowledge our separate existence as a government. We are satisfied that the revolution is now a complete success; and no matter to what extremity the contest be pushed, we have no doubt of the ultimate and complete triumph of the South. We hope there will be no desertion or difference of opinion amongst our own community in regard to the great question before us. We are willing to forget all of the past that is unpleasant to any loyal citizen. Let each and all of us stand firm for Virginia, as a unit in this her greatest trial. Let no seditious one whisper any purpose of dividing the State. Virginia expects every man to do his duty.

Kanawha Valley Star, April 23, 1861

A BETROTHED COUPLE TAKE DIFFERENT SIDES

Clarksburg lawyer John James Davis was a delegate to the Virginia House before the war began and he opposed secession. His fiancée, Anna Kennedy, had strong Southern sympathies. At the outset of the war, John found himself a friend of the Union in a seceded state, while the Southern sympathizer Anna found herself residing with her family in Maryland, a state that remained in the Union. Despite their political differences, John and Anna wed in the middle of the war, and a photograph of the couple is below. In these letters John and Anna exchange their views on the conflict before their marriage.

Clarksburg, VA
April 20, 1861

My dear friend,

You do not know how sad I am tonight. Darkness, gloom and blood hang over the future, and how it will all end the Almighty alone knows. Before you hear from me again or perhaps, before this reaches you, my own state may be drenched in blood—I feel just as if my hopes and aspirations were blasted. My country, the Union, to preserve which I would have laid down my life, is gone—gone beyond the hope or reconstruction—Your father's prediction has been fulfilled. You and I are no longer citizens of the same government—at least so far as the action of the Va. Convention can make us so, we are foreigners. I hope <u>we</u> shall never be so in feeling. Va. <u>has</u> seceded. Madness ruled the hour, and our people are now to fight the battles of South Carolina up on their own soil. You doubtless have heard of all that has transpired in our state. The wildest excitement and confusion prevails. Despondency and gloom are visible in the countenances of everyone, and none know what to do, or what the end will be.

Oh, for an arm of strengthened wisdom to reunite our once glorious and happy Union! I cannot believe that this government has so soon answered the design of Him who treats the follies and passion of men as less than nothing. You are still in the Union and I hope your people will be guided by the dictates of reason and patriotism, and not be led away by passion and prejudice from the Stars and Stripes, the emblem of peace, greatness, and nationality. There may be hope for us yet, the act calling the convention provides that its action shall be submitted to the people for ratification or rejection. They may refuse to ratify the ordinance. I hope they will. I am writing tonight, first because I wanted to talk a little to you, as you have occupied my thoughts for several days, and then again, because this may be the last letter you will receive from me from some time. You may think that strange, but I'll tell you why. As we have seceded as a state, it is almost certain that our mail facilities will be at once cut off, and there will be no communication between this and those States that have not seceded. So if there should be any interruption of our correspondence you will know to what cause it is due. The State may make some arrangements for transporting the mails but then they will be a little uncertain. You must not suppose that I will forget you, nor must you attribute the failure to receive a letter, if such a thing should occur, to my neglect or indifference. I hope the storm that is howling around us will soon be over and then—what —————Let that dash speak.

I saw Miss Amelia this evening. She told me of having received a letter from you &c. I made her promise to write to you tomorrow morning. My illness was not as protracted as I supposed it would be when I wrote. Tomorrow if the day be fair, I will go to Lumberport to make a speech and at night to Shinnston. I shall battle for the Union as long as there is any hope at all. You are not a secessionist, I believe. My brother has been writing that he would come home if Virginia seceded. I wrote to him today to stay where he is. I think I can better protect and defend our home and fireside than one of his rash and ardent temperament. He is almost, if not quite as ardent as Miss Emma.

About noon today, Maj. Jas. M. Jackson hung out on the top of his house, the Southern Confederacy flag. Our people were very indignant and the excitement became so intense that he took it down in a few hours. . . .

I am going to be right good tonight and not punish you with a long letter. You should feel very grateful for it.

Well—remember me to Miss Emma, your father, Ma &c., and send up an humble petition to the Great Disposer of events that our country may be spared the dreadful calamity that hangs over it.

Now you owe me two letters. Let me see if you pay your debts promptly.

<u>Ever</u> your friend
Jno. J. Davis.

* * *

Baltimore, Maryland
April 22, 1861

Dear friend,

I have just received your letter. I too am heartsick. You have of course heard our troubles here. Thank God, however, we are almost a unit here and have no feuds among ourselves. Indeed, Mr. Davis, if you were but here now you too would feel it better to secede immediately, than live under the administration of such a weak villain as I believe Lincoln to be. I have loved the Union, you know I have loved it, but O I hate the present government and whatever so weak an arm as mine can do shall be done to shake its fetters off. I am trembling now so that I can scarcely write. I am not alarmed but I have been in a perfect fever of excitement since Friday.

... Do not think however that because I am now a secessionist, I would not count it one of the happiest days of my life if I could see our country united again. But this I regard as an utter impossibility. I am not more sure that the sun will set tonight, than I am that it will never again rise upon the United States—it makes me sad, but I am sure of it. If we are now foreigners, we will not be so many days. Gov. Hicks has at last called the Legislature and I would not care to be the man who would vote against immediate secession, in the present state of the public mind. I wish you were with us more. Father is very much excited—calm as he has always been before—he is of course a secessionist. I was very glad he had not his pistol with him Friday. He has worn it ever since, and has enlisted in the Home Guards for the sake of getting a musket, he says. Fire arms are not to be had for love or money, except by the companies as every store of the kind has been completely swept out. ...

As I said before I am not alarmed—very many families have already left the city—we will stay to the last. If Father only were not so blind, I would not object to his enlisting, though of course we cannot help feeling somewhat uneasy on his account. My brothers are mere children. I have been out this morning—everything is quiet now. Uniforms and fire arms are of course to be seen everywhere, but no one notices them now and ladies are out as usual. ...

Well, I guess I had better stop talking about it. I am afraid you will think me now more political than is quite ladylike. ...

O Mr. Davis I believe I <u>am</u> a coward (I would not tell you this if I thought you would believe it) I have been talking very bravely but I must confess that when my excitement cools off a little and I think calmly of the danger I feel something very much like fear. I do not think I am in any personal danger. If the city is bombarded, we will have notice and can quit, but father is very rash and is now fully aroused and then even if he remains in the Home Guard, and stays to protect us, there are so many families who will be made desolate. It is horrible. If father were a Christian, I could bear it better. I am so thankful I have no one else to be alarmed for.

When will you be called into action, I wonder. Mr. Lewis said he was safe so long as you, a taller man, were in the company. Of course though you are a Unionist, you will fight for your state, won't you? O me! I believe I take delight in torturing myself with all sorts of forebodings—I think and talk of it so incessantly, and I have written already five pages on the subject. I feel as if some terrible thing were hovering above me and drawing nearer and nearer every moment, and there is no escape. If I was sure we were right as Emma is, I believe the consciousness of that would support me, but I think the secession movement wrong at the beginning and it can bring nothing but wrong and trouble with it. Nevertheless, now that to remain in the Union is to remain with Northern Abolitionists. I say let me go—peaceably if we can—forcibly if we must. I do pray, but it is with a very weak faith I fear. I know that out of all this evil our Father will bring good, I know that He will make the wrath of man to praise Him. I know that He reigneth forever and that "as the mountains are round about Jerusalem, so is the Lord round about them who fear him." I know all this and most heartily I believe it and feel the peace His word brings, but then I know that He has often for some good reason permitted men's passions to desolate whole nations, and I cannot help shrinking from the scourge. I try to say Thy will be done—I will trust Him. He can save us, and He knows best what will prove best for us—perhaps it is well we cannot choose. . . .

I must stop now. I have involuntarily written in a hurry, as if the mails could close before I get this in. I am sorry that what may be my last letter should be so doleful, but it is fitting that it should be so. Remember me to my friends.

Write if you can, and if you must fight, don't get shot if you <u>are</u> the tallest man.

I am <u>ever your</u> friend,

Anna Kennedy

* * *

Clarksburg, Va.,
May 17, 1861

My dear *friend,*

See how I italicized that word friend—Are you satisfied now that you have not lost the title which you claim to be "inalienable?" My pen has a great inclination sometimes, to be more familiar, but lest I offend (?) I restrain it. . . .

... Do you remember those verses in Ruth? Some invisible—super human power prompted when a reference was made to them. And have you ever entertained a suspicion that I would not be as faithful a friend as Ruth. Difference of opinion ought not and must not make us disagree upon the one point.— that we are friends. If I err in opinion on subjects of interest to us all, it is an error occasioned by a lack of ability to perceive what is right, and not from any improper motive. I wish to do what is right if I can. Whatever opinions I express are the honest convictions of my mind. And I am willing to concede to others the same honesty of purpose and motive. I hope I shall never become so perverse and obstinate in opinion as to be deaf to all reason, and when others convince me that I am wrong, I am willing to abandon my false position and assume that which reason clearly demonstrates is right. . . .

Davis Family Papers, 1946, folder 1, West Virginia and Regional History Center, West Virginia University, Morgantown

Despite their disagreement on the wisdom of secession, Anna Kennedy and John Davis were married in 1862. John initially supported the movement for West Virginia statehood but turned against it after Congress demanded the new state emancipate all enslaved people as a condition of admission to the Union. Courtesy of West Virginia and Regional History Center, WVU Libraries.

A UNION "MORE ODIOUS THAN ANY TYRANNY"

Citizens of Guyandotte in Cabell County gathered on April 20, 1861, to celebrate Virginia's secession. Although enslaved people accounted for less than 3 percent of the county's population, and only one resident owned more than twenty enslaved people, the peculiar institution figured large in the gathering's reasons for supporting secession. Waving the flag of Virginia, sewn by local women for the occasion, the citizens vowed to prepare for their defense and resistance to "abolition rule."

PUBLIC MEETING AT GUYANDOTTE—FLAG OF VIRGINIA HOISTED.

At a meeting of the volunteer companies, citizens of Guyandotte, Va., and vicinity, held on the 20th April, 1861, Peter C. Buffington, esq., presiding and Capt. H. H. Miller, secretary; a large number of people of Cabell county being present, the flag of Virginia made by the secession ladies of Guyandotte, and Lewis Peters, esq., artist, was raised on the bank of the Ohio in front of the Planter's Hotel. It went up amid the enthusiastic applause of the multitude and the rejoicing of the ladies, a large number of whom were present. The flag was raised by Elijah Rickets and John W. Ong, Sr., two of the oldest citizens of the place.

Rev. St. Mark Russell was called to address the meeting, who promptly responded. While he was portraying the causes that should impel the secession of Virginia, in his us[u]al animated and eloquent style, he was interrupted by the arrival at the wharf of a steamer and a report that the Convention had passed the ordinance of secession, upon which more deafening shouts now rose on the banks of the Ohio than went up from the meeting. Salutes were fired for the Confederate States and President Davis.

The speaker was again called to the stand. He rejoiced and thanked God, that we were once again free; and in conclusion expressed the hope that Virginia would be as united as that meeting was in hearty approval of the action of the Convention.

L. H. McGinnis, esq., of Logan, was then called for who rose and in a masterly and el[o]quent manner portrayed the wrongs we have endured; the unparalleled sacrifices we have made; and the extraordinary system of legislative encouragement we have acquiesced in towards our heretofore sister States of the North to save a Union which he now declared is more odious than any tyranny ever established over men.

Advertising to the cause of the disruption, the speaker declared that it was a duty we owe to the States themselves; that we were bound by the most sacred obligations to conserve the institution of slavery; it was indispensible to the civilization of the African. He argued elaborately that we had not only the plainest recognition in the Old and New Testament of property in slaves, but all history proved it right and favored by Providence. The revolution of 1776 proved it, and that of 1861 would prove it.

As our fathers enlisted under the banner of Washington, a slaveholder, fighting for the freedom of the white and the slavery of the black race; we should rally under General Davis who is also a slaveholder, against Lincoln *the first,* who, like George the third, and yet bolder in his demands is opposed to *African* and in favor of *American Slavery.* And alluding to Virginia, and her flag waving over his head, and her great efforts to preserve peace, he said that while the old and justly renowned Commonwealth stood as a mediator between the contending fires of revolution, a mercenary soldier had been thrown into her bosom to reduce her to military subordination. And now that she had bravely turned upon her invaders; he made a powerful appeal to Virginians to stand by the mother of States and her flag, and declared that he would be foremost to hang the traitor that dared insult the flag that floated over their heads. His sentiments were responded with the utmost enthusiasm. . . .

Dr. A. B. McGinnis, was called, who responded in an eloquent review of the causes, rise and progress of resistance to abolition rule in Guyandotte and vicinity. He had taken his stand months ago for independence as the only cure for the political disease that threatened the existence of our institutions and liberties:

He rejoiced to be joined by many of those who had denounced him for his "secession madness." He argued at length, the importance of Union of the South; but above all unions the union of Virginia was most essential to her salvation.

Amid the most enthusiastic applause the meeting adjourned to the Town Hall.

G. D. Warren, esq., was called and responded in a practical and glowing description of the present proud position of Virginia. He declared amid tremendous cheering, that the time for division in Guyandotte had passed; that those who were not for Virginia in her sovereign, independent position, were against her in toto; and would now be marked as her enemies; that if any such existed in Guyandotte they would be treated as traitors.

Capt. H. H. Miller, of the Home Guard, also addressed the meeting.

Hon. William H. Buffington responded to the call of the meeting in a brief, practical and forcible review of the crisis.—He, however, said the time for argument had passed, and pressed in a most eloquent manner the necessity of immediate preparations for defense. He said he had long believed that such a crisis was inevitable. That the Puritanic intolerant sentiment of New England, of which he gave a most glowing description, was incompatable with the brave and generous spirit of the Cavaliers of James river; that could they not be united long under the form of free government. He declared he would defend the flag of Virginia to the death; and his sentiments were greeted with enthusiastic applause. . . .

_{Kanawha Valley Star, April 30, 1861}

THE FREE-SOILERS OF CEREDO STAND THEIR GROUND

While the pro-secession voices appeared to rule the roost in Guyandotte, just a few miles west lay the small free-soil community of Ceredo, founded by Massachusetts abolitionist Eli Thayer, who had already established the Massachusetts Emigrant Aid Society in 1854 to encourage antislavery families to move to Kansas to secure that territory as a free state. Thayer launched his second experiment in free-soil colonization in far-western Virginia in the hopes that the economic success of a community that relied upon free labor would demonstrate to other Virginians the superiority of a free-labor economy over a slave labor one. With Lincoln's victory in the 1860 election, proslavery residents of Guyandotte soon turned a hostile eye toward their "abolitionist" neighbors to the west. This excerpt from a letter published back in Thayer's hometown in Massachusetts in 1862 reveals the fear members of the tiny free-soil community of Ceredo felt in 1861.

In February last [1861], nine others and myself were threatened with expulsion from the "sacred soil" of the Old Dominion for voting for Lincoln: all residents of Ceredo. The coal-oil excitement for a time withdrew attention from us; but in May the war against us raged fiercer, and some of the marked ones left for fear of violence. I had leased some land, and planted corn, and potatoes, and beans, and did not at all relish the idea of leaving. . . . My courageous wife agreed with me that it was better to stay, for we might in that course do more for the good cause than in any other way. And it was certain that many of our acquaintances, natives of Virginia, who were at heart for the Union, needed all the encouragement we could afford. We decided that it was better to stay and "fight it out" than to be driven away because of our devotion to the old Government.

In June and July the excitement was all the time increasing, and by the middle of the latter month it was publicly stated that the "Lincolnites" of Ceredo *must* leave, and notices to that effect were sent to us. We sent back word to them to "come on," we were prepared for them, (but we were not, though,) and defied them. We had been somewhat encouraged in this by Union men in Ohio and Kentucky, and the secessionists thought we had some strength unknown to them, and did not then dare to come to put their threats in force.

For several weeks in the middle of summer we watched every night for the coming of the indignant secessionists. They looked for us to submit and take the oath of allegiance to the Southern Confederacy, or leave. It was during this time of fearful peril (for we had sworn to stand by each other and resist to the death, if necessary) that everything else was forgotten. All business was abandoned. The farmers who had been influenced by our position and action, left their crops and joined us in consultation and watch. They were made to understand that they were risking all their property and their lives, and perhaps the lives of their families, by joining us. But they pledged themselves willing to make the sacrifice, if need be for the sake of the Union. Our fears were reasonably increased by the treatment of Union men in the adjoining counties, and we did not hope for mercy. The enemy outnumbered us who would *fight* more than three to one; yet our bold stand and defiant declarations kept them back. For many nights my wife did not retire to rest with any certainty that she would not be aroused before morning by the torch and bullet of the rebel guerrillas now organized in three different places in our own county, and in large numbers in the next and nearest county above us. A little band of twenty-five and sometimes thirty or more, when our country neighbors came in, stood on guard through many summer nights, with such arms as we could pick up, waiting to resist the attack of three hundred or more. But I have no doubt we should have made a desperate resistance. We had become so exasperated by the infamous threats of the rebels, and so incensed at their conduct toward Union men up the country, that we all felt that it was our solemn duty to resist.

Then began the organization of a regiment. One of the old residents was urged to take the lead in this; we New Englanders pledged ourselves to sustain him. It was a fearful undertaking, but we had the right kind of a man to lead off, and it was successful. This, however, drove away from us some who had acted with us only to defend our homes and firesides, not to begin the aggressive or offensive. The rebels were of course indignant that we should attempt to have a military force in the "abolition" village of Ceredo.

The Independent (Worcester, MA), February 20, 1862

THREE

Opening Gambits

THE FIGHT TO control western Virginia began as soon as the Virginia Secession Convention endorsed secession on April 17, 1861. The events in Richmond that day forced free White western Virginians to decide whether their primary loyalty was to the nation or their state. For enslaved African Americans living in the region, the news of the state's secession and the war brought risks and opportunities. The region's enslaved people understood that the issue of slavery was at the heart of the conflict. They also knew about the failed attempt to spark a slave insurrection at Harpers Ferry just eighteen months earlier.[1] Yet they could not be confident that the Northern White population who had voted into power a president and party committed to containing the spread of slavery would embrace the emancipation of those toiling in servitude in the rebellious states. Most would bide their time to see how things played out.

Virginia's most hot-headed secessionists were eager to strike quickly. The opening military moves from leaders on both sides would determine the fate of western Virginia and of the free and enslaved peoples who called the region home. The government in Richmond struck first, acting to secure the armory at Harpers Ferry even before the citizens of Virginia voted on secession. Lincoln's government pursued a more cautious approach, hesitating to move troops into the state before the May 23 referendum on secession for fear that aggressive action might drive more western Virginians to the Confederate side.

Across the state, the vote for secession was endorsed by a significant majority, but most northwestern voters opposed it, even with the addition of the language repealing the unequal taxes on slave property that the eastern elite enjoyed. On June 14, Virginia governor John Letcher issued a proclamation to the citizens of western Virginia urging them to accept the decision of the majority of Virginia voters. He acknowledged that "there has been a complaint among you that the eastern portion of the State has enjoyed an exemption from taxation to your prejudice," but asked westerners to recognize the eastern vote for a fair tax policy to be a "display of magnanimity" and to switch their allegiance to the Confederacy.[2]

Union general George B. McClellan, assigned to lead the Department of the Ohio, would be the first military leader in charge of any western Virginia campaign, and he moved with his characteristic caution, a position Abraham Lincoln, his commander in chief, fully endorsed at this early moment.[3] In what would prove to be the first contest between two important foes, Virginia put Robert E. Lee in charge of the efforts to secure western Virginia. Lee moved quickly, seeking to recruit Confederate units in Wheeling, Grafton, and Harpers Ferry, key towns along the Baltimore and Ohio Railroad. These early efforts gave the Confederate leadership hope that the bulk of fighting-age men of the region would rush to arms for the new Confederacy, but Confederate recruitment soon stalled after the first Union forces moved into the state in late May.[4] McClellan's characteristic caution won the day.

The ground fight for control of western Virginia in 1861 primarily focused on efforts to secure three regions: Harpers Ferry and the lower (northern) Shenandoah Valley, the Monongahela Valley, and the Kanawha Valley.[5] Virginia's Confederate leaders believed securing the area around Harpers Ferry was critical to maintaining sovereignty over all of Virginia. Located at the confluence of the Potomac and Shenandoah Rivers, and bisected by the Baltimore and Ohio Railroad, Harpers Ferry held strategic value that went beyond its industrial and arms-making capacity. But lying along the river and surrounded by steep hills on all sides, it was difficult to defend, and the Confederates opted to cart away what functioning machinery the small federal force that had been stationed there had not destroyed before fleeing. The town changed hands several times during the war. The surrounding agricultural land in the lower Shenandoah Valley also proved to be a significant vulnerability for the Union, as the Shenandoah Valley was part of a large "Great Valley" that extended deep into Pennsylvania, providing an easy route of invasion of the North by Confederate armies. Furthermore, the agriculturally rich Shenandoah Valley, with its fields of wheat, large stock of cattle, and abundant orchards, earned it the nickname "the breadbasket of the Confederacy," and it helped sustain Southern armies early in the war.[6] As a result, the lower Shenandoah Valley figured significantly in the strategic efforts of both armies throughout the war.

From Harpers Ferry the Baltimore and Ohio Railroad (B&O) extended into Virginia's northwestern counties and to the Northern Panhandle, stretching across the second strategic region, the Monongahela Valley. At Grafton, the Northwestern Virginia Railroad split from the B&O and extended west to Parkersburg on the Ohio River. Control of these lines not only secured Virginia's northwestern counties but, under Union control, would serve as an important link between the eastern theater of war and the human and material resources of the Ohio Valley. That strategic value should not be underestimated, and the lines proved to significantly benefit the Union's developing grand strategy later in the war. Virginia Confederates would need to control this line and occupy Wheeling in the Northern Panhandle if they were to have any hope of keeping Virginia's northwestern counties, a task made more challenging by the fact that loyalty to the Union, and connections to the Northern economy, were stronger in this region than in any other part of Virginia. Despite early efforts by Confederate Virginia to recruit troops in the Wheeling area, the prospects of Confederate control were never good. For the Union, maintaining control of the B&O railway and protecting it from Confederate sabotage was a priority. As a result, the first Union campaign in western Virginia occurred in the Monongahela Valley, which the B&O traversed. By the end of 1862, it was clear that the Confederates' ambition to control this region was unrealistic, and for the remainder of the war the Confederacy settled for destructive raids on the rail lines, which could render the B&O, temporarily at least, of limited use to the Union war effort.

The third important theater for military conflict lay in the Kanawha Valley, which extended from the Ohio River through Charleston—an important center of salt production—and southeast to Gauley Bridge, near the confluence of the New and Gauley Rivers. At the outset of the war General McClellan envisioned the Kanawha Valley as a promising pathway for the invasion of eastern Virginia.[7] But the challenging geography and the divided loyalties of the local population would limit its utility to the Union. Nevertheless, Confederates also found their efforts to secure the valley for the South regularly thwarted. Despite repeated invasions, the Kanawha Valley remained under Union military control for much of the war. This was critically important to the eventual efforts to pursue independent statehood for West Virginia (see chapter 5), but the limits of Union control were also evident in the fact that the valley never proved an easy path for invasion of Confederate Virginia. Union forces in western Virginia failed in their early efforts to strike southward to seize the Virginia and Tennessee Railroad, which remained a critical supply route for the Confederacy for most of the war.[8]

During the first two years of the war, both the Union and Confederate governments viewed western Virginia as strategically significant, although not necessarily their highest priority. Efforts by the Union to hold the region securely were sometimes undone when units stationed in the region were reassigned to other theaters deemed more critical. Likewise, Confederate attempts to retake and hold the region were sometimes thwarted by a lack of military forces devoted to the area. Western Virginia experienced several small and moderate-sized military engagements between the two armies, but not one of the Civil War battles scholars would consider "mega-battles"—those with casualty numbers of ten thousand or more men—occurred within the region. The war in western

Virginia was primarily a war of scouting raids and small-scale skirmishes. In 1861 and 1862, both armies could point to important battlefield victories in the region. But early Union military successes in the spring and summer of 1861 laid the groundwork for West Virginia statehood, with most, but not all, of the counties that would become part of the future state of West Virginia under Union control at the end of the war's first year. Notable exceptions were the Eastern Panhandle, which changed hands frequently, and Greenbrier and Monroe Counties in the southeast, where enslaved labor played an important part of the agricultural economy and the White population remained overwhelmingly loyal to the Confederacy.

The fate of western Virginians' enslaved people was bound up in Northern war strategy. The position of President Lincoln and the federal Congress regarding enslaved African Americans began evolving almost as soon as the war had begun. In his cautious First Inaugural Address, Lincoln, speaking directly to citizens of border slave states that had not seceded from the Union—and also to western Virginians—repeated a statement he had made in previous speeches during the campaign: "I have no purpose, directly or indirectly, to interfere with the institution of slavery in the States where it exists. I believe I have no lawful right to do so, and I have no inclination to do so."[9]

But as soon as the war to suppress the rebellion sent soldiers into slave states, the situation became more complicated. In May of 1861, at Fort Monroe, Virginia, on the Chesapeake, Union general Benjamin Butler encountered hundreds of enslaved African American men, women, and children seeking refuge and protection behind Union lines. "I am in the utmost doubt what to do with this species of property," he declared, before noting that many of the men had escaped from forced labor in Confederate military camps. Butler ultimately decided to treat them as "contraband of war," offering them protection and compensating them for their labor.[10] In the same week, McClellan launched his invasion of western Virginia, and he issued explicit orders to his officers to respect civilian property in western Virginia, including "property" in slaves, and to actively suppress any potential "negro insurrection." McClellan's order is included in this chapter.

In August of 1861, the federal Congress passed the first Confiscation Act, affirming that the military should provide protection to any enslaved people who had been working for the Confederate military before fleeing. This was the first step in a long process toward making emancipation a war policy, but interpretation of the act lay in the hands of Union field commanders, who held a wide variety of positions on the issue of slavery. The ambiguity meant that enslaved people who considered taking advantage of the chaos of war to self-emancipate could not always count on finding support by fleeing to Union encampments.

Nevertheless, many enslaved and free Black men offered their services to the Union army. In late October of 1861, just two months after Congress passed the first Confiscation Act, a runaway going by the name of Ben climbed to the top of Cheat Mountain, where he surrendered to federal pickets. Ben did not provide a last name, perhaps because he was uncertain what the soldiers might do with him, and he considered that being returned to his master might be one result. Instead, Ben sought to negotiate a deal. He had valuable intelligence on the size and location of Confederate forces in the area, and he was willing to share it in exchange for a guarantee of his freedom. Robert Huston Milroy, the brigadier general in charge of the Union force on top of the mountain, held strong antislavery views, agreed with the terms, and allegedly christened him "Benjamin Summit" for the location where he gained his freedom. He worked at the camp, served as a guide for raiding parties, and later in the war enlisted in a United States Colored Troops unit and fought for the Union.[11]

Other enslaved people in western Virginia had to make their own choices about how to respond to the war. In Greenbrier and Monroe Counties in the

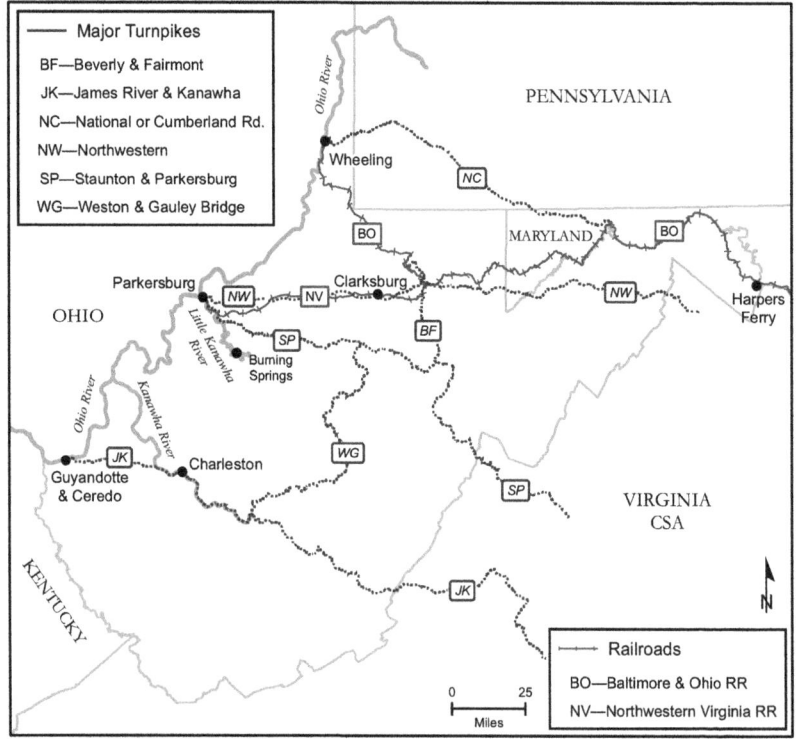

Major turnpikes and railroads in West Virginia, 1860. Map by Brian Balsley.

southwestern part of the region, African Americans comprised more than 10 percent of the population, most of them enslaved. Individual acts of self-emancipation began as soon as the war started. For Whites supporting the Confederacy, enslaved and free African Americans represented both a potential danger to their cause and an exploitable asset. Some Virginia counties began impressing African Americans into labor in Confederate armies early in the war. In 1863, Virginia's assembly passed an act that made impressment of enslaved people a statewide policy. While African American males served with Confederate armies, none were recognized as soldiers during the war. Rumors of Black Confederates circulated in both the North and South during the war, but the Confederate government rejected proposals to arm African American men in exchange for freedom until the very last months of the war.[12]

CONFEDERATE RECRUITMENT BEGINS

In the absence of a large standing army before the Civil War, Virginia relied on a local volunteer militia to maintain order, and in the Southern states, militias doubled as a patrol force to keep the slave population under control. Aiming to quickly build an army, the government in Richmond called on local militias to fill out the ranks of early regiments. Two days after the Virginia Secession Convention passed the secession ordinance, and before it was ratified by popular vote, the Kanawha Riflemen, a militia company from the Charleston area, met and pledged their support for Virginia.

MEETING OF THE KANAWHA RIFLEMEN.

At a meeting of the Kanawha Riflemen, held in the town of Charleston on the 19th day of April, 1861, Captain George S. Patton, presiding, Lieutenant Fitzhugh offered the following preamble and resolution:

Whereas an unjust and unnecessary war had been forced on the country by the administration at Washington, in which our State may be required to take part; we, the Kanawha Riflemen, hereby declare it to be our fixed purpose never to use our arms against the State of Virginia, or any other Southern State, in any attempt by said administration to coerce or subjugate them; and we hold ourselves ready to respond to every call that may be made on us to defend our State and section from hostile invasion; therefore, be it unanimously resolved,

That we hereby tender the services of this Company, to the authorities of the State, to be used in the emergency contemplated in the foregoing preamble—

Which preamble and resolution were unanimously adopted. . . .

On motion, resolved, that these proceedings be published in the Kanawha papers, and that a copy thereof be sent to the Adjutant General of the State.

George S. Patton, Pres't.
John Dryden, Sec'y.

Kanawha Valley Star, April 23, 1861

THE ARMORY AT HARPERS FERRY

Former Virginia governor Henry Wise was determined to bring Virginia into the Confederacy and was impatient with slow progress being made at the Virginia Secession Convention. On April 16, a day before a second scheduled vote on secession was to occur at the convention, Wise ordered Virginia soldiers moved toward Harpers Ferry by rail in preparation for seizing the arsenal at Harpers Ferry and its weapons production facilities. He had no authority to do so. On April 17, shortly before the vote was to take place, Wise took the podium and delivered a fiery speech, brandishing his horse pistol and informing the convened delegates that Virginia troops were just fifteen minutes outside of Harpers Ferry, prepared to act. The convention endorsed secession that evening and scheduled a state referendum on the issue for May 23. Wise's troops did not wait for the referendum but seized the armory the following day.[13]

AFFAIRS AT HARPER'S FERRY.

The 18th of April, says the Charlestown Free Press, proved another great event in the history of Harper's Ferry. A rumor was in circulation that several thousand Northern men were to arrive on that day to take control of the United States Armory. This rumor created much excitement and caused the calling out of the 2nd Regiment of Volunteers, under Col. Allen. This report, however, was not sustained by fact.—On Thursday morning Col. A. M. Barbour, a member of the State Convention from Jefferson county, and John Seddot, Esq., a member of the Legislature from Stafford county, arrived there and stated that the Convention had passed an Ordinance of Secession, and that the Governor of Virginia had ordered the Volunteers out for the purpose of repelling the Federal authorities in the event of an effort to re-inforce the command already there, and that Virginia intended taking possession of the Armory, &c.

This caused much excitement, as the citizens of that place were under the impression that an unlawful seizure of the property was to be made, and were determined to oppose the supposed invasion. In the meantime, however, troops were gathering from all parts of the Valley; and Lieut. Jones, commander of the Federal forces who had been stationed for several months at Harper's Ferry, finding that he would be compelled to evacuate, commenced his preparations for the destruction of the property.

A Mr. Kingsbury, a member of the Ordnance department, had been some 30 hours before sent there as Superintendent in place of Col. Barbour, who had resigned. He and Lieut. Jones had been busily engaged in their designs for the destruction of the property. The operatives were directed to leave the shops, with the assurance that they should resume work the next day.—The gates leading to the Armory were then closed upon them, and sentinels posted, whilst the Superintendent and Lieut. Jones employed their forces in removing foot bridges, from the canal to prevent ingress, and preparing for blowing up the buildings by placing kegs and sacks of powder in them. This was done without the knowledge of those outside. Powder was conveyed in bed ticks to the Arsenal buildings, whilst great quantities had been scattered over the floors of the shops, and barrels of it placed in such position as to demolish the entire establishment as well as destroy those who might approach.

After this, they placed sentinels some two or three miles at different points to watch the approach of the Virginia forces *en route* for the Ferry. A sentinel hailed Col. Allen and his command, and when the Col. ordered to charge upon him, he rode off rapidly, and before the Regiment reached the Ferry, Lieut. Jones had fired the buildings, and he and the Superintendent made tracks for Pennsylvania. The two Arsenal buildings with about 14,000 guns were destroyed. Only a portion of one of the shops was injured, although a deep laid plan had been made to destroy the entire Armory. The wheel for forcing the water was placed in operation, and by the great exertion of the citizens and military, the flames were prevented from spreading, although at much risk of life, as trains of powder had been spread in every direction. The fire broke out about 10 o'clock on Thursday night.

Had the scheme of Lieut. Jones succeeded, there is no telling the loss of life which would have ensued. Hundreds, perhaps would have been killed or wounded in the explosion which he contemplated.

Several thousand guns were not injured, and are in possession of Virginia.

The greater portion of the Machinery of the Armory has been taken down and removed. In a short time the shops will present nothing but an open space—and stand as a monument of the past. It is to be regretted that such a move was made, as one company of volunteers might have been armed every day.

Staunton Spectator, May 7, 1861

SWITCHING ALLEGIANCES

At the outset of the war, James W. Johnson enlisted in the 22nd Virginia but quickly had a change of heart. After joining the Union army, he ascended to the rank of captain and finished his service in 1865 as a captain in the 3rd United States Colored Troops. He summarized his service in this brief letter requesting discharge in the summer of 1865. He was granted an honorable discharge and returned to West Virginia.

Gen[eral]

 In answer to your questions I have the honor to report that I am a native of the state of Virginia. I have had but little education. What I have I procured by my own industry having gone to school but three months. I was at the breaking out of the late rebellion a member of the 22nd Virginia State troops. I was ordered by one Henry A. Wise a rebel leader to join my Regt which I refused to do and was arrested and my property seized. I was released in June 1861 and sent to the Ohio river. I then joined Gen. Cox's division Army of the Kanawha as a scout and guide in which capacity I served until the spring of 1862. When I organized the first company of the 13th Regt. Virginia Infty loyal and served with this Regt as Captain until July 1863. When I went before General Casey's Board and was assigned to duty with the 3 U.S.C.T. I will add here that I answered under the commands of Gens. Cox, Crook & Scammon in West Virginia.

 I was present at the siege of Wagner, Morris Island [then] joined Gen. Seymour's Florida Expedition in Feb 1864. Have served in this state since. I am now 27 years of age.

 I have offered my resignation and have no desire to remain longer in the Service. I have been on detached service for a number of months of late and I am in no way prepared to pass an examination in tactics &c.

Very Respectfully
Your Obdt Servt
J W Johnson
Capt 3 U.S.C.T.

<small>James W. Johnson to Brigadier General E. P. Scammon, June 27, 1865, GLC02214.390, Gilder Lehrman Institute Collections, New York</small>

A MINISTER FEARS SLAVE INSURRECTION

Located in the southeastern corner of present-day West Virginia, Monroe and Greenbrier Counties were Trans-Allegheny counties that retained some similarities with the Shenandoah Valley counties to their east. Despite their hilly topography, a form of plantation agriculture emerged in the flatter parts of these counties before 1860. More than 10 percent of the population of each of these counties was enslaved, and some enslavers commanded the labor of fifteen or more enslaved persons on their farms. Most of the White population of these counties supported the Confederacy throughout the war. Primary sources that explicitly reveal the viewpoints of African Americans in western Virginia are difficult to come by, so it is sometimes necessary to try to draw information about the region's enslaved population through the filter of free White writers. The Reverend S. R. Houston served a congregation in the ironically named town of Union, Monroe County, at the outset of the war. Excerpts from Reverend Houston's diary reveal his concerns about the local African American population in the first months of the war.

December 3, [1860]—Demons at the North and South seem bent on our ruin as a nation. I have not yet entirely despaired of the Republic. Some great good is to come out of this terrible convulsion, I think.

December 15—Dined with Major Echols, A.T. Caperton, and Dr. Waddell. Talked a great deal about the unhappy state of our country. Civil war and perhaps servile war seemed to us all extremely probable. Trade is paralyzed. Thousands thrown out of employment threaten to plunder in the cities for bread.

December 25—Can't do much these Christmas times. Heard that the captain of our patrol had received letters warning him of an intended insurrection on the part of the negroes. . . .

April 18, [1861]—The Presidents, Lincoln and Davis, have both issued their proclamations, calling out the forces of their respective confederacies. Our convention has passed an ordinance of secession. The other border states will doubtless follow. Then there will be a united South against a united North. And I trust that as the folly of undertaking to subjugate fifteen states is patent, the war cannot last more than a few months at most. Very great excitement extending among the people. . . .

April 27—Rumored that Fort Pickens is taken by the South with a loss of 1000 men. It is thought that the South has already made an assault on Washington. An insurrection among the negroes on the Kanawha is apprehended. In other places free negroes are enlisting in the Southern army.

May 15—The stage driver brought intelligence that a disturbance among the negroes in Lewisburg has just occurred, and that the leader of the revolt with many others has been put in jail. It has produced something of a panic among us. Patrol walks the streets till midnight. Our two guns and a large horseman's pistol have been loaded.

May 16—A meeting of citizens to form more efficient police. Never did I see so gloomy a time.

May 17—General muster. About 400 men on parade.

May 18—We have heard that some of the negroes of Monroe are implicated in the disturbance at Lewisburg. Their real designs we cannot tell. Under such circumstances most persons always fear the worst. Floating reports of discontent among the negroes are producing a great deal of uneasiness in neighboring counties, but no organized bands have been discovered.

May 19—Had little sleep last night. Our home dangers more feared by some than by the invading North.

May 20—Court day but no business done. War rules everything in the land. Almost all our schools and colleges are broken up.

May 21—Another company being formed, but its character does not promise much.

May 22—Our volunteer companies highly commended for their good order and discipline. Have heard that the negroes express a strong dislike for the sermon I lately preached, proving that the war on our side, being defensive, is a just one.

May 23—Only two votes against secession in this precinct. The Panhandle and some of the northwestern counties will probably go the whole length with the North. Perhaps this is best for Virginia. Currently reported and believed at the North that someone placed an image of a negro on the statue of Washington at Richmond as a symbol of the Southern Confederacy....

May 31—Vote against secession in northwestern counties much greater than anticipated....

June 8—Apprehension of servile insurrection, etc., etc....

June 29—Negro leader at Lewisburg hung yesterday....

December 31—Several negroes have left their homes in this neighborhood and made their way, it is thought, to the Federal army. They will never find as comfortable and happy homes as they have left.

<small>S. R. Houston, "A War Diary," in Oren F. Morten, *A History of Monroe County West Virginia* (Dayton, VA: Ruebush-Elkins, 1916), 168–73.</small>

REUBEN PUT ON TRIAL FOR PLANNING SLAVE INSURRECTION

Reverend Houston was not alone in his fears that the war might encourage enslaved people to rise up and secure their freedom. Shortly after the war began, rumors of a slave insurrection swept adjacent Greenbrier County. An enslaved man named Reuben was tried and convicted for hatching an alleged plot. His execution is mentioned in Reverend Houston's diary above. There were more than 1,500 enslaved people in Greenbrier County in 1860 owned by more than 250 different enslavers. While many enslavers in the county claimed more than ten people as property, John Withrow, identified in the court transcript as Reuben's enslaver is listed in the June 1860 slave schedule as possessing just one enslaved person, a fifty-year-old man. This was probably Reuben. The records of the trial included testimony from other African Americans in the community.

Virginia.

Pleas before the Justices of Greenbrier County court, at the court house thereof on Monday the 27th day of May, 1861.

Be it remembered that heretofore to wit that on the 14th day of May 1861, a certificate was filed with the clerk of this court in the words & figures following, to wit:

"Greenbrier county, to wit

To the clerk of the county court of said county—I, M. Arbuckle, a Justice of said county, do hereby certify, that I have this day committed Reuben, a slave, the property of John Withrow, to the jail of this county, that he may be tried before the county court of said county for a Felony by him, committed in this, that he did, on the day of plot and conspire to rebel and make insurrection in said county.

Given under my hand this 14th day of May 1861.

M. Arbuckle J. P.

And now at this day, to wit at a court continued and held for the county aforesaid, at the court house thereof on the day and year first herein mentioned to wit, on the 27th day of May 1861. Commonwealth

against

Reuben (a slave, the property of Jno: Withrow)

On a certificate of committal for plotting & conspiring to rebel & make an insurrection. The prisoner was this day led to the bar in custody of the Jailer of this court, and being arraigned pleaded not guilty, whereupon the court having heard the testimony, is of opinion that said slave Reuben is guilty of the felony for which he stands committed. Therefore it is considered by the court, that he be hanged by the neck until he be dead, and that execution of this judgment be made and done upon him the said slave Reuben by the sheriff of Greenbrier County, on Friday the 28th day, of June next, between the hours of ten in the forenoon and two in the afternoon of the same day, and that he be publickly executed. The court doth certify said slave to be of the value of three hundred dollars.

And it is ordered that the testimony, taken in writing in the trial be certified &c.

Memo: Upon the rendering of its judgment by the court, the counsel for the prisoner moved the court for a new trial upon the ground:

1st. That the judgment of the court is against the law—

2d. The judgment of the court is against the law &

3. The judgment of the court is against the law and evidence—which motion was overruled by the court.

The evidence taken down in writing on the trial, is in the words following, to wit: "Commonwealth

vs

Reuben (Slave of John Withrow)

Jordan (a slave) being sworn, saith—I was talking to Reuben about three weeks ago yesterday, and I was telling him I was going with master Cyrus Creigh, he said, after the cavalry started there would be a row kicked up nearer than Harpers Ferry, and said with what arms they had and with what fire they could throw out they could take Lewisburg—mentioned Campbell had two shot guns and Bill had two Pistols, and Mr Arbuckle's John & Mr Rader's Peter, but did'nt say whether they were engaged in—I commenced the conversation by saying Master Cyrus Cary, was going to Harpers Ferry, and he asked me what he was going there for; I told him he was going there to be in a battle or be ready for one, and he said that if there was a battle at Harpers Ferry, there would be a bigger one nearer home—

Cross examined

I never told any white person about it except Master Robert Arbuckle, Mr Beard & Capt Rader, until I was questioned; and the conversation was on Sunday near the Methodist Church, just after preaching—I was at the Campmeeting last fall on the Mountain; was not drunk, nor Reuben did not try to get me away—I had a fuss with Henry Curry, but I dont think Reuben was near—

John Withrow. The morning after Reuben was arrested I went to my stable and found the door unlocked—Reuben usually kept the door locked—I went in, found the door between my stable and my carriage house forced open and found a part of the stable floor torn up—The back door of the stable was forced.

James Withrow—The night Reuben was arrested a search was made at my house and we found four Pistols in the room where Campbell & his wife stayed, one five shooter and three single barrels and a good deal of shot, powder, Bullets & a box of caps—all the barrels of the Pistols were loaded.

John Toothman—Reuben said to some black hands in the cornfield as he passed me, "I will be damned if any white man shall be master over me"—I didn't hear any of the conversation except that much—I am positive as to the language—it was this month that the conversation took place—Mr Estill &

myself were dropping corn—I told it to Mr Mathews, Mr Estill & I think to some person else—

James H. Arbuckle—I raised Jordan and could rely upon him as a witness—he drinks some times, but has'nt drank any for some time—he has an affection of the throat—

Matthew Arbuckle—I am acquainted with Jordan and have known him from a child—would have no hesitancy in the world in relying upon his as a witness—

Jim (a slave of Saml Price Esqr) sworn for the defence—I was'nt with them (the hands in the cornfield) all the time—didn't hear Reuben say any thing about a white man being his master—I was dropping ashes & wasn't with them all the time—I was right after Mr Toothman & not with the coverers—

Alfred (a slave of Mrs Erskine) sworn—I was working with Reuben in the cornfield—I didn't hear the remark made about any white man ruling over or being his master—I never heard Reuben say any thing about destroying Lewisburg when the Cavalry left, or anything about having arms or any thing like that—I was plowing & not with the coverers—

Dr Thos Creigh—So far as I have ever heard of Jordan I consider him a boy of truth

Caesar (a slave of Archd. Edgar) sworn for the defence—I dont know that Jordan & Reuben ever had any quarrel—I did hear they had a quarrel twelve or thirteen years ago—Reuben advised me not to associate with him—I never told this to Jordan—they never quarreled in my presence—

A true transcript of the record

Teste.

JOEL MCPHERSON Clk.

Transcription of trial record in the case of *Commonwealth v. Reuben,* Greenbrier County, May 27, 1861, Executive Papers of Governor John Letcher, Pardons, June 1861, Acc. 36787, State Government Records Collection, Record Group 3, Library of Virginia, Richmond

"THE PEOPLE OF GREENBRIER ARE AMONGST THE MOST LOYAL OF THE STATE"

While Confederate officials were disappointed by the level of support for their cause in some of the northwestern counties, they found strong support for the Confederacy in Greenbrier and Monroe Counties. The presence of hot spring resorts in the region may have strengthened its ties to eastern Virginia, as members of eastern elite families traveled to these western Virginia spas to bathe in the health-restoring waters.

LETTER FROM WHITE SULPHUR SPRINGS.

White Sulphur Springs, June 12, 1861.

The people of Greenbrier are amongst the most loyal of the State. The recent alarms aroused their patriotic indignation to a very high pitch, and they rallied with great alacrity to the defence of their country. They are a hardy and powerful pattern of men. There are no better marksmen, and they will be amongst the most brave and efficient of the army of the Southern Confederacy. It is gratifying to witness the loyalty of a county which depends so much on the people of the South. Within her borders is the great Mecca of health—the White Sulphur Springs.—Here the beauty and the chivalry of the South have always congregated, and here they will continue to hold their annual reunions. How much would it be deplored were they surrounded by traitors to the cause of the South when they met here? It would, indeed; be a strange thing that such a place, so sustained and visited by the pride of the South, should be rendered odious by infidelity to the cause of the Southern people. Greenbrier is true, however, and has given the best proofs of her fealty. She has sent a number of companies to the field. These, with those now ready to join General Wise in his westward march, constitute nine companies mustered by this faithful old county, which, though for Union till Lincoln's proclamation, is now as true as steel to the cause and will make her deeds in the second great struggle for liberty historic.

To-day the second company mustered from this locality, took its departure for Lewisburg, to await the advance of Gen. Wise. This company bears the name of the place, being called the White Sulphur Rifle Company. . . . Just before the departure of the company a beautiful flag was presented to it on behalf of the ladies of Dry Creek and Anthony's Creek[.] Miss Mary Eakle was chiefly instrumental in this tribute to the company, as she has been in the presentation of two other flags to other companies. She has devoted herself with all a woman's ardor to the glorious cause of her country, and has been incessantly engaged with a number of her female friends in making flags and uniforms for the gallant volunteers. She has canvassed her district and raised liberal subscriptions to the cause. Her noble example deserves applause. J. A. Cowardin, Esq., of the Dispatch, presented the flag, on behalf of the ladies, and was responded to by Capt. McCann, on behalf of the company. . . . The parting scene was touching. The lady relatives of the patriotic young men were present, and though they willingly parted with them to go to their country's defence, still it were impossible to suppress the natural emotions at the separation.

A large delegation of the locality went up on Monday to the foot of the Alleghany Mountain, to welcome Gen. Wise to Western Virginia; but they were disappointed. He is expected here to-morrow, when he will be received with unbounded enthusiasm.

D.

Daily Dispatch (Richmond), June 18, 1861

"THE FREEDOM PURCHASED BY YOUR FATHER'S BLOOD"

Virginia's Confederate leadership was divided on whether people loyal to the Confederacy who found themselves in regions occupied by Union forces should engage in guerrilla tactics, which were deemed a violation of the rules of civilized war. But some commanders viewed them as essential to secure the independence of the Confederacy. Colonel Daniel Ruggles, an early advocate of irregular warfare, evoked the memory of the American Revolution in justifying guerrilla warfare in some circumstances.

Fredericksburg, Va., May 11, 1861

In conformity with instructions from headquarters of Virginia forces, volunteer companies of infantry and riflemen will be received into the service of the State for the period of one year from April 25, 1861. . . .

The companies of volunteers presenting themselves are expressly enjoined to conform in every essential particular in their organization, armament, and equipment to the requirements stated in the instructions for mustering volunteers into service. . . .

The policy of the State, as clearly indicated by the proclamation of the governor and the ordinances of the Convention, is to rely mainly on the organized and disciplined volunteer forces, in conjunction with the Provisional Army of Virginia. The readiness with which the people of this department have responded to the call for volunteers induces the hope that, save upon the emergency of actual invasion, the militia will not be called out; but, should that contingency arise before precise instructions are communicated, full reliance will be placed on the bold hearts and strong arms of a united people to make each house a citadel, and every rock and tree positions of defense, thus efficiently aiding the organized forces, by communicating by telegraph and concentrating by railway at the endangered point in such numbers as to sweep from our borders the insolent invaders. Called to command a border district of Virginia, now threatened with invasion and subjugation by a lawless tyranny, which, over a violated Constitution, would march to conquest and carnage, it is esteemed not less the post of honor than of danger. Brave and loyal men of that district which has given to freedom a Washington, Madison, Monroe, Lee, Mercer, and others, whom, both in camp and council, the world has recognized as among the noblest defenders of constitutional liberty, you are called upon to rally for the defense of your homes and firesides; your wives and children; the ashes of your mighty dead; the freedom purchased by your fathers' blood, and the soil and sovereignty of your old Commonwealth. Give force and efficiency to your patriotic ardor by aid of discipline and organization; substitute prudence and policy for passion, and by your devotion to liberty, regulated by law, vindicate before the nations your claim to exercise the inalienable right of self-government.

Daniel Ruggles,
Colonel, Provisional Army, Commanding Virginia Forces.

The War of the Rebellion: A Compilation of the Official Records of the Union and Confederate Armies, ser. 1, vol. 2 (Washington, D.C.: Government Printing Office, 1880), 833–34

"I HAVE ORDERED TROOPS TO CROSS THE OHIO RIVER"

Federals were slow to move into western Virginia for fear that the early arrival of Union troops in the region might push some western Virginians into the arms of the Confederacy. They believed that allowing western Virginians the opportunity to cast their votes in the secession referendum without the threatening presence of Union troops might consolidate loyalty to the Union. A majority of Virginia voters affirmed the Ordinance of Secession, but majorities in many northwestern counties voted no on the issue. General George B. McClellan issued two statements to the people of northwest Virginia through the widely circulated Wheeling Daily Intelligencer. *The first, presented below, addressed the residents of western Virginia. The second spoke to the Union troops he had ordered into western Virginia, urging them to treat the loyal populace with respect.*

Headquarters, Department of the Ohio, May 26, 1861.

To the Union Men of Western Virginia:

Virginians: The General Government has long enough endured the machinations of a few factious rebels in your midst. Armed traitors have in vain endeavored to deter you from expressing your loyalty at the polls. Having failed in this infamous attempt to deprive you of the exercise of your dearest rights, they now seek to inaugurate a reign of terror, and thus force you to yield to their schemes and submit to the yoke of the traitorous conspiracy dignified by the name of the Southern Confederacy.

They are destroying the property of citizens of your State and ruining your magnificent railways. The General Government has heretofore carefully abstained from sending troops across the Ohio, or even from posting them along its banks, although frequently urged to do so by many of your prominent citizens. I determined to await the result of the late election, desirous that no one might be able to say that the slightest effort had been made from this side to influence the free expression of your opinion, although the many agencies brought to bear upon you by the rebels were well known.

You have now shown under the most adverse circumstances that the great mass of the people of Western Virginia are true and loyal to that beneficent Government under which we and our fathers have lived so long. As soon as the result of the election was known the traitors commenced their work of destruction. The General Government cannot close its ears to the demand you have made for assistance. I have ordered troops to cross the [Ohio] river. They come as your friends and brothers—as enemies only to the armed rebels who are preying upon you. Your homes, your families, and your property are safe under our protection. All your rights shall be religiously respected.

Notwithstanding all that has been said by the traitors to induce you to believe that our advent among you will be signalized by interference with your slaves, understand one thing clearly—not only will we abstain from all such interference, but we will, on the contrary, with an iron hand, crush any attempt at insurrection on their part. Now that we are in your midst, I call upon you to fly to arms and support the General Government.

Sever the connection that binds you to traitors. Proclaim to the world that the faith and loyalty so long boasted by the Old Dominion are still preserved in Western Virginia, and that you remain true to the Stars and Stripes.

Geo. B. McClellan,
Maj. General, U. S. A., commanding department of the Ohio.

The War of the Rebellion: A Compilation of the Official Records of the Union and Confederate Armies, ser. 1, vol. 2 (Washington, D.C.: Government Printing Office, 1880), 48–49

"REPRESS ALL ATTEMPTS AT NEGRO INSURRECTION"

McClellan also sent telegrams to his officers who led regiments in the invasion. His order to Colonel Benjamin Kelley, in charge of the 1st Regiment Virginia Volunteers, which was to move on Fairmont, is below. McClellan sent similar telegrams to Colonel James Irvine of the 16th Ohio, who would cross from Bellaire to Wheeling to support Kelley by securing the Baltimore and Ohio Railroad; and to Colonel J. B. Steedman of the 14th Ohio, who was to cross the river at Marietta and occupy Parkersburg.

Col. B. F. KELLEY,
First Regiment Virginia Volunteers, Wheeling:

If you have reliable information that bridges of the Baltimore and Ohio Railroad have been burned, you will at once procure transportation on that railroad, and move your whole command, including the separate companies of Virginia volunteers not attached to your regiment, as near to Fairmont as can be done without endangering the safety of your command. Leave a sufficient guard to protect the bridges and other structures most liable to destruction. Colonel Irvine, of the Sixteenth Ohio, is ordered to cross the river and support you. Telegraph me constantly as to the state of affairs, and how much support you need. Conduct the preliminaries of your movement with as much secrecy as possible, and see that the telegraph conveys no intimation of it in any direction. *Consult Major Oakes frequently.* The move must be made with the greatest promptness to secure the bridges. Take at least one week's rations. Accouterments will follow you to-morrow. I count on your prudence and courage. Preserve the strictest discipline. See that the rights and property of the people are respected, and repress all attempts at negro insurrection.

GEO. B. MCCLELLAN,

Major-General, U. S. Army, Commanding Department.

The War of the Rebellion: A Compilation of the Official Records of the Union and Confederate Armies, series 1, vol. 2 (Washington, D.C.: Government Printing Office, 1880), 46

BATTLE OF PHILIPPI

A Union rout of Confederate forces near the town of Philippi in Barbour County was a small affair but had significant implications. In a county whose citizens were divided in their support, the Union victory assured local Union supporters of protection and silenced local Confederates. Furthermore, it increased McClellan's reputation as the Union's "young Napoleon." McClellan was nowhere near the battlefield but directed operations from Ohio. Confederate newspapers in Richmond downplayed the significance of the victory, but it appears to have blunted Confederate recruitment efforts in the area. Newspaper reports on Philippi also exposed another common problem with war reporting: the telegraph allowed for battlefield accounts to quickly appear in newspapers across the region and nation, but also encouraged the spread of misinformation. Contrary to early stories, Colonel Benjamin Kelley was not killed at the battle of Philippi but was wounded. He returned to military service a few months later.

HEADQUARTERS DEPARTMENT OF THE OHIO,
Cincinnati, June 3, 1861.

I have just received a telegram, dated to-day, from General T. A. Morris, Indiana Volunteers, commanding United States troops at Grafton, Va., in which he says:

We surprised the rebels, about two thousand strong, at Philippi this morning. Captured a large amount of arms, horses, ammunition, provisions, and camp equipage.

The attack was made after a march during the entire night in a drenching rain. The surprise was complete. Fifteen rebels killed. The gallant Colonel Kelley, of the First Virginia Volunteers, I fear, is mortally wounded. No other important casualties on our side.

The dispatch from General Morris informs me that the troops at last advices were in hot pursuit of the rebels.

GEO. B. MCCLELLAN,
Major-General, Commanding.
Colonel E. D. TOWNSEND, Assistant Adjutant-General.

<small>The War of the Rebellion: A Compilation of the Official Records of the Union and Confederate Armies, ser. 1, vol. 2. (Washington, D.C.: Government Printing Office, 1880), 64–65</small>

BATTLE AT PHILLIPPI

Fifteen Virginians Killed. Col. Kelly Killed.

Baltimore papers of Tuesday came to hand last night. They contain the following details of a fight at Phillippi, Va., but as the report is by the way of Cincinnati, and has undergone the revision of the Federal authorities, it must be taken with many grains of allowance:

Cincinnati, June 3.—Two columns of troops, commanded by Col. Kelley, of the First Virginia Union Volunteers of Wheeling, and Col. Crittenden, of Indiana, left Grafton early last night, and after marching about twenty miles through a drenching rain, surprised a camp of 2,000 Confederate troops at Phillippi, Va., a town in Barbour county, on the Tygart's Valley River. The surprise was complete, the Confederates fleeing and leaving fifteen dead bodies on the field.

The Union troops captured a large amount of arms, horses, ammunition, provisions and camp equipage. At the last advices the Federal troops were in hot pursuit of the Confederates, and there will probably be many of them taken prisoners. Col. Kelley was mortally wounded, and has since died. Several other of the Federal troops were slightly wounded. . . .

[A gentleman just arrived from Washington informs us that the report of a battle is false. A skirmish, however, had taken place near the point named, in which Col Kelley was killed. Further evidence of the incorrectness of the report is, that there were no horses of any account in or near Phillippi. The probability is, that on the arrival of reliable information from our own forces, we shall have altogether another coloring to this affair.]—*Eds. Enquirer.*

Richmond Enquirer, June 7, 1861

"YOU WERE THERE ON A REGULAR *DRUNK*"

Unionist Marcia Phillips lived in the divided town of Buckhannon. Her husband, Sylvester Bunyan Phillips (referred to as "Syl-" in this entry), served as a captain in the 3rd West Virginia Volunteer Infantry during the first years of the war. Marcia recounts the delight Unionists had in taunting local Confederates after the victory at Philippi.

JUNE 14TH, 1861

A body of U.S. Troops from Philippi, about 1500 marched into Buckhannon this evening, intending to quarter there. They were received with heartfelt joy, by the inhabitants, or the Union part of them, I might say. The people of the country as they marched through brought out milk and other refreshments to them. They had thirty baggage wagons and 1 cannon, one of the self same pieces, that played such a pretty tune in the astonished ears of the rebels at Philippi, before they were routed and sent from there. . . . They said Buckhannon was the first decent place they had seen since they had left their homes, and were much pleased with it. One of the Artillerymen, who came into town first, called out to the others as they came in, "*Boys, White Folks live here.*" Syl- was talking on the streets, with one of the Artillery men "a great stalwart good natured fellow" Syl- said he was. They were talking of the Philippi skirmish. "By the way," he said, "I understand that Col. Loudin the secession Col. resides in Buckhannon." Syl- replied in the affirmative and looking up the street at that instant, he espied the Colonel coming down leading his little girl. "There he comes now," said Syl- "Shall I give you an introduction?" "No," replied he, "I desire the pleasure of introducing myself to him." When the Col. came up the artillery man jumped up from where he was sitting and advancing to him, exclaimed, "And is it possible, that this is Col. Loudin, late of Philippi, the *Bloody* Colonel as our boys call him?" Loudin grunted out an affirmative answer, when his persecutor continued, "Give me your paw, Col.," and shaking it heartily continued, "The last time I saw you Col., you *was* running most beautifully." "And how would you like, Col., to see your old cap? A very pretty cap it was, Col., very pretty feathers, *but* Col. Loudin, you *can't have it*. I've sent it on to Cleveland by way of Wheeling and many is the masquerade ball, I shall appear at, in your cap next winter." The Col. did not know what to say. He was completely nonplussed.—He finally grunted out something about "he had never seen an army before and just thought he'd go down with the boys and see the Confederate army and have a little spree." "Oh yes, I understand," replied the artilleryman, "You were there on a regular *drunk*." (he is a notorious drunkard.) Loudin tried to excuse himself, but the more excuses he made, the more it poured into him.

<small>Marcia Louise Sumner Phillips Journal, Collection No. 1846, pp. 2–3, West Virginia and Regional History Center, West Virginia University, Morgantown.</small>

"THE UNION MEN ARE GREATLY IN ASCENDANCY HERE"

Brigadier General R. S. Garnett describes the impact of an early Union victory on Confederate recruitment in western Virginia.

BRIGADIER GENERAL R.S. GARNETT TO ROBERT E. LEE

Headquarters, Department of Northwestern Virginia, Camp at Laurel Hill, Va.,
June 25, 1861.

... I have been, so far, wholly unable to get anything like accurate or reliable information as to numbers, movements or intentions of the enemy, and begin to believe it an almost impossible thing. The Union men are greatly in ascendancy here, and are much more zealous and active in their cause than the Secessionists. The enemy are kept fully advised of our movements, even to the strength of our scouts and pickets, by the country people, while we are compelled to grope in the dark as much as if we were invading a foreign and hostile country. My hope of increasing my force in this region has, so far, been sadly disappointed. Only eight men have joined me here and fifteen at Colonel

Heck's camp—not sufficient to make up my losses by discharges, etc. These people are thoroughly imbued with an ignorant and bigoted Union sentiment.

R.S. Garnett
Brig.-Gen'l Provisional Army Commanding.

<small>Reproduced in Theodore F. Lang, *Loyal West Virginia from 1861 to 1865: With an Introductory Chapter on the Status of Virginia for Thirty Years Prior to the War* (Baltimore: Deutsch Publishing, 1895), 59</small>

"WE ARE ENEMIES TO NONE BUT ARMED REBELS"

While the presence of Union troops in northwestern Virginia appears to have slowed Confederate recruitment, underground resistance to Union occupiers quickly emerged, despite McClellan's efforts to reassure western Virginians that his troops presented no threat to their persons or property. Union soldiers became the targets of insurrectionary violence, and McClellan was compelled to issue a warning to those engaged in guerrilla activities.

PROCLAMATION OF MAJOR-GENERAL MCCLELLAN.

HEAD-QUARTERS DEP'T OF THE OHIO,
GRAFTON, VIRGINIA,
June 23, 1861

To the Inhabitants of Western Virginia:

The army of this Department, headed by Virginia troops, is rapidly occupying all Western Virginia. This is done in co-operation with, and in support of such civil authorities of the State as are faithful to the Constitution and laws of the United States. The proclamation issued by me, under date of May 26th, 1861, will be strictly maintained. Your houses, families, property, and all your rights will be religiously respected. We are enemies to none but armed rebels, and those voluntarily giving them aid. All officers of this Army will be held responsible for the most prompt and vigorous action in repressing disorder and punishing aggression by those under their command.

To my great regret I find that the enemies of the United States continue to carry on a system of hostilities prohibited by the laws of war among belligerent nations, and of course far more wicked and intolerable when directed against loyal citizens engaged in the defense of the common government of all. Individuals and marauding parties are pursuing a guerrilla warfare, firing upon sentinels and pickets, burning bridges, insulting, injuring and even killing citizens, because of their Union sentiments, and committing many kindred acts.

I do now, therefore, make proclamation and warn all persons, that individuals or parties engaged in this species of warfare, irregular in every view which can be taken of it, thus attacking sentries, pickets or other soldiers, destroying public or private property, or committing injuries against any of the inhabitants because of Union sentiments or conduct, will be dealt with in their persons and property, according to the severest rules of military law.

All persons giving information, or aid to the public enemies, will be arrested and kept in close custody; and all persons found bearing arms, unless of known loyalty, will be arrested and held to examination.

GEO. B. MCCLELLAN,

Maj. Gen'l U. S. A., Comd'g Dept.

Wheeling Daily Intelligencer, June 25, 1861

"WE DO NOT DOUBT THAT YOU WILL IN DUE TIME SWEEP THE REBELS FROM WESTERN VIRGINIA"

While Philippi might have been more skirmish than battle, McClellan secured a more decisive victory against the Confederates on July 11, 1861. The Confederates held and had fortified two key mountain passes—Laurel Hill and Rich Mountain—blocking any Union advance toward the Shenandoah Valley. McClellan directed his subordinates to surround Confederate lieutenant colonel John Pegram's forces at Rich Mountain, and in a two-hour battle Union soldiers split the Confederate ranks, compelling Pegram and many of his men to surrender while others escaped. On Laurel Hill the vulnerable Confederate force fled and Union forces pursued, defeating them two days later at Corrick's Ford. The victory enhanced McClellan's growing reputation, and after the humiliating Union defeat at First Manassas ten days later, McClellan was summoned east to take charge of the much larger Army of the Potomac. The victories at Rich Mountain and Corrick's Ford also secured Union control of the Staunton–Parkersburg Turnpike, an important route from northwestern Virginia to the Shenandoah Valley. Lee's effort to reverse these losses in the late summer failed at Cheat Mountain, and Confederate forces spent an unusually long and cold winter freezing in the mountains.

Washington, DC July 13th 1861

Maj. Gen. McClellan,

The General-in-Chief, and what is more, the Cabinet including the President, are charmed with your activity, valor, and consequent success and of Rich

Mountain the 11th, and of Beverley this morning. We do not doubt that you will in due time sweep the rebels from Western Virginia, but we do not mean to precipitate you, as you are fast enough.

Winfield Scott

The War of the Rebellion: A Compilation of the Official Records of the Union and Confederate Armies, ser. 1, vol. 2 (Washington, D.C.: Government Printing Office, 1880), 204

"ALL THE SONS OF BITCHES IN THE CONFEDERATE ARMY"

Twenty-year-old James E. Hall of Barbour County joined a Confederate unit called the Barbour Greys shortly after the Virginia Convention voted for secession. The Greys became Company H of the 31st Virginia Infantry on May 14, and Hall was assigned the rank of fourth corporal. The diary he kept begins with great earnestness for the Confederate cause. "Hardships, heretofore and even now unknown, will evidently follow every camp occupant," Hall speculated, "and scenes of carnage and death await a soldier's soliloquy. Be it so. We will go farther and consider our lives as a small offering for our native land!"[14] After the defeats at Philippi and Rich Mountain, and Lee's failure to reverse Union gains at Cheat Mountain in September, Confederate forces in the region retreated to the mountains, where they endured a very cold and very wet fall and winter. Corporal Hall's enthusiasm for the cause quickly waned, and he frequently considered leaving the army. Nonetheless, he stayed, even returning to the army after spending months in a Northern prisoner of war camp. He remained in the army until the war's end, being released from duty after witnessing Lee's surrender at Appomattox.

Sept. 7 . . .

If I should be so unfortunate as to be slain in any battle, and if any (blackhearted) kind Yankee should find this on my carcass while looking for other things of far greater value, of which I have not any amount, I will be much obliged to him to send it to Miss Emma I. Hall, Elk Creek, Barbour Co. Va. I will be much obliged to any persons to do likewise, if they should find it after I lose it.

James E. Hall
Camp Bartow, Sept. 7, '61

NOV. 6, 1861

This is a very disagreeable day. The mountains in the distance are covered with snow. I expect we will have to winter here. If they do keep our Regt. here they will never get another Western Va. volunteer. We have been badly treated. I will have various scores to settle after the war is over.

Nov. 13 . . . I feel like never writing any more. I have quit hoping to ever see our subjugated county as it was once. I feel more like throwing down my gun and cursing the hour I was born to witness such a condition of affairs, than of doing anything else. Unless there is some action soon, I will answer to my name—at a distance! I have a strong idea of getting drunk tonight. I would sure, if it was to be had this side of Yankeedom. Will and Mike are off somewhere on the sick list. I feel somewhat indisposed myself—every time there is a fight on hand! But I have not gone yet! Bud and I console ourselves over a large two-gallon bottle we keep on hand, but which is empty nearly all the time. I wonder if they at home ever think about us. But I wonder more, what they would think if they were to see me with my large vial filled with whiskey!

Nov. 18 . . . Whew! How cold it is this morning! . . . It is now night. We have received marching orders. Our destination is undoubtedly fixed for the top of Allegheny Mountain. Not to save the life of Gen. Loring, and all the sons of bitches in the Confederate Army, would I volunteer again! Not many know where we are going, but I—being a *high private*, find out many things. Bud and I are going to back out in the morning—but not until we get our large bottle filled!

Nov. 19 . . . Bud and I did not leave this morning. . . . If ever I again see J.E. Hall in a muster roll, I will be *tite* when it is put there. A man dies every now and then in our Regt. I felt extremely sorry for one poor fellow who was lying in a tent without any fire. He had the fever, but was suffering greatly from extreme cold. Sickness is more to be dreaded by far in the army, than the bullets. No bravery can achieve anything against it. The soldier may sicken and die, without receiving any attention but from the rough hands of his fellow soldiers. When he is buried he is soon forgotten. Not a stone is raised to tell his living name, age, or race.

James E. Hall, *The Diary of a Confederate Soldier*, ed. Ruth Woods Dayton (n.p., 1961), 11–37

THE KANAWHA VALLEY

The Confederates had hoped to capture and hold Charleston and the Kanawha Valley from the beginning of the war. The Kanawha Salines could be a valuable resource, as salt, used as a preservative, was always needed by armies on the move. Furthermore, the salt manufactories around Charleston depended heavily upon enslaved labor, so many, but not all, of the town's economic elite sympathized with the Confederacy.

SALT—RECAPTURE OF KANAWHA.

The supply of salt is becoming a seriously mooted question. The value of the article imported into the United States during the year ending June 30, 1860, was $1,431,141.—The official tables do not give the quantity; but, estimating the sack at two-and-a-half bushels, and at a dollar-and-a-half in price, the quantity was about 2,335,235 bushels.—If we suppose one-third of this quantity to have been imported for Southern consumption, the supply required for the Southern market over and above what is manufactured within the Southern States, would be 778,412 bushels. Whence this extraordinary supply is to be obtained, is a question of some interest.

The works near Abingdon, in Washington county, in this State, have heretofore manufactured about three hundred thousand bushels a year. Owing to the high freights on the Virginia and Tennessee Railroad, this supply has nearly all gone off in wagons through the country, and upon boats down the Holston river. Several hundred thousand additional bushels would have been manufactured for the Eastern market, but for the railroad freights, which brought the price in Petersburg and Richmond up to a figure too high for competition with the foreign article.

The blockade may remove this difficulty and preparations have been completed for increasing the annual supply produced at those works by about three hundred thousand bushels, which will all come East, unless the cheaper transportation on the Holston river than on the Virginia and Tennessee Railroad, and the strength of the demand in the West, shall direct it all in the opposite direction. At all events, from this source alone will 300,000 bushels of the 778,000 deficiency be supplied to the Southern markets.

The only other accessible source of supplying Virginia is the Salines of Kanawha. Unfortunately, the Valley of the Kanawha is now in the hands of the enemy, Gen. Wise having been obliged to fall back to Lewisburg before a far superior force, and, as is also said, for want of ammunition. General Floyd has marched to a point four miles west of Lewisburg, and is ready to advance in conjunction with General Wise again into the Kanawha country; but is obliged to await his third regiment, which is detained at Bonsack's Depot, fifty miles west of Lynchburg, awaiting arms from Richmond, being fully equipped in every other respect. The joint forces of these two Generals will still be only half of that of the enemy, unless they be largely reinforced by militia, who will be badly armed.

With the Kanawha Valley in possession of the South, the great quantities of salt manufactured there, and heretofore sent to the West and Northwest, could be diverted to our Eastern markets. We are not informed of the amount of the production of the Kanawha Salines, but believe it has heretofore been about 2,500,000 bushels a year. It is certainly very large, and from this source alone could the remaining 500,000 bushels of the deficiency of supply caused by the blockade be obtained for the South.

Thus Western Virginia alone can supply the whole deficiency of the salt supply of the South, provided only adequate steps be taken to hold possession of the Kanawha Valley.—This single object alone is worth a costly military expedition, and yet, unfortunately, this is the very portion of Western Virginia that has been most neglected. The recapture of the dreary country penetrated by McClellan and Roscencranz is of secondary importance. But the possession of the rich and beautiful Valley of the Kanawha, with its prolific Salines, which has been overrun by Cox, is of primary importance. No portion of the State of equal extent is half so important, and we look with great interest to the operations of Generals Floyd and Wise. . . .

Daily Dispatch (Richmond), August 20, 1861

FOUR

The Rules of War

*O*N MAY 25, 1861, Adam Snyder, the political editor of the Lewisburg, Virginia, *Greenbrier Weekly Era*, announced he had "gone to war," joining a Confederate unit organizing at Harpers Ferry. He was marching off "to defend the sacred soil of our loved Old Virginia" against the "infamous, wicked, and mercenary horde" that would soon be invading his state.[1] In his absence, the *Weekly Era* ceased publication. In May of 1862, Union forces under General George Crook occupied the Confederate-sympathizing town of Lewisburg and defeated an effort by a Confederate force under General Henry Heth to retake it. Several soldiers from the triumphant 44th Ohio discovered the abandoned press and decided to launch a new paper, *The Yankee,* to let the local population know who was now in control. The tone of the editorials in the short-lived paper was boastful, but also reflected the growing antagonism between Union soldiers and civilians in the areas they occupied. An editorial entitled "Plain Talk" warned the local citizenry to "abjure the forbidden fruit of anarchy" and swear allegiance to the Union. "Brothers! . . . the 'milk and water' policy that was pursued last summer was found ineffectual and is to be abandoned. A citizen who refuses to take the oath of allegiance to the United States government is an enemy of it, and we are here to suppress these enemies."[2]

The American Civil War took the lives of roughly 750,000 Americans, and many histories have emphasized its violence, brutality, and lawlessness. Still other historians have argued that leaders on both sides of the conflict at critical times sought to check this violence, especially against civilians, and operate within the rules of war.[3] But General Crook was not one of these leaders. Crook had taken command of Union forces in the Kanawha Valley in the fall of 1861, and in his memoir he recalled the abundance of "cowardly bushwhackers who would waylay the unsuspecting traveler and shoot them down with impunity." At first his men tried to capture the bushwhackers alive and send them to Camp Chase, a prisoner of war camp in Columbus, Ohio. But Crook claimed that these men were soon released and came back "fat, saucy, with good clothes, returning to their old occupation with renewed vigor." Soon his men stopped returning from patrols with any suspected bushwhackers alive, maintaining that their prisoners had an unfortunate mishap on their way back to camp, slipping in a stream and breaking their necks or getting "killed by an accidental discharge of one of the men's guns."[4] It appeared that one year into the war in western Virginia, the policy of restraint toward civilians that McClellan had advocated was being abandoned by commanders like George Crook, a veteran of the more ruthless Indian Wars in the American West.

Three areas of contention between the Union and Confederate governments regarding the rules of war persisted throughout the conflict. First were questions about the treatment of civilians, including suspected spies, saboteurs, and guerrillas in regions occupied by military forces. The treatment of civilians in occupied territories was intimately tied to the activities of guerrillas and irregular units within these regions and the extent to which the warring governments encouraged and sanctioned these activities. For many of those loyal to the Confederacy, the use of guerrilla tactics to defend against a Northern invasion had great appeal.[5] Confederate leaders, however, were more ambivalent. They viewed guerrilla tactics as dishonorable and worried about how uncontrolled irregular units might undermine military discipline, draw soldiers away from formal units, and even risk turning civilian populations against their cause. In western Virginia, the failure of Robert E. Lee to reverse Union gains in the region at the battle of Cheat Mountain forced a recognition that Union military occupation would not be easily ended. This limited the Confederate government's ability to recruit additional soldiers to the regular units and to protect Confederate sympathizers from hostile actions carried out by Union armies or Union-sympathizing civilians. By the spring of 1862, the Virginia government in Richmond concluded that Union military occupation of large swaths of northwestern Virginia meant the prospects for recruiting more men for military service in the region were unpromising. The Virginia legislature's solution was to pass the Virginia Ranger Act, which allowed for the creation and recognition of irregular units when they consisted of men from only occupied regions of the state. The act also set out rules for these units' operation in an effort to exert more control. The Virginia Ranger Act became the model for a Partisan Ranger Act passed by the Confederate government a month later.[6]

For Union forces occupying areas with a substantial presence of hostile civilians, saboteurs, and guerrillas, the pressing questions involved what constituted just treatment of civilians. McClellan's spring 1861 orders that soldiers treat civilians and their property with respect soon gave way to harsher and more indiscriminate actions as the Union occupiers became targets of guerrilla violence. Over time, many Union soldiers grew wary even of the armed local home guards who claimed to be fighting on the same side. Yet these locals could be useful sources of intelligence about enemy movements, and even more valuable as guides during scouting raids into areas where the Confederacy retained the loyalty of much of the populace. But when locals were motivated by a desire to exact personal justice for wrongs committed by their neighbors, they could be difficult to restrain, even if the regular Union soldiers were inclined to do so. Furthermore, there always remained doubts about the true loyalties of these rough-looking armed men.

The second area of contention was the status of enslaved people. While the Southern position that the enslaved were just another form of civilian property remained fixed throughout the war, the Union position continued to shift. McClellan embraced the Southern viewpoint at the outset, going as far as to order his officers to suppress any "negro insurrection" that might break out in the chaos of a Union invasion. With the passage of the first (August 6, 1861) and second (July 17, 1862) Confiscation Acts, Congress continued to expand the grounds under which enslaved people fleeing to Union lines could be held as contraband of war. During the first two years of the war, field commanders had a fair amount of discretion regarding the treatment of those who fled enslavement.[7] Those who emancipated themselves and crossed through Union-occupied regions of western Virginia could not be certain how they would be received in Union camps. For the large community of self-emancipating African Americans who found protection in the contraband camp of Union-controlled Harpers Ferry, as well as the many African Americans who were living effectively as free people along the Kanawha in 1862, the temporary Confederate reoccupation of Harpers Ferry and Charleston in the fall placed them in jeopardy of reenslavement.[8] When Lincoln's Emancipation Proclamation went into effect on January 1, 1863, declaring all persons held in bondage in rebel-controlled territories to be free, Confederates were outraged, but the proclamation applied largely to areas where the Union army had no ability to enforce it. Notably, Lincoln's proclamation exempted most of the Virginia counties that would become part of the state of West Virginia. For enslaved people in rebel-controlled regions, the proclamation was effectively an invitation to self-emancipate by fleeing to Union lines.

But Lincoln's proclamation also permitted the enlistment of African American men into the Union army, which raised a third area of contention between the two warring sides. Confederates charged the Union with inciting "servile war," an act White Americans, Northern and Southern, had condemned as barbarism a few generations earlier, when Lord Dunmore offered freedom to any enslaved person toiling on a rebel plantation in exchange for fighting for the Crown. Confederate president Jefferson Davis's response was to declare that

Black men in Union uniforms, along with the White officers who commanded them, could be executed when captured. In practice, Confederate forces often executed Black Union soldiers on the spot. Those who were not killed faced enslavement. The Confederacy's refusal to recognize that the rules of war applied equally to Black as well as to White prisoners of war prompted the suspension of prisoner exchanges between the two sides in the last two years of the war. It also meant that the risks of war were greater for Black soldiers than for White ones, including the roughly 220 Black West Virginians who enlisted in the 45th United States Colored Troops regiment in the summer of 1864.[9]

Uncertainties about what was permissible and impermissible under the rules of war led the Union War Department to commission jurist Francis Lieber to draft a single document outlining the "rules" of war. Issued in April 1863 as "The General Orders No. 100: Instructions for the Government of the Armies of the United States in the Field," the Lieber Code outlined the rules armies must operate under when imposing martial law on civilian populations, as well as the treatment of irregular fighters, spies, prisoners of war, and deserters. It defined the terms under which "hard war" tactics could be used against hostile civilian populations, legitimizing some of the harsher tactics deployed by Union military officers against civilian property in regions where armies faced saboteurs and insurgents. It also affirmed the legitimacy of Lincoln's Emancipation Proclamation as a legal tool of war and declared the Confederate practice of racist discrimination against Black soldiers to be a violation of the laws of war. While the rules enshrined in the Lieber Code were not accepted by the Confederacy, in the decades after the Civil War much of the Lieber Code was incorporated into the rules of warfare issued by other Western nations and accepted as part of international law.[10]

"OUR HOUSES HAVE BEEN FORCIBLY ENTERED AND ROBBED"

Union victories in the summer of 1861 placed much of northwestern Virginia under Union control. Residents of Hardy County were deeply divided in their sympathies, and its Confederate-allied citizens issued a plea to the Confederate government to send forces to drive out Union occupiers they accused of abusing them. Lee's failure at Cheat Mountain to reverse Union gains—just a few days after this plea was issued—was certainly disappointing news to those in the county who retained an allegiance to eastern Virginia.

SEPTEMBER 10, 1861. To His Excellency JEFFERSON DAVIS, President of the Confederate States of America:

The undersigned, citizens of Hardy County, Virginia, desire to call your attention to the exposed and suffering condition of our county. We have been invaded for the past two months by Northern thieves. Our houses have been forcibly entered and robbed. Our horses, cattle, and sheep in large numbers driven off. Our citizens arrested, carried off, and confined, only because they are loyal citizens of Virginia and the Southern Confederacy. Our cattle, sheep, and horses, to the amount of $30,000, have been forcibly taken from us and appropriated to the support of the Army of the United States.

Our county, unfortunately, is divided, the western portion being disloyal. The Union men, as they call themselves, have called upon Lincoln for protection. He, in answer to their call, has sent amongst us a set of base characters, who not only protect the Union men, but under their guidance are committing acts unheard of in any country claiming civilization. We have been wholly unprotected and unable to protect ourselves. Our enemies have met with no resistance. We do not complain, as it is perhaps impossible to give protection to all who are suffering like depredations; but we would suggest whether the interest of the Confederacy, apart from the large private interest involved, does not require the protection of our beef, our pork, and our corn for the use of the Southern Army. General Lee is now drawing his supply of corn from us. There is perhaps no valley in America of the same extent that produces more fat cattle and hogs than the valley of the South Branch. Were we protected in the possession of our property we should be able to supply the Army with several thousand cattle and hogs and at the season of the year when the supply from other sources fails; but if no protection should be given us, and the present state of things suffered to go on, we may well despair not only of feeding the army, but of feeding ourselves. Our enemies, not content with driving off our cattle and sheep by hundreds and our horses in numbers, are to-day, we are most reliably informed, engaged in thrashing out the crops of wheat of some of the farmers of Hampshire.

We have been hoping for relief from General Lee's army in Western Virginia; that the necessities of General Rosecrans would compel him to withdraw his forces from us. In this we have been disappointed. We find still a force on our border acting with the Union men sufficient to rob us. The Baltimore and Ohio Railroad at New Creek Station is but about 30 miles from our county seat and so long as that point is suffered to remain in the possession of the enemy we must be insecure. We placed ourselves under the protection of the Confederate States with a full knowledge of our exposed situation, being a border county, yet relying upon the ability and willingness of our more Southern brethren, who are less exposed, to defend us.

We now would most earnestly call upon you, the chosen head of the Confederacy, for relief and continued protection, if not inconsistent with more important interests.

JACOB VAN METER ET AL.

The War of the Rebellion: A Compilation of the Official Records of the Union and Confederate Armies, series 1, vol. 5 (Washington, D.C.: Government Printing Office, 1881), 845–46

A VIRGINIA "SASSESH"

Born in Poland, Ohio, Andrew Jackson Duncan enlisted in the 23rd Ohio at the outset of the war, which was sent to western Virginia in July of 1861. While he experienced a few small battles, he spent most of his time as an occupier. This pencil sketch appeared in the diary he kept during his time in western Virginia.

Andrew J. Duncan journal, 1861, William L. Clements Library, University of Michigan, Ann Arbor.

BATTELLE CALLS FOR WEST VIRGINIA LEADERSHIP

Gordon Battelle was a Methodist minister serving a congregation in Clarksburg, western Virginia, before the war. Born and educated in Ohio, he was a rare voice for abolition in western Virginia and a college friend of Francis Pierpont, the first governor of the Reorganized Government of Virginia (the provisional government formed by western Virginia Unionists in the wake of the statewide vote for secession). In October of 1861 Pierpont sent his friend Battelle to investigate conditions in Union camps, and in November he became chaplain of the First (West) Virginia Infantry. The First Virginia was indeed the first unit organized in the state, but it was not composed exclusively of Virginians. A sizable minority of its soldiers hailed from Ohio and Pennsylvania. Its first commander, Benjamin F. Kelley, was not a native Virginian but had lived in Wheeling for some time. Here Battelle offers Pierpont some insight into the problems that out-of-state soldiers present as an occupying force and speculates on the potential value of homegrown Virginia leadership in the occupying armies.

Romney Va. Dec 26, 1861

My Dear Governor,

I arrived here on Tuesday evening, and found all in fine spirits in anticipation of a pleasant Christmas—I believe I spent the day as pleasantly as on any similar occasion for many years—

Thinking you would be pleased to hear from the Virginia First Regiment— . . . The discipline in the regiment is admirable; —not a rail is burnt by our boys—while they are hauled in open day to other camps all around us by the wagon load, and in spite of his standing general order against it. By the way the Brigade needs a commander. Gen Kelly is sick at Cumberland. . . . We need and ought to have soon an experienced and efficient military man in active command of the forces here.

And this leads me to remark upon what has struck me with some force in all my personal observations of the working of things—in my Cheat Mountain trip and since. Our neighbors from the Western States have done us an invaluable service in coming to our relief when they did and as they did. I of course fully appreciate our great indebtedness to them. But here they are away from home—they are among the "sesesh"—almost anything is lawful and proper in their eyes, as against the rebels—and they failed to discriminate as clearly as do our own Va troops between Union people and rebels. They will after the war is over go home to see this region probably no more—but our own troops, with all their hatred against the rebels—as intense probably as that of the others—nevertheless feel that they will live with this people when the rebellion is put down. Whatever derelictions the war produces—they will stay here—not only to see it—but in some sense to feel it—as strangers not identified with us will not. . . . if we had a General of Division—or at least a commander of brigade, identified with our people, of the right stripe . . . <u>it would be a vast gain to the Union cause</u> among us. I do frankly state the difficulty, & what I conceive to be a remedy. The how to get at it, I confess I am wholly ignorant of—I leave that entirely with you—I know of no person who can well be spared for such a responsibility even if he could be gotten into it, and I certainly have no "ax to grind" in tendering to you that suggestion. I offer them with much diffidence, as having impressed my own mind from first to last in my personal observations of the needless havoc and destruction which this war is producing among us in some localities. Perhaps I overstep the bounds of propriety—civil and military in writing thus—in my present situation—even in a private letter to you—I know however that I may confide in your discretion[.]

. . . I hope you will hear a good account some day of the "Virginia First." Excuse this long letter and believe me as ever

Your old friend
G. Battelle

Francis Harrison Pierpont Papers, West Virginia and Regional History Center, West Virginia University, Morgantown

"A GLORIOUS TRAMP"

Ohio native Thomas Taylor kept up a regular correspondence with his wife, Netta, and did not hesitate to share with her the brutal details of a scouting raid he led into territory populated by many Confederate sympathizers.

Camp Scott, Va., October 16, 1861

My Dear wife,

Last night had a glorious tramp in the wilderness but I had not remained there forty days and forty nights. I had been a scout. I had a most superb guide, James R. Ramsey, whose son had been shot by bushwhackers and suffered to remain in the road five days and watched around it so as to show his friends. Then they stripped him of all his personal effects, all his horses, cattle, cows, tools and everything and since the 4th of June he has not been permitted to remain at home but has been hunted from place to place like a wild beast. Such a man had I for a guide. I had another man for a guide who had a brother-in-law shot and had been served in the same manner. These men were burning with vengeance, hate rankled in their breasts and manifested itself in their unflagging steps and their intense earnestness to secure prisoners or come within good range of them. Oh, how strong is this passion, this desire for revenge. I left camp Sunday morning with ten men and Lt. King, marched over a very rough country, was reinforced by five men, marched until twelve o'clock at night when we came to the house of a notorious scout by the name of David Nutter. I surrounded his house, knocked at the door and after a long time received an answer and ordered them to open the door, they obeyed and I walked in the room, it was as dark as rooms generally are in the night, the lady said she had no light, no candles, and could get none. I told the boys to get me some wood, they at last got a board, I made a fire, then I took some splinters, looked under two beds and gave the torch to Lt. King to look under another, he did so and came out and set down. I cross-examined the lady but could get nothing out of her save that her husband was at his brother's beyond the Meadow River; then I told her that Gen. Floyd[11] had sent me out after unionists and told me to get her husband as a guide, this had a soothing effect, was like "oil on troubled water" and she became quite communicative, but her stories did not satisfy me and I asked King what he saw, he said a man. I then lit up the torch and by its feeble light looked under the bed, after a while I saw a man, standing on all fours, his back close up to the tick. I cocked my musket and brought the muzzle so it looked him right in the eyes and told him to come forth. He did so, he was the wildest looking man I ever saw and all from fright. I asked "your name sir: Nutter" said he. "David" asked I, "yes" said he. Put on your britches said I he obeyed, then I ordered him to put on his shoes and coat. While he was doing that, I took his rifle which was standing by the bedside with the accoutrements on, slung the pouch across my shoulder and ordered him out of the house, then I had him tied and away we started, before starting however, I told his wife if she told anyone about our visit the consequences should be visited on her husband's head. On we plodded until we got near Odells, then I gave Lt. King nine men and with eight men went to Odells and sent King to Jones and another. At Odells Mill we had the same time about fire and light, searched the house completely but found nothing there, then we went over to Camp Chilly where we remained one hour, waiting for another division. After it came up we started off through the woods, the moon had gone down and we lost ourselves in a laurel brake on the side of the mountain. Lt. King found a candle and I had matches, therefore we struck a light, found the path and went on. We reached a Unionist by the name of Mr. Hypes who had recently escaped from the "secesh" prison house and was informed that the chief of the rebel scouts was at home and was going to leave that day. I wanted him so I told the boys I wanted six of those who felt able, to go with me. Six stepped out and with a guide we started. We went about a mile, then I gave them proper instructions and let the guide go back. As we struck, the opening daylight was fully on us and I saw the blue smoke curling up in all sorts of fantastic shapes that are pleasing to the eye and the dog having let loose his gab, we started on double quick, two of the men could not get to the place assigned them on account of a bog, by accident I happened to beat the boys to the house and without stopping to look, I cocked my gun went up a passage between the kitchen and the back room and knocked. No response, thereupon I opened the door and stepped in as smiling as you please. I asked if Mr. Annick lived there. I had my gun covering him all the while, he said, "no." I queried John T. Annick and came to a rest he said "yes," he rose from the table and I thought as he raised, the devil was in him. I followed him up and did not give him time to get his rifle, but he opened the front door and then to him, Oh Horrors! He met Lt. King with his revolver, and turned to me and said, "I'll get my coat," passed into the room, I at his heels, made a spring and caught the door, just as I caught it entered the dining room, his wife got between us in our race and how I got over her, I know not. I got to the door and stepped out, just as I stepped out a bullet whizzed within an inch of my head, the fellow did not stop, I pulled up my gun and shot and after that saw blood start in two places apparently on his back, not stopping then he was shot at a third time, when I was following him at a run. At the third shot he fell and hallowed "Oh! Oh! Oh!" I got up to him and although I wanted to kill him I couldn't do it while he was helpless. I saw his wife and two small children by her and another in her arms and I felt deeply for her children but made her be quiet. We dressed the wounds and found that one of the bullets had passed entirely through his body and came out near the right arm, that the second had passed through his right arm. I think he is dead by this time as he appeared to bleed inwardly. . . .

<small>Thomas Thomson Taylor Papers, MSS 7, Ohio History Connection Archives and Library, Columbus.</small>

IN PURSUIT OF CONFEDERATE BUSHWHACKERS

Sargeant John T. Booth of the 36th Ohio Volunteer Infantry was an obsessive documentarian of his unit's war experience. In addition to keeping his own regular diary, he frequently asked others in the unit to share their diaries and quoted extensively from them. The original manuscript diaries are lost, but a typescript in the archives of the Ohio History Connection reveals that Booth continued to revise and add to his diary account in the years after the war.

Wednesday. New Years Day. Six companies, C. D. E. F. G. and K., went on a scout on the Sutton Road. Colonel George Crook; Lieutenant-Colonel Melvin Clark; Adjutant Lindener and Assistant Surgeon Whitford accompanying the expedition. The early morning was cloudy, pretty windy, gusty, and chill. Sergeant Melvin C. True and I, as usual, by comparison of notes, revised each others diaries. I, and my help, cooked rations up to three o'clock, or later this morning. . . .

We, upon arriving at the foot of Powell Mountain, halted and there took dinner. As we were crossing Powell Mountain the sun was shining clear and bright, presenting a beautiful scene, a vision of beauty to the lover of nature, and her handiworks. . . .

That night, having crossed Powell Mountain,—we . . . went into bivouac at a "Ford" of the "Big Birch River," in a large meadow. I described this spot on which we were encamped . . . as a large "Delta" shaped tract of level lowland. This Delta shaped Meadow is surrounded by high, sharp peaks; topped with immense, giant rocks.

Thursday, Jany, 2nd. The night was a bitterly cold one. In the night the winds blew so hard that we could scarcely keep our blankets over us and the sparks flew so fast, thick, furious and promiscuously that they almost took on the appearance of tongues of flame, of huge dimensions. Many blankets and over coats were practically ruined by being burned in so many places by the sparks that found lodgement in their folds.

This morning the Colonel and Staff and Companies C and K returned to Camp. The other four companies, under the Command of Captains Hollister and Jewett Palmer proceeded toward the source of the "Big Birch River."

About Ten A.M., a man was seen running from us. He was halted, but did not stop; the consequence was, that he was fired upon and wounded in the neck; not seriously however. We continued our advance movement until mid-day, whereupon we were halted for dinner. After dinner, Captain Hollister, (an ex-Methodist divine (?) made us a pithy, and very good little speech; telling us that Colonel Crook's orders were that every thing along the road was to be burned. Shortly thereafter, we resumed the march at the same time endeavoring to—the best of our ability—, obey Colonel Crook's orders. At or near Four o' clock P.M., our advanced guard sighted a body of armed men coming down the road ahead of us. We immediately filed left—up the hillside. The ground lay almost perpendicular and of quite a heighth before reaching the crest. Having skirmished along that mountain side to distance of fully half a mile; we returned to a house not far distant, prepared eat our suppers and camped for the night.

Friday. January, 3ed. This morning upon starting, skirmishers were thrown out some distance, in advance, on either flank, covering the mountainsides on each side of the diminishing stream as well as it's valley. Upon advancing in this order about two miles our advance fired two shots. A short distance yet in advance they fired three more shots, effecting, thereby the killing of two of the enemy,—two rebels. It was here that we passed quite a breast work constructed of logs quite tactically situated, so as to be hidden from our view among the hemlocks and dense foliage, at same time effectually commanding the approach, by the road, upon which we were marching. Soon after we came to a farm. Here we simply burned every thing of worth, burnable. The destruction was complete.

At a distance of about half a mile farther on we came to a section, locally known as "The Glades;" embracing an area of three miles in length, to, from, probably fifty or sixty rods, to as much as half a mile in width. I presume it covers about one and a quarter square miles. At upper end of this area known as "Glades" we encountered a considerable body of the enemy and a sharp skirmish ensued.

The enemy was posted in the timber, to right of the road. We attacked, and drove them across the run onto the hill beyond, pressing hard upon the enemy. It was here that one of Company D's men came upon a reb of large stature and of immense strength. D's man knocked his antagonist down with his rifle, reached down and despoiled his prostrate foe of revolver and with it shot the rebel dead.

The case was somewhat remarkable. I was told that the Bushwhacker, for that is what he really was, had singled out this man, (Price, I think his name was), of Company D as his, the reb's victim, but whose victim, in turn of events he became. Such is the uncertainty of results in such strife.

The Bushwhacker had on, or about his person, a perfect arsenal; to wit: a loaded rifle; a revolver, it loaded with five balls, and an immense home-made bowie-knife. The remarkable part of it was that the reb was actually killed by a man with an empty gun.

The enemy was constantly pressed and when driven from this hill, crossed the Glades, to another hill on our left and opened up a brisk fire directly upon Company G. As the firing proceeded we, immediately, were subject to a raking fire. We hurriedly got out of that and gained the timber they had just left.

Companies E and F took their stations on the hill the enemy first left, (i.e. the first hill the enemy left), Company D took position in front of the enemy, but not out of range. This formation of forces placed our enemy under a crossfire which advantage we proceeded to put into effective execution.

When we started to cross the run into the timber, their balls flew like singing hailstones over our heads and around about us. None of us, however, were hurt at this time.

The Bushwhackers now set up a yelling and hallooing, such as is supposed to reign in pandemonium, not on earth, thinking a yank was thus easily to be frightened. We are not Chinese to be defeated by yells, horrible noises, hideous banners etc. We raised no objections to their waste of good breath, but worked our good Enfield rifles with a gloriously, hearty good will and for all they were capable of. This was the kind of noise to scare, that we set up, and it worked, for us, all right, for out of sight they got a "2—40" pace as our rifles played the tune of crackity bang, as they departed.

We then burned a store, a house, barn, and all out lying buildings before we moved on. In this spirited little fight we had two men slightly wounded. Their wounds were soon properly cared for by our Assistant Surgeon Captain Whitford.

During the melee, and later, we could see their dead and hear the agonizing cries of their wounded, even above the sound of the firing, altogether, creating a scene of no inconsiderable interest to the Neophyte in such business. It was Company G's first baptism of fire. She acquitted herself nobly.

It was also the first time the other three companies had met the enemy face to face in deadly combat. As with Julius Ceasar, "*Veni Vidi Vici,*"—, so it was with us.

Again we moved on. This time about a mile. Here we burned a number of buildings, amounting to quite a settlement. An incident is said to have occurred here, I give it place in my diary because the active agent told the story as I have written it.

"Here****W.H. Thornton, after telling the people to vacate the house, they refused. One of the women jumped into bed, vowing she would not move. Thornton, finally said, he'd throw hot coals upon the bed. Calling him pretty stiff names, she defied him. Thornton took up a wooden shovel, that stood by the fire place, took upon it a lot of hot wood embers and tossed the hot coals on the bed. The woman flew of and out, seemingly forgetting all she had threatened. The goods were set out and the house burned!"

This whole country is intensely rebel. While burning these houses and other buildings, we were again fired upon, One of Company F's men was wounded in a lower limb.

Captain Jewett Palmer sent a squad with orders to burn a certain lot of buildings. As the squad under charge of Seargeant Thomas J. Stanley . . . crossed the ridge, a man, hid in some bushes, fired into the squad, wounding Sergt. Stanley in the right wrist. The man that fired that shot never fired another—he died in his tracks an instant later. The Captain sent a second squad, as relief to first, the wounding of Stanley was avenged and all the buildings here about burned, the women supplying a requiem, to the departing buildings, in loud, bitter and angry shouts and hurrahs for "jeff davis," and the "southern confederacy." In the intervals, they gasped for breath, catching it upon kindly thought of us, calling us by the endearing name of "BRUTE"

From here we turned our steps and faces toward Summersville, burning everything, that fire would destroy along the line of march. Creating a broad path, marked with desolation and ruin, the ear marks of that grim visaged war they had, so uncompromisingly compelled the North to unwillingly engage in. To night we halted at a house said to be twelve miles from Summersville.

Saturday, 4th Jany. After a nights rest we set out this morning for Camp, where we arrived after noon,—Heroes—in Comrades eyes having had our initiatory battle, and felt well toward ourselves concerning results. It is impossible to accurately determine the enemy's loss. Certainly it was not less than eighteen or twenty, in killed, a good round dozen wounded. (Joint diary of True and Booth).

Later reports came into Camp, brought by "Union Home Guards" that the enemy lost at the Glades fight on the 3rd, thirty or more in killed and twenty-four in wounded. To say the four Companies gave a very good account of themselves, is uttering truth, nought else.

Diary, pp. 99–106, collection 180, John T. Booth Papers, Ohio History Connection Archives and Library, Columbus

GREYBACKS AND BUSHWHACKERS

John T. Booth wrote this piece for publication in the Marietta Home News, *his hometown newspaper, to educate its readers on the types of western Virginians he encountered.*

Dear Home News,

There is nothing of general interest to relate; but, perhaps, a description of the peculiarities of the people and their manufacturers will not be altogether unreadable; so here goes!

"The Greybacks" are a race peculiar to, and indiginous to the Western Virginia hills. When you see a man here, dressed in the "homespun" of our ancestors, wearing deer skin moccasons and a black, lop-rimmed, felt hat, with a piece of red flannel tucked under the band, you may swear he is a "Grey-back," or, as denominated by himself, a "Home Guard!" Why in the name of common sense, they claim the last title, I am unable to say, for whenever they receive an injury from a Bushwhacker, they run to us and make a doleful face, and want us to avenge them. My opinion of this sect is this; when Federal troops occupy the country, they are good, sound, Union loving citizens, and believe in exerting every power to put down the rebellion; but when Floyd or Wise is here, they are as good secessionists, and, in the elegant vernacular of Western Virginian secessh, believe in "hanging every d——d Yankee and abolitionists this side of h-ll." There may be exceptions,—I speak of the generality.

"The Bushwhackers"—No doubt you have heard of these. They are mostly of the poorer classes. The richer people disdaining to fight so much after the fashion of savages, joined the regulars, as they are called, under Floyd and Wise, during the fore part of the summer. The nest of bushwhackers nearest to us, is in Webster County, about fourty miles up the Gauley River. Their depredations consist chiefly in horse stealing, cow stealing, and robbing defenseless women of their means of subistance and, occasionally, firing from the mountain sides on our men as they pass. We never take any of their class prisoners. They have murdered our men and we have retaliated.

"Manufacturers"—The principal article manufactured by the natives appears to be Corn-bread,—"Corn-pone." This is brought into the Camp nearly every day, and the soldiers buy it for change. The bread is of two kinds; viz: "Dodgers" and "Pone." Those cakes resembling in shape, an egg are termed by the "Grey-backs," "Dodgers," while the soldiers have more aptly denominated them—"Cannon Balls." A member of the Field Band informed me a few days since that he ate a chunk of "dodger" just a week before that time, and he thought from the way his stomach felt, it would last him yet a week to come.

There is a painful rumor in Camp that General Rosecrans is about issuing a "General Order," prohibiting the further use of this favorite bread, as an article of food, by the soldiers, and adopting it in the Ordinance department, as a more effective missile, when fired from a cannon, than the famous conical ball, now so popular with our artillerists. I know these same "dodgers" have contributed more to thin the ranks of the Thirty-Sixth regiment than the enemy. The "Pones," which are a decided improvement on the last article are fashioned like our old wheaten loaves, and from their peculiar shape and hardness are termed by the boys "Grind-stones." They answer a very good purpose in setting their teeth on edge.

There is another article produced here, though not to so great an extent as those before mentioned, which is, nevertheless, important. I allude to "Dried apple-pies." To give you a just idea of them, I would say that two circular pieces of leather, fresh and undried from the tan, sewed together at edges and stuffed with pumice from a cider press,—resembles our Virginia pies more than anything else I can think of. Why, only the other day (January 11th, last) I saw two fellows "battling" each other over the head, with those same sole-leather pies, and, it was evident to all, the boys were damaged more than the pies.

> Diary, pp. 134–36, collection 180, John T. Booth Papers, Ohio History Connection Archives and Library, Columbus.

VIRGINIA RANGER ACT

In March of 1862, Virginia's state government passed the Virginia Ranger Act to exert more control over irregular Confederate units operating in Union-occupied parts of the state. The law became a model for the Partisan Ranger Act, passed by the Confederate government one month later.

CHAP.26—AN ACT TO AUTHORIZE THE ORGANIZATION OF TEN OR MORE COMPANIES OF RANGERS.

Passed March 27, 1862.

1. Be it enacted by the general assembly, that the governor of companies of this commonwealth be and he is hereby authorized to commission ten or more captains, and not exceeding twenty, and twenty or more lieutenants, and not exceeding forty, citizens of the counties in this commonwealth now in the possession of the enemy; with authority to raise ten or more companies, and not exceeding twenty, of one hundred men each, to be composed exclusively of men whose homes are in the districts overrun by the public enemy, within the limits of said counties, who shall enlist for twelve months in the service of this commonwealth, to act as rangers and scouts on our exposed frontier near the lines of the enemy, and in that part of the state overrun by the armies of the enemy, with the view of cutting off their marauding and foraging parties, and giving protection to the loyal citizens of the state. Whenever either of said captains and two of Companies organized, how said lieutenants, to be commissioned first and second lieutenants, shall enlist seventy-five men, they shall be organized into a company, and the captain shall make report thereof, with a list or enrollment of his men, with the names of four sergeants and four corporals (to be appointed by him), to the adjutant general, who shall furnish the said company with such arms and ammunition as can be procured. When four

of said companies shall be organized, the officers thereof shall elect a major; when six shall be organized, the officers thereof shall elect a lieutenant colonel; when ten shall be organized, the officers thereof shall elect a colonel. The officers so elected shall be commissioned by the governor as major, lieutenant colonel and colonel of said rangers and scouts. And the said officers and privates shall receive the same pay as is allowed to the privates and officers of the infantry by the Confederate States, from the return of the list and enrollment of said company to the adjutant general, and the time they shall be armed and equipped for and engage in active service.

2. The said officers and rangers shall be under the command of the governor, and shall conform their operations to the usages of civilized warfare: provided the enemy on their part shall conduct the war according to the usages of civilized war. The commandants of companies shall report their operations to the officer in command, who shall report thereon to the governor.

3. The said companies shall be placed in such positions along our northern, western and northwestern frontiers from which they can give the greatest annoyance to the enemy, and the greatest protection to our loyal citizens, in such detached parties, of one or more companies or parts of a company, as will most promote the public interest.

4. Whenever the said rangers shall be in the neighborhood of a confederate army, they shall be subject to the orders of the commandant of the same, and shall always co-operate with the movements of said army when ordered to do so: provided, however, that the provisions of this act shall not impair or interfere with the laws providing for the quota of Virginia to the confederate army.

5. This act shall be in force from its passage.

Acts of the General Assembly of the State of Virginia, Passed in 1861–2, in the Eighty-Sixth Year of the Commonwealth (Richmond: William F. Ritchie, 1862), 51–52

THE SQUIRREL HUNTERS

The presence of irregular units and guerrillas, most without uniform, in western Virginia vexed federal occupiers. Charles Lieb, who served as quartermaster in the region during the first year of occupation, incorporated this unflattering image of western Virginia locals in his memoir.

"We were only Hunting Squirrels."—Page 93.

Charles Lieb, *Nine Months in the Quartermaster's Department; or, The Chances for Making a Million* (Cincinnati: Moore, Wilstach, Keys, Printers, 1862), 93

"POOR HEART-BROKEN LOOKING CREATURES"

The family members of those who fought in irregular guerrilla units could not count on any government to support or advocate for them should their loved ones be killed or imprisoned or their family property seized or destroyed. Buckhannon resident Marcia Phillips was loyal to the Union, but she nonetheless had some sympathy for the widows of local Confederate guerrillas.

JUNE 7TH, 1862

Lieut. Lewis of the 10th Va. was here to see if I would rent the office to him for a couple of women from Webster County. Their husbands were Guerillas and were killed last spring and our troops destroyed their property, and burned their house, as they had been harboring Rebels. The women begged the soldiers to take them to Buckhannon, where they thought they might support themselves, by washing for soldiers. I had let one of the Beverly merchants set several boxes of goods in there,—these were moved into my dining room by the Lieut. and a soldier, and this P.M. the women arrived. They are poor heart-broken looking creatures. One of them is only 17 years old. Within the last few months, she has lost her child, husband, father and 3 brothers. Surely, these men's rebellion, cost them very dear.

These notorious Guerillas, Ben Haymond, Perry Hays, and George Silcott have largely been captured and taken to Camp Chase. I regret that our men did not shoot them, right down and not give themselves the trouble of bringing them into camp.

<small>Marcia Louise Sumner Phillips Journal, p. 122, Collection 1846, West Virginia Regional History Center, West Virginia University, Morgantown</small>

RUTHERFORD B. HAYES ENCOUNTERS "CONTRABANDS"

Lieutenant Colonel (and future president) Rutherford B. Hayes's 23rd Ohio entered western Virginia in July of 1861. By December they were established at a winter camp at Fayetteville in the Kanawha Valley, and many enslaved people in the region saw an opportunity to strike for freedom. Congress had passed the first Confiscation Act in August of 1861. Under this act, any enslaved person who had fought with or worked for the Confederate military could be declared free from obligations to their masters by Union commanders in the field. Hayes was personally hostile to slavery, and during the winter of 1861–82, many runaways appeared in his camp. His liberal interpretation of what the first Confiscation Act empowered him to do was not shared by all Union commanders. Hayes revealed his empathy and admiration for the runaways who entered his camp in many of his letters home (including the following letter to his uncle Saris Birchard) and in entries in his private diary, which follow.

Camp Union, Fayetteville, Virginia December 19, 1861.

Dear Uncle:—Yesterday morning a party of contrabands started for Ohio. It is not unlikely that some will find their way to Fremont. Allen, a mulatto, with his wife and one or two children, is one of a thousand—faithful, intelligent, and industrious,—will do for a house servant—would just answer your purpose. His wife can cook—is neat and orderly—a most valuable family, you will find them, if you put them into the new house, or anywhere else. If you don't want them, you can safely recommend them. Quite a number have come to me, but these are the pick of the lot. They have another black man and wife with them who are well spoken of; I do not know them. It is, of course, doubtful whether Allen will find you; I think he will. I send him because I think he will just answer your purpose.

They will all be entitled to freedom, as I understand the rule adopted by our Government. Their master is a Rebel, and is with Floyd's army as a quartermaster, or the like, being too old for a soldier. These people gave themselves up to me, and I let them go to Ohio. The rule is, I believe, that slaves coming to our lines, especially if owned by Rebels, are free. Allen gave me valuable information as to the enemy. These facts, if necessary hereafter, can be proved by members of Captain McIlrath's Company A, Twenty-third Regiment, Cleveland, or of Captain Sperry's Company H, Ashtabula County. Of course there is little present danger of attempt to recover them under the Fugitive Bill, but it may be done hereafter.

You, perhaps, know that Dr. Joe took a contraband to Cincinnati. These people do not go to Cincinnati, preferring the country, and fearing relatives of their master there. The party start for Galion in company with the servant of one of our men; from here, they will probably get to you.

Sincerely. R.B. Hayes
S. Birchard

* * *

THURSDAY, JANUARY 2, 1862.

... Major Comly reports finding about one hundred and twenty muskets, etc., concealed in and about Raleigh; also twelve or fifteen contrabands arrived. What to do with them is not so troublesome yet as the East. Officers and soldiers employ them as cooks and servants. Some go on to Ohio.

Nobody in this army thinks of giving up to the Rebels their fugitive slaves. Union men might perhaps be differently dealt with—probably would be. If no doubt of their loyalty, I suppose they would again get their slaves. The man who repudiates all obligations under the Constitution and laws of the United States is to be treated as having forfeited those rights which depend solely on the laws and Constitution. I don't want to see Congress meddling with the slavery question. Time and the progress of events are solving all the questions arising out of slavery in a way consistent with eternal principles of justice. Slavery is getting death-blows. As an "institution" it perishes in this war. It will take years to get rid of its debris, but the "sacred" is gone.

FRIDAY, JANUARY 3, 1862, FAYETTEVILLE, [WEST] VIRGINIA.

. . . Charles, an honest-looking contraband—six feet high, stout-built, thirty-six years old, wife sold South five years ago,—came in today from Union, Monroe County. He gives me such items as the following: Footing boots $9 to $10. New boots $18 to $20. Shoes $4 to $4.50. Sugar 25 to 30 [cents a pound]. Coffee 62 ½, tea $1.50 soda 62 ½, pepper 75, bleached domestic 40 to 50 [cents a yard.] Alex Clark [his enslaver is a] farmer near Union (east of it), Monroe County, one hundred and fifty (?) miles from Fayetteville—fifty miles beyond Newbern. Started Saturday eve at 8 P.M., reached Raleigh next Monday night; crossed New River at Packs Ferry. (Packs a Union man.)

Companies broken up in Rebel army by furloughs, discharges, and sickness.[12] Rich men's sons get discharges. Patrols put out to keep slaves at home. They tell slaves that the Yankees cut off arms of some negroes to make them worthless and sell the rest in Cuba for twenty-five hundred dollars each to pay cost of war. "No Northern gentlemen fight—only factory men thrown out of employ." They (the negroes) will fight for the North if they find the Northerners are such as they think them.

Union is a larger and much finer town than Fayetteville. Some Fayetteville people there. People in Greenbrier [County] don't want to fight any more. . . .

They "press" poor folks' horses and teams not the rich folks'. Poor folks grumble at being compelled to act as patrols to keep rich men's negroes from running off. "When I came with my party, eleven of us, in sight of your pickets, I hardly knew what to do. If you were such people as they told us, we would suffer. Some of the party turned to run. A man with a gun called out halt. I saw through the fence three more with guns. They asked 'Who comes there?' I called out 'Friends.' The soldier had his gun raised; he dropped it and said: 'Boys, these are some of our colored friends,' and told us to 'come on, not to be afraid,' that they were safe. Oh, I never felt so in my life. I could cry, I was so full of joy. And I found them and the major (Comly) and all I have seen so friendly—such perfect gentlemen, just as we hoped you were, but not as they told us you were."

<small>Diary and Letters of Rutherford B. Hayes, ed. Charles Richard Williams (Columbus: Ohio State Archeological and Historical Society, 1922), 2:163–76</small>

A LOYAL BLACK FARMER MAKES A POSTWAR CLAIM

In 1871 President Ulysses Grant established the Southern Claims Commission to allow loyal Southerners who had property confiscated by federal armies to seek compensation. Allen Campbell was a free Black farmer born in Monroe County and lived there most of his life, leaving with the federal army in 1864 after the government of Virginia began pressing free and enslaved Black people into labor for the Confederate army. Claimants had to provide evidence of their wartime loyalty to the Union cause in order to secure an award.

Question: What is your name, your age, your residence and how long has it been such, and your occupation?

Answer: . . . My name is Allen Campbell. I am near about 50 years of age I can't give it exactly and my residence is Monroe County and have lived in Monroe pretty much all my life. During a part of the time I lived in Ohio that was during the war. I am a farmer by occupation. . . .

Question: Where were you born? . . .

Answer: . . . I was born in Monroe County about 4 miles from Union.

Question: Where were you residing and what was your business for six months before the outbreak of the rebellion, and what was your business and where did you reside and what was your business from the beginning to the end of the war? . . .

Answer: I was living at A.R. Humphreys in Monroe County. I was engaged in farming. At the beginning of the war I resided at A.R. Humphreys in Monroe County engaged in farm work. I lived there about a year and then went to Mrs. Sally Ann Hosphean in Monroe County and I worked there on the farm until May 1864 when I left with the Union troops and went to Ohio. I lived in Gallipolis a while, in Pomeroy a while. At Gallipolis I did gardening and worked in Mr. Laugley's Mill and in Pomeroy I worked at the saltworks as a hand. Before I went on through to Ohio, I worked a short time in the Kanawha Valley. I don't remember why I went from Mr. Humphreys to Mrs. Hosphean's unless she gave me better wages. The reason I left Monroe County and went to Ohio was because I didn't want to go into the rebel service and the reason I changed about after leaving Monroe was in the expectation of getting better wages.

Question: On which side were your sympathies during the war, and were they on the same side from beginning to end?
Answer: . . . My sympathies were on the Union side from the beginning of the war.

Question: What favors, privileges or protections were ever granted you in recognition of your loyalty during the war, and when and by whom granted?
Answer: . . . No particular favors that I know of. I left here with the Union troops they permitted me to go with them. . . .

Question: Who were the leading and best known Unionists of your vicinity during the war? Are any of them called to testify to your loyalty . . . ?
Answer: . . . A.R. Humphreys and Hiram and Mrs. Hosphean and others these two are called to testify to my loyalty.

Question: Were you a slave or free at the beginning of the war?
Answer: . . . I was free all my life.

Question: Were you present when any of the property charged in this claim was taken?
Answer: . . . I was present and saw it actually taken. I was riding a grey mare the same charged in the dawn she was about six years old when I was met by Arville and Crooks forces and one of the soldier told me get down when he took my horse.

Question: Was any complaint made to any officer of the taking of any of the property?
Answer: . . . When I came near Union I made complaint to a Major I don't remember his name. He told me to watch when they come back and if I could see it he would try to get it back for me. I never seen it after it was taken.

Question: Were any vouchers or receipts asked for or given?
Answer: No. I did not know that I was entitled to a receipt and never asked for any.

Question: Begin now with the first item of property you just said you saw taken. . . .

Answer: The property taken was a grey mare about six years old + about 15 hands high and in splendid order she was taken on the Union and White Sulphur Turnpike road by one Averill + Crooks forces. I met a squad of 10 or 12 calvary in the wood about five or six miles from Union one of them asked me whose beast I was riding. I told him it was mine he said his horse was broke down and he reckoned he would have to have it. He told me to get off which I did he then took my horse got on it and started off and that was the last I seen of it. His horse he sent back to the camp war Union, by me where, by direction of Henry Johnson who belonged to the command turned loose. I don't know the names of any of the officers belonging to the command except Averill + Crooks. The command belonged to Averill. There were no officers present when the property was taken if there were I didn't know them from others. From what the soldier said who took my horse. I believe it was necessary for the use of the Army. The Army had been on a raid into Virginia and on their return stopped near Union to rest up and a great many of their horses were pretty much broken down. The horse taken from me was worth at the time $125.00 and I consider that being its market value in United States money....

Witness   Allen his X mark Campbell

                                                                       M & Kester Specl. Com.}

Allen Campbell Testimony to the Southern Claims Commission, microfilm, pp. 16–25, roll 1, target 14, Monroe County, West Virginia, National Archives and Records Administration, College Park, MD

GENERAL JACKSON GIVES GOD THE GLORY

Stonewall Jackson's September 1862 victory at the battle of Harpers Ferry was largely bloodless, with the vast majority of the 12,613 Union casualties the result of mass surrender rather than killed and wounded. The deeply religious general credited God with his victory. In his summary of what the victory secured him, he failed to mention the roughly 1,000 African Americans who had been living in a large contraband camp in the city, for whom Confederate victory meant reenslavement.

Headquarters Valley District, September 16, 1862

Colonel: Yesterday God crowned our arms with another brilliant success on the surrender, at Harper's Ferry, of Brig.-General White and eleven thousand troops, an equal number of small arms, seventy-three pieces of artillery, and about two hundred wagons. In addition to other stores, there is a large amount of camp and garrison equipage. Our loss was very small. The meritorious conduct of officers and men will be mentioned in a more extended report.

I am, Colonel, your obedient servant,
T. J. Jackson
Major-General.
Col. R. H. Chilton,
Assistant Adjutant General.

The Rebellion Record: A Diary of American Events, with Documents, Narratives, Illustrative Incidents, Poetry Etc. (New York: G. P. Putnam, 1863), 5:448.

HARPERS FERRY CONTRABAND CAMP STEREOGRAPH

Thousands of enslaved people from the Shenandoah Valley fled slavery during the war, and perhaps hundreds of them sought shelter in this contraband camp in Harpers Ferry. Their fate received little attention in the Northern or Southern press after the town was surrendered to Stonewall Jackson in September 1862.

Photograph by John P. Soule, Library of Congress

"WITH THE INFLUX OF REBEL TROOPS CAME THE HUMAN HYENAS IN SEARCH OF LIVING PREY"

Abba Goddard, a Maine woman who came to Harpers Ferry to manage a hospital in town, reveals the psychological effect Stonewall Jackson's invincible reputation had on Union soldiers in Harpers Ferry, and perhaps also on their officers. Goddard also provides some glimpse into the largely unrecorded fate of the African American community in Harpers Ferry after the surrender.

A LETTER FROM HARPER'S FERRY, SEPT. 20, 1862

Ed. Press:—Dear Sir:—When I wrote you last, I little thought that letter was to be the hyphen connecting me with the outside world for three mortal weeks. But so it proved. The next day our empty hospital quarters were turned into barracks and occupied by some three hundred scared, weak-backed cowardly sneaks, who became suddenly afflicted with crick-in-the-back, pain-in-the-stomach, weakness in the knees, &c.,—contracted in anticipation of a visit from Stonewall Jackson.

It was laughable, however, to see how rapidly they recovered the day afterward, when it was discovered that the said "Stonewall" was paying his special attention to Frederick,—a city some twenty-two miles below us. This news gave us all breathing time, and for nearly two weeks we looked for reinforcements daily—only hoping meanwhile that our doubtful commander would be superseded. It proved, however, that we hoped against hope. The surrender which occurred Monday, A.M., Sept. 15, at 7 1-2 o'clock precisely—had been a foregone conclusion for two weeks. But I anticipate. I had, as you know, got ready to leave this post, and hoped for a glimpse of dear old Portland, before another Sabbath sun.

Thursday, the 4th, the Railroad bridge at Monocracy was blown up;—of course journeying was out of the question. Our hospital being re-occupied, I transferred three hundred sheets and pillow-cases, two hundred shirts, fifty bed sacks, fifty quilts, seventy-five pillows, one hundred handkerchiefs, two cases of bandages, eighteen quarts of currant jelly, &c., &c, to the Steward of the regiment, occupying the quarters, and removed my personal effects to the house formerly occupied by Quartermaster Dodge and family, just opposite the hospital.

Day by day for two weeks, we waited for a turn in the tide. On Saturday the 13th, a tremendous firing commenced on Maryland Heights, about 9 o'clock, lasting some three hours. The musketry then ceased on both sides, and our gunners had the field to themselves. They continued to fire at intervals until 5 P.M., *not provoking, however, a single shot in reply;* yet, to the indignant surprise of every one, at that hour, the stars and stripes were pulled down, our cannon spiked, our men retreating, and the key to our defence completely abandoned. After that hour, during Saturday, not a rebel appeared in sight, nor at any time during the siege did a rebel appear again on the heights. Col. Ford of the 32d Ohio, has the honor of ordering the abandonment of the post, and the lookers on devoutly pray it may be the last time he will have the opportunity to disgrace himself in a public capacity.

Our loss Saturday was ten killed, and about sixty wounded. Of the killed two perished by the bursting of a shell that was being rammed home,—so that our great loss—as reported, was not enough to warrant a surrender so long as we still had eleven thousand effective men. Sunday morning, Sept. 14, the cannonading on our part was resumed, but elicited no reply until 2 1–2 P.M., when, to the astonishment of all, the enemy opened on us from two batteries from Loudon Heights.

During some two hours the fall of shot and shell on both sides was incessant. At this time, I think I may conclude myself as having been in great personal danger; no less than four shells and a slug falling within ten feet of me. For about two hours, "they peppered us." As fast as a shell fell, I picked it up, and intend to carry home my own four or five proofs of narrow escape in time of peril. Some of our hospital tents were riddled by shell, but fortunately not one exploded, and consequently nobody was hurt. When we heard them whizzing, we dodged, and so escaped. Seriously, however, had one or either of my proportion of shell exploded, my epitaph would have been written long ere this. After the first fire, one feels quite composed. The boys laughed to see me go and pick up my shells; the slug, a piece of iron six inches long, being so hot I could not hold it. I held onto my trophies, however, and would have volunteered gathering the entire crop, had I supposed our gunners would have re-mailed them to Loudon Heights. Sunday passed, and Monday dawned. Our killed and wounded of Sunday were—0!

Monday A.M., at daylight, the enemy opened from four points, and our batteries returned the fire. Not a shot took effect, and not a man was wounded, when Col. Miles,—the gallant—as the Clipper has it, hoisted a handkerchiefs upon a pole as a signal of surrender.

Perhaps—that signal was not soon enough observed—and, *perhaps* it was. Anyway, the enemy gave us one more shell, and the Colonel's leg being in the way, as a consequence he was fatally wounded.

The rage, the indignation, the surprise, the mortification of eleven thousand men, *and one woman,* it is impossible for me to describe.

Not a musket had been fired, not a foe had been met. Only a "splendid artillery duel"—and a surrender. That is all!

"They say" we were short of ammunition.—In the street below were six four-horse teams, loaded with ammunition, and *I saw four wagonloads* stowed away Sunday, at *midnight,* in a room not a stone's throw from the table at which I am now writing.

We had hundreds of thousands of pounds of ammunition, and eleven thousand Enfield rifles, not one of which was used. If this is being short, I confess I don't understand the meaning of the word.

"They say," also, we were short of rations. Well, the rebels carried away hardbreak, rice, coffee, sugar, molasses, pork, beef, and beans, for three days steadily, and then finished up by burning car load after car load of rice and beans; the air even now is full of the odor of burning beans.

I am not telling you guess-work, nor "they say," when I assure you we could have held out ten days longer, had Col. Miles so ordered. Instead of a word of encouragement to our men, I am told that Monday morning, an hour before the surrender, Col. Miles sent up to the entrenchments, and told the men it would be useless to fight. As they would all be in h— in less than an hour. My informants are Capt. Ward, and Lieut. G.A. Banta, of the N.Y. 12th,—two brave, but mortified officers, who took breakfast with me the next morning.

Finding on Monday that the rebels were to get everything, and having seven pieces of "animated ebony" to feed, I obtained a two horse wagon, went to the commissary stores, loaded up coffee, tea, sugar, rice, bacon, and candles, &c., &c., and had it driven home.—While loading, Stuart's cavalry came up, and asked what I was getting. I said, "by the cartel private property is to be respected."—"Oh yes," they replied, and rode off. I was stopped no less than three times while going through the street with the team,—but the "private claim" was quite sufficient protection. As a consequence I have been able to feed nineteen people, the entire week, and will do the same for a week to come, by which time, please Heaven, we may find a rescue.

The mortification of the surrender was in a degree compensated for to the soldiers in the death of Col. Miles. But there is one feature in the case for which there can be no compensation. It is well known that the slaves follow in the wake of our army; an immense number of poor God-forsaken creatures had sought protection in the Ferry, but Col. Miles had invariably refused to let them pass over the B.&O.R.R., always promising their masters that they should sometime be returned to them. Indeed, he had ordered the return of some, but the troops rescued them, and ducked the owner, so that slave hunting for the time being was abandoned.

But with the influx of rebel troops came the human hyenas in search of living prey. Every nook, corner, cranny, barn, and stye has been searched, and men, women, and little children in droves, have been carried off.

Our hospital laundresses, and our men servants, without a word of warning, were seized upon and carried home, or shut up in the [Charles Town] jail.

In this matter, however, secesh is at fault to the tune of seven, to my personal knowledge. I am almost tired of night-watching, and my revolver begins to grow heavy. It holds but five balls, but before secesh gets my seven ebonies, my body will pay for the two balls wanting. Oh, this traffic in human flesh! Heaven send the day when the African shall cease to be born with black skin. For this let Christians pray, instead of wasting breath in behalf of hard-hearted masters, for I am morally certain it would require a lesser miracle to change the skin of the negro, than the hearts of their owners.

This has been an anxious week. We have buried seventeen men just opposite my window, under an apple tree, without shroud or coffin. The rebel surgeons took sheets, shirts, bandages, &c., from the hospital, together with several jars of currant jelly; but upon the whole, robbed us of less than could be expected. Yesterday they wholly evacuated the town; but, from the rapid cannonading heard in the distance, we judge they have found an avenger.

As they blew up the R.R. bridge, and burned the pontoon, of course there is no such thing as getting away from this place, unless we ford the river. This I am not prepared to do, as my notions of personal salvation involve the saving of my chest of clothing, and good Mr. Jewett's keg of tamarinds, which keg goes to Baltimore with me, and I am not able, as yet, to carry as much upon my back.

I had "hearn tell" of the secesh army, but God forbid my ever looking upon such an ungodly crew again. Just suppose a meal bag draggled through the mud, dipped in bacon fat, and stuffed with rags, animated, and you have a decent representation of a live secesh; especially the live part—for the vermin frequently dropped from their clothes as they walked the street. Faugh! and then to think they drove our troops out of town like cattle! Well, it may be as secesh says; they say our men are so well dressed they don't dare fight, for fear of spoiling their clothes. I am sorry I cannot return the compliment.

Portland Daily Press, October 1, 1862

THE FATE OF HARPERS FERRY'S CONTRABAND COMMUNITY

Excerpts from Richmond newspapers the week after the capture of Harpers Ferry provide a few brief facts on the fate of Harpers Ferry's African American community after the surrender. In general, it received little attention in the press.

SURRENDER OF HARPER'S FERRY.

... Another account, received late last night, says that the surrender took place on Monday morning last at 10 o'clock. The firing commanded as early as 5 o'clock in the morning. Shortly after, the Yankee sent out a flag of truce, proposing a conditional surrender; but our firing did not cease when another flag was sent proposing an unconditional surrender, when the firing ceased. General Miles, the Federal commander, is reported to be wounded. The results of this surrender, according to this last account, are as follows: 12,000 Yankee 12,000 Enfield rifles, 50 cannon, 100 four horse team a number of fine artillery horses, a large quantity of ammunition, some quartermaster and commissary stores, and 1,000 "contrabands."

Daily Dispatch (Richmond), September 20, 1862

* * *

THE CAPTURED NEGROES.

In our reports of the surrender of Harper's Ferry we noticed the capture of a large number of contrabands who had taken refuge with the Yankee thieves at that point. Many of these negroes belonged to citizens of Jefferson and adjoining counties. A letter before us states that one gentleman from Clarke, who had lost 31 negroes, found 28 of them in this lot.

Daily Dispatch (Richmond), September 22, 1862

* * *

FROM HARPER'S FERRY.

Two car-loads of negroes arrived in this city yesterday, by the Central Railroad, direct from Harper's Ferry. Included in the number were men, women, and children. They are the property of citizens of Virginia living in the vicinity of the Ferry, and are part of those found with the Yankees after their capitulation to the forces of Gen. Jackson. Their masters propose to offer them for sale in Richmond, not deeming them desirable servants after having associated with the Yankees.

Daily Dispatch (Richmond), September 24, 1862

CONFEDERATES OCCUPY CHARLESTON IN 1862

The arrival of Confederate forces in Charleston in September 1862 set off a panic. Some of the officers serving under Confederate general William

Loring, who oversaw the occupation, were natives of Charleston and the Kanawha Valley. They had scores to settle with former neighbors who they felt persecuted them when the city was under Union control, and possibly with former enslaved workers they now deemed disloyal. Loring issued orders promising civilians that their peace and property would be respected, orders that were not welcomed by some of his subordinate officers. During their short occupation the Confederates established a newspaper, The Guerilla. The paper reprinted an article that first appeared in an Ohio newspaper describing the impact of the Confederate invasion on Unionist families, and especially African Americans.

LATEST NORTHERN NEWS

We clip the following accounts of . . . the exodus of the enemy from the Kanawha Valley, from the Cincinnati *Commercial* of the 19th: . . .

EXODUS FROM THE KANAWHA.

During the past few days the Kanawha and Ohio rivers, between this point and Gauley, have been full of flatboats, bateaux, skiffs, rafts, and all manner of buoyant conveyance, laden with the families of Unionists, who find themselves compelled to flee on the approach of the Confederate army, fearing the rebel General will carry into execution his recently made threat to hang every citizen "Yankee" he found in the Kanawha Valley. Hundreds of people who two years ago were the quiet possessors of large farms, are now driven away from home in a condition bordering on destitution. Unable to remove the farm stock, they are obliged to leave behind them what they depended on for subsistence during the coming winter. Arriving at Gallipolis, or elsewhere, most of them have to seek a charitable home among strangers—a few only, comparatively, have relatives or friends to live with. It is a pitiable sight to see families set adrift, with their little lots of household furniture, to find a home, they know not where—and all because their father of their husband would not renounce his allegiance to the Government of his fathers. The rebels in Western Virginia have declared themselves unsatisfied with anything less than armed resistance to the Federal power on the part of citizens whom they meet in their raids. It will not do to say you have not taken sides either way, or that your sympathies are with one side or the other. They demand active participation in their cause, and "confiscation," robbery and outrage are the punishments for Federalism. The whites are not the only emigrants from the Kanawha Valley. The negroes have absconded in hundreds, and few less than a thousand have left their disloyal masters to inquire as to their whereabouts and wonder at the answer. The darkies have constructed the most ingenious kind of sailing craft, and in the efforts to elude the rebel advent, which they have learned to dread greatly, have entrusted themselves to the most fragile of home-made vessels. I heard an escaped contraband say, today, that he came down the Kanawha fifty miles on a log, but that he would rather drown than remain with his master, who is in Loring's army and is expected home in a few days.

The rebels, the darkies say, have threatened death to the negroes of the Kanawha Valley, whom they accuse of having kept the Federal forces posted as to Confederate movements coming within their knowledge. The acts and orders of some of our Generals ought certainly to acquit the colored race of the charge of acting as spies for us. There is certainly a conflict of opinion on the subject between the Napoleons of the two sides. General Halleck holds that negroes give information to the rebels, and issues his fiat that they be excluded from the Union lines.

The Guerilla (Charleston), September 29, 1862

CONFEDERATE MAJOR GENERAL'S PUBLIC ORDER

Confederate major general William Loring issued a general order instructing his men on how to treat residents with Unionist sympathies.

General Order No.—

The com'dg General feels deeply sensible of his obligation to treat all persons in arms against the Confederacy, and who may fall into his hands, with the utmost humanity required by Christian charity and the usages of war. In like manner all citizens who obey the laws and repudiate their treason, will be treated with the clemency declared in the Commanding General's Proclamation. He has heard, with deep mortification, that in a single instance this rule has been departed from by the unauthorized order of one of his officers; but the wrong done will be promptly punished and redressed.

All persons who have received arms of the public enemy are invited to bring their arms into camp, and if they choose, take service in the defense of the country. No punishment will be imposed on such persons.

By order of
MAJ. GEN. LORING
H. Fitzhugh, Chief of Staff.
Sep 26-tf
GENERAL ORDER.
Headquarters, Dept. of Western Va., Charleston, Va., Sept. 14, 1862.

The Guerilla (Charleston), September 29, 1862

FIVE

The Movement for Statehood

*T*HE UNION'S military successes early in the war provided space for pro-Union western Virginians to establish a functioning independent government and to shape the region's political future. Less than a month after the Virginia Convention voted to secede from the Union on April 17, loyal western Virginians gathered in Wheeling on May 13 to decide what to do. Harrison County's John S. Carlile called for the formation of a new state, but the majority concluded it would be unwise to do so before voters had an opportunity to vote on secession in a May 23 referendum.[1] That referendum passed across the state but failed overwhelmingly in many western Virginia counties. Open voting, where a voter's choice was visible to anyone at the polls, probably contributed to landslide decisions for or against the measure in specific localities.

Loyal western Virginians reconvened at the Second Wheeling Convention on June 11 and created the Reorganized Government of Virginia on June 19, issuing a "Declaration of Rights of the People of Virginia" to explain their act. By August, the movement for separation from Virginia had gained steam, and a committee on the division of the state proposed a new thirty-nine-county state to be named "Kanawha." After the proposal was put before voters in the proposed new state, a first constitutional convention gathered at Wheeling on November 26 to begin the work of state creation.

Among the questions to be settled was the new state's name. The dismemberment ordinance passed at the Second Wheeling Convention had used "Kanawha," but that name already represented one of the state's counties and a river. Considerable debate resulted in the choice of "West Virginia."[2]

More debate surrounded the proposed boundaries. Support for the Union was strong in the northwest and Northern Panhandle and weak to almost nonexistent in some of the southwestern counties. In the counties that eventually became part of the new state of West Virginia, fate was not simply determined by popular feeling. It was also tied to Union strategic interests and outcomes on the battlefield. This was especially true in the lower (northern) Shenandoah

Valley, which is today part of West Virginia's Eastern Panhandle. The area included Harpers Ferry and the strategically important Baltimore and Ohio Railroad. After much debate, on December 13 the convention affirmed that West Virginia would include the originally proposed thirty-nine counties, plus the southern counties of Pocahontas, Greenbrier, Monroe, Mercer, and McDowell, where support for the Confederacy remained strong. Seven additional counties in the east would be added if voters there chose to join the new state. Jefferson, Berkeley, Morgan, Hampshire, Hardy, and Pendleton Counties did so, but under conditions of Union occupation that no doubt affected the outcome. The seventh, Frederick County, changed hands between Confederate and Union forces repeatedly during the war and never held an election; it remains part of Virginia today.

Delegates crafted a state constitution that retained many of the features of Virginia's structure, with a few significant differences. Rejecting the old Virginia county court system, which had placed too much power in a governor-appointed elite, West Virginia's constitution made county and state offices elective. The governor's term was set at two years, but without term limits. The existing legislative structure consisting of county-level magistrates, circuit courts, and a supreme court of appeals remained, as did a guarantee of suffrage to all White men over age twenty-one. A desire for public education resulted in a provision for free schools as soon as economically feasible.[3]

The question of slavery and its future in the new state also needed to be resolved. In a 2023 monograph on the creation of West Virginia, Scott A. MacKenzie argues that at the outset, White western Virginians shared strong proslavery views with White eastern Virginians and only sought to create a new state within the Union because they believed it was the best way to protect the institution of slavery. According to MacKenzie, a proslavery, pro-Union consensus quickly broke down only after Lincoln announced his plan for compensated emancipation for slaveholders in loyal border regions. The hardships of war and the actions of self-emancipating enslaved peoples also contributed to a sudden shift toward embracing emancipation by 1863.[4] Support for the MacKenzie thesis can be found in the examples of early statehood advocates like Carlile and John James Davis (whose letters appear in chapter 2). Both were proslavery and believed a federal Union was the best protection for the institution.

However, while recognizing slavery's presence in almost every western Virginia county in 1860, most historians of the state have documented periodic tensions, going back decades, between elite eastern slaveholders and western Virginians, as well as actions of western Virginia's self-emancipating enslaved people during the war years, to explain western Virginia's state builders relatively quick acceptance of emancipation as a condition of statehood.[5] Some were eager to rid the region of an institution they believed had caused much political strife. Methodist minister Gordon Battelle offered several resolutions to the constitutional convention in the winter of 1861–62, proposing gradual emancipation and recommending that all African Americans in the state be resettled abroad, but these were tabled by members of the convention not ready to address the issue. The proposed state constitution ratified unanimously by the convention on February 18 included a compromise position—it would prohibit the entry of any new African Americans into the state, whether enslaved or free.[6] In May the General Assembly of the Reorganized Government of Virginia and Governor Francis Pierpont consented to the formation of the state. Virginia senator Waitman T. Willey of Morgantown formally presented the U.S. Senate with a petition requesting statehood on May 29. Carlile, Virginia's other senator and a member of the Committee on Territories, drafted the statehood bill.

Events on the national level would complicate (West) Virginians' decisions regarding the future of slavery in the state. While Abraham Lincoln made it clear in his First Inaugural Address and throughout the first year of the war that he did not intend to dismantle slavery where it already existed, Union setbacks at Manassas in the summer of 1861 and in the Peninsula Campaign during the spring of 1862 resulted in louder calls in the North to embrace a policy of emancipation of enslaved people as a strategic necessity. Lincoln first publicly proposed a plan for compensated emancipation for slaveholders in the loyal border states in March of 1862, then more dramatically issued a preliminary Emancipation Proclamation in September, to take effect on January 1, 1863. The presidential proclamation declared that all persons held in bondage in states and regions under rebellion were to be forever free. While loyal western Virginia was exempted from this, the new proclamation was widely understood as a shift in Union war aims. A Union victory in this war would accelerate the end of slavery everywhere. West Virginia could not become a state without congressional approval, and it seemed increasingly unlikely that an antislavery Congress would approve the creation of a new slave state.

Concerns about the changing national climate regarding the future of slavery may have influenced the revised draft of the West Virginia constitution that emerged from Carlile's Senate Committee on Territories on June 23, 1862. Much to the surprise of many advocates of West Virginia statehood, the new draft proposed adding fifteen counties to the new state. The additional counties were in the Shenandoah Valley, where the institution of slavery was far more entrenched. It was also a region that remained partially under Confederate control. Carlile's proposal did call for gradual emancipation in the new state but required approval by a new constitutional convention in which delegates from all sixty-three of the proposed counties had a voice. The proslavery Carlile, who had been among the first and loudest proponents of a separate state at the outset of the war, now appeared to be attempting to sabotage statehood by adding a number of proslavery counties to the proposed state. The addition of fifteen additional Shenandoah Valley counties was rejected.

Massachusetts senator Charles Sumner proposed an amendment that would emancipate all enslaved people on July 4, 1863, but this amendment was defeated.[7] Ultimately, Virginia's other senator, Willey, and Ohio senator Benjamin F. Wade proposed a compromise amendment on slavery that would come to be called the Willey Amendment: all enslaved people under the age of twenty-one on July 4, 1863, would become free on their twenty-first birthday. With this compromise, the U.S. Senate voted to approve West Virginia's statehood on July 14, 1862, and after much debate the House of Representatives followed suit, approving the admission of West Virginia on December 10. President Lincoln signed the bill creating the new state on December 31, 1862.

The voters of western Virginia went to the polls on April 4, 1863, with Senator Carlile urging them to reject statehood. In an election boycotted by western Virginians who supported the Confederacy and in which nine counties (mostly in the far southern reaches of the new state) submitted no election returns, voters ratified the West Virginia constitution 28,321 to 572.[8] Decades of resentments against the elite, large planters of the east, resentments hardened by the conviction that these planters' arrogance was responsible for all the current suffering and chaos secession had wrought, appeared to have allowed supporters of the new state to discard whatever proslavery views they had held in the past. Carlile's defection from the statehood movement he created was indeed significant. But more significant is how few of West Virginia's leaders followed him out the door.[9] In the wake of the vote, Lincoln issued a proclamation on April 20 that set the date for statehood sixty days hence. On June 20, 1863, the state of West Virginia entered the Union.

"THE PECULIAR SITUATION OF NORTHWESTERN VIRGINIA"

Harrison County attorney and enslaver (and later U.S. senator) John S. Carlile had been present at the Virginia Convention and voted against secession. Returning to Clarksburg, Carlile helped organize the northwestern region's resistance to the Virginia secession decision.

NORTHWESTERN VIRGINIA.

Great Movement in Harrison County for a Separate Organization in the Northwest from the Seceders.

Convention Called in This City on the 13th of May.
From the Clarksburg Guard, Extra

At a large and enthusiastic meeting of from 1,000 to 1,200 of the citizens of Harrison county, assembled at the Court House upon a notice of forty-eight hours, on Monday, April 22, 1861, the following preamble and resolutions were adopted without one dissenting voice.

PREAMBLE.

WHEREAS, The Convention now in session in this State, called by the Legislature, the members of which had been elected twenty months before said call, at a time when no such action as the assemblage of a convention by legislative enactment was contemplated by the people, or expected by the members they elected in May, 1859, at which time no one anticipated the troubles recently brought upon our common country by the extraordinary action of the State authorities of South Carolina, Georgia, Alabama, Mississippi, Florida, Louisiana, and Texas, has, contrary to the expectation of a large majority of the people of this State, adopted an ordinance withdrawing Virginia from the Federal Union: and whereas, by the law calling said Convention, it is expressly declared that no such ordinance shall have force or effect, or be of binding obligation upon the people of this State, until the same shall be ratified by the voters at the polls: and whereas, we have seen with regret that demonstrations of hostility, unauthorized by law, and inconsistent with the duty of law-abiding citizens, still owing allegiance to the Federal Government, have been made by a portion of the people of this State against the said Government: and whereas, the Governor of this Commonwealth, has, by proclamation, undertaken to decide for the people of Virginia, that which they have reserved to themselves, the right to decide by their votes at the polls, and has called upon the volunteer soldiery of this State to report to him and hold themselves in readiness to make war upon the Federal Government, which Government is Virginia's Government, and must in law and of right continue so to be, until the people of Virginia shall, by their votes, and through the ballot-box, that great conservator of a free people's liberties, decide otherwise: and whereas, the peculiar situation of Northwestern Virginia, separated as it is by natural barriers from the rest of the State, precludes all hope of timely succor in the hour of danger from other portions of the State, and demands that we should look to and provide for our own safety in the fearful emergency in which we now find ourselves placed by the action of our State authorities, who have disregarded the great fundamental principle upon which our beautiful system of Government is based, to wit: "That all governmental power is derived from the consent of the governed," and have without consulting the people placed this State in hostility to the Government by seizing upon its ships and obstructing the channel at the mouth of Elizabeth river, by wresting from the Federal officers at Norfolk and Richmond the custom houses, by tearing from the Nation's property the Nation's flag, and putting in its place a bunting, the emblem of rebellion, and by marching upon the National Armory at Harper's Ferry; thus inaugurating a war without consulting those in whose name they profess to act; and whereas, the exposed condition of Northwestern Virginia requires that her people should be united in action, and unanimous in purpose—there being a perfect identity of interests in times of war as well as in peace—therefore, be it

Resolved, That it be and is hereby recommended to the people in each and all of the counties composing Northwestern Virginia to appoint delegates, not less than five in number, of their wisest, best, and discreetest men, to meet in Convention at Wheeling, on the 13th day of May next, to consult and determine upon such action as the people of Northwestern Virginia should take in the present fearful emergency,

Resolved, That Hon: John S. Carlile, W. Goff, Hon. Chas. S. Lewis, J. Davis, Lot Bowen, Dr. Wm. Dunkin, W. E. Lyon, Felix Sturm, and James Lynch be and are hereby appointed delegates to represent this county in said Convention.

JOHN HURLEY, Pres.

J. W. Harris, Sec'y.

Wheeling Daily Intelligencer, April 25, 1861

THE WHEELING CONVENTIONS

In May and June leaders of western counties who opposed Virginia's secession met at Wheeling to draft a formal response to the Virginia Convention's secession decision. The first meeting occurred before the May 23 voter referendum on secession, and some in attendance discouraged a move to separate from eastern Virginia before that vote. After the statewide vote affirmed secession by a large majority—with significant opposition in the northwest—delegates returned for the Second Wheeling Convention in June. On June 13, John S. Carlile drafted a "Declaration of the People of

Virginia," *pronouncing secession illegal and calling for the reorganization of the government of Virginia, which became known as the Reorganized Government of Virginia.*[10]

DECLARATION OF THE PEOPLE OF VIRGINIA REPRESENTED IN CONVENTION IN WHEELING

June 13, 1861

The true purpose of all government is to promote the welfare and provide for the protection and security of the governed, and when any form or organization of government proves inadequate for, or subversive of this purpose, it is the right, it is the duty of the latter to alter or abolish it. The Bill of Rights of Virginia, framed in 1776, reaffirmed in 1830, and again in 1851, expressly reserves this right to the majority of her people, and the existing constitution does not confer upon the General Assembly the power to call a Convention to alter its provisions, or to change the relations of the Commonwealth, without the previously expressed consent of such majority.—The act of the General Assembly, calling the Convention which assembled at Richmond in February last, was therefore a usurpation; and the Convention thus called has not only abused the powers nominally entrusted to it, but, with the connivance and active aid of the executive, has usurped and exercised other powers, to the manifest injury of the people, which, if permitted, will inevitably subject them to a military despotism.

The Convention, by its pretended ordinances, has required the people of Virginia to separate from and wage war against the government of the United States, and against the citizens of neighboring States, with whom they have heretofore maintained friendly, social and business relations: It has attempted to subvert the Union founded by Washington and his co-patriots in the purer days of the republic, which has conferred unexampled prosperity upon every class of citizens, and upon every section of the country: It has attempted to transfer the allegiance of the people to an illegal confederacy of rebellious States, and required their submission to its pretended edicts and decrees: It has attempted to place the whole military force and military operations of the Commonwealth under the control and direction of such confederacy, for offensive as well as defensive purposes.

It has, in conjunction with the State executive, instituted wherever their usurped power extends, a reign of terror intended to suppress the free expression of the will of the people, making elections a mockery and a fraud: The same combination, even before the passage of the pretended ordinance of secession, instituted war by the seizure and appropriation of the property of the Federal Government, and by organizing and mobilizing armies, with the avowed purpose of capturing or destroying the Capitol of the Union:

They have attempted to bring the allegiance of the people of the United States into direct conflict with their subordinate allegiance to the State, thereby making obedience to their pretended Ordinance, treason against the former.

We, therefore, the delegates here assembled in Convention to devise such measures and take such action as the safety and welfare of the loyal citizens of Virginia may demand, having mutually considered the premises, and viewing with great concern, the deplorable condition to which this once happy Commonwealth must be reduced, unless some regular adequate remedy is speedily adopted, and appealing to the Supreme Ruler of the Universe for the rectitude of our intentions, do hereby, in the name and on the behalf of the good people of Virginia, solemnly declare, that the preservation of their dearest rights and liberties and their security in person and property, imperatively demand the reorganisation of the government of the Commonwealth, and that all acts of said Convention and Executive, tending to separate this Commonwealth from the United States, or to levy and carry on war against them, are without authority and void; and the offices of all who adhere to the said Convention and Executive, whether legislative, executive or judicial, are vacated.

Wheeling Daily Intelligencer, June 14, 1861

"YOU HAVE BEEN CONVENED IN EXTRAORDINARY SESSION"

Delegates to the Second Wheeling Convention established the Reorganized Government of Virginia and selected Marion County resident Francis Pierpont to serve as governor of the reorganized state. In this address to the new legislature, Pierpont pondered the momentous changes and difficult path ahead for the politicians and citizens of western Virginia.

Gentlemen:

You have been convened in extraordinary session in midsummer, when, under other circumstances, you should be at home attending to pursuits incident to this season of the year. The exigencies with which we find ourselves surrounded demand your counsels.

I regret that I cannot congratulate you on the peace and prosperity of the country, in the manner which has been customary with Executives, both State and Federal. For the present, those happy days which as a nation we have so long enjoyed, and that prosperity which has smiled upon us, as upon no other nation, are departed.

It is my painful duty to announce that the late Executive of the State, with a large part of the State Officers, Civil and Military, under him, are at war with the loyal people of Virginia, and the constitutional government of the United States. They have leagued themselves with persons from other States, to tear down the benign governments, State and Federal, erected by the wisdom and patriotism of our fathers, and under which our liberties have so long been protected. . . .

But while we are passing through this period of gloom and darkness in our country's history, we must not despair, or fold our hands until the chains of despotism shall be fastened upon us. . . . Our spirits must rise above the intimidation and violence employed against us. . . . If we manfully exert ourselves, we shall succeed. There is a just God who "rides upon the whirlwind and directs the Storm." Let us look to him with abiding confidence.

The fact is no longer disguised, that there has been in the South, for many years, a secret organization laboring with steady perseverance to over turn the Federal Government, and destroy constitutional liberty in this country. . . . The cry of danger to the institution of Slavery has been a mere pretext to rouse and excite the people. In abandoning the Constitution of the Union, the leaders of the movement must have known that they were greatly weakening the safeguards and protection which were necessary to the existence of that institution. It has been urged that Secession was necessary to protect the slave interest of the South. . . .

—Executive Chamber

July 2d. 1861.

Francis Pierpont, "Address to the Senate and House of Delegates of the Commonwealth of Virginia," July 2, 1861, Record Group 13, Library of Virginia, Richmond

THE STATEHOOD REFERENDUM

The Reorganized Government of Virginia put the issue of statehood before the voters on October 24, 1861. The vote for statehood was overwhelming: 18,408 to 781, or 96 percent of votes in favor. But just 34 percent of potential voters turned out. Open voting in a time of war and division likely kept most dissenters away from the polls. Voters also chose delegates for a new constitutional convention at this time.

THE ELECTION TO-DAY

(Statehood Referendum)

We can add nothing to what we have already said about the election that comes off today. The issue is plain, and the minds of those who have thought about the matter at all are made up. We have no idea there will be a full vote in this county. The people have had too much else to think about, important as is the election. The war has swallowed up all other subjects—even those of every day necessity. Out in the interior the vote will be larger and much more unanimous for division we expect. Indeed we hardly think there will be any serious opposition to it where the matter has been properly presented and understood.

Our advice from Monongalia, Marion, Preston, Taylor, Harrison, Ritchie, Wood, &c., &c., lead us to believe that the vote will be pretty much all one way. We should regret to see any serious opposition. We ought to be all unified for division, for it is a matter that concerns us all vitally, and tough to band us together like brothers.

Discussion on the subject has ended. Division has been shown in all its advantages, we think, and we have yet to know that it has one single draw back or disadvantage. If ever there was a measure that appealed to every interest of a people for a united, enthusiastic and hearty support, it is the measure of division.

All that we have to say, then, is, voters of Ohio County, consider only your own best interest, and improve to-day the golden opportunity for which you have to often longed, of organizing a separate State.

Wheeling Daily Intelligencer, October 24, 1861

"THEY ARE AFFLICTED WITH MADNESS"

An editorial in the Clarksburg National Telegraph *revealed the complex attitudes Unionists in western Virginia continued to hold toward the institution of slavery, even in the second year of the war.*

"WHOM THE GODS WOULD DESTROY THEY FIRST MAKE MAD."

If this ancient and classic adage be true, there are thousands now in the Southern Confederacy whose destruction is foredoomed, for it is evident from the action of the secession leaders that they are afflicted with madness.—They have indulged in ambitious dreams of power until their minds have lost their balances, and they have greedily seized upon that which will prove their destruction. They profess to be fighting for their rights in slavery when they are doing the very thing that will injure the institution and should they prove successful, would destroy it.

Just contemplate a moment, the condition of the eleven States, which have gone through with the humbug process of passing secession ordinances, would be in, if the United States Government were to acknowledge their independence and let them set up for themselves. Each State would be convinced that secession was a sound doctrine, that is, secession would be orthodox in every State in the new Confederacy. Every governor would, upon becoming a little offended at the Government, recommend secession, and it would be adopted, and consequently, the boasted Southern Confederacy would soon be divided into little factions, eternally waring with each other. They would have no Fugitive Slave Law to interpose in their favor, when their slaves escaped into the free states, and, consequently they would have a *Canada* upon their borders into which their slaves could escape when they chose. The British and French Governments would then show that all their pretended sympathy was but for effect—that they only wished to embarrass and divide the Government of the United States—that further than this, they had no sympathy with the South or its institutions.

Slavery in the United States has always been respected by the other nations of the earth, because it has always had a Federal Government to protect it, but let the Southern States become an independent nation, based upon slavery, and it will then be seen that the nations of Europe will have no sympathy for them, but on the contrary, will do all they can to embarrass and fetter them. The British Government, especially, is opposed to African slavery, and should it now become an ally of the Rebels, it will only be for the purpose of attempting to destroy the Government of the United States, and of reducing the slave States to a state of dependence. The worst possible thing that can happen for the people of the Southern States, and, especially for posterity, would be acknowledging their independence.—They would immediately establish a strong Aristocracy or a Monarchy and every man who was not fortunate enough to own slaves, would be denied the privilege of the elective franchise. Slavery would be the grand desideratum in everything. It would be the stepping stone to both official and social position. A man, to be a free man, would be compelled to be a slave owner. Such a degree of oppression would be exercised over the poorer claims that it would be insupportable, and frequent and sanguinary rebellions would be the consequence. But it is unnecessary to say any more on this subject, for we presume our readers have heard and read discussions upon this subject until they are wearied of it. But they must permit us to tell them that there is great danger of secession damning the cause it is pretending to save.

National Telegraph (Clarksburg, VA [WV]), January 3, 1862

SENATOR WILLEY'S CONCERNS

Waitman T. Willey, a prominent attorney from Morgantown, Monongalia County, was elected to the U.S. Senate by the legislature of the Reorganized Government of Virginia in 1862 and later by the legislature of West Virginia. In Congress he worked tirelessly on behalf of statehood, but as this letter to Preston County businessman Harrison Hagans details, he worried about the movement's political timing and how the controversial issue of slavery would shape the debate over West Virginia statehood.

Washington City
May 7th 1862

H. Hagans Esq.

Dear Sir: I have just recd. Your letter of the 2nd <u>Inst</u>. I was somewhat surprised that you did not seem to be "aware of my position," in reference to the question of the new state. I had supposed that no one who knew anything about my opinions on any subject, could be in any doubt in this respect. The only matter of doubt with me was, whether our application was not made too soon, to ensure its success. . . . I have now, nor shall I relax a single effort to secure the admission of the new state, if it is possible to be done.

But I am sorry to have to inform you that the present prospect . . . by which our admission is opposed are various. I will mention a few of them.

1st. The border slave state members . . . oppose us; because they say that the movement is simply an abolition scheme; and that it will operate against the loyal sentiment of the south, on which we must rely for reorganising law & order there, in the restoration of the southern states to the Union.

2nd. The abolitionists oppose us, because they say that it is a proslavery scheme to add another slave state to the Union, and two more proslavery senators to the U.S. Senate.

3rd. The members from the large middle states, and New York, oppose us because they say they are unwilling that this territory now embraced within the boundaries of Virginia, should become entitled to four senators instead of two, as at present.

4th. Many, from all quarters oppose us, because they say the legislature at Wheeling representing little more than the counties embraced in the new state, and being far less than a majority of the whole state of Virginia, is not a legislature such as is contemplated in the constitution of the U. States, to give its "consent." . . .

In consequence of these, and other objections—such as the policy of Mr. Sumner & his followers, who are for remitting all the seceded states back to a territorial condition—you must perceive that the prospects of admission are not very flattering. But, sooner or later we must, and we will have a new state....

As to the general question of slavery, you are correct, when you supposed I am no pro-slavery man. But it must be plain to any man of reflection that by no possibility would the state of "West Virginia," remain a slave state any length of time.... It would, even without legislation, virtually disappear in 25 years. But the first session of the legislature, would probably, pass a law of gradual emancipation. But while I am no pro-slavery man, yet as a senator of the U. States, sworn to support the constitution of the U. States, no pressure of policy or expediency can so far stifle my sense of responsibility to my country & to God as to cause me to forget that oath. And whilst, no man will less regret the legitimate & necessary results of the war in the destruction of slavery yet by no act, or vote of mine, in violation of the constitution, shall I aid in its abolition. Whereever the constitution protects it, I, in my official action here am bound to protect it. I assure you I am not disposed to protect it anywhere else....

But no anti-slavery man need give himself any further trouble, in my opinion. The fate of slavery is sealed. Its own friends have destroyed it. I told the secessionists at Richmond a year ago that such would be the result. So let it be— Henceforth, the great question will be <u>Colonization</u>. This will be a necessity. The two races, except in the relation of slave & master cannot exist in harmony in the same body politic.

But I fear, if I write on, the labor of reading this long & lusty scrawl, will be as fatal to you, as the war to slavery; but when I assure you that I have been compelled to take from the hours usually allotted to sleep, the time to write it, you will be assured, that I, at least was desirous of responding to your letter.

Be pleased to remember me to Mrs. H. and all the members of your family. I shall always be pleased to hear from you on any subject.

Yours Truly,

W. T. Willey

Waitman T. Willey to Harrison Hagans, 1361, West Virginia and Regional History Center, West Virginia University, Morgantown

GRADUAL EMANCIPATION AND STATEHOOD

The issue of slavery continued to be a stumbling block in the path to West Virginia statehood. Senators Benjamin F. Wade of Ohio and Charles Sumner of Massachusetts insisted on emancipation of all the region's enslaved people before statehood could be achieved, as adding a new slave

state to the Union was unacceptable. The Reorganized Government of West Virginia's two senators, Waitman T. Willey and John S. Carlile, could not agree on a response. Carlile argued that even a gradual emancipation measure had to be directly approved by voters in West Virginia, while Willey proposed an amendment to the proposed state's constitution, outlining how gradual emancipation would be implemented.

The children of slaves born within the limits of this State after the fourth day of July, eighteen hundred and sixty-three, shall be free; and all slaves within the said State who shall, at the time aforesaid, be under the age of ten years, shall be free when they arrive at the age of twenty-one years; and all slaves over ten and under twenty-one years, shall be free when they arrive at the age of twenty-five years; and no slave shall be permitted to come into the State for permanent residence therein.

_{"An Act for the Admission of the State of 'West Virginia' into the Union, Dec. 31, 1862, and for Other Purposes," in *The Statutes at Large, Treaties, and Proclamations of the United States of America* [. . .], vol. 12, ed. George P. Sanger (Boston: Little, Brown, 1863), 634, https://www.loc.gov/item/llsl-v12/.}

"YOU HAVE DESERTED OUR JUST AND HOLY CAUSE"

The revised constitution containing the Willey Amendment on the abolition of slavery in West Virginia was presented to a reconvened constitutional convention on February 12, 1862. Waitman T. Willey gave an impassioned speech urging support, but some delegates initially wanted to consider compensating slaveholders loyal to the Union cause. John S. Carlile led opposition to the amendment, but it passed by unanimous vote on February 17, removing the last hurdle to attaining statehood. Once it was inserted in the document, on July 14, 1862, the statehood bill received U.S. Senate approval, by a vote of 23 to 17. Carlile voted no, a position that angered many of his constituents. The man who was among the loudest and earliest advocates of West Virginia statehood now came to be seen as a traitor to that cause by many voters. The anti-Carlile backlash even affected his associates. John J. Davis, a Harrison County attorney and a member of the Reorganized Government's House of Delegates, was a friend and associate of Carlile, and he received anonymous hate mail for supporting Carlile's turn.

August 16, 1862

John J. Davis

Sir, Since coming in town I have learned that you have deserted our just and holy cause by upholding John Carlile in his nigger doctrines. The less you say hereafter the better it will be for you if you respect your personal safety. A word to the wise is sufficient.

By one who will stand by the Union in <u>any emergency</u>.

* * *

March 9th 1863

Sir: You're in danger—be <u>slightly</u> careful of your conduct. Your course is entirely repulsive to all patriots & sensible men, therefore this advice: I view you as a personal friend, therefore I advise you to desist from being too ambitious in your new state feelings—or rather anti new state sympathies.

<small>John J. Davis Papers, West Virginia and Regional History Center, West Virginia University, Morgantown</small>

"A STRANGE CEREMONY"

Buckhannon resident Marcia Phillips described the local reaction to John S. Carlile's turn against the new-state movement.

AUGUST 2, 1862

On this day, a strange ceremony was performed by the soldiers and the citizens, hanging John S. Carlile (Traitor to the new state, he once advocated so zealously) in effegy. The long procession went slowly up Maine Street, the drum and fife playing the *rogues* march, and the prisoner blindfolded, sitting in the cart upon his coffin, surrounded by his guard.

<small>Marcia Louise Sumner Phillips Journal, p. 129, West Virginia and Regional History Center, West Virginia University, Morgantown</small>

"I BELIEVE THE ADMISSION OF WEST VIRGINIA INTO THE UNION IS EXPEDIENT"

The fate of the West Virginia statehood movement rested in the hands of President Abraham Lincoln. The unusual and extraordinary circumstances of its creation—during a civil war in which two political entities claimed to represent the state of Virginia, one of which no longer recognized the authority of the old federal government and its constitution—raised constitutional questions about the process to be followed. The emergency of war also raised questions about the expediency of recognizing West Virginia statehood. Would West Virginia statehood help or hinder the administration's prime objective—the restoration of the Union? In late December, Lincoln polled the members of his cabinet and asked them to share their thoughts on the questions of whether recognizing West Virginia as a separate state was constitutional and expedient. Lincoln's cabinet was divided on both questions. Below is Lincoln's response after reviewing the opinions of his cabinet members.

The consent of the Legislature of Virginia is constitutionally necessary to the bill for the admission of West Virginia becoming a law. A body claiming to be such Legislature has given its consent. We can not well deny that it is such, unless we do so upon the outside knowledge that the body was chosen at elections, in which a majority of the qualified voters of Virginia did not participate. But it is a universal practice in the popular elections in all these States to give no legal consideration whatever to those who do not choose to vote, as against the effect of the votes of those who do choose to vote. Hence it is not the qualified voters, but the qualified voters, who choose to vote, that constitute the political power of the State. Much less then to non-voters, should any consideration be given to those who did not vote, in this case: because it is also matter of outside knowledge, that they were not merely neglectful of their rights under, and duty to, this government, but were also engaged in open rebellion against it. Doubtless among these non-voters were some Union men whose voices were smothered by the more numerous secessionists; but we know too little of their number to assign them any appreciable value. Can this government stand, if it indulges Constitutional constructions by which men in open rebellion against it, are to be accounted, man for man, the equals of those who maintain their loyalty to it? Are they to be accounted even better citizens, and more worthy of consideration, than those who merely neglect to vote? If so, their treason against the Constitution, enhances their Constitutional value! Without braving these absurd conclusions, we cannot deny that the body which consents to the admission of West Virginia, is the Legislature of Virginia. I do not think the plural form of the words "Legislatures" and "States" in the phrase of the Constitution "without the consent of the Legislatures of the States concerned" has any reference to the new State concerned. That plural form sprang from the contemplation of two or more old States contributing to form a new one. The idea that the new state was in danger of being admitted without its own consent, was not provided against, because it was not thought of, as I conceive. It is said, the devil takes care of his own—Much more should a good spirit—the spirit of the Constitution and the Union—take care of its own—I think it can not do less, and live.

But is the admission into the Union, of West Virginia, expedient. This, in my general view, is more a question for Congress, than for the Executive. Still

I do not evade it. More than on anything else, it depends on whether the admission or rejection of the new State would, under all the circumstances tend the more strongly to the restoration of the National authority throughout the Union. That which helps most in this direction is the most expedient at this time. Doubtless those in remaining Virginia would return to the Union, so to speak, less reluctantly without the division of the old state than with it; but I think we could not save as much in this quarter by rejecting the new state, as we should lose by it in the new. West Virginia. We can scarcely dispense with the aid of West Virginia in this struggle; much less can we afford to have her against us, in Congress and in the field. Her brave and good men regard her admission into the Union as a matter of life and death. They have been true to the Union under very severe trials. We have so acted as to justify their hopes; and we can not fully retain their confidence, and co-operation, if we seem to break faith with them. In fact, they could not do so much for us, if they would.

Again, the admission of the new State turns that much slave soil to free; and thus, is a certain, and irrevocable encroachment upon the cause of the rebellion.

The division of a State is dreaded as a precedent. But a measure made expedient by a war, is no precedent for times of peace. It is said that the admission of West Virginia is secession, and tolerated only because it is our secession. Well, if we call it by that name, there is still difference enough between secession against the Constitution, and secession in favor of the Constitution.

I believe the admission of West Virginia into the Union is expedient.

Abraham Lincoln, "Memorandum on West Virginia," draft, December 31, 1862, Abraham Lincoln papers, Series 3, General Correspondence, 1837–1897, Library of Congress

A SOLDIER VOTES FOR WEST VIRGINIA

The revised West Virginia constitution was placed before voters in an election in which many soldiers were able to vote for the first time. West Virginia voters endorsed the revised constitution overwhelmingly, with 28,321 votes for and just 572 against. West Virginia's Union soldiers cast 7,828 votes for the measure from their camps.

Winchester, Virginia
March 19th 1863

Dear Mother:

I feel considerably used up from the effects of the march to West Va to vote on the new State constitution. There was one man in our company who showed his ignorance enough to vote against it.

Father was taken quite ill while on the trip with pleurasy in the side, but at this time is recovering very fast. . . .

At Kewtown we <u>confiscated</u> a rebel sutler wagon which we found consealed in the woods.

During the past weeks there has been quite a reinforcement at this place. There is no news of any interest going on here at this time.

Frank starts home this morning, to be gone ten days.

I wish you would send me two pair socks, one quire of the best letter paper in Harrisville plain, one pack of envelopes plain white, and a neck tie, and a pocket knife. The Sutlers here have nothing of any kind but they ask a dollar, cotton neck ties one dollar, Bartow knives same, every thing else same proportion.

I still think that Father and I will get home probably in a year from this, though we would like to come sooner.

Our love to you all.

Your Most obedient Son

Tom

<small>Tom to Dear Mother, March 19, 1863, 43818, Library of Virginia, Richmond</small>

"ADMITTED INTO THE UNION ON AN EQUAL FOOTING"

With the passage of the March vote on the constitution, Lincoln proclaimed on April 20, 1863, that in sixty days West Virginia would become the nation's thirty-fifth state.

By the President of the United States. A Proclamation.

Whereas, by the Act of Congress approved the 31st day of December, last, the State of West Virginia was declared to be one of the United States of America, and was admitted into the Union on an equal footing with the original States in all respects whatever, upon the condition that certain changes should be duly made in the proposed constitution for that state; And, Whereas, proof of a compliance with that condition, as required by the Second Section of the Act aforesaid, has been submitted to me;

Now, therefore, be it known, that I, Abraham Lincoln, President of the United States, do, hereby, in pursuance of the Act of Congress aforesaid, declare and proclaim that the said act shall take effect and be in force from and after sixty days from the date hereof.

In witness whereof, I have hereunto set my hand and caused the Seal of the United States to be affixed.

Done at the city of Washington, this twentieth day of April, in the year of our Lord one thousand eight hundred and sixty-three, and of the Independence of the United States to eighty-seventh.

ABRAHAM LINCOLN.
By the President;
WILLIAM H. SEWARD,
Secretary of State.

Collected Works of Abraham Lincoln, vol. 6 (New Brunswick, NJ: Rutgers University Press, 1953), 181

"THE BOGUS GOVERNMENT"

Western Virginians who sided with the Confederacy considered the whole independent statehood movement and Lincoln's Emancipation Proclamation legal frauds. Henrietta Fitzhugh Barr, an enslaver from Ravenswood on the Ohio River, remained defiantly in support of the Confederacy during the war years. She frequently expressed her sympathies and discussed her political views in a diary she kept during the first two years of the war.

DECEMBER 17, 1862

Today one of the soldiers came in bringing me a letter from Aunt Eliza which this Lieut. had taken from the [Post Office] and opened and read. Saying there was "nothing" to him in it. The intolerable insolence of these people is almost beyond endurance. There is the second offense of its kind within a week. In former times it was a penitentiary offense to open a letter. But everything like law, order or decency is subverted under the Lincoln Government—it is reported that the new state of [West Virginia] has passed both houses of Congress. But the President will veto the bill on the grounds of its "unconstitutionality." This is the most laughable joke Lincoln ever was guilty of. Even the Union people are a little dubious for the same reason but are in favor of it, as one of them said "because of military necessity." . . .

January 1st, 1863. . . . Today Lincoln's proclamation of freedom and equality to the negroes goes into effect. I do not apprehend any serious consequences from this new act of tyranny. All that could be done by the meddling abolitionists to render this unhappy race discontented and miserable has been done. They have failed in their efforts to produce servile insurrections, which the Southern people justly dread more than anything in regard to the war. Anarchy and confusion rule supreme at the Federal Capitol. . . .

January 2nd, 1863. The news reaches us and is hailed with joy by abolitionists that Lincoln has signed the bill for the new state of West Virginia. The joy of the aforesaid will not be very long lived if present indications are to be relied on.... The Yanks are quaking with fear at the idea of the Emperor Napoleon acknowledging and assisting the S. Confederacy....

March 26th, 1863. This is the day set apart by the Bogus Government, for the election for the new state. I understand quite a large number of votes was polled; all in favor, only one against it and that one was Michael Kouns. Who would have thought it? We have not heard the returns from the other precincts. It is all a ridiculous farce. Those will be better off who do not vote at all. (Written on the margin of the page) Later—Mr. Kouns only voted against the Wiley amendment.

May 28th, 1863. Today there is an election going on for officers under the new state. From Gov. down to constable is to be voted for. No doubt the candidates will all be elected as they will MEET with no opposition. They are uniform in their sentiments, i.e., they are all Black Republicans.

May 30th, 1863. Ed Mahan is said to be elected to the state senate, a small majority over Andy Flesher. There is no particular choice between the two men. They are both uncompromising Black Republicans and in other respects are as mean as gas broth. Keeny represents us again in the Legislature. The Union ticket for Gov. etc, were, of course, elected as there was no opposition.

The Civil War Diary of Mrs. Henrietta Fitzhugh Barr (Marietta, OH: Marietta College, 1963), 17–23

BIOGRAPHIES OF SOME OF THE FIRST WEST VIRGINIA LEGISLATORS

The Wheeling Daily Intelligencer *offered brief biographical sketches of many of the first politicians elected to the new state's bicameral legislature in the first months after statehood was achieved. These short biographies offer insights into the paths various West Virginia leaders took toward embracing statehood, and also the process by which statehood advocates secured legitimacy for their cause.*

THE FIRST WEST VA. LEGISLATURE. HOUSE OF DELEGATES. SKETCHES PERSONAL, POLITICAL AND BIOGRAPHICAL.

LEWIS BALLARD, from Monroe.

Lewis Ballard, the member of the House from Monroe county, is a native of Virginia, and of the county he now represents....

He opposed the call for the convention that passed the secession ordinance, and in the face of threats of hanging voted against that ordinance when it was pretended to be submitted to the people. He did all in his power to induce others to vote against it, but when the die was cast, and he was powerless for good, he silently acquiesced in the great wrong that had been done, and quietly pursued his business as merchant and the farmer. But this he was not long permitted to do. On the evening of the day on which the first battle of Bull Run was fought, Floyd's brigade, then overrunning that region, encamped a short distance from his house. Though as stated, Mr. Ballard had been quiet and inoffensive since the breaking out of hostilities, the reels cherished deadly hostility against him. A gang of Floyd's ruffians surrounded his house, and suspended a rope on which they proposed to hang him, but he had been advised of their intentions, and made his escape. They broke open his store and robbed him of several thousand dollars worth of goods, some money and valuable papers. They broke into his cellar and carried off some 800 or 1000 gallons of apple brandy, that article being in great demand in Floyd's army. They also entered his house and drove his family from it and robbed it of everything portable.

After remaining concealed for some days, Mr. Ballard returned home upon assurance by prominent secesh citizens of protection and indemnification for loss. He sought permission to leave the State with his family, but was positively refused. In the early part of August, 1861, he was arrested for "treason to the State of Virginia." He gave bail in the sum of $4,000 to await the action of the grand jury. The jury indicted him for "treason to the Confederate States." He renewed his bail and there the matter ended. He remained at home until the federal troops approached the neighborhood, when he was arrested by order of a militia general and sent to Richmond. On the 8th of January, '62, he was landed in an old tobacco warehouse, known as "the gangrene hospital," where four other citizens were confined, amidst mud, filth and lousy deserters from the rebel army. In about a month he and several others were removed to another warehouse and finally to the notorious Libby prison, where he remained till the middle of May. When they were sent to Salisbury, N. C., where he remained till the 8th of January last, just a twelve month from the time he landed in the tobacco warehouse at Richmond. How much longer he would have been kept no one knows, but he and a companion took French leave by breaking out of prison. For some three days and nights they wandered around Salisbury, the weather being so cloudy they could not shape their course, and at the end of that time they were but twenty miles away. The weather cleared up, however, and they struck northward, and after a long and tedious journey, reached the federal lines at Fayette Court House, Va., Mr. Ballard stopping with his family a few hours.

Since Mr. Ballard's escape through the federal lines, the rebels have carried off and sold all his movable property they could get hands on. What he suffered during his twelve months' imprisonment tongue or pen could hardly tell. Fortunately he was able to procure money from home through a former partner in business, who was in the Legislature at Richmond, and who, though as enemy, could not refuse this aid. Without this he thinks he could not have lived through. While in prison he was often solicited to take the oath to the Confederate government, and as often refused. No charge was ever made against him except that he was loyal to the Union.

Mr. Ballard was elected to represent Monroe county, by some fifty refugees, who held an election at Charleston, Kanawha. The Committee on Credentials have not reported on his case but he will undoubtedly be permitted to hold his seat.

He is not a member of any religious denomination, but, if looks are any index to character is evidently a man of correct moral principles.

There are about 200 refugees from Monroe within the Federal lines. The first representation this county had in any loyal assembly since the breaking out of the rebellion was in the Parkersburg Convention; the next was in the present Legislature. Yet fully one-half the population is represented as loyal, though they have no means of expressing it.

Politically, Mr. Ballard has always been an old Whig, though he strongly opposed Knownothingism and voted for Breckinridge in 1860. He was always strongly pro slavery, till convinced that the predominance of slavery and the stability of the Government are incompatible.—He would favor indemnity to loyal slave owners in West Virginia for any real loss they may sustain by emancipation, but thinks the increase in the value of lands &c., will cover all losses. Mr. Ballard is emphatically the friend and advocate of the Union and of the new State, and is essentially anti-slavery, especially so far as that question relates to West Virginia. It would be very strange, if after his two years experience with rebels fighting to enlarge the dominion of slavery, he was anything else.

Wheeling Daily Intelligencer, July 15, 1863

* * *

SENATE. SKETCHES PERSONAL, POLITICAL AND BIOGRAPHICAL. BY AN OBSERVER

JOHN J. BROWN.

MR. BROWN is a resident of Kingwood, Preston County, and is one of the Senators representing the district of Monongalia, Preston and Taylor. . . .

Mr. Brown has been a democrat ever since his eyes were greeted by the light—voted for Cass in 1848, and Pierce in 1852, Buchanan 1856, and Breckinridge in 1860, which is undoubtedly a strong democratic record—a little too strong, Mr. Brown thinks, for he very much regrets the last vote. Like a great many others . . . he was deceived, but has learned a valuable lesson in politics. . . .

He declared his opposition to the ordinance of secession, took the stump against it, and labored with all his power until the day of election to defeat it, and had the satisfaction of seeing Preston county vote about as follows: For secession 63; against it 2,300. He was a candidate for the Legislature in the spring of 1861, but declined, principally for the reason that he did not care about going to Richmond to represent his constituents among traitors; was elected to the June Convention of 1861, which restored the State Government; was a member of the late Constitutional Convention, of which he was one of the best members, approved its Constitution and labored for its adoption. He opposed the Battelle resolutions, believing that time would eradicate the institution of slavery, and voted with all the members for the clause prohibiting slaves from coming into the State; found that the salvation of West Virginia depended upon the admission of the New State; and, willing to sacrifice all personal feelings for that, he, at the re-assembled session of the Convention, voted for gradual emancipation, and urged it before the people. . . .

Wheeling Daily Intelligencer, July 24, 1863

* * *

THE FIRST WEST VA. LEGISLATURE. HOUSE OF DELEGATES. SKETCHES PERSONAL, POLITICAL AND BIOGRAPHICAL.

NATHAN GOFF, from Harrison.

Nathan Goff, one of the delegates from Harrison, was born in Otsego county, New York, in 1798. . . .

Mr. Goff has been nearly all his life the holder of some responsible official position—having been three years a sheriff, nine years a magistrate, twenty-four years acting marshal, and during thirty years of his life, superintendent, treasurer and commissioner of schools for Harrison County.

He is now and has been for years president of the corporation of Clarksburg, and it may be added, as worthy of mention, that he is also president of a Bible Society in his native town.

Mr. Goff is one of the wealthiest men of his county, and acquired his wealth by his own energy and diligence. He has lost heavily by the war, partly by the general depression it had occasioned in stocks, and partly by debtors running away to rebeldom.

In politics he has always been a whig, and voted for Bell and Everett in '60. As an abstract question he has always believed slavery wrong, but as a practical question has opposed its abolishment. Owns two house servants himself. Thinks however that the Government is worth much more than slavery, and if necessary to save the Union is willing every slave in it shall be emancipated. He has been from the beginning firm and consistent in his opposition to the schemes of the rebels, and so great and general was the confidence of his constituency in him that he was brought out against his will and elected without opposition, by a numerically larger vote than was received by any other member of the House....

Wheeling Daily Intelligencer, August 21, 1863

* * *

THE FIRST WEST VA. LEGISLATURE. HOUSE OF DELEGATES. SKETCHES PERSONAL, POLITICAL AND BIOGRAPHICAL

ALFRED FOSTER, from Wirt.

Alfred Foster, the delegate from Wirt, is a native of that county, which formerly constituted part of Wood. He is 43 years of age....

He had been a thorough Whig, up to '56, when he joined the Knownothings. His county has always been largely Democratic, and it speaks well for Mr. Foster's personal popularity at home that the democracy of his county gave him a liberal support despite his Whig and Know-nothing proclivities.

Respecting the institution of slavery, Mr. Foster has been heretofore pro-slavery in his views; has thought that slavery was a great evil, but not necessarily a sin under all circumstances; was opposed to interfering with the institution in any way, and wanted to let the owners of slaves manage them in their own way. He opposed secession, and voted against the ordinance and labored for its defeat.—Has long been favorable to making a new State out of Western Virginia; and goes warmly for supporting the Administration in putting down the rebellion by force....

Wheeling Daily Intelligencer, September 3, 1863

"ONE 'WHO TREADS ALONE'"

John S. Carlile continued to serve as one of the senators for a state whose creation he now opposed, alienated because of the dismantling of the institution of slavery. After the war he retired to his farm near Clarksburg, where he died in 1878.

[Clarksburg] 24th Nov. 1863

My Dear Wall,

    Last night's mail brought me yr. favor 19th inst. the one of the 10th with Boyards enclosed reached me several days ago. Of course I will send you the Globe every day and if you can think of anything else that would interest you I beg you to write me for it. I dread the winter, I shall feel like one "who treads alone." Even now there is nothing at my home outside of my own family that interests me but your letters. If you could only write daily, I would be better pleased. I shall leave friday week for Washn. The Gettysburg nunnery would disgrace a people who could be disgraced but we long since touched the bottom. Barbarous heathenism alone could exterminate one race for the purpose of liberating another and that other an inferior race. The North has all become yankeeized and we know the Yankee will not fight for honor but he will fight for a dollar. It is the property of the south they covet and are fighting for. Let their be a break down in the finances and then radicalism will not be so popular. I am writing in the printing office & hurriedly will postpone till I see you a general talk, I send you the Patriot regularly every friday. Do you get it.

                                                              Yr. friend
                                                              Jno. S. Carlile

John Snyder Carlile to "Wall," November 24, 1863, 395.35, Library of Virginia, Richmond

SIX

Women and the War

*L*AURA JACKSON ARNOLD became a minor celebrity in western Virginia during the Civil War. The sister of Thomas "Stonewall" Jackson—one of the Confederacy's most famous military leaders—did not share her brother's allegiances. "I was a Union woman from the crown of my head to the soles of my feet," she reflected in an interview years later.[1] Laura did what she could to support the Union war effort. She spent long days caring for the wounded after the battle of Rich Mountain. Throughout the conflict she welcomed Union officers into her home, some of whom visited simply because they were curious to meet the loyal Union sister of the famous rebel Stonewall. The frequent visits from Union officers to the Arnold home grated on her husband, Jonathan Arnold, who began the war as a tepid Unionist but became increasingly disaffected from the Union cause after Lincoln issued the Emancipation Proclamation. In October of 1863, Jonathan exploded into a rage. He threatened "to blow her brains out," then physically assaulted Laura. About a week later, possibly motivated by a desire to protect Laura from further abuse, Union officials arrested Jonathan for spying for the Confederacy and placed him under house arrest in Clarksburg. This was the effective end of her marriage, although an ugly legal divorce followed in 1870, with Jonathan charging her with infidelity during the war. These accusations made their way to her sister-in-law Anna Jackson, who confronted Laura about them in a letter. Anna wrote that she was "grieved to say that I have heard some things of you which have surprised & disturbed me beyond measure, & if they are true, I never want to see you again." Anna asked Laura to deny these stories, but it appears she had already made up her mind about her sister-in-law, in large part based on the political stand she took during the war. She reminded Laura that she had "disapproved of my precious Husband's cause, & differed with him in the conviction that he was doing his duty in defending his home & State from invasion, & turned all your sympathies from him in what he believed was a holy & righteous cause. . . . I do not want to see you. There could be no congeniality of feeling between us."[2] In Anna's mind, Laura had twice failed in her womanly duties—to support the two most important men in her life, and to support the righteous cause of the Confederacy.

Some historians have argued that the crisis of the Civil War pressed women into new roles and, by their courage and devotion to the cause, it elevated their status and expanded their opportunities. Others have challenged this narrative, noting the many examples of women facing backlash when they stepped out of their traditional domestic sphere and into new roles, where they could "find themselves cast as despised and morally suspect 'public women.'" Laura Jackson Arnold certainly experienced both reactions to her public behavior during the war, revered by Union officers and soldiers for her loyalty to the Union even as some allied with the Confederacy impugned her moral character. Historian Nina Silber has argued that both of these interpretations of women's experiences in the Civil War contained a certain truth, that women found both "new opportunities and a new form of subordination" during the crisis.[3]

Arnold was not alone in facing judgment. In September 1861 the *Wheeling Daily Intelligencer* reprinted a piece from a Cincinnati newspaper criticizing "Unpatriotic Mothers" who discouraged their sons from enlisting. "The mother who, in this great emergency, will restrain her son from defending his country, forgets the highest, the noblest duty of woman," the writer declared.[4] Women who earned a living as prostitutes among the troops or sold alcohol and other restricted products to soldiers were also criticized as undermining the war effort.

Despite the increasing visibility of women, the idea persisted that war did not concern them and that they should be shielded from its costs. Historian Stephanie McCurry has written that "there are few ideas more powerful in western culture than the idea that women are outside of war." In the case of the American Civil War, it is a fiction "that shaped the conflict itself." Viewing women as innocent was, according to McCurry, bound up in ideas about the rules and limits of war.[5] One such rule was that civilized belligerents must protect women from the violence of war. Still, the growing recognition during the war that civilians, including women, the largest group of noncombatants, could significantly aid the enemy resulted in the revision of the Union's "rules of war," as noted in chapter 4. No longer would women's innocence be presumed.[6] One manifestation of this was the extension of oath-taking requirements to women, a practice that became common in western Virginia by August 1862.[7]

When violence came to their communities, some women fled in advance of occupying armies, but more often it was the men who fled, leaving women behind to protect family property, expecting the invading army to follow rules of war that shielded women from violence. In these situations, women frequently concealed weapons, food, and other supplies from hostile forces and even hid their male relatives. In a region where the war was primarily characterized by occupation, scouting, and raiding, West Virginia women frequently found themselves at risk of soldier violence as they attempted to protect their property or their loved ones. No place in West Virginia was safe from military raids or occupation during the war. Many West Virginia woman experienced the ordeal of an invasion of their homes by armed strangers. They could be forced to take in and feed soldiers from either army, and even soldiers from "friendly" forces might plunder their orchards, steal personal property, or physically or sexually abuse them, despite "rules" forbidding these behaviors. For African American women, the chaos of war and evolving Union policies regarding enslaved people created opportunities to flee the sites of their enslavement for contraband camps like the one at Harpers Ferry, for towns under Union occupation, or even Union camps, where they might find protection in exchange for domestic work supporting the armies. But they, too, faced increased threats of abuse from soldiers.

Women provided support to armies on both sides of the conflict in a variety of ways. They provided material support, either individually or as parts of local aid societies. Some took outside employment as nurses, teachers, or clerks. Furthermore, the responsibility for maintaining homes and farms, caring for children, and handling the family finances while husbands and military-age sons were away at war generally fell to women. Women often played a critical role in intelligence. At the most basic level, a woman could share or refrain from sharing important intelligence when questioned by military officials in either army. But some served more actively as agents of intelligence, acting as spies, carrying important correspondence, or even engaging in acts of sabotage like cutting telegraph wires. Some acquired local, national, or even international notoriety for their efforts during the war. Martinsburg's Maria Isabella "Belle" Boyd, who spied for the Confederacy, was the most famous of these, publishing her memoir in London in 1865 and touring on the lecture circuit. Most women spies, of course, went undetected, or when exposed earned only local notoriety. Engaging in violence against the enemy was perhaps the most transgressive activity women engaged in. West Virginia produced a few female bushwhackers, including Nancy Hart, the "Lady Guerilla" who rode with the Confederate-allied Moccasin Rangers. Stories about the "discovery" of women masquerading as male soldiers appeared in newspapers with regularity and were often reprinted in other cities. There is evidence of at least 250 women soldiers fighting for the Union or the Confederacy, and the number may have been higher.[8] A few wrote their own stories, but most of what we know about these individuals is filtered through documents written by men. Women who took on these roles were often the object of a patronizing curiosity, but also were treated with condescension and suspicion.

THE LADIES OF WHEELING CONTRIBUTE TO THE CAUSE

While many women acted individually to support soldiers from their community, others organized collectively to support their side.

A REPORT OF THE LADIES UNION AID SOCIETY, FROM THE TIME OF ITS ORGANIZATION, MAY 28TH, TO NOVEMBER 29, 1861.

The following articles have been made and donated to the soldiers in the field, and their families, and to the prisoners at Camp Carlile: 389 flannel shirts, 178 check shirts, 400 havelocks, 152 pairs socks, 200 handkerchiefs, 108 comforts, 74 pair pillow slips, 50 woolen hoods, 20 neck comforts, 500 needle cases, 4 pair pantaloons, 1 vest, 1 blanket, 2 boxes lint, 1 box bandages, 200 towels, 1 pair suspenders, 1 silk dressing gown, 1 woolen do, 17 pairs drawers.

Work on Hand.—33 comforts, 50 pairs socks, 1 woolen dressing gown, 20 needle books, 5 flannel shirts, 5 cotton shirts, 3 pairs drawers, 5 towels, 25 pillow cases, 18 sheets, 1 blanket, 1 quilt, 10 feather pillows.

MONEY DONATED TO THE FAMILIES OF SOLDIERS.

1st Ward	$82 00
2nd Ward	$4 00
4th Ward	$27 00
5th Ward	$112 00
Ritchietown	$10 00
Island	$5 00
[Total]	$240 00

The Society would respectfully solicit contributions, and especially such articles as yarn, gloves, mittens and socks, or the money to provide material for the same. These articles will be indispensable to the comfort of soldiers on the approaching cold weather. Belle Morrison, Sec'y.

Wheeling Daily Intelligencer, November 30, 1861

LADIES AT MORGANTOWN

In April and May of 1863, Brigadier Generals William "Grumble" Jones and John D. Imboden invaded Union-occupied West Virginia to disable the Baltimore and Ohio Railroad, create havoc, rally support for the Confederacy, and enlist new recruits. When Jones's forces arrived in Morgantown, they were not received warmly by the women of the town.

The Ladies At Morgantown.—The ladies of Morgantown, and especially, we rejoice to say, the younger and unmarried portion, acquitted themselves with great credit during the recent raid of the rebels into that goodly place. The invaders inclined to be gallant and desired to propitiate the ladies, but it was in vain. They would not be propitiated. When they sung it was the "Star Spangled Banner" or it was "Hooker is our Leader," and when they played it was the Union edition of "Maryland! My Maryland!" and other such tantalizing performances. Never a song or a note could the secesh get in praise of their miserable cause and its miserable bunting, and when they insisted they were tartly told that Morgantown was not the place where they could make an impression. We wish all our West Virginia ladies would treat the rebels this way whenever and wherever they make their appearance. No influence would be more potent, both on the rebels themselves and on public opinion generally. The women of the South have been so many main pillars of the rebellion. All their smiles, beauty and favors have been reserved for active rebels and they have turned the cold shoulder, in fact no shoulder at all, to those who were suspected of sympathizing with the Union. No man can estimate such an influence. It has forced many an unwilling man, who in his heart loved his country, into the ranks to fight against it. Let our ladies here in West Virginia distinguish themselves as much for haughty exclusiveness on behalf of the Union sentiment as their "erring sisters" in East Virginia do against that sentiment.

<small>Wheeling Daily Intelligencer, May 7, 1863</small>

DISREPUTABLE WOMEN

The Civil War era witnessed the most rapid expansion of the sex trade in nineteenth-century America. The presence of large numbers of soldiers in Wheeling resulted in a flourishing industry in prostitution. The approach of the city of Wheeling to this problem was to arrest the owners of the brothels and the sex workers, and not the soldier clients of these establishments.

Arrest of a Number of Disreputable Women.—In accordance with instructions from Mayor Sweeney, the police of the different Wards, on Friday night, made a simultaneous descent upon quite a number of houses inhabited by disreputable women, and twenty odd arrests were made. Elizabeth Archie, Sarah Archie, and Dora Smith, were arrested in East Wheeling, at or near the house of Pat Ryan. Ryan and his wife were also arrested, but paid their fines. The rest were committed to jail by Ald. McCourtney.

At a house on the side of the hill, above Fourth Street, Linn Brady, Cal Brady, Louisa Brady and Elizabeth Carr were arrested and committed to jail by Ald. Robertson.

At a house in the First Ward, officer St. Meyers arrested Mrs. Haymaker, Cinderella Whims and Miss Manigan. They were all committed by Ald. Miller.

One Alex. Craig interfered with the officer whilst the latter was in discharge of his duty. The officer gave Craig a good thrashing, after which he was fined ten dollars by Mayor Sweeney and committed to jail.

The establishment known as Fort Nichols, was also overhauled. John Nichols, Geo. Ritchie and Mrs. Hinckley were arrested and fined.

Wheeling Daily Intelligencer, May 26, 1862

LADY VISITORS FROM PARKERSBURG

By 1862 Union officials in occupied regions across the South expanded the oath-taking requirement to include many women. Any woman married to a rebel soldier or whose loyalty to the Union was suspect might be compelled to take an oath of loyalty to the Union.

Lady Visitors from Parkersburg.—Miss Clarine Smith, Miss Fanny Hopkins, Miss Florida Neal, Miss Norma Smith, Miss Emeline Neal, Miss Alice Neal and Mrs. Geo. Neal, jr., reached this city yesterday morning by the early train from Parkersburg. They refuse to take the oath of allegiance and entertain private opinions on the present state of the country which they express publicly. Upon their arrival here Major Darr asked them if they were ready to take the oath and they said they were not. The whole party was immediately committed to jail. They were placed in one of the comfortable rooms in the lower floor, where they attracted considerable attention during the day. They seemed to be in the best of spirits in the morning, but towards evening some of them expressed their willingness to take the oath.

P.S.—Last evening the rebellious ladies concluded to take the oath and were released upon bail.

Wheeling Daily Intelligencer, August 20, 1862

DISLOYAL WOMEN LOCKED UP

Women found to be engaged in espionage or sabotage for the Confederacy were frequently confined in local jails.

The County Jail—Its Prisoners.—We yesterday visited the county jail and were shown through the establishment by the courteous jailor, Mr. Toliver.— The jail appears to be in pretty good condition in a sanitary point of view, and when the repairs which have been recommended are made it will be perfectly secure. There are now about thirty prisoners in the jail, most of whom are confined for offences against the ordinances of the city. . . .

There are three young women in the jail charged with treasonable practices. Miss Mary Jane Green, Miss Kate Brown and Miss Peck, of Marshall county. The two former, one of whom is quite a violent character, are from Braxton county and are charged with cutting the telegraph wires and carrying rebel letters. The latter, Miss Peck, is charged with uttering treasonable language and refuses to take the oath of allegiance. . . .

Wheeling Daily Intelligencer, November 12, 1862

A PROFANE CONFEDERATE WOMAN

Some women expressed support for their side in ways that challenged the social expectations of women's behavior. Union quartermaster Charles Lieb, who was stationed in western Virginia early in the war (but soon dismissed from service for alleged corruption), published a memoir in 1862 in which he described an impassioned and defiant young Confederate woman who was imprisoned for spying.

Among the prisoners sent to Clarksburg, was a young girl of seventeen, named Mary Jane Green. She resided in Braxton County, and, for a long time, was engaged in carrying a mail between Sutton, the county seat of that county, and the rebel camp on the Gauley. She was illiterate, perfectly fearless, and cordially hated the "Yankee vagabonds," as she termed the Federal troops. She was noted for her profanity, and when, with the rest of the family, she was arrested, cursed and swore like a professional blackleg, or horse racer, declaring she would have the heart's blood of every "Lincoln pup" in Western Virginia. The real cause of the war, and the effect of Secession, having been explained to her brother, he expressed a desire to be permitted to take the oath of allegiance, saying that he had been misled. Mary Jane became furious, forgot all sisterly affection she possessed, denounced him as a coward, and swore that he might take the oath, but that they could not made a d—d Abolitionist of her. When on her way to Clarksburg, in charge of Lieutenant George E. O'Neal, her language was such, he declared, as to almost disgust him with the sex. While confined in prison, she abused passers-by; shouted lustily for Jeff. Davis and the Southern Confederacy, and swore she would have the heart of General Rosecrans, if she were ever released. Kindness did not move, and affection was thrown away upon her. The Secession ladies, who are refined and intelligent, deeply sympathized with her, but permitted the Federal officers to provide her with decent apparel, which she accepted, although coming from those whom she regarded as her persecutors. The people residing in the neighborhood of the jail felt relieved when she was sent to Wheeling. Arrived there, she was taken to the principal hotel, and treated with great kindness; was neatly clad, and, on promising that she would try to do better, was released, and a home obtained for her in a respectable family; but falling in with some Secession friends, she became as bad as ever.

Charles Leib, *Nine Months in the Quartermaster's Department; or, The Chances for Making a Million* (Cincinnati: Moore, Wilstach, Keys, 1862), 95–96

UNION SOLDIERS SEARCH A PRO-CONFEDERATE HOME

Semantha Atkeson, a young woman with Confederate sympathies from present-day Buffalo, Putnam County, wrote in her journal of the day Union soldiers searched her home looking for firearms.

OCTOBER, 1861

What I have said is but a dim shadow of what happened, as I am writing in Oct. of as far back as May & I can't remember half that was nor tell half I remember, One more item of the past. At the beginning of the fruit drying season in Sept. Susie Fry who was here helping us and myself went over to the river to see a steam boat, which happened to be the "Glenwood", we waved at the Pilot who we both knew, we received contempt however & made three cheers "Jeff Davis", now this boat was one employed by the United States government to carry supplys to the army at Gauley; on our way home about a ¼ of a mile from the river, As we crossed the turnpike which runs in front of the house, at some distance from it though, I chanced to look up the road and saw some armed men coming down, and impelled by curiosity we stopped at the gate to see who it was; very soon here they come marching 2 abreast with only an attempt at order, all carrying guns some without locks, and all very rusty and dirty just some old things they had picked up around town; They came on up to the gate and just as they turned to come in it occurred to me to hold the gate, so I placed my hand on it fully determined that if they passed it should be over my dead body or that my hands should be unloosed by force but as they approached the gate my arm fell powerless by my side as if paralized every feeling was benumbed. I knew not why, but there seemed to be a voice saying it would all be well, for what resistance could I a lone weak woman make against 12 brutal men bent on the works of their master "the Devil". I felt it was best to let them take their course, for I knew they dare not lay one hand on me if I treated them with "silent" contempt which I tried to do. I stood gazing on vacantly until aroused by them passing so near me that they touched my robes and my olfactorys warned me of their close proximity by that peculiar odor emitted by very dirty men on a very warm sunny day; I looked at them until they all went through, then I said, "Where are you going?" and one of them said; "Oh just walking about." When I told them that I thought there was room enough in the public road for such a gang of lawless robbers as they, one of them said there was room enough in here too, I said no more but started to the house with Susie across the lawn, and arrived there before them, they having gone along the carriage way. We went in and calmly awaited the [soldiers], They came in at the side gate, surrounded the house, placing a guard of two or three men at each door, then two of them come in at the front door and proceed to search the house, they said for arms but in reality for Father and Dr. Brown. They were safely hid in the cornfield and three guns were among the rocks on "Arbuckle's creek," therefore we made no resistance but suffered them to search as much as they choose; They were the [most] ignorant, offscourings of the earth, I don't think that more than one of them could read, and I doubt very much if any of them could make an attempt at writing. They knew litterely nothing about searching a house; they only looked in the beds & of which they tumbled, as though that was the only place arms could be hid, they did not even look where they were usually kept. They might have been there as usual and they none the wiser for it, their place was in a corner of the library behind the doors there was considerable ammunition in the house but because we did not so proper to put it in the beds they overlooked it. We followed them around keeping our eyes steady fixed on them, which very much [disrupted] them. As they evidently had forgotten that commandment, which says "Thou Shalt Not Steal," they tride to evade us by going to different parts of the house at the same time, but there were indignant eyes on them, for a family of a mother and seven children, were not likely to let anything go unobserved. They did not search the wing of the building except one room beyond the kitchen, where mother kept her [washing] implements; They trembled from head to foot, their joints knocking together, and their limbs unable to support them, they toterd and reeled as a little child, clutching to the furniture as they past, it was only the trembling of the guilty before the innocent. They looked in a closet where lay on the floor a pistol, some dozen bullets, some powder and caps but they were dim, or something, else for they did not see it, and they opened another closet where there was some lead cut in bits in a basket, with a like result. They found a butcher knife in Dr. Brown's room which he used to cut medicen with and took it, one man cut his finger with it and then gave it back, they also stole some aples that they found in the garret. I was looking out to see if there was not some relief from some quarter, as "Jenking"[9] was said to be not far off where they took the apples, my survey was not wholy without its reward for it occurred to me that I would hallo hard for Jenkings which I did clapping my hands, and screaming at the top of my voice. I looked far across the valley at one window then toward a strip of wood at another at the same time calling on Jenkings to be quick as they were about leaving, talking to myself and some invisible power, then calling on sister to fasten the doors downstairs and keep the robers safe then on mother to send a messenger for them such a scatterment you never saw. Sister slammed and banged the doors mother called the boys, that the mob scattered, those upstairs came tumbling down, in the wildest confusion, their hair fairly raising their caps off their heads, those around the house looked in every direction, some of them started to run and were recalled by their capt. who by this time had got down two flights of stairs. We rushed madly down, taunting them with having stolen our apples, and telling that we had a lot more for Jenkings.

<small>Semantha Atkeson journal, Semantha Atkeson Papers, Series II, William L. Clements Library, Semantha Atkeson, Ann Arbor</small>

"REBEL BEAUX COULD NOT SHINE WITH THE UNION GIRL"

Sarah Frances Young lived in a strongly Unionist family along the Kanawha River near the present-day site of St. Albans. Her father, John Valley, was captain of the 11th West Virginia Infantry.

SEPT. 12, 1861

Oh little Journal, I have things to write that make my heart ache! Yesterday evening we heard of some Rebel soldiers in the neighborhood. Ma sent Ben to Coals Mouth immediately to tell Pa, if he had not heard it; but others had informed him and after dark Pa and three of his men pressed some "secesh" horses and borrowed one of Mr. Mynes, who is hiding from the Rebels, to come down in this neighborhood. They had been here but a short time before the men became sleepy, and Pa told them he would watch if they wished to sleep a little while. They all laid on the floor and I thought Pa looked tired. A young lady, Emilie, and myself, told him we would watch if he wanted to rest. He laid down and in the course of an hour we heard horses coming. We wakened Pa directly, and he and the men ran out through the back door, passed around the corner of the house, but seeing too many Rebels to attack they slipped down the hill back of the house into a ravine thickly set with alders. Two of the men ran on. One concealed himself along the fence to get a shot at them. Pa hid in a large bunch of alders. When the rogues stopped they found the horses tied, and asked us, very authoritatively, what those horses were doing here. Ma told them, as they answered her when she spoke to them, that it was an unfair question, and she would not tell them. I never in my life experienced such a time. They stayed around the house about two hours, scouting through the yard and listening; no doubt expecting Pa to come after their horses. I never felt so much like abusing men in my life. One rough, ill-bred fellow would not tell his name. I suppose he was ashamed of it. Burns, one of the set, told Ma his name was Dotson from Guyandotte. All the time they were here they could not move the horses. They were fastened in the back yard, and I reckon they thought Pa would come after them. While Pa was in the alder bush, a large, overgrown horse-thief came sneaking around him, and would stand listening within about ten steps of Pa. Pa said he fixed to shoot him, but he heard some more talking, and he thought he had better not. They came to the house and we talked with them some. Indeed, my heart ached so I could scarcely talk. Old Dotson said he thought he could get married somewhere on this road. I told him Rebel beaux could not shine with the Union girl, but Yankees went like hot cakes. He said, "I think I could make a Secesh out of you." I gave him to understand quite different. He said something about "homespun Yankees." I told him they were home-spun Rebels. He said "I would like to stay about a week and quarrel with you." After a while, the notorious horse thief, and blood-thirsty Rebel, Jim Nounan, came along and called for a candle to search the house. Emilie carried the candle and helped to search, laughing all the time at them. I told Nounan I would not tell him who came here, and if I knew where they were I would not tell him. He said it was immaterial with him, that he only asked for information. I told him he would get no information here. I think he was made, but I did not care. Dotson told us we would have to go to the North with our sweethearts or submit to Jeff Davis. I hope we will never live to see the time. Well, I suppose they got tired of searching and waiting. They bade us good night, wishing us good luck. Em told them when gentlemen called on us we wanted them to come at a fashionable hour, and not scare us to death in the night. I told them I was not glad to see them, and did not wish them any good luck at all. And I don't.

<small>Sarah Frances Young diary, pp. 13–15, Roy Bird Cook Collection, West Virginia and Regional History Center, West Virginia University, Morgantown</small>

"I DREW OUT MY PISTOL AND SHOT HIM"

Maria Isabella "Belle" Boyd was born in Martinsburg in the Shenandoah Valley and turned seventeen years old the year the war broke out. She operated as a spy for Confederate forces, and Stonewall Jackson credited her with providing intelligence that helped the Confederacy win victories in the 1862 Valley Campaign. Imprisoned multiple times, she quickly emerged as the most famous female spy of the war. Fleeing to London in 1864, she published her memoir a year later, accelerating her fame.

THE morning of the 4th of July dawned brightly. . . .

The Yankees were in undisputed possession of Martinsburg; the village was at their mercy, and consequently entitled to their forbearance; and it would at least have been more dignified in them had they been content to enjoy their almost bloodless conquest with moderation; but, whatever might have been the intentions of the officers, they had not the inclination, or they lacked the authority, to control the turbulence of their men.

The severance of the North from the South had now become in feeling so complete, that we Martinsburg girls saw the Union flag streaming from the windows of the houses with emotions akin to those with which the ladies of England would gaze upon the tricolour of France or the eagle of Russia floating above the keep of Windsor Castle. Those hateful strains of "Yankee Doodle" resounded in every street, with an accompaniment of cheers, shouts, and imprecations.

Whisky now began to flow freely; for, amid the motley crowd of Americans, Dutchmen, and other nations, the Irish element predominated. The sprigs of shillelahs were soon at work, and the "sons of Erin" proved that they could use their sticks with no less effect in an American town than at an Irish fair. They set at defiance the authority of those among their officers who vainly interposed to quell the tumult and restrain the lawless violence that was offered to defenceless citizens and women.

The doors of our houses were dashed in; our rooms were forcibly entered by soldiers who might literally be termed "mad drunk," for I can think of no other expression so applicable to their condition. Glass and fragile property of all kinds was wantonly destroyed. They found our homes scenes of comfort, in some cases even of luxury; they left them mere wrecks, utterly despoiled and mutilated. Shots were fired through the windows; chairs and tables were hurled into the street. . . .

Shall I be ashamed to confess that I recall without one shadow of remorse the act by which I saved my mother from insult, perhaps from death—that the blood I then shed has left no stain on my soul, imposed no burden upon my conscience?

The encounter to which I refer was brought about as follows:—A party of soldiers, conspicuous, even on that day, for violence, broke into our house and commenced their depredations; this occupation, however, they presently discontinued, for the purpose of hunting for "rebel flags," with which they had been informed my room was decorated. Fortunately for us, although without my orders, my negro maid promptly rushed up-stairs, tore down the obnoxious emblem, and, before our enemies could get possession of it, burned it.

They had brought with them a large Federal flag, which they were now preparing to hoist over our roof in token of our submission to their authority; but to this my mother would not consent. Stepping forward with a firm step, she said, very quietly, but resolutely, "Men, every member of my household will die before that flag shall be raised over us."

Upon this, one of the soldiers, thrusting himself forward, addressed my mother and myself in language as offensive as it is possible to conceive. I could stand it no longer; my indignation was roused beyond control; my blood was literally boiling in my veins; I drew out my pistol and shot him. He was carried away mortally wounded, and soon after expired.

<small>Belle Boyd in Camp and Prison, Written by Herself (New York: Blelock, 1865), 62–68</small>

THE BUSTLE

Wellsburg native Henry Johnson signed up to fight to restore the Union in 1861. He regarded those from his town who sided with the Confederacy to be contemptible traitors but also had very harsh words for abolitionists in the first years of the war. Johnson was fond of the company of loyal Union women, calling on then whenever he could. Here in a letter to his sister Clara, he describes the efforts by some West Virginia Union women to protect the American flag from marauding Confederates by hiding it in the bustle of their hooped skirts. The bustle was a protrusion at the back of the skirt intended to fill out the woman's derriere. Despite his early hostility to abolition, the letter also reveals his changing views on Lincoln's emancipation policy.

North Mountain Va

Dear Clara:

Your letter of 11th inst. came to hand yesterday. I answer at the earliest opportunity.... Our camp is but five minutes' walk from the station, where reside the Misses Cookus. There are four of the young ladies.... They are real heroines; will do anything for our soldiers or anything against the rebels. When "the rebellion" was here they concealed the American flag by rolling it into a "bustle" and wearing it about town when the soldiers came to search the homes for it.... We remember this plan well when we went down here last spring, and the aforesaid American flag was flying from the window. The young ladies were rather bashful when telling me about their artifice in hiding the flag. They said when the rebels came there their father and brother had to leave and they were compelled to take in their flag. When arose the question, "What shall we do with it?" one suggested that they make a skirt of it, another a pillow, finally a bustle. The latter plan was adopted, and one night, in their room, when all was quiet they waistformed the American flag into a "bustle." They then took it town about watching for the rebel soldiers. When the watch would see them coming she would raise the alarm, and—well the "bustle flag" or "flag-bustle" would—disappear to a safe hiding place to be brought out only when the danger was removed. At one time a Miss Austin, a visitor, a young lady of here also seen, wore it for 3 days + mighty fearful to take it off lest it would be captured. They know here what war is. . . . I am sorry you and Ruth had such an experience with the contraband. I do not think it was owing to the proclamation. I am in for the proclamation "heart + soul," and you know what my sentiment were at home. . . .

With love,
Yours truly,
Henry

Henry Johnson to Clara Johnson, January 14, 1863, Henry Johnson Papers, William L. Clements Library, University of Michigan, Ann Arbor

"ABE'S SAGACIOUS GRIMALKINS"

Buckhannon resident and loyal Unionist Marcia Phillips described several tense days in April 1863 when she was left to guard the family home and property in advance of Confederate brigadier general John Imboden's occupation of the town. Phillip's husband, Sylvester, a captain of a Union regiment, fled along with virtually all of the town's Union men before Imboden's troops arrived.

April 28th, Tuesday. When I opened my eyes this morning, the memory of yesterday seemed like some hideous nightmare, but when I went out and looked around, the desolate appearance of everything, brought back the memory of our defenseless condition, and I burst into a flood of tears. The suspense that we are living in, is dreadful. It is exhausting to soul and body. Everything seems so forsaken and still. The tavern bells and gong have not rung, for there are no boarders to call. Not more than a dozen men remain at home, the rest flying with our retreating army. Heavner's hotel looks so lonely,—all gone but Mr. Heavner, Kate, Ellen and her two children, and Deliliah. I never knew the meaning of loneliness, before.

The Secesh ladies have promenaded the streets in droves all day, and their insolent and triumphant looks have shown plainly that something was on hand....

Just before dark, the dreaded invaders made their appearance. One company of cavalry came in and rode slowly up Maine Street, looking on all sides, fearfully, as if expecting to be fired upon, glancing furtively at every house, as if suspicious that every wall, concealed a masked battery....

I did not dare to go to sleep till very late, and did not undress at all. I put both children in my bed and then towards morning lay down by the fire, which I kept burning all night.

Wednesday, 29th, April. I was awakened by a noise in the street, and going to the window, discovered it to be the Secesh Cavalry galloping up the street. Soon a Regiment of Infantry marched in. I now began to realize the horror of our situation. Crowds of hateful Secesh women are promenading the streets, arm in arm with the dirty scoundrels, and taunting and sneering at every Union person that is visible. I told the children not to go out of the house on any account—Lenny especially, for he was so choked up as to be hardly able to speak above a whisper. I told him that if he became worse and died, there would be hardly friends enough here to bury him. "Mother," he whispered, "I reckon I can go to Heaven just as well, if I am not buried." The child's faith gave me the courage and strength that I needed, and encouragement. I left them upstairs and went below to my work. As I stood on the porch, I heard one of the Secesh women before mentioned, telling some of the Rebels that that was where Capt. Phillips' lived and three of them came through the gate where I was, and accosted me with—"Got any pies to sell?" "No," was my reply....

Soon another one came up to the porch, begging for a little piece of bread, which I gave him. He said his name was "Boggs" of Webster Co. and that my husband's men had shot at him many a time, when they were scouting that county....

... One of them pointed out to me, General Imboden, sitting on his horse by Heavner's sign post. I said to one of them that I should like to [see] the General, for I felt and thought to myself, that I could not stand the suspense. That if they were going to annoy and run over citizens and pillage, and burn, I wanted to know it at once. The soldier went to the General and told him that a lady wanted to see him. He came in accompanied by an old man in a Major's uniform, who introduced himself as Dr Bland, formerly of Weston; then introduced me to General Imboden. I cannot call to mind how our conversation commenced, but I remember of telling him that I was a Union woman, and of the stand my husband had taken.... He told me he had caused my house to be searched, as he wished to take all the Government property that has been left here. Dr. Bland said he was sorry to hear me express myself in favor of the Union. I replied, "I wish to God that you were *all* for the Union." General Imboden then told me that I had a perfect right to my opinion and that I should not be disturbed on account of my principles. Said he, "We do not come to make war upon women and children, or to destroy or burn. I have been sickened at the destruction your Federal army has made in Eastern Virginia. At one fine old family mansion, they have destroyed the rich furniture, some of it a hundred years old, and split to pieces, even splendid pianos thrown out of doors, and used as feed troughs for the Cavalry horses." I thought to myself, "Did they not bring it upon themselves?" but refrained from saying it, for I was in their power, and did not want to incense them too much.

When they rose to leave, the General told me I should be protected; that not a soldier, should enter my house unless invited. The property, cartridge boxes etc., that they took from me had been left on the Portico, and a sentinel placed there and the General gave him orders to admit no soldiers into the house.

In the course of our conversation "Western Virginia" came up. I told the General that I loved West Virginia and hoped that I could make it my home, while I lived, and that I hoped and prayed it might remain in the Union. He replied, "We will not yield one inch of Virginia soil!" I replied, "We do not know yet, how it will terminate." Said he, "Madam, I know how it will terminate. As sure as there is a sun in the heavens, we must, and will hold Western Virginia."

My guard was a grim, surly looking rebel, but he did his duty manfully, and not one of the many who tried coming in would he admit. When they made the attempt to enter, he would draw his gun up to a "charge bayonet" and sternly tell them "You can't come in here. General ordered this house protected and I'm going to protect it." . . .

Just before night, the Rebels mostly left town, and went into camp across the river. They marched out to the tune of "Rio Grande" with their hateful accursed flags flapping defiance and triumph at the dispairing Union people in this God forsaken town.

It was a relief to me to see them going out. Just at dark a heavy rain and thunder storm came on, which added to the loneliness and the gloom. . . .

I will watch for a few nights and see if my Southern brethern can be depended upon, before putting myself in their power, so much as to go to sleep. I guess they are watching too, for I hear them now and then tramping along on the pavement under my windows. They are a little "dubious" about matters and things and don't know how far off, or how near, the "Yanks" may be. "Jeff's mice" are a little suspicious of "Abe's sagacious Grimalkins."[10] An idea of great brilliancy has just occurred to me,—wonder if this is not a good opportunity to decide the question how long anyone can live without sleep.

    Marcia Louise Sumner Phillips journal, pp. 136–49, Collection Number A&M 1846, West Virginia and Regional History Center, West Virginia University, Morgantown

A CONFEDERATE WOMAN IN BARBOUR COUNTY

Samuel Woods was a successful lawyer in Philippi, Barbour County, before the war. Elected as a representative to the 1861 Virginia Convention, he had spoken passionately in favor of secession, drawing the applause and admiration of eastern secessionists (see chapter 2). During the war Woods served in the Stonewall Brigade, leaving his wife, Isabelle, and his children behind in Barbour County, which was under the control of the Union army for the duration of the war. Isabelle managed the family affairs and business dealings as best she could while fending off legal challenges to her property because of her husband's disloyalty. While the Woods family owned no property in enslaved people, Isabelle depended upon hired labor, and leased enslaved workers, to care for their two homes, one in town and another in the country. The country house was destroyed by fire in 1862, possibly set by locals who viewed her husband as a traitor. As you can see in these letters, Isabelle's commitment to the Confederate cause was not as strong as her husband's. She eventually fled western Virginia with her children and reunited with her husband. After the war, the Woods returned to Barbour County and Samuel quickly regained his political prominence, serving as a judge and participating in the 1872 state constitutional convention.

ISABELLA WOODS TO SAMUEL WOODS

Guineau, January 3, 1862.

My dear husband:

I wrote and sent off a letter to you last week, but hearing it was still in this county, and would be until tomorrow, I have concluded to send another, and let you know I've heard from you since. . . .

[Spencer Dayton] is determined to beggar you if possible. He took the lumber we had in the wood house and your broken safe and set them up for sale. . . . Since I wrote last I received ten summons for you to appear at January court. . . . I don't know what I can do about it. The "stay law" of Wheeling does not protect the property of "rebels". I tried to engage Martin to attend to your business, but he refused. Secessionists don't attend the courts or observe their laws at all. I sometimes feel tempted to employ Taft (he and Dayton hate each other), but he abused you so much I can't bear to approach him. I will consult some of your friends and do the best I can. They can't get any personal property, all is sold; and they cannot run away with the land. Mr. Martin does not think anything can be done until March. . . .

I felt very badly at parting with Tilda,[11] but get along better than I expected to. Frank makes the fires in the morning and when it is very cold Mr. T. or Draper puts on big back-logs. Mary and Bell help me very much, too. I couldn't manage to keep Tilda. John Cole has resigned acting as agent for his sister, and she is left to the control of her mistress, and, of course, Robinsons have got Tilda on the same terms they had her when we got her. I offered to pay all that was due and give good security for the time I might have her this year, but they said no one in the county could hire her until times were better. They hinted at security for $1000, but I wouldn't give that if I could. If the Federal troops keep possession of this county much longer, there won't be a slave left. If the soldiers have ravaged our town they have left a great deal of money in the county. Jane has fared well by them.

. . . The children were delighted with the letter. I can truly say they are good children, and great company and comfort for me. Hop has been at Alice Johnson's for two days and I miss him very much. Sam Holt is down here. He likes to stay with Hop.

I feel so much better since I heard from you. I did not get a letter from the 16th of September until the 1st of January.

Bell N. Woods.

* * *

ISABELLA WOODS TO SAMUEL WOODS

Philippa, Feb. 19, 1862.

Dear Sam:

I'm living in our house in town again after an absence of eight months, but it does not look or seem like my old home. I feel as if I were living in a deserted village among strangers and enemies, friendless and almost homeless, but God has been a friend in days when I didn't trust Him and I don't believe He'll forsake me now when I lean upon Him and Him alone.

I have often wished I could meet you if only long enough to tell you how I've suffered since we parted. I have often wished, too, you had never left home. You would have been imprisoned, but been released before this, and we might have had a peaceful year of domestic happiness, and malicious Union people would not have been gratified at seeing all we had destroyed and scattered.

On the night of the 8th of February Trimble's house was burned to ashes, and everything valuable I had in it,—my carpets, dishes, best bed clothes, and the big box I kept upstairs packed full of everything I valued most; my jewelry, twelve dresses and dress patterns, window curtains, parlor chairs, all my fine night clothes and underclothes, the family Bible and pictures, our letters, books I valued most, and many other things I can't think of now. They were put there when I first moved. I felt unsettled and let them remain. Many think the house was set on fire, but I doubt it. Mr. and Mrs. Trimble were from home. The children were aroused from sleep from the roaring of flames. They saved only a few bed clothes and feather beds. Many persons have given to them and they are comfortable again. I went up in the night and took the children to my house and moved to town. The corn crib was saved (the meat and corn). Trimble talks of building where the old house stood, but I will not give a cent to help. I haven't collected all my money yet, but feel that it is safe. The things you desired me to take to Cass' house had been removed but a few hours before it was burned. That has, in some degree, reconciled me to my loss. If I had only saved *that box* I wouldn't care so much for the other things. Indeed I would rather they were in ashes than that they should be set up at public sale. Next court Strickler's and Reger's furniture is all to be sold for debt they say.

You have been sued more than a dozen times since the first of January, '62. Kincaid has sued for his claims on this house. I don't know how long they will let me have it, but they will have trouble to get me out. Campbells lived in it all winter to take care of it, and they had no place to go, so I gave them the upper story and your office. I have room enough and feel better to have a family in the house with me. Of course, there will be much that is unpleasant, but I do not expect to be content or happy.

I wrote I had lost Tilda. Martha Johnson has been staying with me for a few days.

Atherton, the constable, says Trimble is a richer man than you are. He owns the best part of that farm, and would like to get his deed, but doesn't believe I'd let him have it—wonders if it was burned. Alf Wilson has been at Campbells to learn if they heard me say your papers were destroyed.

I wrote to you that Trimble's wagon and buggy had been found and taken off by the soldiers. I would make an effort to get the buggy but it would be executed for debt. Jane got a long letter mailed in Meadville, and I got several through the mountains. The children got theirs. I wish you would set down their ages and preserve it. I'll get their pictures again.

I haven't seen Nes Hardin since I showed him your account, nor John Williamson since you left home. Frank Snodgrass wouldn't settle with me. He'll stay as long as he pleases. . . .

I was glad to see a postage stamp of the Confederate states. I kept it and sent five cents.

Lynch's house is published for sale, and Reger's. Henry Barron lives in his house. John Thompson keeps store in Holt's house, pays rent to Jane. McClaskie keeps store too. Goods sell high, all cash,—unbleached cotton and calico 20 and 25 cents a yard; everything at the same rates. I have sold them my corn, and if I can get it brought up I will get goods for it. I got $35 for hay, all I'll get, and it will pay for the expense of curing it. Benjamin Wilson wrote to me he had been driven from his office for nine months, and confined to bed for two, but he was better and hoped soon to let me have some money. Sarah Jane sent me $100. I'll return it the first opportunity. I thought it was your money when I got it. . . .

There is one company of soldiers in town, but they are civil men. March court there will be a great time selling "sesesh" property. Auvil's books and bedsteads were sold last court. God grant that these days are almost past. May He protect and defend you.

* * *

ISABELLA WOODS TO SAMUEL WOODS

Philippa, May 16, 1862

My dear husband:

I have just received your letters dated April 2nd and 3rd, the first I had since the one you wrote me just before leaving Richmond. I got one from Porterfield after the retreat from Romney, and one from Mrs. Neal after the retreat from Winchester. Before receiving your letter I had been trying to go to you, but intended leaving the children and returning as soon as possible. The reason will suggest itself to you. I wrote to Pierpont asking his assistance. He replied that there were no passes given now, that W. G. Brown had gone in person to the Secretary of War to get a pass for Sarah Jane and was refused. I wrote to Carlyle, but have had no answer yet. I have a friend who has promised to get W. T. Wiley to use his influence, but have little hope of success. When I heard of the retreat from the mountains I hired a man and sent him to Bowman to buy me a horse, but couldn't get it until he planted his corn, and before I had time to get another, the northern army again had possession of Monterey. I will still keep trying and may yet succeed. I intend next to appeal to the Union men of this town (the highest officer I ever see is the Captain), but I must tell you that for the first time in my life I want to *live here,* and have you *come home,* and outlive the odium that some malicious persons have tried to blast you with, and hinder them from fattening upon our substance. Where do you expect to make a final and successful stand? The Yankees say in the Gulf of Mexico, and I must confess

I very much fear it will not be in Virginia. I know how reluctantly you will leave this state, particularly if I cannot get to you. I have been talking to some of your friends—Union men, so-called. They think you might remain safely where you are. If you should ever be arrested, the charge of "treason" cannot be *lawfully* sustained against you. The only evidence is a letter you wrote Dan Auvil which Dayton carries around, and that was written *before* the Ordinance of Secession was passed, and therefore cannot convict.

I think from what I hear there will be some proposition to the men from the west of Virginia. I hope you may all be united, and determine calmly and cooly not to be driven from your families, your home and property, perhaps, forever. After I was told the conscription law was enforced in the E. S. I felt very uneasy. You must keep your promise to me. I have no hope of the South conquering without foreign intervention. . . .

My dear husband, I found *One Friend,* that friend that sticketh closer than a brother. He has always been near, and when I remember He is your friend too, I enjoy that "peace" of mind that passeth all understanding, and my constant prayer is that He will yet unite us. . . .

I will write other letters and send to different points, hoping you may get one.

Your wife,

B. N. Woods.

R. W. Dayton, ed., *Samuel Woods and His Family* (n.p., 1939), 60–72.

QUARTERING TROOPS

It was not just enemy soldiers who disrupted the lives of West Virginia women during the war. Supposedly friendly forces often depended upon locals to house soldiers, and these uninvited guests were sometimes a great imposition upon the women required to board them.

February 3rd, 1863

By Telegraph from Gauley to Capt Botsford, AAG

There are some cavalry men of Harrison County quartered in the house who make me very miserable. They are ruining the house & they are burning all my coal & have treated me very meanly. Will you please see Genl Scammon & have them moved way somewhere else. Please answer & Oblige very much. Yours truly

Jane T. Hale to James L. Botsford, February 3, 1863,
Collection of Eliakim P. Scammon, 23rd Regiment, Ohio, Infantry,
Gilder Lehrman Institute Collections, New York

A UNION WOMAN TRAVELS THROUGH WEST VIRGINIA

New Hampshire–born Eliza Ann Otis was an avowed enemy of slavery before the war began, revealing in her journal in 1860 that she was a fiercely partisan Republican in the upcoming presidential contest and declaring that "there is an 'irrepressible conflict' waging, a conflict between the mighty hosts of evil, and the opposing battalions of freedom and of right."[12] Her husband, Harrison Gray Otis, shared her passion for the causes of union and antislavery. He enlisted as a private at the outset of the war and had been promoted to major by war's end. In 1863, Eliza traveled through the Kanawha Valley to visit her husband, who was encamped at Gauley Bridge. Her journal reveals that she found the scenery on her journey through the Kanawha Valley awe-inspiring, but she was less enamored of some of the people who occupied this landscape.

SEPTEMBER 1, 1863

. . . We rode on while those giant hills seemed to have closed all about us. I never saw a view quite like it before. One wouldn't think there could be an opening found any where. Behind and before us, on our right hand and on our left, they looked as if they had joined hands. . . .

There were a few fine old residences scattered along the Valley on either bank of the river. Some times where there is a rich sweep of meadow land, and the mountains have fallen back from the stream these homesteads peep out from behind giant poplars, or the dark sighing cypress, or rich holly with a cheerful well-to-do air that is not the least in the world in sympathy with War or its desolation. The sun shines on them as brightly as ever, and the rich harvests come to them, and the pampered, selfish souls which they shelter are at ease, caring nothing for a Nation's peril—sympathizing only with its foes.

Meeting a little girl with a bright, sunny face, and a look of intelligence that interested me, we stopped for a few words with her.

Simple, artless and frank, as childhood always is in its perfect trust, the child amused us with her innocent prattle—her confidential story of a baby brother, whose rosy, dimpled feet, so wonderful in her loving eyes, were just beginning to walk. "It was so funny"—it made her and darling mama—the prettiest and "goodest" mama the world ever saw laugh so to see baby brother toddle along. She wishes we could see him too. "And where do you live, little one?" "O over there where those great trees are—don't you see?"

"Yes, and you have a pretty home, have you not? And you are a good little Union girl and your papa and mama, are they Union, too?"

The great blue eyes looked up into our own—and over the pretty face that looked so innocent of all guile came a half smiling, half serious look as she answered, "O we'se Union when the Union soldiers is here, and we'se Secesh when the Secesh soldiers came."

"Isn't there an ample commentary in that simple reply on the loyalty of the people in this Valley?" said I to my friend as we rode onward.

"Yes, Loyalty here is generally a thing of policy rather than principle. It's an outgrowth from the pocket, an execrescense that is tolerated, that isn't lopped off, because it is balanced by dollars and cents."

"There's a deep undercurrent of hatred to our Cause flowing as steadily and surely through this Valley as the waters of the Kanawha flow—moving along often without a ripple on the surface, but daily upheaving."

<small>Architects of Our Fortunes: The Journal of Eliza A. W. Otis, 1860–1863, with Letters and Civil War Journal of Harrison Gray Otis, ed. Ann Gorman Condon (San Marino, CA: Huntington Library, 2001), 218–20.</small>

"A SPY SENT FROM PRINCETON"

Because of legal proscriptions and social expectations regarding their treatment by military authorities, women were particularly effective conveyors of information for both sides. A young woman from Princeton revealed how lucrative operating as a spy could be.

By Telegraph from Gauley, April 13, 1863

To Genl Scammon

That youngest girl that was caught at Fayette with woman's clothes on told a woman at the 91st hospital that she was a spy sent from Princeton—got 100 dollars every trip & this was the fourth one & that she was here about 2 weeks ago & the secesh gave 30 dollars when she left Princeton this time.

A A Sloane

Co. D 34th O.V.I.

"AN IDEAL SPECIMEN OF THE 'FEMALE SOUTHERN CONFEDERACY'"

Women were also frequently called upon to search suspected female spies. Unionist Marcia Phillips recounts being called upon to search and question a woman suspected of spying for the Confederacy.

WEDNESDAY, JUNE 10TH, 1863

Nothing special from the stampede of last night. I think it must have been a gang of Bushwhackers, trying to slip in after horses and plunder. Kate H. was here this afternoon and while we were chatting, Mr. Poundstone came and told us the soldiers had just arrested a female spy, and he wanted Kate, Ellen, Mrs. Gibson and I to go and search her. He said he wanted me to give her a real *talking-to*. Well we went and searched her but found nothing, as she had been running about town a long time before she was arrested, and had probably dealt out her rebel mail. She was an ideal specimen of the "female Southern Confederacy" that we read of in Orpheus C. Kerr.[13] She raved and foamed and said she expected to be shining in glory while we were burning in hell, and many other elegant and refined remarks. She ran over the usual formula about "Nigger war, Black republicans, Lincoln hirelings, &&." I told her crazy talk would get her into serious trouble and if those were indeed her sentiments, she had better leave and go to Dixie at once. We had a long talk, but to no avail. There are none so blind as those who *will not see*.

_{Marcia Louise Sumner Phillips journal, pp. 158–59, Collection Number A&M 1846, West Virginia and Regional History Center, West Virginia University, Morgantown}

"BOGUS SOLDIERS"

Some women disguised themselves as men to experience the war as soldiers. Most of those soldiers discovered to have female genitalia were arrested, confined, and questioned about their allegiances. Because their actions were viewed as deceptive, they were often assumed to be guilty of other crimes like prostitution or spying. Little is known about the persons who called themselves James Johnson and Frank Glenn in the brief report below or about their motivations.

Office of the Provost Marshall.
Military District of Harper's Ferry, Va. Sept 12th 1864

St. Col. John Wooley
Prov. Mar. Mid. Dept. 8th A.C.
Colonel,

>I have the honor to forward to you, under guard
Two (2) Female Prisoners, Bogus Soldiers <u>entitled</u>
Kate alias James Johnson, and Eliza Frances alias Frank Glenn.
They were arrested for loitering about the camps dressed in the U.S.

uniform, & claiming to belong to Co. "K," 1st W. Va. Cav. It is reported that they have another companion if not several, of the same "persuasion" who will be "gobbled" as speedily as possible by the military authorities—I would respectfully recommend that you make a levy on some of the generous feminines of Baltimore, for a proper suit of wearing apparel, for the benefit of these wayward damsels.

Very respectfully,

Your Obdt Servt

A Pratt

Capt. & Prov. Marshal

Alonzo D. Pratt to John Wooley, September 12, 1864, Mss2P8882a1, E. Claiborne Robins Jr. Library Collections, Virginia Museum of History and Culture, Richmond

"IN THE SHAPE OF A FEMALE"

Harry Fitzallen enlisted in at least three separate Union infantry regiments—the 23rd Kentucky, the 92nd Ohio, and the 8th Ohio, as well as one West Virginia cavalry unit—before being arrested and accused of serving the Confederacy, a charge Fitzallen denied.[14]

Office of Provost-Marshall-General,
Wheeling, December 24, 1862.
Col. W. Hoffman, *Commissary-General of Prisoners.*

Sir: I have the honor specially to report the receipt of a prisoner of war sent here by Brigadier-General Crook in the shape of a female wearing male apparel charged as a spy for the rebels, arrested in the streets of Charleston, Va. Her statements are contradictory, at one time asserting she was in the rebel army, at another time affirming she served with the Twenty-third Kentucky Volunteer Infantry, U.S. Army. She is a course-looking creature, scarcely answering the description of *la fille du regiment.* I have placed her in the Ohio County jail for the present, ordered clothes for her suitable to her sex, and await your order regarding her.

Very respectfully,

Jos. Darr, Jr.

Major and Provost-Marshal-General.

* * *

Respectfully referred to Colonel Doster, provost-marshal, to know if he can provide for the within-named woman in the Old Capitol Prison if she is ordered to this city. Please return this letter.

W. Hoffman,

Colonel Third Infantry, Commissary-General of Prisoners.

[Inclosure.]

* * *

A FEMALE SOLDIER IN CUSTODY—AN EVENTFUL CAREER.

Among the prisoners brought up yesterday on the steamer Bostona, No. 2, was the somewhat famous female soldier, Harry Fitzallen, of whom our readers have doubtless heard something through the Cincinnati papers. Harry, who was dressed in a tightly-fitting cavalry uniform, was taken to jail yesterday soon after his arrival, when the provost-marshall, Major Darr, with a view of ascertaining if possible the truth in relation to the charge that has been made against Harry of being a rebel spy, held in an interview with her.—During the conversation she said her name was Marian MCKinziey. She was born in Glasgow, Scotland. Her mother died when she was an infant and her father removed with her to this country, when she was only four years old. Her father dying a short time after reaching New York[,] Marian was left alone upon the world and managed to make her living in various ways, as she expressed it. She educated herself and studied for the stage but finding the profession of actress not exactly suited to her taste she traveled about from place to place engaging in divers employments. Shortly after the breaking out of the war she enlisted in a Kentucky regiment at Newport and served two months. Upon her sex being discovered she had to quit. She enlisted several times after this in as many different regiments and was several times arrested. The last time she was arrested in Charleston, Kanawha County, in men's apparel, by the provost-marshal. She says that she has brothers and sisters residing in Canada. Upon being asked what part of Canada her relations inhabited she declined to answer, saying: "This sensation will have publicity enough if it has not already and I do not wish the innocent to suffer for the guilty." When told that she would be detained until her statements could be corroborated she said. "Very well. I cannot help it. The only way in which I have violated the law is in assuming men's apparel. The injury that I have done is principally to myself."

She speaks fluently and uses the best of language, and is evidently an educated woman, well skilled in the iniquities of the world. She visited this city about three years ago, under the name of Miss Fitzallen, and in the character of a prostitute. She says she went into the army for the love of excitement and from no motive in connection with the war, one way or another. She is about twenty-five years of age, and very short and very thick. She has heretofore acknowledged that she has been engaged in the rebel service but now denies the soft impeachment. As there are several suspicious circumstances connected with the case Harry will be furnished with appropriate clothing and detained until all doubts are removed.

<small>Official Records of the War of the Rebellion, ser. 2, vol. 5 (Washington, D.C.: Government Printing Office, 1899), 121–22</small>

"WANTS HOOPS"

When women were arrested clad in a soldier's uniform, male officials acted quickly to provide them with gender-specific clothing and encourage them to wear it. On a few occasions, the arrested soldiers rejected the women's clothing.

WANTS HOOPS

Harry Fitsallen, of whose arrest we gave some account not long ago, and who is still confined in jail, refuses to wear the women's clothing purchased for her by the Provost Marshal, but clings to the cavalry pea-jacket and pantaloons in which she soldiered through the Kanawha Valley. The reason assigned is that she is not provided with hoops.

Another female prisoner, Mary Jane Green, the gentle maiden from Braxton county, is also very much put out on the same account, and both girls are very rebellious.

<small>Wheeling Daily Intelligencer, January 20, 1863</small>

* * *

ANOTHER LOT OF PRISONERS—"A WOMAN IN THE CASE."—Yesterday seventeen rebel prisoners arrived in the city and were placed in charge of the Provost Marshal, Major Darr. . . .

There also arrived on the boat another female cavalry soldier who was sent to the county jail for safe keeping. Major Darr had an interview with the woman yesterday afternoon when she gave him something like the following account of herself: Her name is Mary Jane Prater and she is only seventeen years of age.

She was born in Tennessee, but came to Cincinnati when she was "a little bit of a chap" and has since been residing with her aunt, a Miss Prater, who keeps a Millinery establishment at the corner of Smith and Fifth streets, Cincinnati. She left Cincinnati about three months ago and went to Gallipolis, where she met a couple of soldiers belonging to the 2nd Virginia Cavalry, named Emerson Sears and Benj. Fortney, who persuaded her to put on soldier's clothes and enlist in their company. She took the advice of the soldiers and went with the company up to Charleston where she was arrested and has since been confined in jails and guard houses. Upon being asked something in relation to the streets of Cincinnati she hesitated to answer, saying that she had lost all her senses in guard houses and jails. Maj. Darr asked her if she would wear female apparel without hoops. (This question was asked in view of the late mutiny upon this account among the female prisoners) Miss Prater said she didn't know. She would see how she looked first. She was inclined to be sportive in her manner, and considering all things was very much unconcerned. She is evidently well versed in the wickedness of the world for one so young. She will probably be sent to a house of refuge.

Wheeling Daily Intelligencer, January 23, 1863

SEVEN

Enduring a Long War

$\mathcal{D}$AVID SHAFER of Preston County enlisted in the 7th Virginia Infantry, a Union regiment organized in the fall of 1861. "The Bloody Seventh," as it came to be known, was composed of men from the Northern Panhandle and Monongahela Valley counties of Virginia, as well as from several bordering Union states. Renamed the 7th West Virginia after statehood was achieved, it participated in some of the war's deadliest battles, including Antietam, Fredericksburg, Chancellorsville, Gettysburg, and Grant's 1864 Overland Campaign. In a letter Shafer penned to Lydia Bishoff, a friend back home, just weeks after the war's bloodiest battle, Antietam, he wrote of his sorrow that Preston County soldier John Foglesong, her cousin and his friend, had been killed in the battle. He expressed his longing to come home but did not know when he might be able to get back to Preston. "I would like to be there with you and to go to the apple cuttings. . . . There is no place like old Preston, that is the place for me and shall be as long as I live." In a second letter to Bishoff just a few weeks later, Shafer shared his views on Lincoln's Emancipation Proclamation, which had been announced in the wake of the Union victory at Antietam. "There is quite a stir among the soldiers here," Shafer wrote. "They don't like old ab[e]s procklamation. I don't like it so durned well my self, for if they go to free the dam black cusses I shall go, with good many more, for I shall not fite for the black cusses."[1]

Shafer was not alone in his hostility to Lincoln's Emancipation Proclamation. Many other Union soldiers shared this sentiment in the fall and winter of 1862–63. Anti-emancipation feelings spiked, and so did desertion rates, in the Union army that winter. It was not just the perception that the goals of the war had changed. Hard marching, exposure to harsh conditions, and a series of costly battles increased soldier homesickness and made many question why they were still fighting. Desertion rates in the Confederate army also escalated during this hard and bloody winter. Military historians have examined the question of soldier persistence in war. Why did some stay in the fight, and why did some desert? James McPherson examined ideological motivations of Civil War soldiers by reviewing the private letters of hundreds of soldiers. He found that for most Confederate soldiers, support for the institution of slavery was not debated, and they saw themselves fighting for freedom from Northern tyranny. For Union soldiers the belief in the sacredness of the Union was the most common political sentiment they shared. The issue of slavery, on the other hand, divided Union soldiers. Nevertheless, across the four years of war McPherson found that of those Northern soldiers who expressed views on slavery in their letters, more than twice as many supported the emancipation policy as opposed it. But his study surveyed letters from soldiers across the Union and probably did not reflect the views of western Virginia's Union soldiers, who came from counties where slavery was present before the war.[2]

Political viewpoints may not have been what drove soldier persistence, for either North or South. Many historians have emphasized the nonideological reasons soldiers continued to fight, including masculine identity, concerns about their reputations back home, or loyalty to their closest comrades.[3] Soldiers wrote home to tell their loved ones about the hard marching, the exposure to the elements, and the terribleness of battle and frequently expressed their homesickness. Long periods in camp between engagements provoked boredom, and to pass the time, they sang and made up songs, played pranks on each other, and engaged in other distractions.

Back in western Virginia, civilians were adjusting to new political realities and continued to cope with the indignities of war. With military occupation came infringement on personal liberties. Hungry armies taxed the resources of the communities they occupied. Civilians lived with the fear of raids from regular or irregular units from either side. They despaired as they read regular news reports of the local men wounded or killed in battle. Some western Virginians opposed independent statehood, or one of the conditions that came with it—the end of slavery in the new state. Critics of the Lincoln government or even statehood became increasingly vocal and were derided as "Copperheads" by those in the community who still supported the Union government. Ironically, the increasingly frequent expressions of dissent in hometown papers may have helped unify soldiers in the field, who took public criticism of the war effort personally. Such feeling may have motivated the soldiers of the 7th West Virginia to send a letter, included in this chapter, to their local newspapers in the spring of 1863.

On March 26, 1863, western Virginians were called upon to vote for or against the creation of a new state—one that would set slavery on the path to extinction. While the voters overwhelmingly affirmed statehood, residents of nine counties, mostly in the far south, returned no votes at all. Even in counties where support for statehood was strong, dissenters mostly boycotted the referendum.[4] Confederate military leaders hoped to disrupt the movement toward statehood by launching a cavalry raid into the region. In late April, Confederate brigadier generals William "Grumble" Jones and John D. Imboden launched a coordinated invasion of western Virginia, hoping to "liberate" western Virginia communities and to disrupt the process of West Virginia statehood. They also were optimistic that such a raid would yield new recruits among those in western Virginia increasingly disaffected with the Lincoln administration. A third goal of the Jones-Imboden raid was to seize or destroy resources and to disable infrastructure currently supporting the Union war effort. Jones and Imboden did in fact leave a path of destruction in their wake, burning bridges, stealing supplies, and tearing up rail lines. But the raid ultimately failed to achieve any of its objectives. The statehood process continued, and on June 20 West Virginia formally entered the Union as the thirty-fifth state. The raiders claimed to have recruited six hundred new soldiers, but these were partially offset by desertions among the raiders. Destroying oil wells and setting the Little Kanawha River on fire at Burning Springs, described in this chapter, were among the most dramatic acts of destruction to occur during the raid. The damage the raids inflicted upon the strategically important Baltimore and Ohio Railroad (B&O), however, was quickly repaired.

Throughout the war, the B&O was a critical route for moving supplies and men from midwestern states to battlefields in the eastern theater. The privately run company was among the most efficient railroads under Union control, and the company's executives were committed to maintaining and quickly repairing the line after each Confederate act of vandalism. The Union military leadership came to depend heavily upon the B&O during the war, and as a result the company's profits doubled between 1860 and 1864.[5] In September 1863, after the Union Army experienced a great defeat at Chickamauga, the B&O was at the center of a dramatic plan to rescue William Rosecrans and the Army of the Cumberland by rapidly shifting twenty thousand soldiers and their equipment from the eastern theater to Chattanooga, where Union forces were under siege. Secretary of War Edwin M. Stanton approved the ambitious plan to achieve this feat in just ten days. He directed the leadership of the B&O to assist in the complex logistics. The stretch of the line that crossed the mountains of West Virginia presented some of the greatest challenges, as a train engine could only pull about half as many cars and maintain only about half the speed through this portion of the route. The relatively new technologies of telegraph and rail were deployed with near perfection to ensure that adequate rail cars were available at the right time at various points along the route.[6]

The presidential election of 1864 provided both West Virginia's soldiers and civilians with a last opportunity to demonstrate their persistent support of this long war. This would be the first presidential election in which most deployed soldiers were able to vote from their camps. The new state of West Virginia embedded the soldier's right to vote in its 1863 constitution, an idea that was novel at the beginning of the conflict. The 1864 campaign pitted Abraham Lincoln against George McClellan, his former general, who was still beloved by many soldiers. Lincoln's majority among civilian voters across the North was significant, but among soldiers he may have secured as much as 80 percent of the vote. Partial data on West Virginia soldiers in the Army of the Potomac put the vote for Lincoln at over 90 percent. Many historians have concluded that the soldier vote was evidence that by the fall of 1864, soldiers overwhelmingly supported Lincoln and his policies, including emancipation. A 2014 study has challenged this, noting that there was no secret ballot and soldiers might have been pressured by their officers to support Lincoln, and also that the vote might more accurately reflect soldier anger at Democratic war critics than enthusiasm for Lincoln and his policies.[7]

The ultimate outcome of the war, in West Virginia and elsewhere, was determined by the capacity of the Union and Confederate armies and the civilian societies that supported them. In West Virginia in the fall of 1864, Lincoln secured all five of the new state's electoral votes, besting McClellan in the popular vote by more than a two-to-one margin. His reelection dimmed the prospects of Confederate victory.

ENDURING WAR IN THE 7TH (WEST) VIRGINIA

Daniel Swisher was the cousin of David Shafer, mentioned in the introduction to this chapter. Both resided in Preston County. In this letter to his sister, Swisher reveals his homesickness and fatigue, questions what he is fighting for, and contemplates desertion. Swisher did eventually desert the army, in the weeks after experiencing the battle of Gettysburg.[8]

Bolivar Heights Near Harpers Ferry
Saturday Evening
October 19th, 1862

Dear Sister

After a long and tedious march it seems as if I am permitted time enough to answer your letter which I received a few days ago and had not time enough to answer until the present time. Hope you will excuse me for not writing sooner. We made a reconnaissance towards Winchester to find out where the Rebel company was. We whipped them out of Charlestown and came back to camp again. I am somewhat tired to day by fatigue and hard marching. We was called out of bed at midnight to march and its raining very hard but we had to put up with it. Lydia Anne, I see in your letter that you wished for me to come home. Indeed, I would if I could but as it is I can't. I am waiting to see whether old Abram is going to put his proclamation into execution. If he does I am not a going to stay I will have something to leave for. But as long as I am fighting for the right cause I would rather die at the point of the enemy's bayonet than to have the name of a deserter. But if I see that I can't stand it I am coming [home] anyhow. But the way we are situated here I can't get away without being caught. Me and Dick are tent mates together and we have planned out our future welfare that is if old abraham is going to free the niggers. I did say and say again that I won't fight to free the niggers. I believe that is what they have been trying to do ever since the war commenced and if I see it is their [idea] I am agoing to desert in spite of old Abe and all his Abolition Army. I never could ascertain what they meant to do until now and it can be distinctly seen that they mean to free the niggers. If it be the case I am as big a Rebel as those that are fighting against them. Lyd, you do not know how much good it would do me to see you all once more. I only wish I could see the children at the mill, they are always in my mind. If I could only get to see them, I could rest awhile with satisfaction, but so I can't. If I live and keep my health you must not be surprised to see me at home. Before many months elapse, Lydia Anne, I want you to do one favor for me without fail and that is get your likeness taken and send it to me and when I get paid off I will pay you for it what it cost you. You can send it by mail if no other way. No more at present I still remain

Your Affectionate
From your brother Dan
Daniel Swisher
To Lydia A. Bishop
Answer soon sooner soonest.

Daniel Swisher to Lydia A. Bishoff, Bishoff Collection, Gilder Lehrman Institute Collections, New York

THE 7TH (WEST) VIRGINIA RESPONDS TO WAR CRITICS

For soldiers far from home, reading pieces in their local papers that criticized the Union war effort could be dispiriting, and debates over the emancipation policy and the decision to enlist African American troops, in conjunction with a growing sense of stalemate in the war, all magnified the critical press. In the spring of 1863, many Union units published statements declaring their support for Lincoln's war plan and condemning the critics. The 7th (West) Virginia, encamped near the bloody fields of Fredericksburg and awaiting the beginning of the spring campaign, issued its own statement just days after loyal western Virginians voted for West Virginia statehood. The soldiers mailed it to their hometown papers so their communities knew where they stood.[9]

WHAT THE 7TH VIRGINIA THINKS ABOUT THE WAR—A VERY STRONG AND COGENT EXPRESSION OF LOYALTY.

Headquarters 7th Va. Vols.
Camp Near Falmouth, Va.,
March 30, 1863

Editors Intelligencer:
... A meeting of the officers and soldiers of the 7th Reg't Va. volunteers in their camp on the bank of the Rappahannock river in Stafford county, Virginia.... The committee reported the following which was read and unanimously adopted:

WHEREAS, Standing as we are on the banks of the Rappahannock near the graves of many of our near and dear friends we are solemnly impressed with the justice of our cause and the goodness of God, and believing as we do that no people since the creation of man have had more important duties to perform than has fallen to our lot, and while we are suffering hardships and privations, and while we regret our separation from our friends, we cannot but rejoice that it has fallen to our lot to live in this important period in the history of our country and that we are endowed with a will to do our duty to the Government rendered sacred by the blood of our fathers, and to which we owe our unparalleled prosperity.

While regretting the cause of our troubles and miseries as much as any men, we know that nothing but treachery of those in whom confidence had been misplaced by a prosperous, industrious, confiding and unsuspecting people produced this rebellion against this Government and that our troubles were brought on without any cause on the part of the Government. But it is left to us of the nineteenth century to witness a rebellion of aristocrats and office holders against the best Government on earth, and our great surprise is that this rebellion should meet with so much favor by any people. At no time and under no circumstances has this Government failed to perform its duty towards all its citizens. And if it was not for armed traitors in the South encouraged by doughfaced sympathizers in the North, we could all be at home enjoying the comforts of peace and happiness. We are surprised at the wanton and wicked conspirators of the North, their meeting professing to be democratic. Sueing for peace with traitors meets with our unbounded disapprobation.

We are pained to hear of these humiliating proceedings in some of the Northern and Northwestern States, but we are proud that no such proceedings have been carried on in Western Virginia, where traitors and their evil designs are best known.—We are rejoiced at the withering rebukes sent to those servile creatures by our brother soldiers from Ohio, Pennsylvania, Indiana and other States, who came to our assistance in the hour of trial; and from our inmost hearts, we say, well done, thou good and faithful servants, to our common cause. We pledge ourselves to stand by you and return with you, if necessary, to put down treason wherever it may raise its hydra head.

We give our solemn and firm warning to all honest people to beware of those who profess to be for the Union, and talk about compromises and peace with armed traitors. It is only a trick of aiders and abettors of treason—a mean effort on the part of disappointed politicians to redeem promises made to traitors. . . . This and kindred outrages on the part of traitors, brought to our regiment over one thousand gallant soldiers, who left their once peaceful and happy homes, leaving behind them kind parents, wives, children, brothers and affectionate sisters. And through the divine dispensation of Providence, we, as did the patriots of the Revolution and others, have had to look upon the pale faces of our dead comrades at Romney, Bloomer's Gap, Front Royal, Harrison's Landing, Antietam and Fredericksburg.

Although our ranks have been thinned by hardships and privations as well as upon the battle-field, we have not forgotten the tears of those we left behind us and the interests of generations yet unborn, nor have we forgotten the pledges made to our country on leaving our homes. . . .

We look upon this as the proper time and place to express our unqualified disapprobation of every measure calculated to cripple the Administration in its efforts to sustain the Government. This rebellion must be put down at all hazards, let it cost what it may. Therefore,

Resolved, That the peace meetings of the North are but a repetition of the kindred song "no coercion," which was sung by so many at the commencement of this unholy rebellion, by the sympathizers of treason, while traitors were deliberately robbing the Government and arranging their plans for desolation and ruin, by which they were enabled to establish a reign of terror over a portion of our country, unparalleled in the civilized world. . . .

Resolved, That we see nothing in the administration of our government that is either tyranny or usurpation. . . .

Resolved, That we have more respect for the open and avowed enemies of our country in the rebel ranks than for those sneaking and cowardly traitors in our rear who are staying at home and who have not the manhood to shoulder the rebel musket and fight like men, but will aid the traitors by holding peace meetings, thereby crippling the administration in its efforts to put down this rebellion and restore the constitution and the laws....

Resolved, That we are in favor of a vigorous prosecution of the war until every rebel shall be compelled to lay down his arms and submit to the laws of our country. Though our hardships may be many, and many of us may never see our homes in this world; we have the pleasing consolation that we are in the discharge of our duty. We are unconditionally opposed to all who are not in favor of the government and a vigorous prosecution of the war....

Resolved, That we are not unmindful of our good and devoted friends at home, who assisted with such energy to wrest Western Virginia from the conspirators.—Your kindness will ever be held in grateful remembrance, and it is our earnest hope that your favors may be properly appreciated by all concerned, and that you may long live to enjoy the blessings of free people.

Resolved, That our motto is "the Union and the Constitution, and the new State of West Virginia forever."

Wheeling Daily Intelligencer, April 10, 1863

THE DAILY LIVES OF SOLDIERS

For western Virginian soldiers on both sides of the conflict, the soldiering life often meant finding distractions from the boredom of camp life. To keep themselves entertained in the long periods when nothing much was happening, soldiers composed songs and wrote poems. Some songs, like "Nicholas Blues" below, sung by the Confederates, were meant to remind soldiers of what they were fighting for. At other times soldiers wrote comic pieces like "The Lost Dorg," composed by members of the Union 5th Virginia Volunteer Infantry to distract themselves from the politics of the conflict.

"Nicholas Blues"

But little do good people know,
What we poor soldiers undergo,
Whilst we are struggling to be free,
From Abolition tyranny.

Whenever called, we have to go
Through mud and ice, through rain and snow;

We have to march both night and day,
On frozen ground we have to lay.

Our native homes and friends so kind,
Are far away and all left behind;
No friend to soothe our sorrows now,
Or wipe a suffering soldier's brow.

Our rations, too, will well compare,
With all the other kinds of fare
A stern decree has spoke and said,
That we must live on beef and bread.

The battle-field it has no charms,
When silence breaks to a clash of arms;
The cannon's roar, the musket's peal,
Proclaims a bloody battle-field.

The battles rage with fearful roar,
Our comrades fall to rise no more;
In conflicts sore we have to be,
To pay the price of Liberty.

This conflict sore would soon be past,
And we would all get home at last,
Had Dixie's sons all been true,
To fight against old Lincoln's crew.

Amalgamation they must try,
And for the UNION still they cry;
Our brothers now we have to scorn,
And hate the day that they were born.

Two years ago we volunteered,
The soldier's fate have always shared;
And now we pause to count the cost,
And mourn the men that we have lost.

In Summersville we plighted hands,
To fight old Lincoln's thieving bands;

All other honors we refuse,
We still are called the Nicholas Blues.

James McNeill, Civil War Song Sheet, "Nicholas Blues," West Virginia and Regional History Center, West Virginia University, Morgantown

* * *

THAT DOG.—The wagoners of the 5th Va. had a good dog—that is, they say it was a good dog. I do not know how they came to have him in their possession; I know they had him long enough to become attached to him. And of course when he was lost a great sensation was produced in the social circle of the wagoner's mess. I have been requested to write some poetry that would commemorate the character, virtues and usefulness of their late canine companion, with an allusion to the manner of his loss. I cannot write poetry so I treat the subject in doggerel.

C.B.W.

The Lost "Dorg"

The wagoners had a favorite dog,
And a favorite dog was he.
He would watch a mule or chase a hog
As faithful as any dog could be.
This dog was not large nor very small,
He had two eyes, and was not blind.
He had four legs, which made him tall
And he carried a splendid tail behind.
He was gentle, and brindle in color was he,
In fact one of the very best of dogs,
As any observant man could see.
When he went out a-chasing hogs.
The wagoners were to Charleston sent,
And the dog was taken along to scout,*
(And it was a very unlucky day he went)
For when "Dog-Leg" got in the dog got out,
And couldn't not never more be found!

The Knapsack, October 8, 1863

EXCERPTS FROM *THE KNAPSACK*, 1863

The 5th Virginia Volunteer Infantry (later called the 5th West Virginia Volunteer Infantry) was recruited in Ceredo, Virginia, in September and

October 1861. While Ceredo was founded as a free-soil colony by New England Congregationalists and Massachusetts congressman Eli Thayer in 1856, Ceredo and Wayne County residents made up a minority of the regiment, with many volunteers coming from Ohio and eastern Kentucky. The 5th spent most of the war in West Virginia and, in 1863 while stationed at Gauley Bridge, produced a weekly newspaper entitled The Knapsack. *The 5th's origins in a small free-soil colony did not seem to significantly influence the viewpoints of members of the regiments. Issues of* The Knapsack *rarely discuss the issue of slavery, and the handful of references to African Americans in its pages are mostly disparaging. These short pieces provide a glimpse of camp life during a time when there was little military action.*

THE WAR IS AT AN END

The soldier is like everybody else, looks with anxiety to the moment when the above sentence can be heard re-echoing throughout the land. Yet he does not want that desirable end accomplished on the basis of a shameful and humiliating treaty of peace, like that for which the so-called Democracy is working now and aiming at.—

The rebels must acknowledge the corn ere we accept any terms of peace. We want a peace which will extinguish rebellion in this country forever, and establish *Liberty and Union* in its stead. Until that can be accomplished, we want to hear nothing of peace; nor do we want to hear anything of the advocates of the peace party at the present day, a resolve which Mr. Vallandigham will find clearly demonstrated in the next election in Ohio and other States.

_{The Knapsack, September 10, 1863}

* * *

LOCAL COLUMN

If any of our friends at home could just light into our camp some fine moonlight night, they wouldn't doubt but we had moral and social privileges. First, as to the moral. Thanks to the powers that be, here and below, there isn't a pint of whisky within camp or within twenty miles of it,—and hasn't been as we nose on for ever so long. If we are not every one 'sons of temperance,' in principle, we are tetotalers in practice. Hence we have sober men, therefore no guard-house for two months. As the peace, quiet and order would strike them, they would most likely find the chaplain by the color stand singing and playing psalms, hymns and spiritual songs, with a large group seated in the moonlight who love to hear the voice of prayer and some verses from the Good Book.

If then our visitor was a lady and had a taste for social privileges, and would go down under the hill to the bakery boys, they would hear a fine cotillion, three violins, bass viol doing the most scientificist cowtillions, pokers, waltzes, etc., to which the boys are tripping the lightest kind of fantastic toes. You ladies who think that graceful, civil and hilarious dancing can't be done without the "feline gender," are deluded—although the boys do say that a good floor would be better than a dirty drill ground;—and above all a due mixture of hoops and crinoline would add ineffably—but what's the use in making a man's mouth water for what he can't help? It's huge fun any way, and harmless as huge, and if you do not think so just come and see a man "call off" in a stentorian voice from the house top in a cloud of dust, and the rocks and hills resound.

We are grieved that our little brothers are not here to help the boys kill rats of nights.

J.L.

The Knapsack, October 8, 1863

"A BURNING RIVER, CARRYING DESTRUCTION TO OUR MERCILESS ENEMY"

> *The Jones-Imboden raid of April and May 1863 dominated the news and struck fear into the hearts of loyal western Virginians. Despite being outnumbered by Union forces four to one, the raiders inflicted over eight hundred casualties while suffering just one hundred of their own, made off with substantial herds of cattle and other valuable resources, and left a path of destruction wherever they went. But the biggest impact of the Jones-Imboden raid was psychological, causing many to wonder if the war would ever end. One of the more dramatic moments of the raid occurred at Dripping Springs, where Jones ordered his men to set fire to the oil derricks and barges along the Little Kanawha River. In his official report on the raid, Jones describes the extent of the damage. The impact on those who witnessed it is powerfully described in the memoir of John Opie, a cavalryman on Jones's raid.*

William E. Jones

Headquarters Valley District
Near Harrisonburg, Va. May 26, 1863

. . . From here we moved onto Oiltown, where we arrived on May 9. The wells are owned mainly by Southern men, now driven from their homes, and their property is appropriated either by the Federal Government or Northern one. This oil is used extensively as a lubricator of machinery and for illumination. All the oil, the tanks, barrels, engines for pumping, engine-houses, and wagons—in a word, everything used for raising, holding, or sending it off was burned. The smoke is very dense and jet black. The boats, filled with oil in bulk, burst with a report almost equaling artillery, and spread the burning fluid over the river. Before night huge columns of ebony smoke marked the meanderings of the stream as far as the eye could reach. By dark the oil from the tanks on the burning creek had reached the river, and the whole stream became a sheet of fire. A burning river, carrying destruction to our merciless enemy, was a scene of magnificence that might well carry joy to every patriotic heart. Men of experience estimated the oil destroyed at 150,000 barrels. It will be many months before a large supply can be had from this source, as it can only be boated down the Little Kanawha when the waters are high. My orders were in all cases to respect private property, irrespective of the politics and part taken in the war by the owners. Horses and supplies were to be gathered indiscriminately. Two saw-mills (private property) were burned by my order—one, at Fairmont, was engaged on a contract with the Federal Government in making gun-stocks, and had on hand many thousands; the other, at Cairo, would have been used to repair the damages done the railroad. I am aware my orders were in a few instances disobeyed. The library of Pierpont was burned, in retaliation for a like act on the part of the ambitious little man. One or two stores were plundered, but as far as practicable the goods were restored.

From Oiltown we marched by Glenville and Sutton to Summerville, where the command of General Imboden was again overtaken. Our exhausted condition and exhausted supplies rendered homeward movements necessary. Our marches henceforward were easy, and little of interest occurred.

In thirty days we marched nearly 700 miles through a rough and sterile country, gathering subsistence for man and horse by the way. At Greenland and Fairmont we encountered the enemy's forces. We killed from 25 to 30 of the enemy, wounded probably three times as many, captured nearly 700 prisoners, with their small-arms, and 1 piece of artillery, 2 trains of cars, burned 16 railroad bridges and 1 tunnel, 150,000 barrels of oil, many engines, and a large number of boats, tanks, and barrels, bringing home with us about 1,000 cattle, and probably 1,200 horses. Our entire loss was 10 killed and 42 wounded, the missing not exceeding 15.

Throughout this arduous march the men and officers evinced a cheerful endurance worthy of tried veterans. They have shown a skill in gleaning a precarious subsistence from a country desolated by two years of oppressive tyranny and brutal war that would have won the admiration of the most approved

Cossack. With such troops the country of the enemy can be reached at almost any point....

W.E. Jones,
Brigadier-General, Commanding

Official Records of the War of the Rebellion, vol. 25, pt. 1 (Washington, D.C.: Government Printing Office, 1889), 120–21

* * *

A few days after the charge made upon our rear guard by the enemy, we reached a place called Oil Town, where many oil wells had been sunk. When we arrived at this place, we found much oil and whiskey; when we left, there was neither oil nor whiskey there. The two most combustible fluids known to science are coal oil and corn whiskey. The men were ordered to destroy both of these useful fluids, as they were considered contraband goods. This they did in the usual way—they drank the whiskey and fired the oil. They first lighted the tanks, which exploded, throwing the fire and oil in every direction. Finally, the wells became ignited, either by design or accident. Great pillars of flame, resembling pyramids of fire, rose to a prodigious height in the air from the burning wells, lighting the surrounding country for miles. These pillars, or pyramids, of flame, after ascending separately some distance in the air, seemed to unite in one great sheet of fire, and it looked as though the firmament was one vast conflagration. This appalling and supernatural spectacle was beyond conception or description. It was, in appearance, the flames of an expiring world, and I believe that the men would have so considered it, but for the fact that it was of their own creation.

The fire also extended to the river, which was soon enveloped in flames, containing many colored lights. The current carried the flames over the waterfalls, producing the most fantastic shapes and figures, resembling fiery demons, dancing upon the surface of the river, ever and anon disappearing in the darkness and again appearing, when on a line with one's vision. The men were greatly relieved when we left this scene of desolation, and many a man that night dreamed of h—l and of a personal devil.

John Opie, *A Rebel Cavalryman with Lee, Stuart and Jackson* (Chicago: W. B. Conkey, 1899), 135–36

TROOP TRANSFER ACROSS WEST VIRGINIA

In September of 1863 the War Department, under Secretary Edwin M. Stanton, needed to quickly transfer the 11th and 12th Corps of the Army of the Potomac—more than twenty thousand troops and all the supplies they would need—from Virginia to southern Tennessee in the wake of the Union's disastrous defeat at Chickamauga. The extraordinary feat of logistics was carried out in roughly eight days through masterful planning and the use of the relatively new-to-war technologies of the telegraph and rail. The feat could not have been accomplished without the use of the Baltimore and Ohio Railroad line extending through western Virginia. Without this rapid redeployment, the city of Chattanooga and the Union troops held in siege there might have fallen to Confederate foes, severely undermining efforts to take the war to Atlanta and beyond. The telegram messages below reveal the complexity and size of the operation, and the challenges the War Department faced.

Camden Station, Baltimore, Md., September 26, 1863—11 a.m. (Received 1.20 p.m.)
Hon. E.M. Stanton, Secretary of War:

The first three trains, over 60 cars, with 2,000 men, passed Martinsburg, 100 miles west of Baltimore, at 8.45, 9.15, and 9.45 this morning, in good order. The men have ben promptly and fully supplied there by the commissary with coffee and other rations. Some twelve trains, with nearly 7,000 men, have now (11 a.m.) passed the Relay House, 30 miles from Washington. The first trains will be due at Benwood, Ohio River, to-morrow (Sunday) before dark, and may get there by noon. Everything so far working well, with complete success. We have telegraphed ahead to Ohio, and the responses indicate the fullest condition of readiness at Bellaire to receive and dispatch. Everything satisfactory.
W.P. Smith, Master of Transportation, (Copies to Major-General Hooker and Col. D.C. McCallum)

* * *

War Department, September 26, 1863—2.50 p.m.
William P. Smith, Camden Street Station, Baltimore:

A thousand thanks for the diligence and ability manifested in the movement. I cannot tell how much obliged I am to Mr. Garrett and yourself, and your subordinates. If there is no hitch in the west all will go well, I hope.
Edwin M. Stanton

* * *

Camden Station, Baltimore, Md., September 26, 1863—5.20 p.m. (Received 5.30 p.m.)
Hon. E. M. Stanton, Secretary of War:

The first three trains named in my dispatch to you of 11 o'clock this morning passed Cumberland before 4 o'clock this afternoon, continuing to make excellent time, while obeying our precaution to avoid excessive and unsafe speed. I will continue to send you these bulletins throughout the movement. We have now delivered, within forty-eight hours, at Washington over 340 seated cars for troops, besides other cars, which embrace three-quarters of the provision for the whole movement. The remainder will be forthcoming with equal promptness.

W.P. Smith (Copies to Major-General Hooker and Col. D.C. McCallum)

* * *

War Department, September 27, 1863—4 p.m.
Col. Thomas A. Scott, Louisville:

The first train reached the Ohio at Bellaire this morning. All of the Eleventh have gone forward, and are beyond Cumberland by this time. Part of the Twelfth Corps have also gone forward. The whole force will be moving tonight. I have directed Mr. Smith to advise you of the rate of movement, from which you can calculate better than anyone else. General Hooker starts in the morning for Louisville.

Edwin M. Stanton

* * *

Camden Station, Baltimore, Md., September 27, 1863 (Received 11.50 a.m.)
Hon. E. M. Stanton, Secretary of War:

At 9.15 this a.m. we had started from Washington for the west 12,600 men 33 cars of artillery, and 21 cars of baggage and horses. The first four trains, with 2,500 men, reached Benwood, the end of our line, 412 miles from Washington, at 11 this a.m., and continuing to move at the ratio expected by us, or two hours less than our promise of forty-four hours through. At Benwood a substantial and superior bridge of scows and barges, strongly connected, is in full readiness to make the transfer across the Ohio, and adequate cars are waiting at Bellaire.

W.P. Smith

* * *

Camden Station, Baltimore, Md., September 27, 1863. (Received 12.50, p.m.)
Hon. E.M. Stanton, Secretary of War:

Our agent at Grafton has orders, he says, to hold all the Third Division, Eleventh Corps there until General Schurz arrives. May I suggest that this kind of thing will cripple your whole movement? I have therefore given a peremptory order to our agent that the trains shall not be so held unless his order comes from you.

W.P. Smith (Same to General Hooker)

* * *

War Department, Washington City, September 27, 1863—1 p.m.
William P. Smith, Esq., Baltimore:

You have done right. Order your men to disregard every order that presumes to interfere with you, and let me know who gave the order referred to in your telegram.

Edwin M. Stanton, Secretary of War

* * *

Camden Station, Baltimore, Md., September 27, 1863—1.35 p.m. (Received 2.10 p.m.)
Hon. E.M. Stanton:

Your response to my dispatch received. I thank you for your prompt way of sustaining us, which has induced me to send the following order to every chief agent and officer upon our line:

Some of the military officers having ordered General Schurz's division to wait at Grafton until he came up to join it, the Secretary of War and Major-General Hooker thereupon direct me to order, in their name, that under no circumstances nor any pretext must any train of troops or stores be stopped on the route, unless by accident or other necessity, without their own order. Should any such stoppages be ordered or suggested, show this dispatch as your authority for disregarding it. This is imperative.

This will correct a serious evil, I hope. The origin of the Grafton order for delay shall be sent you.

W.P. Smith (Copy to General Hooker)

* * *

War Department, Washington City, September 27, 1863—4.20 p.m.
Capt. William P. Smith:

You should direct your agents immediately to report to you or the Secretary of War the name of any military officer who attempts to interfere with transportation.

Edwin M. Stanton, Secretary of War.

* * *

Camden Station, Baltimore, Md., September 27, 1863. (Received 9.10 p.m.)
Hon. E. M. Stanton:

The following dispatch was received from our agent at Grafton at 4.45 p.m.:

The order by telegraph to stop the troops here was sent by one of General Schurz's staff. I did not recognize it, and had some difficulty with the general on his arrival here. Had great difficulty in preventing his taking possession of an engine, and running on after the trains to try to overtake them. He has telegraphed from here to Fairmont to have them stop there until he comes up.

To which I have replied as follows:

Conductor of Military Trains, Fairmont:

In the name of the Secretary of War and Major-General Hooker, as well as my own, I direct you to proceed with your trains according to the orders and arrangements made for you by Captain Willard or our agents, without regard to any orders from General Schurz or his staff, or other parties proposing to stop you on any pretext whatever. Let me know at once and distinctly what military officer undertakes to interfere with this order.

W.P. Smith

* * *

War Department, September 27, 1863—9.40 p.m.
Maj. Gen. Carl Schurz, Fairmont:

Major-General Hooker has the orders of this Department to relieve you from command and put under arrest any officer who undertakes to delay or interfere with the orders and regulations of the railroad officers in charge of the transportation of troops.

Edwin M. Stanton, Secretary of War.

* * *

War Department, September 27, 1863—9.40 p.m.
Capt. William P. Smith, Baltimore:

You have done exactly right. I have telegraphed Schurz that he will be relieved and put under arrest if he undertakes to interfere with the transportation. You need not have furnished him an extra, but let him and any other officers who lag behind, get along the best they can.

Edwin M. Stanton

* * *

Benwood, W. Va., September 28, 1863 (Received 10.55 a.m.)
Hon. E. M. Stanton, Secretary of War:

Am I to understand from your dispatch that I am relieved from command? By the displacing of trains and cars at several depots, the different commands have become so mixed up that it would have been highly desirable, and rather expedite matters instead of causing delay, if they should be put in order. No train has been delayed so far, but the above difficulty is causing great inconvenience, which I desire to remedy. An answer to the above question is respectfully solicited.

C. Schurz, Major-General

* * *

War Department, September 28, 1863—1.35 p.m.
Maj. Gen. Carl Shurz, Benwood, via Wheeling:

General Hooker is authorized to relieve from command any officer that interferes with or hinders the transportation of troops in the present moment. Whether you have done so, and whether he has relieved you from command, ought to be known by yourself. The order will certainly be enforced against any officer, whatever his rank may be, who delays or endangers transportation of troops.

Edwin M. Stanton

* * *

Camden Station, Baltimore, Md., September 28, 1863—3 p.m.
Hon E. M. Stanton, Secretary of War:

I beg further report that the troops have been most promptly and successfully transferred from Benwood to Bellaire, with baggage, artillery, and all effects, which were reloaded at once on the Ohio side, and dispatched to Indianapolis. Ample water and coffee have been supplied by the commissaries, as previously arranged, and indeed everything has worked with the most desired success, exceeding our promises and anticipations. So far not one of the thirty trains of nearly 600 cars has been delayed improperly. The only thing we have to regret is that the actual movement exceeds the requisitions by nearly 20 per cent. in men and more than 50 per cent. in horses, though we hope to have no delay of consequence even from this cause.

W.P. Smith

The War of the Rebellion: A Compilation of the Official Records of the Union and Confederate Armies, ser. 1, vol. 29, part 1 (Washington, D.C.: Government Printing Office, 1890), 161–73.

LOCAL NEWSPAPERS ON THE TROOP TRANSFER

The efforts required to prepare for the troop transfer, including the building of a pontoon bridge across the Ohio River, and the sudden and dramatic increase in rail traffic no doubt drew the attention of West Virginians along the way. For the most part, local newspapers kept silent about these activities, probably under the direction of government censors. Nonetheless, the Republican Wheeling Daily Intelligencer revealed critical details about the secretive transfer while simultaneously priding itself on its discretion.

TRANSFER OF SOLDIERS

We learn that about fifteen thousand troops have arrived and are arriving at Benwood going west. The Rattler and the Buck were pressed into the service and taken in charge by Capt A.S. Doane. They are to be employed in building a pontoon bridge at Bellair to facilitate the crossing of the troops. We do not deem it advisable to make known the destination of the soldiers or the direction from which they come.

Wheeling Daily Intelligencer, September 26, 1863

ELECTION OF 1864

As the war moved into its fourth year, Union victory remained elusive. Grant's bloody Overland Campaign in the spring of 1864 resulted in high casualties and failed to capture the Confederate capital of Richmond. By the summer the war had settled into extended sieges at Petersburg and Atlanta, and Lincoln was pessimistic about the possibility of a second term. Despite widespread war-weariness among Northern voters, the Democrats had their own challenges in defeating Lincoln, as the party was divided between factions that supported the continued prosecution of the war and those who were impatient for peace. The party nominated George McClellan as its candidate, who had been beloved by Union soldiers. McClellan's overly cautious approach to the war had been a source of immense frustration to Lincoln, and after McClellan failed to move on Lee and the Confederate army after the victory at Antietam, Lincoln removed him from command. McClellan was a fierce critic of Lincoln but nonetheless a War Democrat. While committed to seeing the restoration of the Union, he opposed Lincoln's emancipation policies, which he believed only hardened Southern resistance and prolonged the war. The Democratic Party's hope that McClellan would secure the soldier's vote and win the presidency was partially undermined by the very vocal Peace Democrat faction of the party, which appeared willing to accept Southern independence if that was what was necessary to end the war. Critics of the Peace Democrats labeled them "Copperheads," after the venomous snake. Another popular term for a Northerner with pro-Southern and proslavery sympathies was "Butternut," generally used to describe poor Whites from southern Ohio, Indiana, and Illinois who had roots in Southern slave states.[10] In the buildup to the fall elections, newspapers covered the meetings of partisans for Lincoln and McClellan.

MEETING TO-NIGHT.

Gen. Willich, of Indiana, an orator and a soldier of reputed worth and capacity, will address his German fellow citizens in their own language this evening, at the Lincoln & Johnson pole place, in Ritchietown.

The General arrived in the city last night, so that there is no mistake about his speaking.

Mr. Bayne, of Pennsylvania, will afterward address the meeting in English. He is also a speaker of a great deal more than ordinary power, as those who heard him at Triadelphia can attest.

The two speakers will meet with the Central Club at their headquarters, at precisely half past six this evening, and will be escorted down by the members, in torch light procession.

This meeting in Ritchietown should be made one of the grandest rallies of the campaign. The little "independent republic" did so well the other day at the election, that we should all go down in great force to-night and do her honor. There are some Union men in the upper end of the city who have never seen how they do things down in Ritchietown, and to gratify their curiosity and at the same time help roll on the ball, they should come to the Club room to-night and join in the procession. . . .

Wheeling Daily Intelligencer, November 1, 1864

* * *

THE RECENT BUTTERNUT MEETING AT MOUNDSVILLE.

Moundsville, W. Va., Oct. 28th, 1864.

Editors Intelligencer:—The whitewashed and self-styled Democracy of Marshall [County] . . . have been for the last two or three weeks moving heaven and earth to get up some kind of demonstration in Moundsville. They circulated flaming posters far and near, and made every effort to insure success for their meetings.

Tuesday, the 26th inst.... About 12 o' clock a meagre few of lonely stragglers, here and there, might have been seen approaching the town and wending their way towards the Court House—looking as terrified as if they were going to the gallows. The hour at last arrived, and the noses carefully counted numbered all the way to seventy three, by counting Mr. J.W. McCarricher several times. This *immense* concourse of seventy three included the delegations from Wheeling and Ohio, and the musicians....

... [The] band performed the prelude, after which a certain Col. Stambaugh, a lately defeated candidate for the Attorney Generalship of Ohio, was called to the stand. He spoke about two hours.... He denounced the Administration, charged the abolitionists with having caused the war, asserted that 1,900,000 men had been killed or otherwise disabled by it, that our national debt would ruin us, that the present war policy was also ruinous, that 40,000 Republicans voted the Democratic ticket at the last Ohio election, that the only hope for peace and union was in the election of McClellan, that the destruction of slavery, instead of being the terminus of our troubles [would be the beginning of them] ... for with freedom the African would aspire to equality with us; that over in Ohio he had seen "beautiful Yankee ladies dancing with, and even parading the streets armlocked with negroes;" that by a decision of a Republican judge negroes are legalized voters in Ohio....

Wheeling Daily Intelligencer, November 2, 1864

"THE VERY EXISTENCE OF THE STATE OF WEST VIRGINIA"

The Point Pleasant Weekly Register *speculates on whether a Democratic victory in 1864 might threaten West Virginia's statehood.*

On Tuesday next, the election for the President and the Vice-President occurs.—The number of Electors constituting the Electoral College, is two hundred and forty-four, of which West Virginia chooses five—one hundred and twenty-three being necessary to a choice. From present indications, Lincoln and Johnson Electors will be chosen from every voting State—there being a bare possibility of their losing those for Kentucky, and New Jersey. The people feel that the war is drawing to a close, and that permanent peace with the Union, is certain to result from the success of the Union party at the polls on the 8th inst. Such a popular verdict evidently, will not only greatly encourage Unionists but hopelessly discourage the great body of those now arrayed against the Union.

From all sources of information, we learn that the main support now of the rebel cause, is found in the hope of the defeat of Lincoln & Johnson at the coming election. They admit that they cannot succeed by force—that they are not strong enough to continue much longer the contest by arms—and that they can secure their independence only by an armistice and negotiations. The success of Lincoln and Johnson will entirely dishearten them. . . .

Here, the canvass both State and National, has been remarkably quiet. The State election being passed, interest is now being directed to the Presidential election. Our citizens were favored on the 1st inst, with an able and eloquent speech from Major R.S. Brown, the Union Elector for this Congressional District, at the Court House, during the recess of the Circuit Court. The Major had a large and appreciative audience who listened with [rapt] attention to his convincing arguments of which we greatly regret we have only room for the following points:

He had a right to speak of matters that relate to the very existence of the State of West Virginia. McClellan and his party say they are in favor of restoring the Union in its original integrity, with West Virginia blotted out, but Lincoln is in favor of West Virginia remaining an original State in the bright galaxy of States. The speaker here gave a history of the Legislation of Virginia, averred a racial conflict existed, and our interest demanded separation. Spoke of the efforts of our ablest men in the Conventions of '29 and '49 to procure a proper representation in the Legislature, but could obtain only a compromise—the mixed basis—'till '65, when by a new convention, we might consider our claims. West Virginia sorrowfully obeyed and payed their exorbitant taxes, hoping that then they might secure that equality so long and cruelly denied them.—

East Virginia in the meantime, built with our money her network of railroads. He here gave instances of unequal taxation. When the time had approached for a convention, East Virginia brought on the war, and had used the railroads against us 'till the government in self-protection destroyed them, and if reunited we would be taxed again to rebuild them. East Virginia attempted to drag us from the Union, but we of the West being denied the protection due for our allegiance, then reorganized the government. . . . The Democratic party ask you to vote for McClellan, though by so doing all this goes for naught. The New State men are all for Lincoln—the friend of the New State. All enemies of the New State are McClellanites. McClellan has no chance of election, but if successful would repudiate the New State of West Virginia. . . .

Weekly Register (Point Pleasant, WV), November 3, 1864

A REFUGEE CRISIS IN THE LOWER SHENANDOAH VALLEY

Union general Philip Sheridan's devastating raid through the Shenandoah Valley in the autumn of 1864, and his victory at Cedar Creek on October 19, 1864, contributed to a growing optimism in the North about the war's end and no doubt aided Lincoln's reelection effort. But the raid also created a crush of war refugees at Martinsburg, Harpers Ferry, and Wheeling, as described in these newspaper reports.

SCENES IN THE SHENANDOAH

A Visit to Martinsburg—The Depopulation of the Valley—Talks with Refugees—Incidente

Correspondence of the New York Post.
Martinsburg, Va., October 29, 1864.

A visit to this town since Sheridan began his operations in the Shenandoah Valley is peculiarly interesting. The place is now held as a military post by our forces, and its population is largely increased by the arrival of refugees from all parts of the valley. Originally it contained between three and four thousand inhabitants. Yesterday afternoon, after obtaining quarters through the assistance of some military friends, I sallied out for a look at the town....

Darkness was near at hand, and the sight was picturesque in the extreme.—Over a space of fifty acres or more were spread unique clusters, hundreds of families of the Valley of the Shenandoah. The government had furnished them with soft bituminous Cumberland coal, which abounds in this region, and each little family had lighted a pile which burned bright, but smoky like a blacksmith's fire, and around it were grouped the few articles of household gear which, like the children of Israel they carried with them from out of Egypt. They were scattered over chests, in the lea of bureaus or behind barricades of tables;...

... A church was taken possession of, the pews bustled out in piles, and there, in long rows on the floor, lay brave uncomplaining fellows, passed from the daring skirmish and fierce shock of battle to the steady suffering of the hospital and the uncomplaining endurance of wounds and sickness, which is so marvelous to all whose duties have brought them among the hospitals of this war....

The railroad, new built and surrounded with tons and tons of heated and twisted rails from former raids, was now lined with refugee families, all "bound for Ohio." The Government gives them transportation for themselves and their effects, and rations to keep them from starving, and thus the Shenandoah valley is cleaned out at the rate of fifty or sixty families a day. The clothes of these people are of the most common kind generally. They go like the children of Israel out of Egypt, and intend to settle in Ohio or some other free western State and go to farming. . . .

With a long freight train loaded with these men and women, with soldiers, freedmen and others, we crept slowly along to Harper's Ferry—but no slower than was safe, we afterwards found; for the train that followed us four hours after, was attacked, robbed and burned by guerillas.—Harper's Ferry was safely reached, and the long assorted cargo of human beings was unloaded and sent hither and thither, while the departing train for Washington bore my snuffling and cold-racked head, body and shoulder, over its single track.

Wheeling Daily Intelligencer, November 3, 1864

* * *

MORE REFUGEES—HOW THEY GOT AWAY AND WHAT THEY SAY.— Another lot of about twenty refugees from different portions of Old Virginia arrived in the city on Saturday. During their stay they were quartered in the Union Campaign Club Room. The most of them are shrewd intelligent men, and a few were original secessionists. They inform us that in order to escape the rebel pickets, they traveled through the mountains for more than a hundred miles without striking a road.—They came in through Greenland Gap, about five thousand men having preceded them on the same route. Some of the men with whom we conversed are from the southern part of the State and others from the eastern part, from neither of which sections are the means of escape so easy. Those who desire to come North have therefore to employ a little strategy, the employment of which is not necessary in the Valley. The last call of the rebel authorities, made about a month ago, was for the men who had been previously detailed to gather crops and carry on indispensable manufactories. They were ordered to report at different places and were allowed to choose a regiment in which to serve. These men selected regiments doing duty in the Valley, knowing that their chances of escape would be better. These men say that Early does not hope to occupy the valley much longer. All the government stores are being removed to Lynchburg.

Two of the refugees of whom we speak, assured us that they had heard hundreds of rebel soldiers say they would desert if Lincoln was elected—that it was no use fighting any longer and that they would not do it.

Wheeling Daily Intelligencer, November 14, 1864

EIGHT

Revolution and Counterrevolution

HISTORIANS REFER to the years immediately after the Civil War as the era of Reconstruction. The big questions of this age included how to restore political autonomy to states that had joined the Confederacy, how and when to reintegrate defeated Confederates into the body politic, and what political and civil rights would be extended to freedmen and freedwomen who before the war lived in bondage. In states that had joined the Confederacy, these issues were first confronted in the context of military occupation outlined in the congressional Reconstruction Acts. For border slave states that remained in the Union, military occupation did not apply. It is worth asking the question as to whether the term "Reconstruction" should be applied to West Virginia, which was born in the war. Historian Eric Foner has argued that Reconstruction began in West Virginia, as new state leaders negotiated with Congress the terms of their admission, specifically in relation to the legal abolition of slavery. In contrast, historian John Stealey has argued that West Virginia's wartime and postwar experience might best be characterized as a "revolution" from 1861 to 1865, when Unionists threw off the yoke of rule by eastern Virginia's slaveocracy, followed by a "counterrevolution" from 1865 to 1872, when conservative forces regained power and reversed some of the political changes implemented under Republican rule.[1]

West Virginia's unique situation as a child of the conflict meant that its postwar politics had slightly different priorities from those of former Confederate states, as well as some similarities with the border states. After Appomattox thousands of men who had waged war on the Union returned to their former homes in West Virginia, which was a frightening experience for local Unionists. Not only were they concerned about outbreaks of more violence, but these returnees represented an existential threat to West Virginia if they sought to return all or parts of the new state to Virginia. That fear shaped West Virginia's postwar politics far more than the second major political issue of the Reconstruction era—the political status of the newly freed men and women. Demographics help explain these priorities. Two-thirds of the state's land mass and 40 percent of the state's 1860 population resided in counties that had voted for secession in 1861. The African American population of the new state was no more than 4 or 5 percent of the total population. Thus, questions of loyalty and disloyalty drove much of West Virginia's postwar politics, and civil rights took a back seat.[2]

West Virginia's Union-Republican leaders recognized that the inclusion of so much territory where majorities had supported the Confederacy made the new state vulnerable. Even in counties where allegiances were strongly divided at the outset of the war, fear of the returnees and their intentions made issues of forgiveness and restoration of political rights fraught. If their civil and political rights were restored, would they try to use them to return West Virginia to the Old Dominion? In some places they did just that. Former Confederates in Jefferson and Berkeley Counties believed their annexation to the new state was not legal and took their case all the way to the Supreme Court. Jefferson County residents also tried to vote in Virginia state elections, and the masthead of the Jefferson County newspaper *Spirit of Jefferson* continued to identify its location as "Charlestown, Va." for many years after the war. Resistance was not limited solely to counties that bordered old Virginia. Men who were dressed in Confederate uniforms in Jackson County "desecrated American flags at Independence Day celebrations at Ravenswood and Sandyville."[3] In response to the defiance of some of these returning Confederates, Union loyalists in at least twelve different communities in West Virginia issued public proclamations or formed vigilance committees to warn those who had joined the Confederate military to not return. Unionists in Marion County drove several former Confederates out of the county, and West Virginia governor Arthur Boreman warned returning Confederates that the state government would not protect them.[4] Some heeded this warning and relocated their families to eastern Virginia. But most did return, and in deeply divided communities like Barbour County they "lived in constant fear of arrest or worse," according to historian John W. Shaffer. "Their private correspondence was subject to search, their property and persons subject to seizure. Church doors were closed to them."[5] But others were bent on exacting vengeance of their own. A few weeks after Lee's surrender at Appomattox, several Barbour County Confederates captured three members of the local Union home guard unit and forced them "to kneel and pray for the Confederacy" before executing them. The crime was in retaliation for the execution of a local Confederate that had occurred several years earlier.[6]

Because of these concerns, the state of West Virginia took early action to keep unreconstructed Confederates disenfranchised. In February 1865, the West Virginia legislature passed a new voting law that empowered any citizen to challenge the vote of anyone they suspected of disloyalty. A challenged person would be required to take a test oath swearing that they had never provided any support for or participated "in armed hostility against the United States, the reorganized government of Virginia, or the State of West Virginia."[7] The 1865 law was followed by several additional laws restricting the vote. Up to 85 percent of voters were disqualified in some counties.

The commitment of West Virginia's Unionist-Republican coalition to the civil rights of African Americans was quite shallow. The first constitution established free public schools for all children, but an early state law called for racial segregation in education. Voting rights were reserved for White men before the state ratified the Fifteenth Amendment.[8] It would be voting restrictions on former Confederates, not issues of race, that sparked the new state's first political upheaval. Moderate Unionists soon became uncomfortable with aggressive restrictions on voting, while their Radical Republican allies dug in their heels. Reports of questionable voter disenfranchisement tactics in the October 1869 elections resulted in growing calls for "letting up" on former Confederates. Relaxed voting rules in 1870 resulted in the Democrats taking the governorship and majorities in the legislature. In 1871 the Flick Amendment ended almost all restrictions on voting for former Confederates. In 1872 Democratic majorities called a new constitutional convention, in which many former Confederates, including Samuel Woods of Barbour County, played an important role. The 1872 constitution reorganized the courts, effectively purging Republican judges, and dismantled the "Yankee" system of townships established in the 1863 constitution. It also enshrined public school segregation, something that was already forbidden by law, and allowed voters to cast their vote by secret ballot for the first time. But efforts to reinstate the word "White" into the qualifications for voting or office-holding failed. While the 1872 constitution restored Democratic control to all branches of state government for a time, the third postwar issue on the minds of West Virginians—economic development—soon scrambled old political allegiances.[9]

Before the war, western Virginians had often expressed frustration with an eastern Virginia–dominated government that prioritized the slave labor economy of that region over the needs of the mostly free-labor west. Richmond, in the minds of many westerners, had been slow to invest in infrastructure in the west and indifferent to its developing industries. Postwar West Virginia would need federal money to rebuild the damaged and limited transportation infrastructure it had. It would also need new influxes of capital and immigrant labor to develop its postwar economy. The politics of economic development cut across old political lines. Former Confederate- and Union-supporting political leaders came together to promote projects they viewed as in the interest of their locality. Railroads, especially, received their attention as "the most efficient engine for economic growth," and "by World War I nearly four thousand miles of track conveyed the heavy equipment necessary to cut and haul the big virgin timber away and connected even the deepest recesses of the mountains to national markets." This market revolution "fractured previous political alignments and stimulated the emergence of a new political culture. The old Confederate-Democrat versus Yankee-Republican split was replaced by pro- versus anti-industrialist factions in both parties, and the industrial factions generally prevailed."[10] These new extractive industries did not distribute the wealth they generated equally. Instead, they used up the bodies of poor West Virginians, Black and White, who laid the rail, drilled the tunnels, cut the virgin timber, and descended deep into the ground to extract the coal, expanding inequalities and creating new dependencies. Documents in this chapter examine these three intersecting issues: the status of African Americans, the rights of former Confederates, and the postwar economic development of the state.

LOYAL WEST VIRGINIANS PREPARE FOR THE RETURN OF DEFEATED CONFEDERATES

As the war neared its end, the West Virginia legislature began to plan for the return of defeated Confederates to the state. Fearful that these men might question the very existence of the new state, they acted to restrict their political rights even before Lee's surrender at Appomattox.

HOUSE BILL NO. 77.

A bill to prohibit Rebels and disloyal citizens from holding any office, either civil or military, in this State.

Be it enacted by the Legislature of West Virginia:

1. That no person who has heretofore voluntarily borne arms, or who may hereafter voluntarily bear arms or engage in armed hostility against the Government of the United States, or of the State of West Virginia, or give aid or assistance to the so-called Southern Confederacy, shall be eligible to any office, either civil or military, within this State.

2. No person who voted for the Ordinance of Secession in the year 1861, and then went into the service of the United States and has been or may be honorably discharged, shall be embraced in this act if he has volunteered prior to the passage of this act.

3. Any person who may hold or attempt to hold any office within this State contrary to this act, on being duly convicted thereof shall be fined, in the circuit court of his county. . . .

4. When any such fines shall be imposed, the cost shall first be paid out of the same and the remainder go into the free school fund of the county in which such fine is imposed.

5. Any person now holding office who may have been guilty of any crime named in this act, shall be dismissed from the same by the Governor's order, and his office supplied by a new election, at the earliest time possible, according to law.

<small>Journal of the House of Delegates of West Virginia (Wheeling: John F. M'Dermot, 1865), n.p.</small>

WEST VIRGINIANS RESPOND TO THE ASSASSINATION OF LINCOLN

The momentary euphoria loyal West Virginians felt upon hearing of Lee's surrender at Appomattox on April 9 was crushed one week later with the shocking news that Lincoln had been killed by a pro-Confederate assassin. The bitterness loyal West Virginians felt likely quelled, in the short term at least, any spirit of generosity toward their disloyal neighbors.

Proceedings in the Circuit Court of Hancock County in Relation to the National Bereavement.

At the recent session of the Grand Jury of Hancock county the following resolutions and response of Judge Caldwell were ordered to be published:

Circuit Court of Hancock County, W. Va.,

APRIL 18, A. D., 1865.

The Grand Jury in attendance at this term of this Circuit Court through their foreman, Hon. J. H. Atkinson, presented to the Court their action in reference to the death of the President, which is ordered to be entered upon these minutes, to wit:

Resolved, That as a Grand Jury, for the county of Hancock, we desire to unite with the loyal men of this country in an expression of sorrow over the said calamity which has befallen us as a nation. Never perhaps in the history of the world has such a fearful tragedy taken place. We mourn to-day a murdered President. An assassin['s] hand, has taken away our Chief Executive. But last week this nation was rejoicing over the glorious victories which had crowned our brave soldiers with glory; over the disenthrallment of patriots from Southern treason, as they came back in crowds to welcome the old flag that is to wave over us an undivided people; and over the prospect of returning peace. To day the land is covered with mourning and filled with lamentations over the murder of our President at the moment he was holding out the olive branch to thousands who had forfeited their lives to the jaws of our country. In this hour we would counsel forbearance, and while we would desire that the majesty of the laws may be maintained, we would remember that vengeance belongeth to the Lord....

Dan'l Donehoo, Clerk.

Wheeling Daily Intelligencer, May 3, 1865

"A GREAT MANY REB SOLDIERS IN THE PLACE"

Peter Mereness of Lowville, New York, served in the 5th New York Heavy Artillery Regiment, which was stationed near Washington in the early part of the war but after November 1863 was engaged in frequent action in the lower Shenandoah Valley. This letter describes the situation in Charles Town, West Virginia, at the war's end.

Charlestown Va April 27th/65

Dearest of all Friends,
Nellie

As I have a few leisure moments this evening I will endeavor to improve them by penning you a few lines in answer to a couple of letters which I rec'd from you a little more than a week ago. I am well as usual and I hope these few lines will find you enjoying the same good blessing. We have made two moves since I wrote to you last first from Maryland to Harpers Ferry and then from H. Fr. to Charlestown, Va we are now situated in a very nice place and I should judge from appearances that it was an exceedingly beautiful place once that is before this cruel war broke out.

I am at my old trade again, I suppose you can guess what it is but nevertheless I will tell you and then you will be sure to know it is cooking. I am cooking for 33 men who are on Provost duty here in the city of Charlestown. I say city it is a place much larger than Lowville.

The great trouble here is that the people here are mostly strong secessh and they turn up their nose when they see any of us around there is also a great many reb Soldiers in the place who have come home on parole.

Nell I am going to Harpers Ferry to morrow and I will get my likeness taken and send in this letter but I do not know as I need to tell you of it for you will see it when you get this letter. I hope you will excuse this poor writing as I am nearly tired out and my hand trembles very bad but I guess you will be able to read all of it except the first page which was written with a steel pen.

I am hearing some beautiful piano music and some singing by some secessh ladies just across the way from here.

I guess you will think that I am never going to write to you any more before you get this letter but the fact of it is I have been so busy since we left the Heights that I could not find time to write to anyone and if I had I should written to you first of all.

What an awful thing has happened within the past three weeks at Washington that most awful crime that was ever committed since I can remember I must draw to a close soon wishing you good health and much Joy good night—with a kiss write soon from Peter Mereness.

To Nellie

Peter Mereness to Helen A. Arthur, April 27, 1865, Peter Mereness Papers, William L. Clements Library, University of Michigan, Ann Arbor

"THEY HAD BETTER NOT RETURN AMONGST US"

Two weeks after Lincoln's assassination, loyal residents of Kingwood warned returning Confederates to stay away.

Kingwood, Preston Co., W. Va.,
April 27, 1865.

Editors Intelligencer:

This being the annual Township election day, the question arose whether those of our citizens who voluntarily left our township four years ago and went to the rebel army, should be permitted to return and live among us, and in order to ascertain the feelings of the people generally, a public meeting was called the object of which was stated and a vote taken and the result was as follows: Out of 60, 56 voted against their returning, and four in favor of their return.

Now, Messrs. Editors, you will please insert the above in your valuable paper so that those rebels may be apprised of the sentiment that prevails amongst our loyal citizens. In order to avoid all trouble hereafter for themselves they had better not return amongst us, as we disown them as citizens, and look upon them as our enemies who would destroy us and the government if they could.

Signed
Many Voters of Kingwood Township

Wheeling Daily Intelligencer, May 4, 1865

WEST VIRGINIA'S FIRST GOVERNOR CONFRONTS POSTWAR CHALLENGES

Arthur Boreman hailed from far-western Virginia counties of Tyler and Wood and was a practicing lawyer in Parkersburg when Virginia seceded from the Union. Boreman was not an abolitionist but opposed Virginia secession. In 1863 West Virginians elected him as their first governor, re-electing him to two additional terms in 1864 and 1866. In 1868 he was elected to the Senate and played a role in ratifying the Fifteenth Amendment, which extended full citizenship rights to African American men. Boreman faced the challenging tasks of dealing with returning Confederate veterans and establishing functional government in regions of the state where none had existed during the war and addressing the fate of Black West Virginians.

BY THE GOVERNOR.

An Address to the People of West Va.

Fellow-Citizens:—The Rebellion has proven a failure. In all its proportions as an organized resistance to the authority of the Government, it is ended. We may not forget by whom, by what means, and in what manner it was inaugurated and has been prosecuted; nor shut our eyes to the ruin, devastation and death that have followed in its train; yet it is not the part of wisdom to brood over the wrongs and evils of the past. Let us rather, as a people who have an interest in the great future, renew our energies to overcome the unfortunate and anomalous condition in which we find ourselves.

In some parts of the States there has been no exercise of civil authority; no mail facilities; no commercial intercourse with the rest of the country for three or four years. It is desirable that these be restored and that the necessity for the presence of a military force be removed at the earliest possible moment. The first difficulty that presents itself here is the presence of the guerilla bands that infest the parts of the States referred to; whose presence inspires such a sense of insecurity that the better part of the community hardly feel safe in attending to their ordinary business, much less in performing the duties of civil officers. The Government recognizes no rebel army now east of the Mississippi river, and an order has been issued declaring these guerillas outlaws, and denouncing against them the penalty of death. And I call upon all persons who desire a return of the security and blessings of peaceful society to aid in hunting them down and bringing them to the punishment so justly denounced against them. . . .

There are others amongst the disloyal now in the State: some of whom have been in arms against the government: who, not withstanding the rebellion, as an organized opposition to the government, has been effectually suppressed, seem to take pride in thrusting their disloyal sentiments before the community. The result is that at times they offend and excite loyal people to violence, and thus get themselves into difficulty; and if protection is not at once afforded them against the violence thus wantonly provoked, the authorities are denounced for a failure or neglect of duty. Now, if such persons wish peace and safety, I would advise them not only to yield a willing obedience to the constituted authorities, both Federal and State, but to be careful to avoid the avowal or manifestation of disloyal sentiments or sympathies, and conduct themselves in such wise that the most exacting will have no ground of complaint against them.

To the loyal people I hardly deem it necessary to say anything. It has been your pride and boast, justly so, that you were the supporters and defenders of the Government of the United States and of the State, and all orders made by them for the vindication of their authority, during the great struggle through which we have passed. Will you not continue that support as heretofore, and prove as you have in the past, that you are the law and order party of this country? The constituted authorities of the United States have made orders respecting the return of paroled rebel prisoners which the loyal people of this State deem invidious and unjust. I have used my utmost endeavors in the proper and legitimate way to have these orders revoked; but thus far without success. You have the right to protest against them and petition for their revocation; but while they remain in force, it is your duty as loyal and law abiding citizens to respect them....

Allow me especially to urge upon all good citizens of the disorganized parts of the State the propriety and necessity of giving their practical aid and co-operation in the restoration of civil authority in their respective counties....

Fellow-Citizens: nature has endowed our New State with all the elements of greatness. The capital, enterprise and labor to develop these resources await invitation to begin and successfully carry on their work. Let us, then, not only restore peace to her borders, but place her in the high road to prosperity, resolve to advance her to the front rank amongst the States of the Union, in wealth, intelligence and power.

Arthur I. Boreman,
Governor.
Executive Department,
Wheeling, W. Va., May 26, 1865.

Morgantown Weekly Post and Monongalia and Preston County Gazette, June 10, 1865

* * *

MESSAGE OF GOVERNOR ARTHUR BOREMAN TO THE SENATE, 1866:

Gentlemen of the Senate and House of Delegates:
You have assembled under more favorable auspices than any preceding legislature in our State. Since the adjournment of the last legislature, the War has been brought to a close by the triumph of National arms and the suppression of the Rebellion. . . . It is a matter of congratulation among ourselves, as of profound gratitude to the almighty God, that through His blessings the War has thus been brought to a successful and happy termination. . . .

REORGANIZATION IN THE STATE.

Permanent civil organization has been restored throughout our own State, except in five or six counties on the extreme eastern border. These have been partially organized, and would have been entirely so, had my efforts to that end been seconded as they should. But I regret to be compelled to state that many of the intelligent and leading participants in the Rebellion, instead of counselling observance of the law, have pursued a course of conduct that has prevented complete organization in the five or six counties mentioned. These parties either became candidates themselves, or induced others who, like themselves, had committed acts of disloyalty, to become candidates for office, at the election in October last; and in a number of cases these ineligible parties were elected. They cannot take the oath of office prescribed by existing law, and as a consequence, these offices are not filled by persons elected by the people, but their functions, are performed, as far as it is practicable to have them performed at all, by appointees.

JUDGE OF NINTH CIRCUIT.

At the same time, an election was held for a judge of the Ninth Judicial Circuit, and Samuel Price, Esq., of the county of Greenbrier, claims that he received a majority of the votes for that office and is therefore entitled to the commission. From some cause unknown to me, I have not received the official returns of the election from all the counties in the circuit, and therefore cannot tell who received the greatest number of votes, but am inclined to think that Mr. Price has a majority. It is well known to me, however, that at the close of the Rebellion, and for some time previous, he held the influential position of Lieutenant-Governor in the rebel government of Virginia, and of course he cannot take the oath of office prescribed by our law. I have, on this account, taken the responsibility of declining to issue a commission to him for the high and responsible position to which he claims to have been elected. I cannot commission to so high and important an office one who has so recently been engaged in efforts to destroy the State and to overthrow the Government of the United States....

ENFORCEMENT OF OATHS OF LOYALTY.

After the war ended and peace was being restored, I entertained the hope that I would be able at this session of the Legislature to recommend the modification of the more stringent laws in regard to the election and qualification of officers; but after what has transpired at the first and only election held since the close of the war in the localities where disloyalty had most prevailed, I cannot make such recommendation. On the contrary I now think it the duty of the Legislature to so amend these laws that their execution may the more certainly be secured. And to this end I recommend, 1st, that you provide for a registry of voters as authorized by the Constitution, Art iii, Sec. 12; 2d, that you declare distinctly that all officers of election shall take the oath of office, prescribed by the act of November 16, 1863, and, if they fail to do so at any place of voting, that the vote where such failure occurs shall be void and shall not be counted; 3d, that you require all the county and the principal township officers to qualify before the circuit court of the county, or the judge thereof in vacation. These amendments, it seems to me, will insure the purity of elections and the due and proper enforcement of the laws. And in order that there may be no failure in the administration of the laws where a person is elected who cannot qualify, and, at the same time, frequent elections may be avoided, it may be proper to amend the law so that vacancies may be filled until the succeeding annual election, instead of holding special elections as now provided by law; and that the vacancies in the principal township offices may be filled, as many county offices now are, by the circuit court, or the judge in vacation.

I know that the passage of the laws to which I have referred has been attributed to a vindictive and unkind spirit on the part of the loyal people towards those who have hitherto committed acts of disloyalty, but I confidently affirm that they were not so intended by those who passed them; nor am I actuated by any such spirit in recommending their amendment and enforcement. When they were passed it was deemed necessary to adopt some measures of protection against the evil influences which those in rebellion were exerting within our State....

THE COLORED PEOPLE.

The recent amendment to the Constitution of the United States completes the abolition of slavery and leaves the colored people' in our midst free, a fact which should be borne in mind and recognized. Under the constitution of our

State they cannot vote or hold office, but they are entitled to security and protection of person and property, which should be guaranteed to them by proper legislation. An important step towards the accomplishment of this purpose, and one it seems to me you should not hesitate to take, is the removal of the restrictions upon their competency as witnesses. Until this act of justice is done, all other guarantees are fruitless, and these unfortunate people are left to the mercy of any one who chooses to inflict injury upon them.

Journal of the Senate of the State of West Virginia, for the Fourth Session, Commencing January 16, 1866 (Wheeling: John Frew, 1866), 5–10

EMERGING RESISTANCE TO RADICAL REPUBLICAN RULE

The wing of the Republican Party that remained committed to holding traitors accountable for their actions after the war and extending rights to freed people came to be called the Radical Republicans, and under Governor Boreman's leadership they temporarily held sway in West Virginia politics. But those who sought a speedy restoration of the political rights of former Confederates and who resisted the extension of rights to freedmen and freedwomen became increasingly powerful in the state beginning in 1866, emboldened by President Andrew Johnson's Reconstruction policies, which were generous toward defeated White Confederates but quite stingy toward the formerly enslaved. In April of 1866, conservative Democrats gathered at Clarksburg to call for an end to "radical misrule."

STATE CONVENTION

Important Proceedings.

Opposition to Radicalism.
Stirring Resolutions.

Organize! Register! Vote!!

The State Convention called by the opponents of radical misrule, assembled at the Court House in Clarksburg, at 10 o'clock a.m. on Thursday, April 12th. . . .

The members of the Convention assembled at 2 o'clock and proceeded to the transaction of business. The report of the committee on resolutions being called for, the committee, through its chairman, Mr. Lamb, submitted the following

RESOLUTIONS

Resolved, That Andrew Johnson has won our confidence by his unwavering devotion to the Union; and we heartily approve his policy looking to the speedy restoration of the Southern States to their constitutional position in the National government, and the re-establishment of peace and civil law throughout the land.

Resolved, That by the Freedman's Bureau bill, and Civil rights bill, the Congressional majority have attempted to subject the tax-paying population of the country to heavy additional burdens, in order to support the negro in idleness and vice, and maintain new "swarms of officers to harass our people and eat out their substance."

Resolved, That the Constitution of the United States is the supreme law of the land, but it is equally supreme in what it reserves as in what it grants; that it has granted to the United States ample powers for national objects and for the common defence against war and insurrection, but has reserved to the several States the care and regulation of civil rights within their respective limits; that, in particular, it belongs to the States to prescribe how contracts may be made, proved and enforced, how real and personal property may be inherited, acquired, used and disposed of, and the life, liberty, property and character of individuals protected; and that while, on the one hand, the central government ought to be supported in the exercise of all its legitimate powers, on the other, the continued existence of the States and the preservation of their rightful authority, are necessary to the liberty and welfare of the American people; yet by the Freedman's Bureau Bill, and Civil Rights Bill, Congress have endeavored, in violation of the fundamental principle of our government, to deprive the State Legislatures and Judiciary of many of their most important functions—an attempt which, if it prove successful, must lead in the end to the abolition of State Governments, as useless and expensive incumbrances to the central despotism at Washington.

Resolved, That by the bills in question, Congress have endeavored, in favor of the negro, to subject the white inhabitants of the country to the continuation of military rule, and the jurisdiction of tribunals foreign to their habits and institutions and destructive of their liberties.

Resolved, That while we could protect the negro in his civil rights and freedom by just State legislation, we are opposed to negro suffrage, because we believe it impossible to support republican government upon a negro constituency; and we regard with abhorrence the policy of the Congressional majority, led by Stevens, Sumner and Wade, and supported by a party in this State, intended to prevent any restoration of the Union until negro suffrage is forced on the several States by Federal authority.

Resolved, That they are *Unionists* who seek to restore the Union, and they are *Disunionists* who seek to prevent its restoration; and he alone is *loyal,* who is faithful and true to the Constitution of the United States and the Constitution of the State.

Resolved, That the Test oaths, Registration act, and the several acts of the Legislature of this State, to suppress freedom of elections, of speech and of the press; to encourage public officers to violate the Constitution, and protect them in so doing; to establish the reign of a single man in the Ninth Judicial circuit, and to prevent a portion of our people from asserting any right by legal proceedings, thus denying them the protection of law, and subjecting them to the fraud, oppression and plunder of pretended loyalists; are unwise, destructive to the welfare and prosperity of the State, and inconsistent alike with the provisions of the Constitution and the principles of free government. . . .

Resolved, That the proposed amendment to the constitution of the State, permanently depriving of the civil and political rights of citizenship, all who, under any circumstances, have given any voluntary aid whatever to the rebellion, must operate most unjustly, and at the same time, disastrously to the interest and welfare of the State. It will, we believe, prevent the re-establishment of peace, order and good government, drive away immigration and capital by causing constant strife and discord among the people—compel a portion of our population to abandon the State, or become the enemies of its government—and lead to new excesses of power and persecution on the part of malignant men, who will regard the ratification of the amendment as sanctioning the system of misrule and extravagant legislation to which we have been subjected. We regard it as unwise, and at the same time cruel and unworthy of a christian people.

Resolved, That the effort of the Radical party to delude voters into the support of such measures, by denouncing their opponents as rebels and copperheads, and raising an outcry that the news State is in danger, is but an artifice to raise false issues—to draw away attention from their own misdeeds—and prevent the voters of the State from calmly investigating the character and effects of the recent acts of legislation.

Resolved, That we earnestly appeal to the voters of the State, without regard to former party names or divisions, to unite in opposition to these measures, and in support of the policy of President Johnson. Organize—Register—Vote. These are the only peacable means to protect and defend civil liberty and popular rights.

After the reading of the resolutions it was moved that they be adopted as a whole. The motion was agreed to with great unanimity and enthusiasm. . . .

Wheeling Daily Register, April 14, 1866

JEFFERSON COUNTY VOTERS TURNED AWAY FROM THE POLLS IN 1869

By 1869, many moderate Republicans had become uneasy with the aggressive tactics local registrars were using to suppress the vote. Here the

Spirit of Jefferson, *a paper that typically presented an unreconstructed viewpoint, reprints an editorial that appeared in the Republican newspaper the Berkeley* Star, *which criticized the excesses of governor-appointed registrars in suppressing rival votes.*

THE OUTRAGE TOO APPARENT

The result of the recent election in this county, the circumstances under which it was held, and the manipulations that preceded it, are too much even for the Berkely *Star,* staunch Republican as it is, in its proclivities. In the last issue we find the following:—

Jefferson County.—The county of Jefferson at the recent election cast 272 votes!!

Here is a county with a voting population of 2,300. Suppose there be in it, and it is a most exaggerated estimate, 600 persons who were so directly or indirectly connected with the rebellion as to exclude them from the right of suffrage, still there remain 1,700 voters at this moment clearly and unquestionably entitled to vote according to the existing laws and constitution of this State. How is it then, that these 1,700 legal voters of the county of Jefferson are reduced to 272? It is by virtue of this infamous and atrocious abuse of the Registration law of which the annals of party crime can afford no parallel. In no part of this Republic is there a more intelligent, refined, educated, and high spirited people than compose the population of Jefferson; and that they should for the last five years have submitted to the infamous proceedings of the Underdonk's and Turner's of that county, is just past comprehension. Will Governor Stevenson further tolerate these crimes against the liberties of his fellow-citizens, and against the laws and the constitution of his State? Will he make himself the further instrument of the perpetration of these enormities? Will the Legislature continue in the hands of the Executive, a power liable to such abuses? Is it the policy and purpose of Governor Stevenson by a system of most unparalleled annoyances and oppressions to drive these people into a state of chronic resistance to the State authority?

We are Republicans, and we wish success to the Republican party, but the abuses and the enormities of which the county of Jefferson has been the theatre, for the past five years, are sufficient to destroy any party on earth, unless it promptly corrects the gross injustice and wrong resulting from the present abuse of the Registration Law.

Spirit of Jefferson (Charles Town, WV), November 9, 1869

ACCUSATIONS OF VOTER SUPPRESSION IN JEFFERSON COUNTY

This document with missing pages appears to be a Jefferson County election official's response to charges that in the October 1869 elections some legal voters were turned away or had their votes destroyed. The author defends the actions of voting officials in two townships in Jefferson County during that election. Open voting was nearly universal at this time, and voters often carried ballots printed by their favored political party into the polls with them. The appearance of voters with a ballot of a different color than the Republican one may have attracted the suspicion of election officials, who challenged these voters' eligibility.

. . . The voters at Chapline & Shepherds township all voted. Some rebels who were at the polls in said townships on the day of the election offered colored ballots which were refused. Others asked whether they could vote and when told if they were challenged they would be obliged to take the test oath required by [the] 56th chapter of the laws of 1865, refused to even offer their ballots. The few persons who asked to have their names placed on the registered list carried their ballots away with them; more of the parties who were refused their votes left their ballots with the Inspector of election except one . . . who laid this ballot in the window at the polls and went off and left it without saying anything. . . .

I further say that all of the parties whose names [are] annexed to the motion of contest did not offer to vote in Shepherd or Chapline Township.

I further say that if the supervisors of Jefferson County excluded any ballots from this count, they had good reasons for so doing, they having a right so to do.

I am informed and deny the lie that at the Charlestown Polls the Inspectors of the election were not appointed according to law [or] that colored ballots that were deposited in the box, which ballots had your name printed thereon were taken out and white ballots put in their stead. That the poll books of Charlestown Township were not delivered by one of the inspectors of said Township to the proper officer of the county, as required by law.

I charge that you together with other copperheads used your best effort to subvert a legal election being held in Jefferson Co. that you disregarded the laws of the state and advised others so to do. . . .

_{Author unknown, "Letter discussing post Civil War party politics in West Virginia," incomplete, GLC08606.07, Gilder Lehrman Institute Collections, New York}

"WEST VIRGINIA REDEEMED!"

After the controversies surrounding the 1869 elections, Republican governor William Stevenson removed some of the barriers to voting so that former Confederates could once again exercise the franchise. Even the enfranchisement of African American voters could not keep West Virginia's Republicans in office, as Democrats were victorious across the state, putting John Jacob in the governor's office and capturing majorities in both branches of the legislature. Radical Republicans in the state laid the blame for defeat on liberal Republicans who had abandoned the Republican cause. Democratic organs like the Charles Town Spirit of Jefferson *crowed about the overturning of Republican rule.*

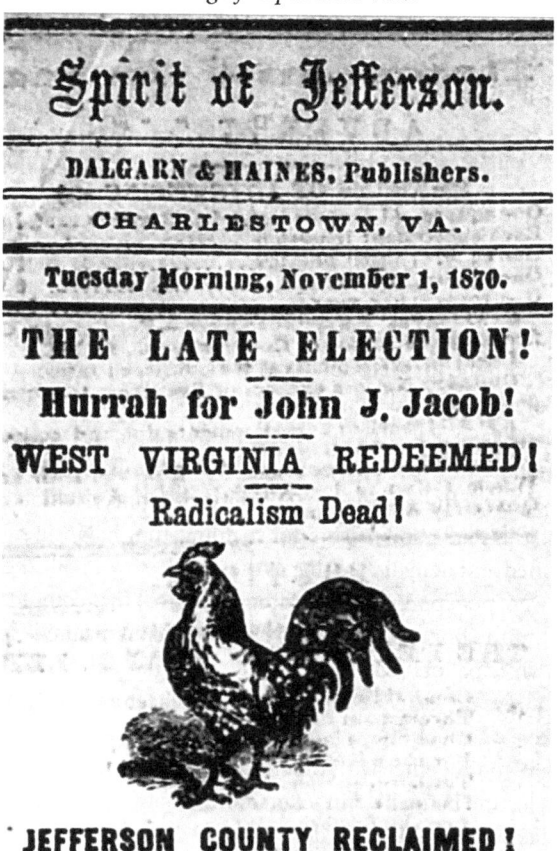

The *Spirit of Jefferson* celebrates the end of Republican rule in the state. Note that seven years after statehood, and five years after the Civil War's end, the newspaper still locates Charles Town in the state of Virginia. Charles Town *Spirit of Jefferson* November 1, 1870. Library of Congress.

THE LATE ELECTION!

Hurrah for John J. Jacob!
West Virginia Redeemed!
Radicalism Dead!

Jefferson County Reclaimed!
The Ball in Motion!

The returns from the gubernatorial election of Thursday last, as far as received, exhibit one of the grandest political revolutions in the history of this country, and indicate pretty clearly that John J. Jacob, the Democratic Conservative candidate for Governor, together with the entire State ticket have been elected by a handsome majority.

Jefferson county, in the election of 1868, gave Stevenson a majority of twenty, but now, with the addition of *four hundred registered negro voters*—who marched in serried ranks to the aid of radicalism—she gives to John J. Jacob a *majority of fifty*.

Berkeley county, in 1868, gave to Stevenson a majority of four hundred and sixteen which is now—notwithstanding the addition of three or four hundred negro votes—cut down to but little over *one hundred*.

In this Senatorial district—Jefferson and Berkeley—the radical candidate, Gold, is elected by a small majority. In Berkeley we elect the Sheriff and one member of the House of Delegates. In Jefferson, we elect the Sheriff, two members of the House of Delegates, Clerk of the Circuit Court, Assessor, Prosecuting Attorney, three Supervisors, and a fourth tied; besides a large majority of the township officers. All this was accomplished without any regular nominations on our part, and in the absence of any organization whatever, whilst, on the other hand, the radical party were drilled to perfection, and voted in solid column. Had every registered Conservative voter cast his ballot on Thursday last, not a single Radical would have been elected in the county.

As will be seen from the telegrams published elsewhere, the news of the State is the most encouraging. Large Democratic gains are reported everywhere, and Jacob's majority already puts up 5,400. We will have a good majority in the Legislature, and secure the election of a Democratic United States Senator, in the place of Mr. Willey.

Thus the death-knell to the vile hordes who have lorded it over West Virginia for the past five years, is sounded. The people have arisen in their might, and the State is redeemed.—*Sic Semper Tyrannis.*

THE NEGROES AND THE LATE ELECTION.

The votes of the majority of the negroes, at the election on Thursday last, were cast as we expected—for the straight out Radical ticket. But we confess surprise at the action of some of this class, for whilst the larger portion of them are ignorant and uneducated, and hence an easy prey to the vilifying scoundrels who have made them their dupes, we had thought that such intelligent colored men as Henry Cooke, James Brady, and others—who make their livelihood from the *white* people alone—would have had more discretion. But we believe that here, as has been the case elsewhere in the South, after the excitement of the first exercise of the right of suffrage is over, that they will give the subject a calm consideration, and drop, as a coal of fire, the miserable carpet-baggers and political tricksters that have been deceiving them thus far, and who have no interest at sake save their own vile greed for office.

<small>*Spirit of Jefferson* (Charles Town, WV), November 1, 1870</small>

"A PARTY . . . DANGEROUS TO OUR EXISTENCE AS A STATE"

Not all West Virginians were happy about the political turn that occurred in the 1870 election. The Republican Point Pleasant Weekly Register *viewed the return of "the corrupt Democracy" as a threat to West Virginia's independent statehood.*

. . . The masses of the American people are too apt to be swayed by their prejudices rather than be controlled by sound reasoning. Particularly was this prejudice exhibited in the election in this State last Thursday, by many casting their votes with the corrupt Democracy, who had up to that day acted with the Republican party. In their blindness, they have by their votes, elevated, in all probability, a party to power in West Virginia, that is dangerous to our existence as a State. A party that in '61 used every possible means to destroy the government—that engaged in hostile rebellion to do so; that caused the death of more than 500,000 citizens of this nation; that caused more than $2,000,000,000 of debt to hang over this Union, and which now oppresses the people from one end of the country to the other. Yes, you, Republicans who have allowed your prejudices rather than your sound judgment to control you, have put power into the hands of a dangerous party in this State, which they will use against you. And mark our word, which you will regret as long as you live. How long do you suppose your Free School law will be enforced by this Democratic party? Don't you know that this party has always opposed the education? Yes, you knew it.

But rather than give up your prejudices, you have by your votes said, "let my children grow up in ignorance." You have by your vote endangered your educational system, for which vote your children will yet curse you. You have listened to the misrepresentations and falsehoods of your enemies. You have believed them. You have voted with your oppressors; and you will receive that reward at their hands your foolish act deserves. . . .

Weekly Register (Point Pleasant, WV), November 3, 1870

THE FLICK AMENDMENT

The rights of former Confederates were fully restored in April 1871 when voters endorsed the Flick Amendment to the West Virginia constitution. Liberal Republican William H. H. Flick had initially proposed it as a kind of compromise. The amendment affirmed the rights of African American men to vote and at the same time fully restored the voting rights of those who had been disloyal during the war. Liberal Republicans' hopes that this action might restore Republicans to power were not realized.

THE QUESTION TO BE VOTED ON TO-DAY.

The people of this State are called on to vote to-day upon a proposition to amend the State Constitution. The purpose of the amendment is two-fold: first to restore the ballot to those now disfranchised for their participation in the rebellion; and, second, to remove the discrimination in the Constitution which limits the right of suffrage to "white" persons, and thereby make that instrument conform to the XVth Article of Amendment of the Constitution of the United States.

The precise terms of the proposed Amendment will be understood, we trust, from the following explanation. Section 1 of Article III of the State Constitution is now as follows:

"1. The *white* male citizens of the State shall be entitled to vote at all elections held within the election districts in which they respectively reside, but no person who is a minor, or of unsound mind, or a pauper, or who is under conviction of treason, felony or bribery in an election, or who has not been a resident of the State for one year, and of the county in which he offers to vote for thirty days, shall be permitted to vote while such disability continues. *No person who since the 1st day of June, 1861, has given, or shall give, voluntary aid or assistance to the rebellion against the United States, shall be a citizen of this State, or be allowed to vote at any election therein, unless he has volunteered into the military or naval service of the United States, and has been, or shall be, honorably discharged therefrom."*

The Amendment proposes to strike that section out and insert in place of it the following:

"1. The male citizens of the State shall be entitled to vote at all elections held within the election districts in which they respectively reside; but no person who is a minor, or of unsound mind, or a pauper, or who is under conviction of treason, felony or bribery in an election, or who has not been a resident of the State for one year, and of the county in which he offers to vote for thirty days, next preceding such offer, shall be permitted to vote while such disability continues."

The effect of this, it will be perceived, is to eliminate from the section as it now stands in the constitution, those portions which we have placed in *italics*.

The negro already has a right to vote in this State by an authority which overrides the denial of it by a State Constitution. He is a voter now, and will continue to be, whether our State Constitution be amended or not. Practically, therefore, the only substantial question involved in the amendment is that of enfranchising the ex-Confederates.

Wheeling Daily Intelligencer, April 27, 1871

LOW TURNOUT FOR THE FLICK AMENDMENT VOTE

The Wheeling Daily Intelligencer *speculates on the cause of voter apathy over the Flick Amendment.*

YESTERDAY'S ELECTION.

The vote yesterday on the proposed amendment to the State Constitution was the lightest ever cast in this city. In the seven city townships from which we have returns only 435 votes were cast all told—less than one-tenth of the full vote of those townships. There was an utter absence of interest; and those who voted did so, we presume, as a matter of abstract duty. We can only regret that so many felt no sense of duty as citizens in connection with the matter submitted to them.

While the indifference shown is to be regretted as a not very healthy indication, it is not by any means unaccountable. The questions involved in a vote were purely impersonal and abstract. It has been often demonstrated that no election which does not involve money or personal success, or both, will excite more than a limited interest. Neither money nor personal interests entered into this election.

Then again it was a peculiarity of the proposed Amendment that it contained features displeasing to a very large number of both parties. It required an unpleasant concession from each. The Democrat was required to concede negro suffrage, and the Republican ex-rebel suffrage. A very large proportion of each party felt reluctant to make these respective concessions, and this reluctance helped very much to make them indifferent about the election and to keep them at home.

No opinion can be formed at present, that is worth expressing, about the result in the State.

<small>Wheeling Daily Intelligencer, April 28, 1871</small>

BUILDING A NEW WEST VIRGINIA

The political rights of former Confederates and freedmen and freedwomen were not the only issues that West Virginians were concerned with at the war's end. Four years of war had taken a toll on the state's infrastructure, and the legislature sought financial support for rebuilding roads and infrastructure from the federal government, noting that "during the recent rebellion, our State, lying on the border, has been peculiarly exposed to the raids of the enemy and the ravages and desolations resulting from the oft repeated tread of advancing and retreating armies, and . . . our citizens have endured sufferings beyond weight or measure."[11] The urge to build a new economy for West Virginia, which many West Virginians believed had been hampered by the slave-centered economy of antebellum Virginia, was strong. Among the priorities was attracting more people and external capital. On March 2, 1864, the West Virginia legislature passed an act "for the encouragement of immigration to this state" and appointed a commissioner of immigration the next day. Over the next several years Commissioner J. H. Diss Debar mailed out "over 18,000 pamphlets, hand-bills, and advertisements, exhibiting the various resources of the state, and our inducements to immigration." In 1870 the state financed the publication of a handbook (see image below) touting the state's advantages. The state seal had been adopted in September 1863, and it depicted an independent farmer and a miner with the state motto, which translates to "Mountaineers Are Always Free."

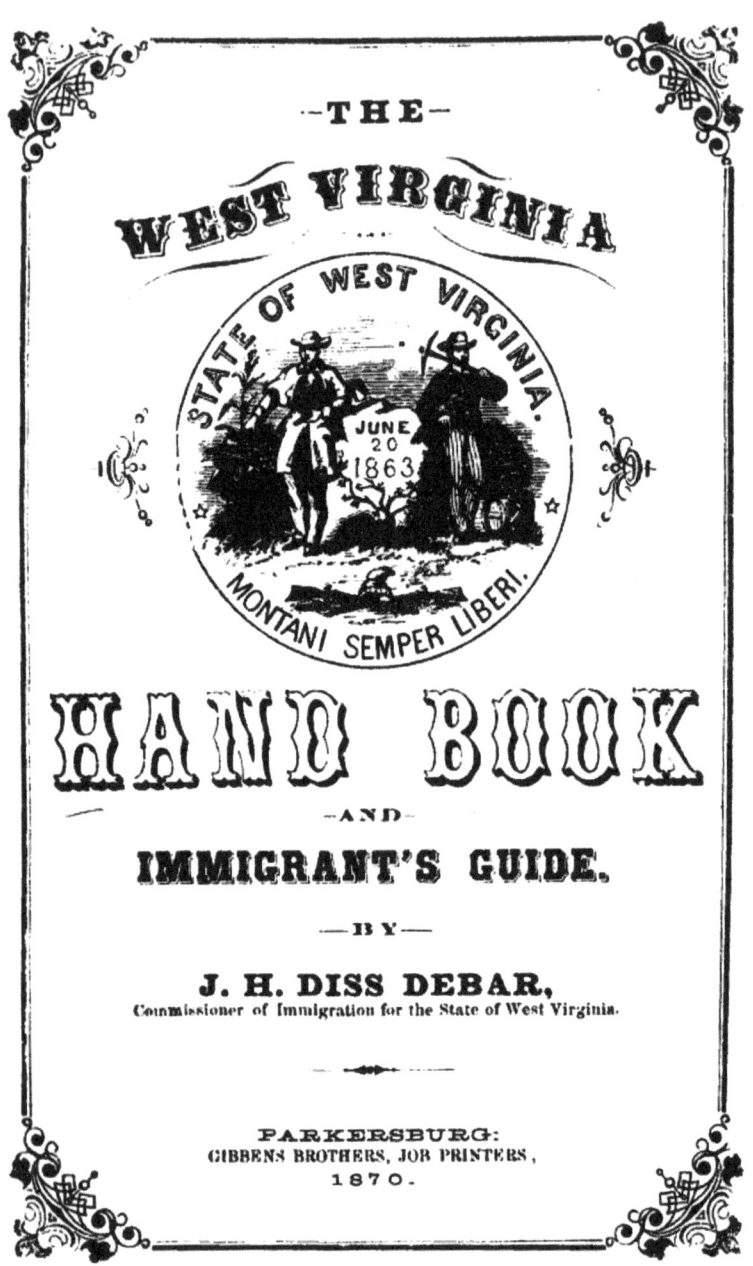

J. H. Diss Debar, *The West Virginia Hand Book and Immigrant's Guide* (Parkersburg, WV: Gibbens Brothers, 1870).

"SHALL WE NOT SHOW OURSELVES WORTHY OF OUR OWN EMANCIPATION?"

In the years after the Civil War, West Virginia politicians embraced railroad building and other capital investment in the state as a path to prosperity and "emancipation." Former enemies joined together to promote this transformation.

At a mass meeting of the citizens of the counties of Monongalia, Marion, Harrison, and Upshur, held at Fairmont, West Virginia, on the 2nd day of November, 1865, W.T. Willey of Monongalia; T.B. Taylor of Marion, Colonel Spates of Harrison; F. Berlin of Upshur; and Colonel Kapp of Greenbrier, we appointed a committee *"to prepare and publish in pamphlet form, for distribution, an address to the people of the State, and to capitalists, on the subject of constructing the proposed road, collecting all the facts in relationship to the mineral wealth and agricultural resources along the route, or contiguous thereto."*

The points designated in the charter for this road are: the Pennsylvania line at or near where it crosses the Mononghela river, Morgantown, Fairmont or Palatine, Clarksburg, Buckhannon, and Lewisburg. It must, therefore, pass through the counties of Monongalia, Marion, Harrison, Upshur, Randolph or Lewis, Webster, Pocahontas, and Greenbrier. The "contiguous" counties are Preston, Taylor, Barbour, Braxton &c. . . .

We proceed now to an examination of the resources of the portion of West Virginia through which it is proposed to carry this great improvement. . . .

It is a remarkable fact that although the territory embraced in the boundaries of West Virginia, has composed part of one of the oldest, if not entirely the oldest State in the Union, and contains within it natural resources unsurpassed by the same amount of territory anywhere else in the United States, we are, nevertheless, almost the hindmost in improvements and development. The richest in natural resources, we are among the poorest in fact. Most advantageously located, geographically, for convenient connections with the best marts of trade and commerce, we have no connections with any of them, excepting those provided ready made by the hand of nature, and by the enterprise of a foreign corporation. Look at another strange fact. In our State there are 8,550,257 acres of unimproved land, and only 2,346,137 acres of improved land. If this were the fault of our own people it were a shame; as it is, it is our misfortune. . . . But it cannot remain. We, too, are in one sense now the freedmen of the nation. We are no longer subject to the domination of that remorseless political and sectional majority which has hitherto withheld from us the means of developing our resources. Shall we not show ourselves worthy of our own emancipation?

Will it be answered that we have not the means to make this road? If we have the will, the means will come. Let us properly invite capital from those who have it to spare. If we take the necessary pains to inform capitalists of the actual natural wealth of our State they will, for their own sakes, come to our relief. They will see, moreover, as all must see, that this improvement is not local, but it is, in fact, national in its character and relations. . . .

If the attention of intelligent capitalists can be properly attracted to these conspicuous advantages, and to the manifold invaluable mineral resources abounding along the proposed route for this road, they cannot fail to see that few enterprises of this character ever presented themselves offering so many great inducements for investment. . . .

But let our fellow-citizens of West Virginia remember the familiar maxim, that if we expect Hercules to aid us we must put our own shoulders to the wheel. The best means of securing the attention and cooperation of foreign capitalists are the zeal, energy, and public spirit which we ourselves bring to the prosecution of the work. . . .

W.T. Willey, Chairman.

Waitman Willey, *Address to the People of West Virginia on the Mineral Wealth and Agricultural Resources of the Route of the Monongahela and Lewisburg Railroad* (Washington, D.C., 1866), 3–8, pamphlet attached to the Waitman Willey diary, West Virginia Collection, West Virginia and Regional History Center, West Virginia University, Morgantown

JOHN HENRY

The end of the war brought a renewed interest in railroad building across West Virginia. Many of the lines were financed by out-of-state capital and built with the labor of freedmen, including some who quickly lost that freedom after being charged with crimes. The Thirteenth Amendment to the U.S. Constitution, ratified in December of 1865, had outlawed involuntary servitude, "except as punishment for crime whereof the party shall have been duly convicted." The ballad of John Henry tells the story of a steel driver working on a railroad tunnel who has a fateful competition with a steam-powered drill to blast a tunnel through rock. Dozens of versions of the song survive, and many place the events at the Big Bend Tunnel, which was completed on the Chesapeake and Ohio Railroad (C&O) near Talcott, West Virginia, between 1870 and 1872. We cannot know for certain whether the song was inspired by actual events and if so where the contest might have occurred. Recent scholarship suggests that Henry was a Black convict laborer sent from an eastern Virginia penitentiary ("the big white house") to work on the C&O and that the event more likely occurred in

Danville, Virginia.[12] The song nevertheless resonated deeply throughout postbellum West Virginia and across the South, as it spoke to the impact of capital and new technology on the experiences of laborers in the late nineteenth century. Melvin T. Hairston of Raleigh, West Virginia, shared this version with folklore scholar Guy B. Johnson in the 1920s.

> John Henry, who was a baby
> Sitting on his papa's knee.
> He said, "The Big Ben Tunnel on the C. & O. Road,
> It is sure to be the death of me."
>
> O shaker, huh turner, let her go down,
> O shaker, huh turner, let her go down.
>
> They took John Henry from the big white house
> And they put him in the tunnel for to drive,
> With two nine-pound hammers hanging by his side
> And the steam drill pointing to the sky, etc.
>
> O shaker, huh turner, let her go down,
> O shaker, huh turner, let her go down.
>
> John Henry was standing on the right hand side
> And the steam drill standing on the left.
> He said, "Before I would let you beat me down,
> I would hammer my fool self to death, etc."
>
> Oh he died with his hammer in his hand,
> Oh he died with his hammer in his hand.
>
> John Henry, he had a woman,
> Her name was Mary Magdalene.
> She would go to the tunnel and sing for John,
> Just to hear John Henrys hammer ring, etc.
>
> Oh he died with his hammer in his hand,
> Oh he died with his hammer in his hand.
>
> Well they took John Henry to the new burying ground
> And they covered him up in the sand,

And I see his little woman coming down the street,
She says, "Yonder lay my steel-driving man," etc.

Oh he died with his hammer in his hand,
Oh he died with his hammer in his hand.

Some said he come from Kentucky,
Some said he come from Spain.
It was written on his tombstone and placed at his head,
"John Henry was an East Virginia man," etc.

Oh he died with his hammer in his hand,
Oh he died with his hammer in his hand.

Guy B. Johnson, *John Henry: Tracking Down a Negro Legend* (Chapel Hill: University of North Carolina Press, 1929), 108–9.

BOOKER T. WASHINGTON: *UP FROM SLAVERY*

Born into slavery in eastern Virginia, Booker T. Washington's family arrived with other migrants to work in the coal mines and salt factories of the Kanawha Valley. In his famous autobiography, he described his childhood in the Kanawha Valley in the postwar years.

. . . My mother's husband, who was the stepfather of my brother John and myself, did not belong to the same owners as did my mother. In fact, he seldom came to our plantation. I remember seeing him there perhaps once a year, that being about Christmas time. In some way, during the war, by running away and following the Federal soldiers, it seems, he found his way into the new state of West Virginia. As soon as freedom was declared, he sent for my mother to come to the Kanawha Valley, in West Virginia. At that time a journey from Virginia over the mountains to West Virginia was rather a tedious and in some cases a painful undertaking. What little clothing and few household goods we had were placed in a cart, but the children walked the greater portion of the distance, which was several hundred miles.

I do not think any of us ever had been very far from the plantation, and the taking of a long journey into another state was quite an event. The parting from our former owners and the members of our own race on the plantation was a serious occasion. From the time of our parting till their death we kept up a correspondence with the older members of the family, and in later years we have kept in touch with those who were the younger members. We were several weeks making the trip, and most of the time we slept in the open air and did our cooking over a log fire out-of-doors. One night I recall that we camped near an abandoned log cabin, and my mother decided to build a fire in that for cooking, and afterward to make a "pallet" on the floor for our sleeping. Just as the fire had gotten well started a large black snake fully a yard and a half long dropped down the chimney and ran out on the floor. Of course we at once abandoned that cabin. Finally we reached our destination—a little town called Malden, which is about five miles from Charleston, the present capital of the state.

At that time salt-mining was the great industry in that part of West Virginia, and the little town of Malden was right in the midst of the salt-furnaces. My stepfather had already secured a job at a salt-furnace and he had also secured a little cabin for us to live in. Our new house was no better than the one we had left on the old plantation in Virginia. In fact, in one respect it was worse. Notwithstanding the poor condition of our plantation cabin, we were at all times sure of pure air. Our new home was in the midst of a cluster of cabins crowded closely together, and as there were no sanitary regulations, the filth about the cabins was often intolerable. Some of our neighbours were coloured people, and some were the poorest and most ignorant and degraded white people. It was a motley mixture. Drinking, gambling, quarrels, fights, and shockingly immoral practices were frequent. All who lived in the little town were in one way or another connected with the salt business. Though I was a mere child, my stepfather put me and my brother at work in one of the furnaces. Often I began work as early as four o'clock in the morning.

The first thing I ever learned in the way of book knowledge was while working in this salt-furnace. Each salt-packer had his barrels marked with a certain number. The number allotted to my stepfather was "18." At the close of the day's work the boss of the packers would come around and put "18" on each of our barrels, and I soon learned to recognize that figure wherever I saw it, and after a while got to the point where I could make that figure, though I knew nothing about any other figures or letters. . . .

About this time the question of having some kind of a school opened for the coloured children in the village began to be discussed by members of the race. . . . [A] young coloured man from Ohio, who had been a soldier, in some way found his way into town. It was soon learned that he possessed considerable education, and he was engaged by the coloured people to teach their first school. As yet no free schools had been started for coloured people in that section, hence each family agreed to pay a certain amount per month, with the understanding that the teacher was to "board 'round"—that is, spend a day with each family. This was not bad for the teacher, for each family tried to provide the very best on the day the teacher was to be its guest. I recall that I looked forward with an anxious appetite to the "teacher's day" at our little cabin. . . .

After I had worked in the salt-furnace for some time, work was secured for me in a coal-mine which was operated mainly for the purpose of securing fuel for the salt-furnace. Work in the coal-mine I always dreaded. One reason for this was that any one who worked in a coal-mine was always unclean, at least while at work, and it was a very hard job to get one's skin clean after the day's work was over. Then it was fully a mile from the opening of the coal-mine to the face of the coal, and all, of course, was in the blackest darkness. I do not believe that one ever experiences anywhere else such darkness as he does in a coal-mine. The mine was divided into a large number of different "rooms" or departments, and, as I never was able to learn the location of all these "rooms," I many times found myself lost in the mine. To add to the horror of being lost, sometimes my light would go out, and then, if I did not happen to have a match, I would wander about in the darkness until by chance I found some one to give me a light. The work was not only hard, but it was dangerous. There was always the danger of being blown to pieces by a premature explosion of powder, or of being crushed by falling slate. Accidents from one or the other of these causes were frequently occurring, and this kept me in constant fear. Many children of the tenderest years were compelled then, as is now true, I fear, in most coal-mining districts, to spend a large part of their lives in these coal-mines, with little opportunity to get an education; and, what is worse, I have often noted that, as a rule, young boys who begin life in a coal-mine are often physically and mentally dwarfed. They soon lose ambition to do anything else than to continue as a coal-miner.

Booker T. Washington, *Up from Slavery* (New York: Doubleday, Page, 1907), 24–39

NINE

Memory

Between 2017 and 2021, a series of public protests occurred at the West Virginia Capitol, with demonstrators calling for the removal of Charleston's oldest Civil War monument: the statue of Stonewall Jackson that occupies the statehouse grounds. Ten thousand concerned citizens signed a petition in support of removal, and someone set a Confederate flag on fire at one event. A local commercial property broker in Charleston declared the Stonewall monument to be "a form of hate speech," and he proposed putting the statue "in the darkest corner of the basement of the [West Virginia] Culture Center, with interpretive signage and the movie '12 Years a Slave' running on a continuous loop in the background."[1] Some West Virginians also called for the renaming of Charleston's Stonewall Jackson Middle School and a Stonewall Jackson Bridge in Hampshire County and for the removal of the Stonewall Jackson monument in front of the Harrison County courthouse. These and other calls for ending the celebration of those who fought to protect and extend the institution of slavery have met with resistance. Conservatives in the state legislature responded by drafting legislation to prohibit "the relocation, removal, alteration, renaming, rededication, or other disturbance" of monuments and memorials on public property without securing permission from the West Virginia State Historic Preservation Office.[2] While these battles over the public memory of West Virginia's war continue, historian Steven Cody Straley noted in 2022 that "the fight to remove Jackson monuments [had] produced mixed results." Charleston has renamed its middle school, but monuments to Jackson still remain on public property in Charleston and in Clarksburg. At the same time, however, conservatives in the legislature have not successfully passed a bill to give monuments broad protections from removal by the people.[3]

Historical monuments are one of the ways groups have tried to shape the "public memory" of the past. Monuments are not neutral, but rather they tell a story or convey a viewpoint. In West Virginia, a state born in the conflict of the Civil War, campaigns to control the public memory via monuments in stone and bronze began shortly after the war ended. The town of Romney in Hampshire County held the first postwar public decoration ceremonies of Confederate graves in the spring of 1866. From that small gathering emerged an effort to raise money and construct a memorial to the Confederate dead, which the citizens of Romney dedicated on September 26, 1867. After some debate, the supporters of this first Confederate monument in West Virginia settled on an inscription that read, "The Daughters of Old Hampshire Erect This Tribute of Affection to Her Heroic Sons Who Fell in the Defense of Southern Rights."[4]

The battle over public memory of the Civil War often began with commemorations of the war dead, in the places they were interred, but eventually moved to more public spaces, like county courthouse lawns and state house grounds. Americans who had allied themselves with the defeated Confederacy were especially eager to establish a sympathetic narrative in the public mind, and Confederate women's groups like the United Daughters of the Confederacy often took the lead in the monument-planting campaign.[5] Campaigns to erect, and much later to remove, monuments and statues in West Virginia followed the same path they did in other American states.

The Romney memorial was the first public monument in West Virginia to promote what historians call the "Lost Cause" narrative of the Civil War, a particular way of understanding the war and its meaning. Historian Caroline Janney has identified six core tenets of the Lost Cause, advanced in monuments, school textbooks, and in popular media: (1) the idea that slavery was not the cause of the Civil War; (2) that slavery was a benign institution and that most enslaved people were loyal to their masters; (3) that Union victory was merely the result of overwhelming material advantages; (4) that Confederate soldiers were heroes who were only defeated by the vastly superior resources of the North; (5) that the leaders of the Confederacy were anointed by God and that the first among these was Robert E. Lee, but western Virginia–born Stonewall Jackson was a not-too-distant second; and (6) that the faithful devotion of White Southern women sustained a righteous cause for four long years.[6]

Across the South, wives and daughters of Confederate soldiers took the lead in public commemoration of the Lost Cause, as they had in Romney.[7] During the first century after the war's end, champions of the Confederacy had great success getting their viewpoint represented in West Virginia's public spaces. About ten Lost Cause monuments were erected across the state before the war's centennial. The dedication of a Confederate soldiers monument in Monroe County in 1901 drew a crowd of twelve thousand. Other West Virginia monuments to the Confederate soldiers were dedicated in Lewisburg (1906), Parkersburg (1908), Randolph County (1913), Hinton (1914), Charleston (1922), and Clarksburg (1953). Two monuments in the state advanced the Lost Cause tenet of the faithful slave. A monument to the Confederate Kanawha Riflemen listed "William Armstead, colored cook, faithful during the war" near the bottom.

Erected in 1922, the Kanawha Riflemen monument was removed in 2020. In 1931 the United Daughters of the Confederacy dedicated a monument to Heyward Shepherd, a free Black resident of the town before the war who was shot by John Brown's raiders. That marker honors Shepherd for allegedly "exemplifying the character and faithfulness of thousands of negros" across the South.

There were also efforts to honor the sacrifices of men who fought to preserve the Union across the state. In 1883, Wheeling dedicated its Soldiers and Sailors Monument, which still stands but has been relocated twice. In 1886, citizens of Hancock County installed a Union monument in front of the county courthouse, listing the names of those who died for the Union and inscribed, "To the Perpetual Memory of the Defenders of the Union, 1861–1865." Honoring the memory of those who fought for the Union cause in Clarksburg, however, met more resistance. In 1907, the Clarksburg chapter of the Ladies of the Grand Army of the Republic launched a fundraising campaign to install a simple monument to a Union soldier in his trademark kepi in front of the Harrison County courthouse. Perhaps because they understood that the Union cause was no longer popular with many of their neighbors, they proposed text for the monument that was more inclusive: "Erected by the Citizens of Harrison County in Memory of Its Soldiers Who Served in All the Wars from 1776 to 1907." Installed in front of the courthouse in 1908, this tepid endorsement of the Union soldier's sacrifice was later removed. The county constructed a new courthouse in the early 1930s, and in 1953 installed a monument to Stonewall Jackson in its front plaza. The monument erected by the Ladies of the GAR now resides in a less prominent location across the street. Clarksburg was the birthplace of Stonewall Jackson, but it was also the site of the first pro-Union convention after eastern Virginians voted for secession. Virtually all the Union monuments erected in the state of West Virginia in the century after the war ended promote a "Union cause" narrative of the war, emphasizing that preserving the sacred Union was the issue at hand, and ignoring the other major result of the war—the emancipation of four million people from bondage.[8]

What explains the relative success of the champions of the Confederacy in getting their viewpoint carved in stone? The early organization and determination of the United Daughters of the Confederacy was critical in getting Confederate monuments erected not just in Southern states but in border states and even Northern states during the decades after the war. Northerners acquiesced to critical elements of the Lost Cause narrative, argues historian David Blight, out of a desire for sectional reconciliation and a shared embrace of white supremacy. However, historian Caroline Janney has argued that resistance to forgetting what the Union fought for did not quickly evaporate. In the case of West Virginia specifically, the postwar redemption of the Confederacy and native son

Stonewall Jackson may have also been facilitated by other concerns. West Virginia historian John Williams explains Lost Cause success as a manifestation of nostalgia for traditional ways during an era of rapid industrial change, and Steven Cody Straley has argued that elevating Jackson as a man of extraordinary Christian virtue and military genius was one way West Virginians responded to increasingly negative stereotypes of mountain people that were ascendant in American popular culture during the twentieth century.[9]

This chapter explores Civil War memory in West Virginia by focusing on the four Civil War monuments that, as of this book's publication, still reside on the statehouse lawn. An image of each monument is presented, along with the inscriptions on the base of each monument and newspaper accounts describing the events surrounding their dedication. Collectively, these four monuments reflect the complex and somewhat unique strands of Civil War public memory in the one state born in this conflict.

STONEWALL JACKSON STATUE UNVEILED ON THE STATE CAPITOL GROUNDS

In the first decade of the twentieth century, a West Virginia chapter of the United Daughters of the Confederacy sought permission from the West Virginia legislature to install a statue of a Confederate soldier on the capitol grounds. After the legislature issued its approval, the Daughters of the Confederacy altered its plan and instead constructed a monument to Clarksburg-born Confederate military hero Thomas "Stonewall" Jackson. The dedication drew a large crowd to the capitol in 1910, and the event was covered by papers from across the state. West Virginia's White-owned newspapers, including the Fairmont West Virginian *and the* Beckley Messenger, *had a different take on the meaning of the event than the African American–owned* Charleston Advocate.

A GREAT SOLDIER.

That the dedication of the statue to Stonewall Jackson was carried on at Charleston on the Capitol grounds without any more interest excited than any similar celebration marks another example of how sectionalism and the old bitterness engendered by the war is passing away. All West Virginians are proud of the career of this one of the greatest military leaders of any war.—Grafton Republican.

Fairmont West Virginian, September 29, 1910

Stonewall Jackson statue. The first Civil War monument installed on the statehouse grounds was not to honor the soldiers who made the state's independence possible but to commemorate those they defeated. Photo by William Kerrigan.

* * *

JACKSON MONUMENT

Unveiled at Charleston Tuesday with Imposing Ceremonies

Participated in By Confederate Camps, State Troops, Cadets, Citizens, and State Officials.

The unveiling of the monument to Stonewall Jackson in Charleston Tuesday was an event of more than ordinary importance from more than one standpoint.

Not only was this the first monument to be erected on the state capitol ground, but it is a peculiar fact that a monument commemorating the memory of a confederate leader should be the first to be erected on the lawn of the capitol of the only state actually created as a direct result of the war in which Jackson won his fame, and in opposition to the cause which he espoused. No more convincing testimony could be asked of the passing of the feeling engendered by that struggle and the reuniting of those who participated in it.

The ceremonies opened with a parade, headed by the Stonewall Brigade Band, of Staunton, Va., which still embraces in its membership some of those who followed through the war the fortunes of the leader whose memory they had met on this occasion to honor, the cadets from the V.M.I. where Jackson was an honored instructor until the outbreak of the war in which his life was sacrificed, a detachment of the national guards, headed by the Second Regiment Band, confederate veterans, citizens and distinguished guests, present and former state officials.

At the close of the parade, the ceremonies connected with the unveiling were opened with the invocation by Rt. Rev. G. W. Peterkin, of Parkersburg, which was followed by a patriotic song by Mrs. J. G. Edwards. The presentation speech made by Gen. Green and the address of acceptance by Hon. John A. Preston, of Greenbrier county. Major General Robert White followed Mr. Preston with an historical and eulogistic address which was the feature of the day's exercises. He was followed by Sir Moses Ezekiel, the sculptor to whose skill the creation of the monument is due, and the formal exercises were concluded with an address by Gen. B. H. Young, song by Mrs. Edwards and the pronouncing of the benediction by Bishop Peterkin.

A number of social events in honor of the many distinguished guests of the city closed the day.

<small>Beckley Messenger, September 30, 1910</small>

* * *

LEADERS HOPELESS

Injection of the Disfranchisement Issue Disconcerts Democratic Bosses. "Lily White" Buttons.

And George Byrne's reminder that party is pledged to support anti-Negro planks in last campaign throws the fat in the fire. (Charles Brooks Smith.)

The "Lilly White" issue has bobbed up serenely and unexpectedly in the campaign in this State. It was a thing almost forgotten and it would not have been thought of but for the Hon. George Byrne, of this city, whose ardent championing of negro disfranchisement was responsible for writing a plank to that effect in the Democratic state campaign of 1908. Mr. Byrne's recalling of that pledge touched off a boom in the Democratic camp, and interfered with plans that the Democratic managers had mapped out and were executing with noticeably good effect.

"The Democratic candidates for the Legislature," says Mr. Byrne, "will vote for a disfranchising amendment, if elected. They are pledged to do this by the Democratic platform, and impelled as well, no doubt, by personal predilections. The Democratic candidates are also in favor of a separate coach law and will no doubt give their support to such a measure."

There are fifteen thousand negro voters in this State, the greatest majority of them residing in the counties along the line of the Chesapeake & Ohio, and the Norfolk & Western railroads. It was that plank in the Democratic platform declaring in favor of disfranchising them, and the votes of that party's representatives in the legislature in favor of a "Jim Crow" coach law, which held the negro vote in line for the Republican party two years ago, and saved that party from defeat, when it was face to face with disaster because of a double-headed state ticket in the field. That is what astute and skillful Democratic campaign managers say, and their view of it is shared by Republican leaders of equal acumen in affairs political.

This year the Democrats, realizing the value of splitting up the negro vote and getting part of it, if possible, started to work early in that direction. It is admitted that they were making decided progress, especially in such large counties as Kanawha where negro voters are numerous, and a factor of sufficient importance to be seriously considered by the leaders of both parties in campaign years. In this—Charleston-Kanawha legislative district—the negro vote seemingly had been pretty well captured by the Democrats, whose well laid schemes to accomplish that very thing, were working out to more or less perfection. Ex-Governor MacCorkle, Democratic candidate for the State Senate in this district, and his law partner and political manager, W. E. Chilton, regarded the work among the negroes with a high degree of satisfaction. It seemed to assure MacCorkle's certain success in a Republican district that was believed to be wavering in its allegiance. Then something happened which knocked their shrewd plans awry.

A few days since the Confederate veterans of the State journeyed to Charleston where, upon the capitol ground, a splendid bronze statue of General "Stonewall" Jackson was unveiled with great pomp and ceremony. Thousands of people attended, and here and there in the throng were seen the heroic survivors of a lost cause attired in their grey uniforms, and upon their lapels shone a button—the "Lily White" button of the last Democratic State campaign. Not only did the old veterans wear these buttons, but many others wore them. There seemed to be plenty of these buttons left over from the campaign of two years ago—that was certain. It created quite a stir among the politicians of both parties.

The following day the Democratic managers hastened to deny that their party had anything to do with the appearance of these buttons, and they charged the Republican leaders with issuing them themselves, and denounced it in strenuous language. The controversy about it still waxes warm.

Then, the Hon. George Byrne moved to the center of the stage where the spotlight struck him fair, and announced that the Democratic platform—the last one of the party—pledged the party, if given the power by the voters, to disfranchise the negroes of West Virginia, and also to enact a separate coach law on all electric and steam railroads within the State. He declared that every legislative nominee of his party was irrevocably pledged to work and vote for the fulfillment of this and all other planks of the platform; that they knew it, personally wanted to have a chance to do it, and that they would do it if given the opportunity by the electorate next month.

The effect of Byrne's frank declaration was electrical in the counties in southern West Virginia, where the race question is decidedly much of a live wire. The Democratic leaders, who are running their party's campaign this year, had been steering clear of mentioning the negro question, and were hoping that it would remain dormant and buried in this off year campaign. But their hopes have been blasted, by the ardent Byrne, who has fought against letting the negro vote and giving him equal rights with whites on railroad trains, for ten years. Mr. Byrne is a Democratic leader of state-wide prominence, a splendid stump-speaker and one of the brightest writers on politics and politicians that there is in the State. He is a very sincere and ardent advocate, and his whole soul is in this particular issue. That many of the Democratic colleagues, who, for the sake of political expediency, do not agree with him in keeping alive that issue, especially in forcing it to the front this campaign when they have strong hopes, doesn't fease Mr. Byrne. He has touched off the fireworks and the rockets are shooting and the pinwheels are whirling, lighting up the political heavens.

The Republican party managers, who had become more or less distressed over the probability of losing much of the negro vote, are melancholy no more. They are smiling at each other and shaking hands with themselves whenever they think of that particular and important phase of the present fight. They have the negro vote intact, cinched as it were, they say. And it looks decidedly that way.

Charleston Advocate, October 13, 1910

THE MOUNTAINEER STATUE

That the first monument to be installed on the West Virginia Capitol grounds was to honor a defeated Confederate general rankled many West Virginians who had fought and suffered to restore the Union. West Virginian members of the Grand Army of the Republic (GAR), a national organization founded to represent Union veterans after the war, began a campaign to raise funds for a monument to loyal Union soldiers at the capitol, but William Seymour Edwards, a local coal baron with high political aspirations, stole some of their thunder by financing a monument to the loyal West Virginia mountaineer. The armed figure represented in the Mountaineer Monument does not wear the typical Union coat and

The Mountaineer Monument on the West Virginia State Capitol grounds commemorates local militias loyal to the Union during the Civil War. Photo by William Kerrigan.

kepi, and Edwards's efforts to construct and install the monument just two years after the installation of the Stonewall statue garnered significant backlash from members of the GAR. Edwards, who often used the title "Col. Edwards," was not in fact a Union veteran. He adopted the title after serving a peacetime stint in charge of a local militia. The two newspaper articles that follow represent the diverging sides of the Mountaineer Monument controversy.

INSCRIPTION ON THE PEDESTAL OF THE MOUNTAINEER MONUMENT

Erected to commemorate the valor of those who on April 15, 1861, in instant response to the first call of Abraham Lincoln formed themselves into the intrepid home guards who held in check unaided the forces of Wise, and Lee, and Jackson, until the federal armies came and driving the Confederates across the Alleghenies made possible the creation of the state of West Virginia; and also of those who as incomparable scouts & riflemen gave themselves to the nation and with dauntless courage and sagacity assisted in assuring to mankind "That government of the people, by the people, for the people, shall not perish from the earth"

* * *

HIS DREAM AT LAST REALIZED

Edwards Sees Statue to West Virginia Heroes Unveiled.
"Montani Semper Liberi"
People of the Mountain State Given Opportunity to Contribute to Fund For Purchase of Bronze Pedestal Upon Which Rests Work of Noted Sculptor—How the Money May Be Contributed.

Charleston, W. Va., Dec. 10.—Beneath sunny skies the ceremonies of the unveiling of the magnificent statue of the typical West Virginia soldier here at the capitol grounds this afternoon took place. The statue, which is in bronze, is the work of the celebrated sculptor, Henry K. Bush-Brown of Washington, and is the gift of Colonel William Seymour Edwards of Charleston to the state. . . . The flag fell slowly away from the exquisite figure. As the great throng of people viewed for the first time the classic outlines a hush fell upon them and then a great cheer burst forth. The work is distinctively the best of the kind ever seen in West Virginia and is so suggestive in its portrayal of the period of the sixties that the most critical persons have nothing but praise for the statue. . . .

The governor's staff was in attendance in full uniform, as were also prominent officers of the national guard with companies of the state militia. Massed bands furnished the music, and picturesque background to the entire scene was the formation of a thousand school children carrying flowers. These children sang "The Hymn of the West Virginians," the state song written by Colonel Edwards. A trained chorus of more than a hundred voices led this inspiring singing. The state militia fired a salute as the statue was unveiled and this brought light to the eyes of the hundreds of Grand Army men who were prominent in the day's program.

The gift of the statue to the Grand Army of the Republic and Women's Relief corps was then formally made by Colonel Edwards in a short but decidedly entertaining address. He said:

"This splendid figure is not intended to represent merely the blue coat and brass buttons that 50 years ago sometimes encased the soldier; it is not intended to parade the personal glory that sometimes, maybe, might decorate the officer to whom chance and occasion may have brought distinction; it is not intended to in any way aggrandize whose of those yet surviving the tears and the glories of Gettysburg, Antietam, or Shilo, or any other of the thousand fields of actual battle, now receive and must ever receive our most reverent homage and tenderest esteem!

"No! No one of these! But the rather, it is intended to represent and does represent that glorious and heroic spirit which stirred the heart of the man within the blue coat; the dauntless courage which lay with the man whom it was given to govern and command; that supreme loftiness of soul which made heroes of the unpretentious citizen and common man and which brought to God's service, the service of human freedom, the militant people of these mountains and valleys, amidst the prayers and rejoicings of a solicitous and grateful world.

"This figure and its pedestal typifies and represents the splendid personality, the unswerving courage, the devotion of a great race, a race great in Colonial and Revolutionary times; a race great in meeting every call made by the nation in every crisis of the nation. . . .

"It is then this militant, fighting soul of the true West Virginian that this noble statue is here to represent.

"This figure stands behind all of the glory, all of the splendor of our West Virginian in war! He is equally the master personality in peace! The calm, strong face, the unfaltering resolution, the coolness and daring, the love of home and country which will meet death or give it ere he will let that blessed flag fall from its uplifted hand, are all embodied here in enduring bronze!

"The figure is that of no single man. It is a composite representation of a yet living type. The gifted sculptor created it in no hurried moment. It is the outcome of successive years of study and travel and association among our finest population in divers parts of West Virginia, where are yet preserved so many splendid types of our militant people. Look upon this face! In it you behold a hundred faces which you have seen and known and yet know.

"The race, the West Virginian, as we know him, as we would wish to know him, lives and will live forever in this imperishable bronze to inspire and glorify the generation of today and also many a generation yet unborn.

"In this noble face and figure you now possess one of the greatest masterpieces of the sculptor's art in America and in the world. It typifies the spirit of the West Virginian." . . .

Pioneer Press (Martinsburg, WV), December 21, 1912

* * *

GRAND ARMY POST TAKES FALL OUT OF EDWARDS CANDIDACY.

Refuse to Accept Much Advertised Monument Unveiled on Capitol Grounds.
Say Movement Savors Too Much of Politics
Hurried Changes to Day's Program Had to be Made and Speeches Revised Accordingly, Governor Glasscock Accepting for State—May Demand Statues Removal.

Charleston, W. Va., December 10 (Special)—Members of the West Virginia Grand Army of the Republic today took a fall out of the candidacy of William Seymour Edwards for the United States senate, refusing to accept the much advertised monument to be unveiled this afternoon on the capitol grounds, a supposed gift of Col. Edwards. Declarations were also made by prominent G.A.R. leaders that the monument unveiled today will have to be moved when the ex-union soldiers are ready to erect their shaft, since the legislature granted them the privilege of erecting a monument and the board of public works designated that as the spot.

The veterans went on record as refusing to accept the memorial on the ground that it does not represent their cause. The bronze figure is that of a sturdy mountaineer, bearing a flag in one hand and an ancient rifle in the other. The veterans declare their monument must represent a soldier. Many veterans further protested that the entire movement savored too much of politics, the unveiling taking place immediately preceding a session of the legislature before which Edwards is a candidate for United States senator.

It was to be a gala occasion at the capitol. Governor Glasscock had ordered out a part of his staff and a military escort was on hand to fire the salute.

Before noon G.A.R. leaders assembled and adopted resolutions refusing to accept the monument and the local camps refused to attend the ceremonies. Hurried changes in the day's program had to be made and speeches revised accordingly. Col. Edwards presented the monument, which was accepted by General Romeo H. Freer, acting as the agent of Edwards and not as a representative of the G.A.R. General Freer then presented the monument to the state, the speech of acceptance being made by Governor Glasscock. The speakers were the same as those on the original program and few who attended knew of the refusal to accept on the part of old veterans.

Owing to the failure of the pedestal to arrive, the figure was unveiled mounted on a wooden pedestal, the other to be substituted when it arrives. Whether or not this will be done, since G.A.R. leaders declare they will demand the monument's removal, is a question.

While understanding that the monument was to be a union soldier's memorial, members of the committee appointed by the state encampment say they were not consulted as to the figure. As members of the women's relief corps assisted in raising finances for the base of the monument, various complications are threatened.

The governor and Mrs. Glasscock entertained the governor's staff at dinner tonight at the governors' mansion.

Bluefield Daily Telegraph, December 11, 1912

UNION SOLDIER MONUMENT INSTALLATION

It would take another eighteen years and the efforts of West Virginia state senator H. Sol White before a GAR-approved monument to West Virginia Union soldiers would be financed and constructed. In the ensuing years, West Virginia commissioned the highly regarded architect Cass Gilbert to design a new capitol and its grounds. The new monument had its critics, including Gilbert, who made it clear he did not welcome the decision to site it on the capitol lawn, as he regarded it as an artless intrusion on his carefully designed space. Senator White, a Union veteran of the Civil War, pressed forward despite this criticism, referring to Edwards's statue of the loyal mountaineer as depicting a "squirrel hunter."

STATUE SNEERING ARCHITECT WILL BE ASKED TO UNVEILING

Senator White Announces Decision to Invite Cass Gilbert to Attend Exercises at Monument to Union Soldier on July 4

The Union soldier monument desired by the West Virginia Grand Army of the Republic did not meet the approval of the capitol's architect. Photo by William Kerrigan.

Senator H. Sol White left here yesterday to attend a G.A.R. encampment at Moundsville. But before the 90-year-old veteran of the Civil war departed he took occasion to say that he intends to invite Cass Gilbert to the unveiling of the new memorial monument that is being erected on the Capitol grounds.

Mr. Gilbert, it will be remembered, is the capitol building architect, who several months ago looked at the drawing of the then proposed statue and called it "a monstrosity." Mr. Gilbert it also will be remembered, called the proposed statue other things and strongly opposed placing it on the capitol grounds.

CHAIRMAN OF COMMISSION

Senator White, on the other hand, is chairman of the memorial commission, created by the legislature and the architect's condemnation of the proposed monument only made him fight the harder for its erection. Senator White said in effect that he knew what a Union soldier should look like because he saw Union soldiers before Mr. Gilbert was born. If he and his comrades wanted a soldier on the march, a soldier on the march they would have. Furthermore, their representative would be a young fellow and he would have ginger in his step and he would carry his rifle and his blanket and other accoutrements.

"SQUIRREL HUNTER ALL RIGHT"

"The squirrel hunter is all right. He had his place in the war, too, but he doesn't represent the Union soldier." The squirrel hunter, in case you don't know, is the present memorial to union veterans on the Duffy Street side of the capitol grounds.

The unveiling exercises of the new monument will be held on July 4 with the G.A.R., United Spanish War Veterans, American Legion and other groups joining in the affair.

And, Mr. White revealed, the Confederate veterans of the Civil War also will be invited to join in the unveiling celebration.

Charleston Gazette, June 8, 1930

* * *

H. SOL WHITE HAS HIS BIG DAY AS STATE GETS MEMORIAL

Veteran Crows Over Statue's Critics When Union Soldier Monument Is Accepted by Lee; Ogden Delivers Address

H. Sol White, Matewan veteran of the Civil war, former state senator, had his big day yesterday.

The 90-year-old chairman of the Union memorial commission was never in greater glory than when he stood before the multitude, on the lawn of the state capitol and saw removed the flag veil from the tall bronze man of battle—replica of a federal soldier marching in full accoutrements. The cord was pulled by his 13-year-old son, H.S. White, jr.

With a few of the grey-haired, blue uniformed comrades of '61 scattered among the guests and speakers on the platform, the elderly man boasted of his fight and the fight of his comrades to make possible the event of yesterday. He told of the legislature appropriating the money for the purchase of the memorial; of the fight against its erection; of the victory of the veterans.

With no slight vein of sarcasm, he referred to the statue as "a monstrosity"—the designation that was given it by Cass Gilbert, capitol architect, who opposed its erection. He referred to uncomplimentary newspaper comment. And then he boasted some more.

NOT READY FOR CALL

Bringing himself erect in his best military fashion the fighting man of another era denied the friendly intimation of an earlier speaker that "these old veterans are ready to answer the final roll call."

"We are proud," he said, "of the praise that has been heaped upon us and upon our work here today and we expect to live to hear many more words of praise."

Laughter burst often from the crowd as Mr. White spoke. At other times his listeners were silent and somber.

OGDEN GIVES HISTORY

It was Sol White's big day, but others joined to make the ceremony complete. H.C. Ogden, in the dedicatory address, recited the history of the state in the great civil conflict.

"West Virginians," he said, "were in every battle of Grant's last great drive. They were in at the very beginning and at the end."

In conclusion the publisher urged that the people learn from veterans the lesson of service to the state.

Attorney General Howard B. Lee, accepting the monument for the state, paid high tribute to the old vets.

"It is a conspicuous honor," he said, "to accept this memorial erected to the memory of both the living and the dead who served their country in that unfortunate fratricidal struggle of the sixties. In so honoring them, we honor ourselves, our state and our country."

HALLAHAN TALKS

Walter S. Hallahan, state senator, told of the legislature's action in appropriating the money for the statue and authorizing its construction.

He told of the courage of the West Virginia soldiers and praised them for their stand in helping to preserve the union.

"Peace," said Senator Hallahan, "is a blessing, but peace at any cost is abominable."

Maj. Gen. John L. Clem of Washington failed to arrive. Other speakers were Dr. L. E. Arnesburg of Uniontown, Pa., past commander-in-chief of the Grand Army of the Republic and Roy K. Stewart of Mannington, designer of the monument.

Four airplanes circled above the monument as the parade that originated in Capitol street reached the grounds for dedication. A large crowd was already waiting on the lawn and more continued to arrive as the morning passed. State and city officials who were not on the speaking list stood like the others with bared heads as the flag drape was taken from the statue. A band played patriotic airs—some of them originations of Civil war days. A few Confederate veterans, invited by Mr. White, mingled in the crowd. State police headed by Chief Harry L. Brooks were present in uniform.

It was a big day for Sol White and his boys in blue.

Charleston Gazette, July 5, 1930

CHARLESTON INSTALLATION OF SAD LINCOLN

On the state's capitol grounds, the centennial of West Virginia in 1963 passed without a monument celebrating the state's birth. A decade later, however, a bronze statue of Lincoln, the president who gave birth to the state, was installed directly in front of the capitol building. The bronze statue was designed by sculptor Fred Torrey and inspired by a somber poem about the president, "Abraham Lincoln Walks at Midnight," by the poet Vachel Lindsay. The resulting statue represented a very different kind of war monument than those erected before it. An image of that monument, and an excerpt from the poem that inspired it, can be found in the introduction of this book.

SHRINE BAND OUT OF PLACE

The Shrine is one of the few remaining fraternal holdouts against creeping racial egalitarianism. It has no black members. There are no indications that it will accept any in the foreseeable future.

As a private organization, the Shrine has a perfect right to be racially selective in its membership. We are compelled to observe, however, that there is something incongruous about the scheduled participation of the Beni Kedem Shrine band in public ceremonies accompanying the unveiling on the Capitol Lawn of a statue of Abraham Lincoln.

The only parallel we can conjure up would be the selection of Cab Calloway to provide the music at the funeral of the late Bull Connor of Alabama.

Charleston Gazette, June 12, 1974

* * *

LINCOLN STATUE IS UNVEILED IN CHARLESTON CEREMONIES

Charleston, W. Va. (AP)—

The statue "Abraham Lincoln Walks at Midnight" was unveiled at about noon Thursday with all the ceremony incumbent on the celebration of the state's 111th birthday.

A color guard of state police, Marines, boy scouts and cub scouts flanked the Charleston Symphony Orchestra on the capital stairs as it worked its way through arrangements of "West Virginia Hills" and "Battle Hymn of the Republic."

A large group of dignitaries was on hand, including Gov. Arch A. Moore Jr., who spoke of the integrity of the former president and of West Virginians, and the new Miss West Virginia, Mary Beth Derry, who grinned broadly under a white diamond tiara and said nothing.

Lincoln was the president who signed the proclamation June 20, 1863, naming West Virginia as an independent state and part of the union. Tuesday's ceremonies on the capitol lawn and steps came exactly on the 111th anniversary of the state.

"We cannot claim his birthplace like those in Kentucky," said Moore to an estimated 600 persons in attendance. "And we cannot claim him as a resident like those in Illinois and Indiana. But we do have a claim on him for his role in the birth of our state."

William S. Bryant, president of the Lincoln Statue Fund Corp., said completion of the project cost $40,000 in cash, plus additional personal funding from those directly involved.

Bryant, former Democratic mayor of Summersville said, "I've been called all kinds of names. I was called a socialist, and about all the things you can be called when you get into something like this. I was even called a Republican."

Bluefield Daily Telegraph, June 21, 1974

* * *

SLEEPLESS AT MIDNIGHT

Of Abraham Lincoln's right to carve West Virginia out of the Old Dominion and set it up in a sovereign existence of its own there was then and still is some doubt.

It took Gettysburg and then that awful stillness at Appomattox to confirm his decision and moot the question, the historic lesson being that the Commander-in-Chief may dare what the President of the United States might not get by with in a state of disunion.

In any case, West Virginia has lived for 111 years by that daring and finally got around to memorializing it in bronze on the Capitol grounds. It is purely a personal quibble that Fred M. Torrey's "Abraham Lincoln Walks at Midnight" belongs better in the subdued light of the rotunda than in the broad daylight of the esplanade.

This is the melancholy, sleepless man, brooding at what he had to do with the power he had sought and won. Least of all did he aspire to the heroics of office, but here he was, setting off for a future whose tragic dimensions he saw more clearly than his more heroic contemporaries. He knew it would be an ordeal.

But for those western Virginians, as for everyone else it was, and for this reason, perhaps it is especially appropriate that it is the troubled Lincoln who stands now at the entrance to the classic symbol of their statehood. History says he was right at nearly every step of the way. At every step, he paid and suffered the price which righteousness exacts.

Charleston Daily Mail, June 24, 1974

* * *

CAPITOL LAWN RIGHT FOR LINCOLN

The nobly executed statue of a brooding Abraham Lincoln finally stands at the State Capitol, the realization of a dream of a few West Virginians who put their hearts and energies into the project.

It is fitting that a sad Lincoln should stand at the Capitol's entrance. West Virginia is a state of Lincoln's creation, a child born out of strife and sadness.

It is an irony that for so many years a likeness of Stonewall Jackson should stand on the Capitol lawn. Jackson, gallant warrior that he was, hardly provides the proper atmosphere for the seat of West Virginia government. Jackson wouldn't have countenanced the existence of West Virginia.

The Capitol lawn, however, can accommodate varied views of what was right and what was wrong about that terrible conflict of a little more than 100 years ago.

It is appropriate, however, that Lincoln should occupy the more prominent place, for West Virginia owes its existence to that tall, powerful, good, and suffering man.

Charleston Gazette, July 6, 1974

STONEWALL JACKSON STATUE RESTORED AND RELOCATED

The prominence of the Lincoln statue along Kanawha Boulevard may have been what prompted champions of the Confederacy to persuade the state to pay the bill for renovating the older Stonewall Jackson statue and relocating it to what had in recent years come to be the "front lawn" of the capitol. The controversial Mountaineer Monument, which also received a publicly financed refurbishment, was reinstalled in a less visible location away from the boulevard.

FACING STATUE OF LINCOLN

Stonewall Jackson Back Home at Capitol

By John G. Morgan. *Staff Writer*

Confederate Gen. Stonewall Jackson is home again in the form of a heroic bronze figure on the Capitol lawn.

But he has a new position with a new wrinkle. He now faces Abraham Lincoln.

To be more specific, the front of Jackson's body is pointed toward Lincoln. But his head is slightly turned, as always, and he looks across the river toward South Hills.

The statue of Jackson is one of three returned to the Capitol lawn after a 175-mile truck ride to the north.

THEY WERE TAKEN to Kingwood, Preston County, where Sheidow Bronze Co. restored them to their original bronze appearance. All of the work, including removal, refurbishing and resetting, was done under a $15,245 state contract with Sears Monument Co.

Memory 255

The other two statues represent a Union soldier, standing as if he had just made a turn during his long vigil at the Capitol, and a symbolic West Virginia mountaineer.

The soldier stands near Kanawha Boulevard and by the site of old Duffy Street near the Governor's Mansion. He looks upstream, also toward Lincoln. This statue was restored to its original position. But Jackson and the mountaineer, formerly on old Duffy Street near the new Science and Culture Center, were placed in new positions.

The mountaineer, modeled after the countenance of Eli "Rimfire" Hamrick and the body of his brother, Ellis, stands at Washington Street and California Avenue. He looks from the lawn directly toward the corner, so that pedestrians along either street may see his countenance.

STONEWALL'S NEW position is at California Avenue and the boulevard. His back is toward California as he is turned toward Lincoln and looking across the boulevard and the river toward the hills.

Actually, Stonewall faced in this same direction when he stood beside old Duffy Steet. Lincoln stands near the boulevard on the wide sidewalk that leads up to the steps to the main entrance of the Capitol. He is about half way between the Union soldier and Stonewall. In the form of the statue, "Lincoln Walks at Midnight," he has been standing there more than two years.

Thus, all three of the statues along the boulevard—Stonewall, Lincoln, and the Union soldier—represent the Civil War period.

Presumably, the instructions to place all of the statues in their present positions were given by Gov Moore.

JACK SEARS of the monument company confirmed only that he did the work according to contract and instructions. He said the locations were approved by Cleveland Benedict, state finance commissioner with control over buildings and grounds.

Sears said Stonewall couldn't see Lincoln if he tried through the present growth of leaves on trees in the Capitol lawn. But when late autumn arrives, the Civil War President would be quite visible to the Confederate general.

New lettering, carved on Stonewall's pedestal Tuesday and readily visible to boulevard pedestrians, shows that he was born Jan. 21, 1824, in Clarksburg, Va., now West Virginia, and died May 10, 1863.

More lettering on the other side of the pedestal will show that the statue was first located on the old Capitol grounds September 27, 1910, and moved to the present Capitol grounds July 25, 1926, and finally to the new location July 20 of this year.

Charleston Gazette, August 4, 1976

Timeline

1830

January — The revised Virginia constitution maintains eastern Virginia's grip on power. Trans-Allegheny delegates vote against it.

1851

October — Reform constitution is ratified, granting more representation to western Virginia.

1859

October — John Brown leads his raid on Harpers Ferry.

1860

November — Abraham Lincoln is elected.

December — Lucy Bagby is returned to Wheeling. She is the last fugitive from slavery forcibly returned to slavery under the Fugitive Slave Act of 1850.

1861

February — The Virginia Secession Convention begins.

Jefferson Davis is inaugurated as president of the Confederate States of America.

March — Abraham Lincoln is inaugurated as sixteenth president of the United States.

April: — South Carolina fires on Fort Sumter.

Lincoln calls for seventy-five thousand volunteers.

Virginia delegates vote for the Ordinance of Secession.

Virginia forces seize the armory at Harpers Ferry.

May — Clarksburg Union meeting is held.

First Wheeling Convention is held.

Virginia voters approve secession.

	George B. McClellan moves troops into western Virginia.
June	The battle of Philippi results in Union victory.
	The Second Wheeling Convention is held.
	Wheeling votes for the Reorganized Government of Virginia.
	Francis Pierpont is elected governor of the Reorganized Government of Virginia.
July	The battle of Rich Mountain ends in Union victory.
	The first battle of Manassas ends in Confederate victory.
	The Reorganized Government of Virginia debates forming a new state.
	McClellan called east to lead the Union war effort. William Rosecrans takes charge of western Virginia operations.
	Congress passes the first Confiscation Act, giving military protection to enslaved people fleeing the Confederate military.
August	The Second Wheeling Convention votes for the new state of Kanawha.
	The 1st West Virginia regiment is mustered out of Wheeling.
September	Battle of Carnifex Ferry results in Union victory.
	Battle of Cheat Mountain results in Union victory.
October	Voters approve the new state of Kanawha.
November	The constitutional convention is held in Wheeling.

1862

May	Waitman T. Willey petitions Congress for the admission of West Virginia as a state to the Union.
July	Congress passes the second Confiscation Act.
September	Confederate occupation of Charleston begins and lasts six weeks.
	Confederates siege and capture Harpers Ferry.
	The Union achieves victory at the battle of Antietam.
	A preliminary Emancipation Proclamation is drafted.
October	Confederate occupation of Charleston ends.
December	The battle of Fredericksburg ends in a Confederate victory.

	Lincoln signs a congressional bill organizing the new state of West Virginia.

1863

January	The Emancipation Proclamation goes into effect.
February	The West Virginia legislature passes the Willey Amendment, establishing gradual emancipation in the new state.
April	West Virginia voters ratify the new state's constitution.
	Confederates launch the Jones-Imboden raids into western Virginia.
June	West Virginia celebrates statehood on June 20.
July	The battle of Gettysburg results in a Union victory.
	The siege of Vicksburg ends and results in a Union victory.
August	Battle of White Sulphur Springs ends in Confederate victory.
November	Battle of Droop Mountain results in Union victory.

1864

May	The Overland Campaign begins in eastern Virginia.
June	The siege of Petersburg begins in eastern Virginia.
August	The first United States Colored Troops unit from West Virginia is formed.
October	Philip Sheridan's raid in the Shenandoah Valley brings an influx of refugees into West Virginia.
November	Lincoln is reelected and wins the state of West Virginia.

1865

January	The Thirteenth Amendment is passed by Congress.
April	Robert E. Lee surrenders to Ulysses S. Grant at Appomattox Court House, Virginia.
	Lincoln is assassinated.

1866

April	Conservative Democrats hold a state convention in Clarksburg and stand against African American civil rights.

1868

November — Grant is elected eighteenth president of the United States.

1869

February — The Fifteenth Amendment is passed by Congress.

1870

November — John Jacob, a Democrat, is elected governor of West Virginia.

1871

April — The Flick Amendment to the West Virginia state constitution is passed, restoring rights to ex-Confederates.

1910

September — A Stonewall Jackson statue is installed on the state capitol's grounds.

1912

December — The Mountaineer Monument is installed on capitol grounds.

1930

July — The Soldiers and Sailors Monument, honoring the Union, is installed on capitol grounds

1974

June — A Lincoln statue is installed on capitol grounds.

Discussion Questions

INTRODUCTION

1. How do you think West Virginia's birth during the Civil War has affected the state's history and shaped some of the popular myths about Appalachian West Virginia?
2. In what ways was West Virginia's Civil War experience distinctive from that of other states? In what ways was it similar to the border states of Missouri, Kentucky, Maryland, and Delaware?
3. What were the four regions of Virginia in 1860? What did they have in common? How did they differ?
4. Consider the part of Virginia that would become West Virginia. What were some of the differences within the region? What factors helped shape these differences?

CHAPTER 1: VIRGINIA'S WEST

1. What is a mountaineer? How does Henry Howe's description of western Virginians fit the common characterization of the mountaineer? Are there aspects of the modern mountaineer identity that are missing from Howe's description?
2. How would you characterize free western Virginians' viewpoints on slavery before 1860?
3. What grievances did western Virginians have with their fellow citizens of the state in the decades before the Civil War? What common values did they share?
4. To what extent did the issue of slavery shape the divisions between White residents in eastern and western Virginia?
5. Were the divisions between eastern and western Virginians greater or lesser by 1860 than they had been in 1830? Do you think the region was destined for independence, even if the Civil War had been avoided?
6. Why do you think the citizens of Cabell County believed that the solution to the threat John Brown's invasion posed was to accelerate the completion of a railway to the Ohio River?

7. Did John Brown's raid on Harpers Ferry divide or unite free Virginians of all regions?

CHAPTER 2: THE REVOLUTION OF 1860

1. The fugitive slave case of Lucy Bagby took place in the context of Lincoln's election victory and South Carolina's decision to secede from the Union. What do you think was at stake in the outcome of Bagby's case for White western Virginians? How do you think Black western Virginians viewed the case?
2. How did western Virginians respond to the decision of the Virginia Convention to secede from the Union?
3. The issue of Southern secession prompted different reactions among western Virginians. How did John James Davis and Anna Kennedy negotiate their differences on the question of loyalty? How did the residents of Guyandotte respond to the presence of nearby Unionists in Ceredo? Can you explain the differences in their responses?
4. What political solutions did opponents of secession in western Virginia propose after the state seceded?

CHAPTER 3: OPENING GAMBITS

1. Why was the fate of western Virginia important to the Confederate states at the beginning of the war? Why did Lincoln and the Union military leadership seek to control it?
2. There are few surviving sources written from the perspective of West Virginia's African American population. To some extent, historians are forced to interpret their experiences through the eyes of White observers. Reading these documents carefully, can we draw any conclusions about African Americans' hopes and fears in 1861?
3. How did military events in western Virginia in the spring and summer of 1861 shape the future of West Virginia? Did they have any significant impact on the course of the larger war?
4. Did George B. McClellan's cautious approach to military occupation in western Virginia yield the results he hoped for? How did Union military occupation of western Virginia in 1861 influence civilian allegiances?

CHAPTER 4: THE RULES OF WAR

1. In what ways did the "rules of war" change in western Virginia over the course of the war?

2. At the outset of the war, Lincoln made it clear that his one objective was to restore the Union. But by the beginning of 1863, ending slavery became a second strategic objective. How did events in western Virginia and other regions occupied by Union forces influence Lincoln's changing war aims?
3. Older histories of the American Civil War typically tell the war's story as a series of mega-battles between regular armies fought on the fields of places like Manassas, Antietam, and Gettysburg. Western Virginians endured the hardships of war for four long years, but only one of the war's mega-battles was fought on West Virginia soil. How did the West Virginia war experience differ from this old narrative of the war?
4. How did occupying soldiers who hailed from other states view the civilian populations they encountered in western Virginia? What did they make of the men who fought in irregular home guard and ranger units?
5. In what ways were western Virginia's African American population affected by Confederate offensives in Charleston and Harpers Ferry in the fall of 1862?

CHAPTER 5: THE MOVEMENT FOR STATEHOOD

1. What were the main arguments made in favor of independent statehood for West Virginia?
2. What factors shaped the boundaries for the new state?
3. John S. Carlile had been a strong opponent of Virginia secession and an early advocate for independent statehood. Why did he turn against the movement?
4. Describe some of the men who were elected as representatives in the first West Virginia government? What were their views on slavery and states' rights before the war? How did their experiences in the war alter their views?

CHAPTER 6: WOMEN AND THE WAR

1. Describe some of the varied ways in which West Virginia's women experienced the war.
2. In what ways did West Virginia women affect the outcome of the war?
3. Did changes to the rules of war have a significant impact on how West Virginia women experienced war?
4. Were ideas about women's proper roles and appropriate womanly behavior challenged during the war years? If not, why not? If so, how?

CHAPTER 7: ENDURING A LONG WAR

1. The third year of the war brought West Virginia statehood and Lincoln's emancipation policy into play. How did these developments affect the war experiences of West Virginians?
2. What impact did the Jones-Imboden raid in the spring of 1863 have on the people of western Virginia? Did it achieve its objectives?
3. What are some of the ways soldiers endured the long war?
4. What did the troop transfer on the Baltimore and Ohio Railroad reveal about West Virginia's strategic value in the Civil War?
5. What was at stake for West Virginians in the election of 1864?

CHAPTER 8: REVOLUTION AND COUNTERREVOLUTION

1. In what ways was West Virginia's Reconstruction experience different from the postwar experience of defeated Confederate states?
2. Why was it difficult for West Virginians to separate the issue of freedmen and freedwomen's rights from the issue of the rights of former White Confederates?
3. What factors enabled former Confederates to regain political power so quickly after the war?
4. In what ways have the Civil War and Reconstruction shaped West Virginia's politics and economy since the war?

CHAPTER 9: MEMORY

1. Supporters of the defeated Confederacy seemed to have been more successful in erecting monuments to their cause than supporters of the Union victors. Why do you think this was the case?
2. In what ways did Black and White West Virginians view the installation of the Stonewall Jackson statue on capitol grounds differently?
3. Why do you think the promoters of the Mountaineer Monument opted not to portray a traditional Union soldier? Why did it provoke so much scorn? When you hear the term today, what do you see as the characteristics of a "mountaineer"?
4. Did the American Civil War help shape modern popular views of West Virginia and West Virginians in any way? If so, in what ways?
5. West Virginia's monuments to the Confederacy have come under attack in recent years. What do you think should be done with them?

Notes

INTRODUCTION

1. Vachel Lindsay, *Collected Poems* (New York: Macmillan, 1925), 53–54.
2. Eric Foner, *Reconstruction: America's Unfinished Revolution, 1863–1877* (New York: Harper & Row, 1988), xvii, 37–39. Foner argues that Reconstruction first began in West Virginia in 1863 with statehood, or possibly as early as 1861, when the statehood process began. John E. Stealey, *West Virginia's Civil War–Era Constitution: Loyal Revolution, Confederate Counter-Revolution, and the Convention of 1872* (Kent, OH: Kent State University Press, 2013). Stealey suggests we consider 1861–65 an era of revolution in West Virginia and the period from the end of the war until the adoption of the 1872 constitution an era of counterrevolution.
3. Mark A. Snell, *West Virginia and the Civil War: Mountaineers Are Always Free* (Charleston, SC: History Press, 2011), 28–30. Snell provides an excellent explanation of the shifting numbers.
4. Daniel E. Sutherland, *A Savage Conflict: The Decisive Role of Guerrillas in the American Civil War* (Chapel Hill: University of North Carolina Press, 2009), ix.
5. Important recent work on women's actions in the Civil War include Thavolia Glymph, *The Women's Fight: The Civil War's Battles for Home, Freedom, and Nation* (Chapel Hill: University of North Carolina Press, 2022); and Stephanie McCurry, *The Women's War: Fighting and Surviving the American Civil War* (Cambridge: Belknap, 2019).
6. Link draws on the concept of "infrapolitics," developed by historian Robin D. G. Kelley, to show how the choices enslaved people made, both before and during the conflict, shaped the political choices enslavers made. William A. Link, *Roots of Secession: Slavery and Politics in Antebellum Virginia* (Chapel Hill: University of North Carolina Press, 2003), 4–5.
7. Kenneth Noe and Shannon H. Wilson, eds., *The Civil War in Appalachia: Collected Essays* (Knoxville: University of Tennessee Press, 1997), xiv–xv.
8. Scott A. MacKenzie, *The Fifth Border State: Slavery, Emancipation, and the Formation of West Virginia, 1829–1872* (Morgantown: West Virginia University Press, 2023).
9. Waitman T. Willey, March 4, 1861, quoted in William W. Freehling and Craig M. Simpson, eds., *Showdown in Virginia: The 1861 Convention and the Fate of the Union* (Charlottesville: University of Virginia Press, 2010), 14.
10. Aaron Astor's *Rebels on the Border: Civil War, Emancipation, and the Reconstruction of Kentucky and Missouri* (Baton Rouge: Louisiana State University Press, 2012) is an excellent study of the racial politics of two important border states. MacKenzie's *Fifth Border State* offers an iconoclastic challenge to almost all previous scholarship written on West Virginia in the Civil War. Christopher Phillips, *The Rivers Ran*

Backward: *The Civil War and the Remaking of the American Middle Border* (New York: Oxford University Press, 2016) broadens the geographic scope by examining conflicting perspectives on both sides of the Ohio River. Two excellent memory studies on border states are Steven Cody Straley, *A Constant Reminder to All: Stonewall Jackson, the Lost Cause, and the Making of a West Virginia Idol* (Charleston, WV: 35th Star Publishing, 2010); and Anne E. Marshall, *Creating a Confederate Kentucky: The Lost Cause and Civil War America* (Chapel Hill: University of North Carolina Press, 2013).

11. Kenneth W. Noe, *Southwest Virginia's Railroad: Modernization and the Sectional Crisis* (Chicago: University of Illinois Press, 1994), 14.
12. Jonathan A. Noyalas, *Slavery and Freedom in the Shenandoah Valley during the Civil War* (Gainesville: University of Florida Press, 2021) effectively demolished a popular conception in the Valley that slavery was not important to its prewar economy.
13. See John E. Stealey, *The Antebellum Kanawha Salt Business and Western Markets* (Morgantown: West Virginia University Press, 2016).
14. Frank S. Riddel, ed., *The Historical Atlas of West Virginia* (Morgantown: West Virginia University Press, 2008), 210–15; Noe, *Southwest Virginia's Railroad* explores the ways the Virginia and Tennessee transformed the economy and politics of the region.

CHAPTER 1: VIRGINIA'S WEST

1. George Washington, "Advertisement of Western Lands, 15 July 1773," Founders Online, National Archives, https://founders.archives.gov/documents/Washington/02-09-02-0207.
2. John Alexander Williams examines the connections between land speculation and patronage in chapter 1 of *West Virginia: A History* (Morgantown: West Virginia University Press, 2001).
3. Otis K. Rice and Stephen W. Brown, *West Virginia: A History* (Lexington: University Press of Kentucky, 1993), 97–98; Kenneth W. Noe, *Southwest Virginia's Railroad: Modernization and the Sectional Crisis* (Chicago: University of Illinois Press, 1994), 20–26.
4. John Carlile, quoted in Theodore F. Lang, *Loyal West Virginia from 1861 to 1865* (Baltimore: Deutsch Publishing, 1895), 4.
5. Noe, *Southwest Virginia's Railroad*, 8.
6. Richard Orr Curry, *A House Divided: A Study of Statehood Politics and the Copperhead Movement West Virginia* (Pittsburgh: University of Pittsburgh Press, 1964), 23.
7. Daniel W. Crofts, *Reluctant Confederates: Upper South Unionists in the Secession Crisis* (Chapel Hill: University of North Carolina Press, 1989), 47–48.
8. For a good summary of the party system in the Jacksonian era, see Harry Watson, *Liberty and Power: The Politics of Jacksonian America*, 2nd ed. (New York: Hill & Wang, 2006).
9. Manisha Sinha's *The Slave's Cause: A History of Abolition* (New Haven, CT: Yale University Press, 2016) is the most complete account of the idea and the movement. Eric Foner's *Free Labor, Free Soil, Free Men: The Ideology of the Republican Party before the Civil War* (New York: Oxford University Press, 1995) remains the best exploration of the free-soil idea. William A. Link, *Roots of Secession: Slavery and Politics in*

Antebellum Virginia (Chapel Hill: University of North Carolina Press, 2003) is an excellent account of slavery's impact on Virginia politics.
10. Mary E. Mauzy and George Mauzy to Mrs. Eugenie Burton, November 8, 1859, typescript, Boyd B. Stutler Collection, West Virginia State Archives, Charleston.
11. Granville Parker, *The Formation of the State of West Virginia, and Other Incidents of the Late Civil War* (Wellsburg, WV, 1875), 1.

CHAPTER 2: THE REVOLUTION OF 1860

1. *Wheeling Daily Intelligencer*, December 3, 1859.
2. "About The Wheeling Daily Intelligencer," Chronicling America, Library of Congress, Accessed December 12, 2024, https://chroniclingamerica.loc.gov/lccn/sn84026844/.
3. "Ceredo," *e-WV: The West Virginia Encyclopedia Online*, last revised April 10, 2024, https://www.wvencyclopedia.org/articles/1040.
4. A good summary of the election of 1860 is Douglas R. Egerton, *Year of Meteors: Stephen Douglas, Abraham Lincoln, and the Election That Brought On the Civil War* (New York: Bloomsbury, 2010).
5. Otis K. Rice and Stephen W. Brown, *West Virginia: A History* (Lexington: University Press of Kentucky, 1993), 115–16.
6. William A. Link, *Roots of Secession: Slavery and Politics in Antebellum Virginia* (Chapel Hill: University of North Carolina Press, 2003), 242.
7. For more on the taxation issue, see William Freehling and Craig M. Simpson, eds., *Showdown in Virginia: The 1861 Convention and the Fate of the Union* (Charlottesville: University of Virginia Press, 2010), 133–52, 204–6.
8. Albert Castell, *Winning and Losing in the Civil War: Essays and Stories* (Columbia: University of South Carolina Press, 1996), 186–87.

CHAPTER 3: OPENING GAMBITS

1. William A. Link, *Roots of Secession: Slavery and Politics in Antebellum Virginia* (Chapel Hill: University of North Carolina Press, 2003), 248–49.
2. Theodore F. Lang, *Loyal West Virginia from 1861 to 1865* (Baltimore: Deutsch Publishing, 1895), 4–5.
3. Ethan Rafuse, *McClellan's War: The Failure of Moderation in the Struggle for the Union* (Bloomington: Indiana University Press, 2005), provides an excellent explanation of McClellan's decisions in western Virginia early in the war. See chapter 5.
4. W. Hunter Lesser, *Rebels at the Gate: Lee and McClellan on the Front Line of a Nation Divided* (Naperville, IL: Sourcebooks, 2004), 36–38.
5. An excellent brief overview is Mark A. Snell, *West Virginia and the Civil War: Mountaineers Are Always Free* (Charleston, SC: History Press, 2011).
6. Margaretta Barton Colt, *Defend the Valley: A Shenandoah Family in the Civil War* (New York: Oxford University Press, 1994), 5.
7. McClellan's early proposal to strike Richmond from a starting point near Gallipolis, Ohio, had it been enacted, would have put western Virginia's Kanawha Valley at the center of Union military strategy. But Commanding General Winfield Scott expressed concern that a major Union invasion might "turn" civilians in the region

toward the Confederacy. The proposal perhaps reflected a poor understanding by McClellan of the challenging terrain such a path would need to cross. See Donald Stoker, *The Grand Design: Strategy and the U.S. Civil War* (New York: Oxford University Press, 2010), 36–38. Rafuse offers a defense of McClellan's early thinking on the Kanawha Valley route as a better political option than invading neutral Kentucky (*McClellan's War,* 96–97).

8. See Kenneth W. Noe, *Southwest Virginia's Railroad: Modernization and the Sectional Crisis* (Chicago: University of Illinois Press, 1994), chaps. 6–7.
9. "First Inaugural Address," in *Collected Works of Abraham Lincoln,* vol. 4 (New Brunswick, NJ: Rutgers University Press, 1953), 250.
10. Glenn David Brasher, *The Peninsula Campaign and the Necessity of Emancipation: African Americans and the Fight for Freedom* (Chapel Hill: University of North Carolina Press, 2012), 36–39.
11. Jonathan A. Noyalas, *"My Will Is Absolute Law": A Biography of Union General Robert H. Milroy* (Jefferson, NC: McFarland, 2006), 26, 56, 75–76; Lesser, *Rebels at the Gate,* 242–43.
12. Kevin M. Levin, *Searching for Black Confederates: The Civil War's Most Persistent Myth* (Chapel Hill: University of North Carolina Press, 2019).
13. Clayton R. Newell, *Lee vs. McClellan: The First Campaign* (Washington D.C.: Regnery Publishing, 1996), 9–11.
14. James E. Hall, *The Diary of a Confederate Soldier,* ed. Ruth Woods Dayton (n.p., 1961), 11.

CHAPTER 4: THE RULES OF WAR

1. *Greenbrier Weekly Era,* May 25, 1861.
2. *The Yankee* (Lewisburg, VA [WV]), May 29, 1862.
3. Daniel E. Sutherland, *A Savage Conflict: The Decisive Role of Guerrillas in the American Civil War* (Chapel Hill: University of North Carolina Press, 2009) is one work emphasizing violence and lawlessness. Mark Grimsley's *The Hard Hand of War: Union Military Policy toward Southern Civilians, 1861–1865* (Cambridge: Cambridge University Press, 1995) emphasizes restraint. Aaron Sheehan-Dean's *The Calculus of Violence: How Americans Fought the Civil War* (Cambridge, MA: Harvard University Press, 2018) toes a middle ground on these issues.
4. *General George Crook: His Autobiography,* ed. Martin F. Schmitt (Norman: University of Oklahoma Press, 1960), 86–87.
5. Sutherland, *A Savage Conflict,* ix.
6. For a discussion of how the Partisan Ranger Act was used, see Robert R. Mackey, *The Uncivil War: Irregular Warfare in the Upper South, 1861–1865* (Norman: University of Oklahoma Press, 2004), chaps. 3 and 5 and the appendix (205–6) for the text of the act.
7. Glenn David Brasher, *The Peninsula Campaign and the Necessity of Emancipation* (Chapel Hill: University of North Carolina Press, 2012) provides a good overview of shifting military policies toward self-emancipating people. George McClellan's conservative proslavery approach was evident in his instructions to his subordinates when he launched his invasion of western Virginia. George McClellan to Colonel

B. F. Kelley, May 26, 1861, in *The War of the Rebellion: A Compilation of the Official Records of the Union and Confederate Armies,* series 1, vol. 2 (Washington, D.C.: Government Printing Office, 1880), 46.
8. Very little has been written about the large contraband camp at Harpers Ferry. Jonathan A. Noyalas, *Slavery and Freedom in the Shenandoah Valley during the Civil War* (Gainesville: University Press of Florida, 2021) provides a great deal of information about the experiences of enslaved people in the Valley during the war. Amy Murrell Taylor, *Embattled Freedom: Journeys through the Civil War's Slave Refugee Camps* (Chapel Hill: University of North Carolina Press, 2018) has little information on the Harpers Ferry camp but provides a broad look at what African Americans experienced in these camps.
9. John Fabian Witt, *Lincoln's Code: The Laws of War in American History* (New York: Free Press, 2012), 29–31, 256–60; Elizabeth R. Varon, *Armies of Deliverance: A New History of the Civil War* (New York: Oxford University Press, 2019), 206–8, 238–40.
10. Witt's *Lincoln's Code* traces the construction of the Lieber Code during the war and the issues that prompted its creation.
11. A Confederate general.
12. From this point forward, Hayes is paraphrasing and quoting information he gleaned from Charles.

CHAPTER 5: THE MOVEMENT FOR STATEHOOD

1. Eric J. Wittenberg, Edmund A. Sargus, and Penny Barrick, *Seceding from Secession: The Civil War, Politics, and the Creation of West Virginia* (El Dorado Hills, CA: Savas Beatie, 2020), 41–43.
2. Otis K. Rice and Stephen W. Brown, *West Virginia: A History* (Lexington: University Press of Kentucky, 1993), 141.
3. Rice and Brown, 141–45.
4. Scott A. MacKenzie, *The Fifth Border State: Slavery, Emancipation, and the Formation of West Virginia, 1829–1872* (Morgantown: West Virginia University Press, 2023), 146.
5. Michael E. Woods, "Mountaineers Becoming Free: Emancipation and Statehood in West Virginia," *West Virginia History,* n.s., vol. 9, no. 2 (Fall 2015): 37–71 offers a notable alternative to MacKenzie's understanding of how the statehood movement came to embrace emancipation, one that emphasizes the actions of enslaved western Virginians themselves and the alliances they formed with Union troops.
6. Rice and Brown, *West Virginia,* 145.
7. Rice and Brown, 147–48.
8. Wittenberg, Sargus, and Barrick, *Seceding from Secession,* 116.
9. Wittenberg, Sargus, and Barrick, 79–82.
10. See Wittenberg, Sargus, and Barrick, chapter 4, for a detailed account of the First and Second Wheeling Conventions.

CHAPTER 6: WOMEN AND THE WAR

1. Laura Arnold, from an interview in 1890 with the *Columbus Dispatch,* reprinted in *The Yazoo Herald* (Yazoo City, MS), August 6, 1897.

2. Mary Anna Jackson to Laura Arnold Jackson, October 21, 1865, Manuscript Acc #102, Stonewall Jackson Papers, Arnold Family Papers, Box 5, VMI Archives, quoted in Larry Spurgeon, "Laura Arnold: Stonewall Jackson's Unionist Sister" (unpublished manuscript, 2020), 16–17, accessed January 1, 2025, https://www.jacksonbrigade.com/wp-content/uploads/2020/05/Laura-Arnold-paper-Final-Draft.pdf.
3. Nina Silber, *Daughters of the Union: Northern Women Fight the Civil War* (Cambridge, MA: Harvard University Press, 2005), 10–13.
4. *Wheeling Daily Intelligencer,* September 4, 1861.
5. Stephanie McCurry, *Women's War: Fighting and Surviving the American Civil War* (Cambridge, MA: Harvard University Press, 2019), 3–4.
6. McCurry, 15.
7. *Wheeling Daily Intelligencer,* August 29, 1862.
8. DeAnne Blanton and Lauren Cook, *They Fought Like Demons: Women Soldiers in the Civil War* (New York: Vintage, 2002), 7.
9. "Jenking"/"Jenkings" refers to Albert Gallatin Jenkins, a congressman from Cabell County in far-western Virginia. Jenkins was from a wealthy slaveholding family and resigned from Congress at the outbreak of the war, forming a mounted company of partisan rangers who harassed federal troops throughout much of the war, at one point invading Kentucky and crossing into Ohio.
10. "Grimalkin" is an archaic term for a cat but also can mean an old, spiteful woman.
11. Tilda was an enslaved woman the Woods family had leased for a year.
12. *Architects of Our Fortunes: The Journal of Eliza A. W. Otis, 1860–1863, with Letters and Civil War Journal of Harrison Gray Otis,* ed. Ann Gorman Condon (San Marino, CA: Huntington Library, 2001), 90.
13. This is the pseudonym of Robert Henry Newell, a popular humorist who wrote satirical pieces about the Civil War. The name was a play on "office seeker," a reference to the many self-serving individuals who sought to advance their careers.
14. Larry G. Eggleston, *Women in the Civil War: Extraordinary Stories of Soldiers, Spies, Nurses, Doctors, Crusaders, and Others* (Jefferson, NC: McFarland, 2003).

CHAPTER 7: ENDURING A LONG WAR

1. David Shafer to Lydia A. Bishoff, October 6 and October 23, 1862, Bishoff Collection, Gilder Lehrman Institute Collection, New York.
2. James M. McPherson, *What They Fought For, 1861–1865* (New York: Anchor Books, 1994), 57–64.
3. For examples of historians who emphasize nonpolitical motives for soldier persistence, see Gerald Linderman, *Embattled Courage: The Experience of Combat in the American Civil War* (New York: Free Press, 2008); Reid Mitchell, *Civil War Soldiers* (New York: Penguin Books, 1988); Reid Mitchell, *The Vacant Chair: The Northern Soldier Leaves Home* (New York: Oxford University Press, 1993); Bell Wiley, *The Life of Johnny Reb: The Common Soldier of the Confederacy* (Baton Rouge: Louisiana State University Press, 2008); Bell Wiley, *The Life of Billy Yank: The Common Soldier of the Union* (Baton Rouge: Louisiana State University Press, 1992); and J. Glenn Gray, *The Warriors: Reflections on Men in Battle* (Lincoln: University of Nebraska Press, 1970).

4. Otis Rice and Stephen W. Brown, *West Virginia: A History* (Lexington: University Press of Kentucky, 1993), 150–51.
5. Earl J. Hess, *Civil War Logistics: A Study of Military Transportation* (Baton Rouge: Louisiana State University Press, 2017), 80, 88, 91.
6. Roger Pickenpaugh, *Rescue by Rail: Troop Transfer and the Civil War in the West, 1863* (Lincoln: University of Nebraska Press, 1998), 7; Hess, *Civil War Logistics*, 191–96.
7. Oscar Osborn Winther, "The Soldier Vote in the Election of 1864," *New York History* 25 (1944): 441, 455. Jonathan W. White, *Emancipation, the Union Army, and the Re-election of Abraham Lincoln* (Baton Rouge: Louisiana State University Press, 2014) challenges conventional wisdom on the meaning of the 1864 soldier vote.
8. David W. Mellott and Mark A. Snell, *The Seventh West Virginia Infantry: An Embattled Union Regiment from the Civil War's Most Divided State* (Lawrence: University Press of Kansas, 2019), 92–93.
9. Mellott and Snell, 117–19.
10. James McPherson, *Battle Cry of Freedom: The Civil War Era* (New York: Oxford University Press, 2003), 31.

CHAPTER 8: REVOLUTION AND COUNTERREVOLUTION

1. Eric Foner, *Reconstruction: America's Unfinished Revolution, 1863–1877* (New York: Harper & Row, 1988), xvii, 37–39, argues that Reconstruction first began in West Virginia in 1863 with statehood or possibly as early as 1861 when the statehood process began. John E. Stealey, *West Virginia's Civil War–Era Constitution: Loyal Revolution, Confederate Counter-Revolution, and the Convention of 1872* (Kent, OH: Kent State University Press, 2013) suggests we consider 1861–65 an era of revolution in West Virginia and the period from the end of the war until the adoption of the 1872 constitution an era of counterrevolution. Richard Curry, *Radicalism, Racism, and Party Realignment: The Border States during Reconstruction* (Baltimore: Johns Hopkins University Press, 1969) does not employ the terminology of "counter-revolution" but aligns with Stealey in noting the return of traditionalists to power in the state in the 1870 elections.
2. Curry, *Radicalism*, xvi–xvii, 99–100.
3. Randall S. Gooden, "'Neither War nor Peace': West Virginia's Reconstruction Experience," in *Reconstructing Appalachia: The Civil War's Aftermath*, ed. Andrew L. Slap (Lexington: University Press of Kentucky, 2010), 216.
4. Caroline Janney, *Ends of War: The Unfinished Fight of Lee's Army after Appomattox* (Chapel Hill: University of North Carolina Press, 2023), 182; Gooden, "Neither War nor Peace," 214–15.
5. John W. Shaffer, *Clash of Loyalties: A Border County in the Civil War* (Morgantown: West Virginia University Press, 2003), 129.
6. Shaffer, 103–4.
7. *Acts of the West Virginia Legislature at Its Third Session, Commencing January 17, 1865* (Wheeling, WV, 1865), 47–48.
8. Otis Rice and Stephen W. Brown, *West Virginia: A History* (Lexington: University Press of Kentucky, 1993), 158.
9. Rice and Brown, 156–61.

10. Ronald L. Lewis, *Transforming the Appalachian Countryside: Railroads, Deforestation, and Social Change in West Virginia, 1880–1920* (Chapel Hill: University of North Carolina Press, 1998), 7–8.
11. *The Miscellaneous Document of the House of Representatives: Printed during the First Session of the Thirty-Ninth Congress* (Washington, D.C.: Government Printing Office, 1866), 35–36.
12. Scott Reynolds Nelson, *Steel Drivin' Man: John Henry, the Untold Story of an American Legend* (New York: Oxford University Press, 2006), 40.

CHAPTER 9: MEMORY

1. *Charleston Gazette-Mail,* June 20, 2019; *Charleston Gazette-Mail,* October 21, 2021.
2. House Bill 2174, West Virginia Monument and Memorial Protection Act of 2021.
3. Steven Cody Straley, *A Constant Reminder to All: Stonewall Jackson, the Lost Cause, and the Making of a West Virginia Idol* (Charleston, WV: 35th Star Publishing, 2022), 3–5.
4. Hu Maxwell and Howard Llewellyn Swisher, *History of Hampshire County, West Virginia from Its Earliest Settlement to the Present* (Morgantown, WV: A. Brown Boughner, 1897), 692–93.
5. See Caroline E. Janney, *Burying the Dead but Not the Past: Ladies Memorial Associations and the Lost Cause* (Chapel Hill: University of North Carolina Press, 2008).
6. Caroline E. Janney, "The Lost Cause," last updated August 26, 2024, *Encyclopedia of Virginia,* https://encyclopediavirginia.org/entries/lost-cause-the/.
7. Caroline E. Janney, *Remembering the Civil War: Reunion and the Limits of Reconciliation* (Chapel Hill: University of North Carolina Press, 2013).
8. It is worth noting that the border states that remained in the Union during the war grappled with somewhat similar challenges as the new state of West Virginia did in commemorating this bloody conflict. There have been a number of excellent studies on Civil War memory in the border states, including Ann E. Marshall, *Creating a Confederate Kentucky: The Lost Cause and Civil War Memory in a Border State* (Chapel Hill: University of North Carolina Press, 2010); Amy Laurel Fluker, *Commonwealth of Compromise: Civil War Commemoration in Missouri* (Columbia: University of Missouri Press, 2020); and David K. Graham, *Loyalty on the Line: Civil War Maryland in American Memory* (Athens: University of Georgia Press, 2018).
9. Janney, *Remembering the Civil War;* David W. Blight, *Race and Reunion: The Civil War in American Memory* (Cambridge, MA: Harvard University Press, 2001); John Alexander Williams, *West Virginia: A History* (Morgantown: West Virginia University Press, 2001); Straley, *A Constant Reminder to All.*

Selected Bibliography

ARTICLES

Buchkoski, Courtney. "'Luke-Warm Abolitionists': Eli Thayer and the Contest for Civil War Memory, 1853–1899." *Journal of the Civil War Era* 9, no. 2 (2019): 249–74.

Engle, Stephen D. "Mountaineer Reconstruction: Blacks in the Political Reconstruction of West Virginia." *Journal of Negro History* 78, no. 3 (1993): 137–65.

Fain, Cicero. "Into the Crucible: The Chesapeake and Ohio Railroad and the Black Industrial Worker in Southern West Virginia, 1870–1900." *Journal of Appalachian Studies* 17, no. 1–2 (2011): 42–65.

Fones-Wolf, Ken. "'Traitors in Wheeling': Secessionism in an Appalachian Unionist City." *Journal of Appalachian Studies* 13, no. 1 (2007): 75–95.

Fredette, Allison. "The View from the Border: West Virginia Republicans and Women's Rights in the Age of Emancipation." *West Virginia History* 3, no. 1 (2009): 57–80.

Hathaway, Rosemary V. "From Hillbilly to Frontiersman: The Changing Nature of the WVU Mountaineer." *West Virginia History* 8, no. 2 (2014): 15–45.

Hulver, Richard A., and William M. Theriault. "McNeill's Rangers in the Public Memory of Hardy County, West Virginia." *West Virginia History* 8, no. 1 (2014): 21–38.

MacKenzie, Scott A. "The Slaveholders' War: The Secession Crisis in Kanawha County, Western Virginia, 1860–1861." *West Virginia History* 4, no. 1 (2010): 33–57.

Moore, George E. "The Battle of Carnifex Ferry: Succession and the War in West Virginia before September 1, 1861." *West Virginia History* 7, no. 1 (2013): 39–74.

Woods, Michael E. "Mountaineers Becoming Free: Emancipation and Statehood in West Virginia." *West Virginia History* 9, no. 2 (2015): 37–71.

Zimring, David R. "'Secession in Favor of the Constitution': How West Virginia Justified Separate Statehood during the Civil War." *West Virginia History* 3, no. 2 (2009): 23–51.

BOOKS

Adams, Sean P. *Old Dominion, Industrial Commonwealth: Coal, Politics, and Economy in Antebellum America*. Baltimore: Johns Hopkins University Press, 2009.

Armstrong, Richard L. *The Battle of Lewisburg, May 23, 1862*. Charleston, WV: 35th Star Publishing, 2017.

Ayers, Edward, *Promise of the New South: Life after Reconstruction*. New York: Oxford University Press, 2007.

Blair, William Alan. *Virginia's Private War: Feeding Body and Soul in the Confederacy, 1861–1865*. New York: Oxford University Press, 1998.

Blair, William Alan. *With Malice toward Some: Treason and Loyalty in the Civil War Era*. Littlefield History of the Civil War Era. Chapel Hill: University of North Carolina Press, 2014.

Blanton, DeAnne, and Lauren M. Cook. *They Fought Like Demons: Women Soldiers in the American Civil War*. New York: Vintage, 2002.

Brown, John, and Louis A. DeCaro. *John Brown Speaks: Letters and Statements from Charlestown*. Lanham, MD: Rowman & Littlefield, 2015.

Carmichael, Peter S. *The Last Generation: Young Virginians in Peace, War, and Reunion*. Civil War America. Chapel Hill: University of North Carolina Press, 2005.

———. *The War for the Common Soldier: How Men Thought, Fought, and Survived in Civil War Armies*. Chapel Hill: University of North Carolina Press, 2018.

Cashin, Joan E. *War Stuff: The Struggle for Human and Environmental Resources in the American Civil War*. Cambridge: Cambridge University Press, 2018.

Chappell, Louis W. *John Henry: A Folk-Lore Study*. Kennikat Press Series in Negro Culture and History. Port Washington, NY: Kennikat, 1933.

Collins, Darrell L. *The Jones-Imboden Raid: The Confederate Attempt to Destroy the Baltimore & Ohio Railroad and Retake West Virginia*. Jefferson, NC: McFarland, 2007.

Cozzens, Peter. *Shenandoah 1862: Stonewall Jackson's Valley Campaign*. Civil War America. Chapel Hill: University of North Carolina Press, 2008.

Crook, George. *General George Crook: His Autobiography*. New ed. Norman: University of Oklahoma Press, 1960.

Curry, Richard Orr. *A House Divided: A Study of Statehood Politics and the Copperhead Movement in West Virginia*. Pittsburgh: University of Pittsburgh Press, 1964.

Dew, Charles B. *Apostles of Disunion: Southern Secession Commissioners and the Causes of the Civil War*. A Nation Divided: Studies in the Civil War Era. 15th anniversary ed. Charlottesville: University of Virginia Press, 2016.

Drake, Brian Allen. *The Blue, the Gray, and the Green: Toward an Environmental History of the Civil War*. UnCivil Wars. Athens: University of Georgia Press, 2015.

Dunaway, Wilma A. *Slavery in the American Mountain South*. Studies in Modern Capitalism. Cambridge: Cambridge University Press, 2003.

Duncan, Richard R. *Lee's Endangered Left: The Civil War in Western Virginia, Spring of 1864*. Baton Rouge: Louisiana State University Press, 1998.

Earle, Jonathan Halperin. *John Brown's Raid on Harpers Ferry: A Brief History with Documents*. Bedford Series in History and Culture. Boston: Bedford/St. Martin's, 2008.

Egerton, Douglas R. *The Wars of Reconstruction: The Brief, Violent History of America's Most Progressive Era*. New York: Bloomsbury, 2014.

Foner, Eric. *Reconstruction: America's Unfinished Revolution, 1863–1877*. New York: Harper & Row, 1988.

Ford, Bridget. *Bonds of Union: Religion, Race, and Politics in a Civil War Borderland*. Civil War America. Chapel Hill: University of North Carolina Press, 2016.

Freehling, William W. *The Road to Disunion*. New York: Oxford University Press, 1990.

Gallagher, Gary W. *The Union War*. Cambridge, MA: Harvard University Press, 2012.

Gallman, J. Matthew. *Defining Duty in the Civil War: Personal Choice, Popular Culture, and the Union Home Front*. Civil War America. Chapel Hill: University of North Carolina Press, 2015.

Graham, Michael B. *The Coal River Valley in the Civil War: West Virginia Mountains, 1861*. Charleston, SC: History Press, 2014.

Guelzo, Allen C. *Fateful Lightning: A New History of the Civil War and Reconstruction.* Oxford: Oxford University Press, 2012.
Hearn, Chester G. *Six Years of Hell: Harpers Ferry during the Civil War.* Baton Rouge: Louisiana State University Press, 1999.
Hettle, Wallace. *Inventing Stonewall Jackson: A Civil War Hero in History and Memory.* Baton Rouge: Louisiana State University Press, 2011.
Horwitz, Tony. *Confederates in the Attic: Dispatches from the Unfinished Civil War.* Vintage Departures. New York: Vintage Books, 1999.
———. *Midnight Rising: John Brown and the Raid That Sparked the Civil War.* New York: Henry Holt, 2011.
Inscoe, John C. *Race, War, and Remembrance in the Appalachian South.* Lexington: University Press of Kentucky, 2008.
Janney, Caroline E. *Burying the Dead but Not the Past: Ladies' Memorial Associations and the Lost Cause.* Civil War America. Chapel Hill: University of North Carolina Press, 2008.
———. *Remembering the Civil War: Reunion and the Limits of Reconciliation.* Littlefield History of the Civil War Era. Chapel Hill: University of North Carolina Press, 2013.
Johnson, Guy Benton. *John Henry: Tracking Down a Negro Legend.* New York: AMS Press, 1929.
Lang, Andrew F. *In the Wake of War: Military Occupation, Emancipation, and Civil War America.* Baton Rouge: Louisiana State University Press, 2017.
Lang, Theodore F. *Loyal West Virginia from 1861 to 1865: With an Introductory Chapter on the Status of Virginia for Thirty Years Prior to the War.* Baltimore: Deutsch Publishing, 1895.
Lesser, Hunter. *Rebels at the Gate: Lee and McClellan on the Front Line of a Nation Divided.* Naperville, IL: Sourcebooks, 2004.
Levin, Kevin M. *Searching for Black Confederates: The Civil War's Most Persistent Myth.* Civil War America. Chapel Hill: University of North Carolina Press, 2019.
Lewis, Ronald L. *Transforming the Appalachian Countryside: Railroads, Deforestation, and Social Change in West Virginia, 1880–1920.* Chapel Hill: University of North Carolina Press, 1998.
Link, William A. *Roots of Secession: Slavery and Politics in Antebellum Virginia.* Civil War America. Chapel Hill: University of North Carolina Press, 2003.
Lowry, Terry. *The Battle of Scary Creek: Military Operations in the Kanawha Valley, April–July 1861.* Rev. ed. Charleston, WV: Quarrier, 1998.
MacKenzie, Scott A. *The Fifth Border State: Slavery, Emancipation, and the Formation of West Virginia, 1829–1872.* Morgantown: West Virginia University Press, 2023.
Mackey, Robert Russell. *The Uncivil War: Irregular Warfare in the Upper South, 1861–1865.* Campaigns and Commanders 5. Norman: University of Oklahoma Press, 2004.
Manning, Chandra. *What This Cruel War Was Over: Soldiers, Slavery, and the Civil War.* New York: Vintage Civil War Library, 2008.
McClellan, George B. *The Civil War Papers of George B. McClellan: Selected Correspondence, 1860–1865.* Edited by Stephen W. Sears New York: Da Capo Press, 1989.
McGinty, Brian. *John Brown's Trial.* Cambridge, MA: Harvard University Press, 2009.

McKnight, Brian Dallas. *Contested Borderland: The Civil War in Appalachian Kentucky and Virginia*. Lexington: University Press of Kentucky, 2006.
McPherson, James M. *Battle Cry of Freedom: The Civil War Era*. New York: Oxford University Press, 2003.
McWhirter, Christian. *Battle Hymns: The Power and Popularity of Music in the Civil War*. Civil War America. Chapel Hill: University of North Carolina Press, 2012.
Mellott, David W., and Mark A. Snell. *The Seventh West Virginia Infantry: An Embattled Union Regiment from the Civil War's Most Divided State*. Lawrence: University Press of Kansas, 2019.
Meyer, Eugene L. *Five for Freedom: The African American Soldiers in John Brown's Army*. Chicago: Lawrence Hill Books, 2018.
Nelson, Scott Reynolds. *Steel Drivin' Man: John Henry, the Untold Story of an American Legend*. New York: Oxford University Press, 2006.
Newell, Clayton R. *Lee vs. McClellan: The First Campaign*. Washington, DC: Regnery Pub., 1996.
Noe, Kenneth W. *Southwest Virginia's Railroad: Modernization and the Sectional Crisis*. Chicago: University of Illinois Press, 1994.
Noe, Kenneth W., and Shannon H. Wilson. *The Civil War in Appalachia: Collected Essays*. Knoxville: University of Tennessee Press, 1997.
Noyalas, Jonathan A. *Slavery and Freedom in the Shenandoah Valley during the Civil War*. Gainesville: University of Florida Press, 2021.
Pickenpaugh, Roger. *Rescue by Rail: Troop Transfer and the Civil War in the West, 1863*. Lincoln: University of Nebraska Press, 1998.
Rafuse, Ethan Sepp. *McClellan's War: The Failure of Moderation in the Struggle for the Union*. Bloomington: Indiana University Press, 2005.
Rice, Otis K., and Stephen Wayne Brown. *West Virginia: A History*. 2nd ed. Lexington: University Press of Kentucky, 1993.
Riddel, Frank S. *The Historical Atlas of West Virginia*. Morgantown: West Virginia University Press, 2008.
Shaffer, John W. *Clash of Loyalties: A Border County in the Civil War*. West Virginia and Appalachia 3. Morgantown: West Virginia University Press, 2003.
Sheehan-Dean, Aaron Charles. *The Calculus of Violence: How Americans Fought the Civil War*. Cambridge, MA: Harvard University Press, 2018.
Silber, Nina. *Gender and the Sectional Conflict*. Steven and Janice Brose Lectures in the Civil War Era. Chapel Hill: University of North Carolina Press, 2008.
Slap, Andrew L., ed. *Reconstructing Appalachia: The Civil War's Aftermath*. New Directions in Southern History. Lexington: University Press of Kentucky, 2010.
Snell, Mark A. *West Virginia and the Civil War: Mountaineers Are Always Free*. History Press Civil War Sesquicentennial Series. Charleston, SC: History Press, 2011.
Stealey, John E. *The Antebellum Kanawha Salt Business and Western Markets*. Morgantown: West Virginia University Press, 2016.
Stephenson, Darl L. *Headquarters in the Brush: Blazer's Independent Union Scouts*. Athens: Ohio University Press, 2001.
Summers, Mark W. *The Ordeal of the Reunion: A New History of Reconstruction*. Littlefield History of the Civil War Era. Chapel Hill: University of North Carolina Press, 2014.

Sutherland, Daniel E. *A Savage Conflict: The Decisive Role of Guerrillas in the American Civil War.* Civil War America. Chapel Hill: University of North Carolina Press, 2009.
Thomas, William G. *The Iron Way: Railroads, the Civil War, and the Making of Modern America.* New Haven, CT: Yale University Press, 2011.
Tucker, Spencer. *Brigadier General John D. Imboden: Confederate Commander in the Shenandoah.* Lexington: University Press of Kentucky, 2003.
Varon, Elizabeth R. *Armies of Deliverance: A New History of the Civil War.* New York: Oxford University Press, 2019.
———. *Disunion! The Coming of the American Civil War, 1789–1859.* Chapel Hill: University of North Carolina Press, 2008.
Washington, Booker T. *Up from Slavery: An Autobiography.* New York: Skyhorse Publishing, 2015.
White, Jonathan W. *Emancipation, the Union Army, and the Reelection of Abraham Lincoln.* Conflicting Worlds: New Dimensions of the American Civil War. Baton Rouge: Louisiana State University Press, 2014.
Williams, John Alexander. *West Virginia: A History.* Morgantown: West Virginia University Press, 2001.
Wittenberg, Eric J. *The Battle of White Sulphur Springs: Averell Fails to Secure West Virginia.* Charleston, SC: History Press, 2011.

Index

5th (West) Virginia Volunteer Infantry, 190–92
7th (West) Virginia Infantry, 181, 184–88
12th Ohio Volunteer Infantry, 103–7
23rd Ohio Volunteer Infantry, 101, 114, 173
36th Ohio Volunteer Infantry, 109–11
45th United States Colored Troops, 99

abolitionism in Virginia: as an accusation to silence dissent, 24, 38–39, 43, 54–56; definition of, 12; failure to distinguish free-soil ideas from, 13; fears of, 37–38, 43, 47–48, 64–67; as an insult, 110, 146, 159, 185, 188, 202
"Abraham Lincoln Walks at Midnight" (poem), 1
Abraham Lincoln Walks at Midnight (statue), 1–2
African Americans: and Confederate armies, 98–99, 125–27; as contraband of war, 71–73, 98, 114–17, 120–27, 155, 165–66; and enlistment in Union army, 98–99; enslaved, 3, 5–7, 10, 12, 16–17, 45, 68, 71–73, 77–81, 121; free, 3, 48–49, 72, 117–19, 237; and postwar civil rights, 206–8, 225–26; and postwar migration to West Virginia, 230–34; and self-emancipation, 98, 114–17, 120, 129–30; and Union army, 115–19, 123–24
agriculture, 6, 11, 14–17, 23, 67, 77, 100, 107, 117, 126, 227–28
Antietam, battle of, 18, 187, 200, 245, 258
anti-secession views in western Virginia, 52–56, 59–60, 66–67, 76
antislavery in western Virginia. *See* abolitionism in Virginia; free-soil ideology
Appalachia, 3–4
Appomattox, surrender at, 92, 206–7, 209–10, 253, 259
Army of the Kanawha (Confederate), 76
Arnold, Laura Jackson, 46, 153–54
Averill, William, 118–19

Bagby, Lucy, 45, 48–52
Baltimore and Ohio Railroad (B&O): and access to eastern markets, 6, 11; Confederate sabotage of, 86, 156–57, 183; Richmond blocks funding, 11; strategic importance of, 69–70, 100, 128–29, 183; troop transfer on, 194–200
Barbour County, 45, 53, 86–87, 92, 169–73, 207–8, 229
Barbour Greys, 92
Battelle, Gordon, 102–3
Bell, John, 44
Berkeley County, 129, 207, 223
Black people. *See* African Americans
"Black Republicans," 13, 43, 58, 147, 176
Board of Public Works, 7, 246
Bolivar Heights, 184
border states, 4–5, 58, 77, 130, 206, 237, 261; West Virginia as one of the, 4–5
Boreman, Arthur, 207, 213–17
Boteler, Alexander, 37–39
Boyd, Maria Isabella "Belle," 155, 163–65
Braxton County, 159, 229
Breckinridge, John C., 44
Bristol, Tennessee, 11
Brown, John (abolitionist), 13–14, 26–37; execution, 33–34. *See also* Harpers Ferry insurrection
Brown, John J., 149–50
Brown, Mary Ann, 31–32
Buckhannon, 88–89, 114, 142, 166–68, 229
bushwhackers. *See* guerrillas

Cabell County, 39–41, 64–67, 261
Campbell, Allen, 117–19
Campbell, Archibald, 42
Campbell, W., of Brooke, 18
Camp Chase, 114
Camp Gauley, 160, 173–75, 190–92
canals, 6, 10–11, 19, 40, 75
Caperton, Allen, 77, 80–81
capitol grounds (West Virginia), 1–2, 238–55

Carlile, John S.: call for formation of new state by, 128, 131–33; and emancipation, 141–42; flip on statehood issue, 130–31, 141–42, 151–52; opposition to secession, 10, 55; as slaveholder, 101, 129
Carnifex Ferry, battle of, 258
cavalry, 47, 80–81, 123, 167–68, 173, 177–80, 183, 192–93
centennial of West Virginia, 1, 251
Ceredo, 13, 43, 66–67, 190–91, 262
Charleston: Confederate 1862 occupation of, 125–27; Confederate sympathizers in, 57, 57–59, 73–74; and salt industry, 93–95
Charles Town, 31–33, 219–24
Cheat Mountain: battle of, 91–92, 98–99, 258; summit of, 72, 102
Chesapeake and Ohio Railroad (C&O). *See under* railroads
Child, Lydia Marie, 34–37
children in war, 30–31, 61, 71, 105, 114–15, 124–25, 161, 166–68, 170–72, 175
civilians: pro-Confederate sentiments of, 53–54, 56–59, 61–66, 76–78, 81–83, 158–59, 160–62; pro-Union sentiments of, 52–56, 59–60, 66–67, 88–89, 162–63, 165–68; as victims of soldiers, 99–101, 103–5, 114, 117–19, 124–27, 156–57, 160–63
Civil Rights Bill of 1866, 218
Civil War memory in West Virginia: "Lost Cause," 236–42, 254–55; the mountaineer, 243–48; Union cause, 27–56
Clarksburg, 151–53, 159–60, 217–19, 235–37, 257, 259; convention, 131–33
Confiscation Acts: first, 71–72, 98, 114–17, 258; second, 98, 258
Constitutional Union Party, 44
constitution of 1830 (Virginia), 9–10, 17–21
constitution of 1851 (Virginia), 9–10, 24–26
constitution of 1863 (West Virginia), 128–31, 142–46
constitution of 1872 (West Virginia), 2, 169
contraband camps, 120, 155. *See also* African Americans: as contraband of war
contrabands. *See* African Americans: as contraband of war
Copperheads, 182, 201, 219, 221
Corrick's Ford, battle of, 91

Covington and Ohio Railroad. *See under* railroads
Cox, Jacob D., 76, 95
Crofts, Daniel, 11
Crook, George, 76, 96–97, 106, 118–19, 177
Cumberland Gap, 6, 8

Davis, John James, 45, 53, 59–64
Democratic Party: in antebellum era, 11–12; during the war, 184–88; in 1860, 43–44, 150, 151; and election of 1864, 200–203; postwar, 208–9, 217–19; return to power of, 221–25; and Stonewall Jackson monument, 240–42
Department of the Ohio, 84
Douglas, Stephen, 44
Douglass, Frederick, 39
Duncan, Andrew Jackson, 101

Eastern Panhandle, 71, 129
Echols, John, 77
elections: congressional election of 1870, 208, 221–25; presidential election of 1860, 46–47; presidential election of 1864, 183–84, 200–203; state elections of 1869, 208, 219–22. *See also* referenda
emancipation, as war policy, 5, 17, 68, 71, 73, 129–30, 140–41, 150, 165, 181–82, 184–85, 200–201
Emancipation Proclamation, 98–99, 130, 146, 153, 181, 258–59, 264
enslaved people. *See* African Americans: enslaved

Fairmont, 86, 193, 198, 229–30
farming. *See* agriculture
Fayette County, 114–17, 148, 175
Fifteenth Amendment, 208, 213, 260
First Wheeling Convention. *See* Wheeling Conventions
Flick Amendment, 208, 225–26, 260
Floyd, John Buchanan: as Confederate general, 94–95, 104, 110, 115, 148; as Virginia governor, 10
free Black people. *See* African Americans: free
Freedman's Bureau Bill, 218
freedmen and freedwomen, 2, 7, 16–17, 205, 206, 217–19, 227, 229, 230

Index 281

free public schools, 129, 208, 233
free-soil ideology, 12–14, 21–23, 24–25, 42–43, 48–52, 66–67, 190–91
Fugitive Slave Act of 1850, 4–5, 12, 48–52, 257
fugitive slaves, 48–52, 114–17, 257
Fund for Internal Improvements, 5

Gallipolis, OH, 117, 126, 180
Gauley Bridge, 70, 72, 160, 173–75, 191–92
Germans, 201
Gettysburg, battle of, 18, 184, 245, 253, 259
Goshorn, William, 48–50
Grafton, 69, 87, 90, 197–98
Great Valley of Virginia. *See* Shenandoah Valley
Greenbrier County: Confederate sympathies in, 71–72, 76–78, 81–83, 96, 129; feared slave insurrection in, 78–81; postwar politics in, 215–16, 229; slavery in, 7, 71–72; and Union occupation of Lewisburg, 96–97; war-weariness in, 116
Guerilla, The, 126–27
guerrillas, 3, 96–98, 105–11, 114, 155, 176, 205, 213–14
Guyandotte, 39–41, 64–66

Hall, James E., 92–93
Hampshire County, 100, 129, 235–36
Hardy County, 99–101, 129
Harper, Frances Ellen Watkins, 45, 51–52
Harpers Ferry: Confederate occupation in spring 1861, 74–75; contraband camp, 98, 120, 124–25, 155; end of the war, 211–12; refugees, 204–5; strategic value during the war, 44–45, 69–70, 129; surrender of Union forces in 1862, 3, 98, 119–24; trade and industry, 6
Harpers Ferry insurrection, 26–29; Brown prepares for execution, 31–32; Child-Mason newspaper debate, 34–37; community reaction, 29–39; execution of Brown, 32–34; political responses, 37–41
Harrison County, 10, 45, 52–53, 128, 131–33, 150–51, 229, 235, 237
Hart, Nancy, 155
Hatfield and McCoy feud, 4
Hayes, Rutherford B., 114–17
Henry, John, 230–32

Herald, Wellsburg, 42, 46–47
home guards, 61–62, 65, 109–10, 207, 244, 263
Howe, Henry, 14–16
Huntington, 43

Imboden, John, 156–57, 166–68, 183, 192–93, 259, 264
immigrants, 164, 201, 208, 227–30
industrial development, 2, 6, 10–11, 23
Intelligencer, Wheeling Daily, 42–43, 48, 147, 154, 200–202, 226
internal improvements, 5, 10–11, 19–21, 39–41, 72, 203, 208–9, 227–30
iron industry, 10
irregular warfare, 3, 83–84, 96–99, 111–14, 182–83, 263. *See also* guerrillas

Jackson, Andrew, 9, 11–12
Jackson, Mary Anna, 32–34, 153–54
Jackson, Thomas "Stonewall," 2, 32–34, 45, 119–21, 125, 153, 163–64, monuments to, 235–40, 255, 260
Jackson County, 146–47, 207
James River and Kanawha Canal, 11, 72. *See also* canals
Jefferson, Thomas, 6, 11
Jefferson County, 31–35, 74–75, 119–25, 129, 207, 219–24
Jenkins, Albert Gallatin, 162
John Brown's raid on Harpers Ferry. *See* Harpers Ferry insurrection
Johnson, Andrew, 217–18
Johnson, Joseph, 10
Jones, William E. "Grumble," 156, 183, 192–94
Jones-Imboden raid, 156–57, 183, 192–94

Kanawha, Army of the, 76
Kanawha, proposed state name, 128
Kanawha County, 47, 56–59, 73–74, 77, 178–80, 241
Kanawha Riflemen, 73–74, 236–37
Kanawha River, 1, 6–7, 9–10, 21, 72, 126–27, 162–63, 174–75
Kanawha Salines, 93–95
Kanawha Valley, 69–70, 93–96, 114, 117, 125–27, 162–63, 174–75, 232–34
Kelley, Benjamin, 85–88, 102–3

Kennedy, Anna, 59–64
Kentucky, 4, 6, 14, 40, 43, 66, 72, 191

Lang, Theodore F., 2, 4
laws of war, 96–99; civilians, 90–91, 97–103, 117–19, 127; enlistment of African American men, 98–99; enslaved people, 98, 114–16; irregular units, 111–14
Lee, Robert E.: and Harpers Ferry insurrection, 29; and the Lost Cause, 236; and surrender at Appomattox, 92, 207, 209–10, 253, 259; in western Virginia, 69, 89–90, 97
Leigh, Benjamin Watkins, 19–20
Letcher, John, 10, 68
Lewisburg, 77–78, 80, 82, 94, 96, 229, 236
Lieber Code, 99
Lincoln, Abraham: assassination of, 210–12; election of 1860, 43–44, 46–47; election of 1864, 184, 200–201, 204–5; and Emancipation Proclamation, 98–99; First Inaugural Address of, 71, 130; in memory, 244, 251–55; militia called up by, 44; on moving troops into western Virginia, 68–69, 82; on slavery, 71, 129–30, 200; and statehood bill, 131, 142–46, 202–3; statue on capitol grounds of, 1–2; western Virginians' views of, 43–44, 56–59, 64–67, 100, 146–47, 165–66, 176, 184–85, 189, 210–12
Lindsay, Vachel, 1, 251
Link, William A., 3
Little Kanawha River, 9, 72, 183, 192–94
Loring, William W., 93, 126–27
Lost Cause, 236–38. See also Civil War memory in West Virginia
Loyal West Virginia (Lang), 2
Lynchburg, 11, 205

Madison, James, 6
Manassas, first battle of, 33, 91, 131, 258
Martinsburg, 6, 28, 155, 163–65, 195, 204–5
Mason, Margaretta, 34–37
Massachusetts Emigrant Aid Society, 43, 66
Mauzy, Mary and George, 13–14, 29–32
McClellan, George B.: early plans for western Virginia, 69–70; election of 1864, 184, 200–203; emancipation, 71–72, 97–98; Philippi, 86–87; Rich Mountain, 91–92; soft war policy, 84–86, 90–91, 97–98; Union troops moved into western Virginia, 71–72, 258
McDermot, John F., 42
McDowell County, 129
memory. See Civil War memory in West Virginia
Milroy, Robert H., 72
Monongahela River, 6
Monongahela Valley, 6, 10, 69–70
Monroe County, 7, 72, 76–78, 81, 116–19, 129, 147–49, 236
Morgantown, 130, 139, 156–67, 229
motto for state of West Virginia, 4, 227, 245
mountaineer, as West Virginia icon, 4, 14–16, 243–47, 254–55, 260
Mountaineer Monument, 243–47, 254–55, 260

New River, 116
Noe, Kenneth, 3–4, 11
noncombatants. See civilians
Northern Panhandle, 6, 13, 42–43, 46, 69–70, 128, 181
northwest Virginia, 7, 10–11, 43–45, 56, 68–70, 78, 84, 89–91, 99–101, 128, 131–33

oath taking: after the war, 207–8, 215–19, 221; during the war, 67, 96, 149, 154, 158–59, 207
Ohio County, 137
Ohio River, 6, 8, 14, 69–70, 72, 76, 84–85, 126, 146–47, 195, 200
Opie, John, 92, 94

Parkersburg, 72, 86, 158, 213
partisan rangers, 3, 97, 111–12, 155, 263. See also guerrillas
patronage. See regionalism in Virginia: political patronage
Philippi, battle of, 86–92, 169, 258
Piedmont region of Virginia, 5–6
"plural voting," 10
Pocahontas County, 16–17, 129
Point Pleasant, 202–3, 224–25
political antislavery. See free-soil ideology
postwar economy, 227–34
Potomac, Army of, 91, 184, 194–95

Potomac River, 6, 69
prices during wartime, 94, 116, 172
Princeton, 175
pro-secession views in western Virginia, 53–54, 56–59, 61–66, 81–83, 92–93
public schools, free, 129, 208, 233
Pulaski County, 7

qualifications for voting. *See* voter qualifications
quartering troops, 173–74

railroads: Chesapeake and Ohio Railroad (C&O), 230–32; Covington and Ohio Railroad, 40–42; Virginia and Tennessee Railroad, 7, 11, 94. *See also* Baltimore and Ohio Railroad (B&O)
Ravenswood, 146–47
Reconstruction, 2, 5, 206–25; civil rights of African Americans, 216–17, 224; civil rights of former Confederates, 213–21; defeat at the polls, 221–25; Flick Amendment, 224–27; return of defeated Confederates, 209–12
referenda: on Flick Amendment, 208, 225–27; on statehood (October 1861), 131, 136–37; on Virginia Ordinance of Secession, 44–45, 68, 74, 84, 128, 133; on West Virginia constitution of 1863, 131, 144–45; on West Virginia constitution of 1872, 208
refugees, 149, 204–5, 259
regionalism in Virginia, 9–13; apportionment of representation, 17–19, 26; cultural and economic differences between east and west, 14–16, 21–23; internal improvements, 19–20, 39–41; "peasantry of the west" insult, 19–20; political patronage, 11–12; privileging of large slaveholder's interest, 19–23; property qualifications, 24–26; unfair taxation system, 17–20
religious faith, 31–37, 59, 61–62, 65, 78, 119–20, 124, 135–36, 173
Reorganized Government of Virginia, 102, 128, 134–36, 141, 258
Republican Party, 12–14, 37–38, 42–44, 46–47, 174; postwar, 206–9, 217–25
Restored Government of Virginia. *See* Reorganized Government of Virginia

Rich Mountain, battle of, 91–92, 153, 258
Romney, 102–3, 172, 187, 235–36
Rosecrans, William S., 100, 110, 159, 183
Ruffner, Henry, 13, 21–23

salt industry, 7, 10, 21, 70, 93–95, 232–34
Scammon, E. P., 76, 173, 175
secessionism in western Virginia, 11, 44–45, 53–65, 73–74, 76–78, 88–89, 92, 110, 159–60, 169–70, 206–7
secession ordinance, referendum on. *See* referenda: on Virginia Ordinance of Secession
second Confiscation Act. *See* Confiscation Acts
"servile war," 31, 35, 43, 77
Seward, William H., 43, 146
Shenandoah Valley, 6, 21, 26, 44, 69, 77, 91, 120, 130–31, 204–6, 259
Shepherd, Hayward, 28
Shepherdstown, 221
slave insurrections, fears of, 29–31, 34–36, 76–81
slaveocracy. *See* slave power
slave power, 7–9, 10, 12–13, 18–19, 24–25, 46–47, 131, 206
Small, Jennie, 16–17
soldiers: camp life, 190–92; conscription, 76; destruction of property, 85, 99–101, 108, 192–94; impressment of property, 117–19; morale, 92–93, 165–66, 181–82, 184–92; motivations for fighting, 184–89, 191; quartering of troops, 173; recruitment, 73–74, 78, 82–84, 89–90, 92, 97; scouting raids, 103–9; searching of homes, 99–101, 103–5, 108–9, 160–66; stealing from civilians, 99–101, 161–62
South Carolina, 44, 47, 54, 55, 56, 57, 59, 132, 257, 262; response to secession of, 47–48
Southern Claims Commission, 117–19
southwest Virginia, 6–8, 10–11, 44, 73, 128
spies, 153; women as, 3, 159–60, 163–65, 175–78
squirrel hunters, 112–13, 247–49
statehood. *See* West Virginia statehood
Staunton-Parkersburg Turnpike, 72, 91
suffrage, universal White male, 9, 17–19, 22, 129
Sutherland, Daniel E., 3

Tavenner, William C., 47–48
taxes, 10, 17–21, 25, 40, 45, 68, 203
Taylor, Thomas, 103–5
Tennessee, 6, 11, 14, 195
Thayer, Eli, 43, 66, 191
Thirteenth Amendment, 230, 259
Tidewater region of Virginia, 5–6, 8
tobacco, 5–6
Torrey, Fred, 1
Trans-Allegheny region of Virginia, 6, 10–11, 44, 76, 257
troop transfer of 1863, 194–99

United Daughters of the Confederacy, 236–38
Upshur County, 229

Valley Campaign, 163–64
Vietnam War, 2
Virginia and Tennessee Railroad. *See under* railroads
Virginia Military Institute, 33
Virginia Ranger Act, 111–12
Virginia Secession Convention, 4–5, 44–45, 52–60, 64, 68, 73–74, 77, 83, 92, 128, 131, 169
voter qualifications, 9, 17–21, 24–25, 208, 216
voting, 128, 136–37, 144–45

Washington, George, 9, 11
Wellsburg, 23, 165
Wellsburg Herald, 42, 46–47
western Virginia, culture and economy. *See* regionalism in Virginia: cultural and economic differences between east and west
West Virginia constitutional convention, 129–31, 139–42, 144–46, 150
West Virginia statehood, 128–31, 146–47; boundaries, 128–29, 131–32; Congress, 130, 132; constitution, 129–30; county court system, 129; Lincoln, 131, 142–46; naming, 128; referendum, 136–37, 144–45, 147; slavery, 129–30, 137–42
wheat, 6
Wheeling, 23, 48–50, 133–36, 156–59, 201–2, 226–27
Wheeling Conventions, 128–30, 133–36
Wheeling Daily Intelligencer, 42–43, 48, 147, 154, 200–202, 226
Whig Party, 11–12, 37, 42, 44, 149, 151
"white basis." *See* suffrage, universal White male
White Sulphur Springs, 82–83, 259
Willey, Waitman T.: and belief that secession threatened slavery, 4–5; at the constitutional convention of 1851, 24–25; and postwar economic development, 229–30; as senator, 130–31, 139–41, 223; at Virginia Secession Convention, 55; and Willey Amendment, 131, 141, 259
Wilson, Shannon, 3–4
Winchester, 144–45, 172, 184
Wise, Henry A.: as Confederate general, 76, 82–83, 94–95, 110, 244; and order to seize Harpers Ferry, 44, 74–75; as Virginia governor, 10, 36, 44
women: African American, 16–17, 48–52, 155, 165; arrested, 157–60, 177–80; as bushwhackers, 155, 159; Confederate, 59–63, 146, 153–54, 157–65, 167, 169–73; interrogation of, 114, 175–76; and local aid societies, 155–56; as nurses, 153, 155; and oath taking, 154, 158; and profanity, 159; and prostitution, 154, 179; and protection of family property, 154–55, 160–73; and rules of war, 154; as soldiers, 155, 177–80; as spies, 155, 158–60, 175; Union, 88–89, 114, 153–54, 157, 162–63, 165–68, 174–75; violence against, 153, 155
Woods, Isabella, 169–73
Woods, Samuel: as postwar judge, 169; as soldier in the Stonewall Brigade, 169–73; at Virginia Secession Convention, 45, 53–54, 169

Printed and bound by CPI Group (UK) Ltd, Croydon, CR0 4YY

03/06/2025

14682894-0001